D1322702

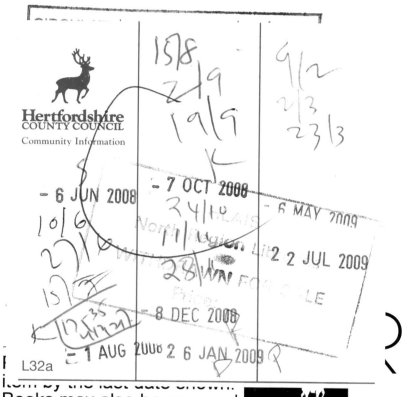
Books may also be renewed
by phone or Internet.

Hertfordshire

From Area codes 01923 or 020:
Renewals: 01923 471373   Textphone: 01923 471599
From the rest of Herts:
Renewals: 01438 737373 Textphone: 01438 737599
www.hertsdirect.org/libraries

FEEL fab FOREVER

THE ANTI-AGEING HEALTH & BEAUTY BIBLE

JOSEPHINE FAIRLEY & SARAH STACEY

KYLE CATHIE LIMITED

contents

PART 2: *HOW TO feel fab* 154

PART 3: *HOW TO be fab* 226

IN MEMORY OF THE ETERNALLY FABULOUS
DORIS FAIRLEY AND FLORRIE ROWE (JO'S GREAT AUNTS)
AND STEFFIE TEPPER CRAN (SARAH'S BELOVED FRIEND)

First published in Great Britain in 1998 by Kyle Cathie Limited,
122 Arlington Road, London NW1 7HP
email: general.enquiries@kyle-cathie.com
website: www.kylecathie.com

This revised edition published 2006

ISBN (10-digit) 1 85626 685 0
ISBN (13-digit) 978 1 85626 685 7

A Cataloguing in Publication record for this title is available from the British Library

Book design by Jenny Semple
Edited by Simon Canney
Picture research by Nadine Bazar & Vicki Murrell
Production by Sha Huxtable & Alice Holloway
Colour reproduction by ChromaGraphics, Singapore
Printed and bound in China by C & C Offset Printing Co Ltd

introduction

JOSEPHINE FAIRLEY has been a Contributing Editor to *The Mail on Sunday*'s *YOU* magazine for 15 years, writing about health, beauty and organic living. She has won the fragrance industry's top prize for journalism, and received an Achiever Award from Cosmetic Executive Women. She is also co-founder of Green & Black's chocolate.

SARAH STACEY is an award-winning journalist and TV documentary producer. She is currently Health Editor of *The Mail on Sunday*'s *YOU* magazine, writing her own column every week, and Vice-President of the Guild of Health Writers UK. Together with Jo, she edits their online beauty and health magazine, www.beautybible.com

THE WORLD OF ANTI-AGEING seems to move at Warp Factor Nine – to quote *Star Trek*'s Captain Kirk! From nanospheres to line-paralysing creams, 'age-defying' foundations to body creams that all claim to lift, firm and smooth our sags and bags. But what the women we speak to, and who e-mail us at www.beautybible.com, want to know is – quite simply – does any of it work? Once again, having embarked on another round of exhaustive testing for this entirely updated edition of *Feel Fab Forever*, we can put our hands on our hearts and say: yes, some of it really does. Having now sent specific anti-ageing products out to over 1,500 women over thirty-five over the last few years – the biggest survey into anti-ageing products ever carried out – we're consistently blown away by some of the responses. Our testers – who are asked to test products on one leg, or one eye, or half their face – frequently e-mail us with: 'Can I start using this on the other side of my face/leg/whatever, because I'm starting to look lopsided!' Of course, it doesn't happen with every product, but when it does, we can't argue. What's more, the products in this book have all been tested by real women, who have the real beauty concerns that go hand in hand with ageing: dark spots, lines and wrinkles, loss of firmness and radiance. (And lots of our testers started as beauty sceptics.) So in this book, we bring you up to date with the latest technology, but more importantly, whether or not those products really do live up to the vast amounts of hype.

Those of you who buy our books – and often write lovely e-mails to our website – know that our approach to health and beauty is about much more than what you smooth on to the outside. If you don't feel gorgeous on the inside, you won't look it. Simple as that. Putting together this book, we spoke to experts in every field – the world's top make-up pros, doctors, complementary health professionals, sleep gurus, nutritionists, and more – so we could share their wisdom with you, all in bite-sized, easy-to-digest chunks.

You'll also discover, throughout these pages, the women who inspire us – and who we hope will inspire you. They're shining examples of everything we believe in: all over 40 years old (well over 40-plus in many cases!), all fab, and all pretty wise and wonderful, if you ask us – glowing with good health, with graceful good looks, bags of humour and endless joie de vivre. We hope you'll enjoy reading what they have to say, from the gorgeously curvaceous Nigella Lawson to Evelyn Lauder, via 75-year-old supermodel Carmen dell'Orefice.

We've found room, too, to squeeze in just about every anti-ageing trick we've ever learned that actually works for us. Now both in our fifties (yikes! How did that happen?), we're often asked how we personally manage to hold back time, so here it is. We hope all this adds up to a book that really will help you feel fab – and look it – if not forever, then for many, many decades to come!

We can thank our lucky stars to be living in the 21st century.

Once upon a time, wrinkles were an inevitable fact of life. Don't get us wrong:

some lines we love – the only way not to get laugh lines is never to laugh.

But today, we can all beam about the fact that skincare and make-up are up there

with rocket science, searching for ways to keep time at bay and even turn

HOW TO *look fab* part 1

back the clock. And – as our 2,500 women testers have discovered – some of it

really works. The dream of younger, fresher, smoother-looking skin has become

reality. So, for the truth about ageing from the world's leading skin experts

and make-up artists – and the lowdown on the 'miracle' products that make

a difference (whether you're into high-tech or ultra-natural) – just turn the page…

WHAT HAPPENS TO OUR SKIN AS WE AGE

20s Skin is settling down after the hormonal upheaval of teenage years, although oil production may still be relatively high. Towards the end of their twenties, many women experience a gradual shift towards dryness – and notice the very first fan of fine lines around the eyes and mouth.

30s More fine lines develop as collagen and elastin start to break down in the skin and the delicate skin under the eyes begins to thin. The complexion tends to become drier, quicker. Broken veins may start to show up, as tiny red dots – and towards the end of this decade, age spots and brown pigmentation marks may start to appear. Pore size may increase and skin may become noticeably rougher and coarser due to sun damage. Under-eye puffiness can start to become a problem – taking increasingly longer to subside.

40s Deeper lines begin to etch around the mouth and eyes, as well as furrows on the forehead; skin loses more of its 'bounce-back' factor (due to a loss of elastin). Circles under the eyes may grow into pouches. Most women's skins become noticeably drier – although around menopause some women experience teenage-style complexion rebellion in the form of increased oiliness and breakouts. As the menopause sets in, skin may become more sensitive – and that may endure till menopause is completed.

50s, 60s and beyond By now, skin starts to acquire true character: fine wrinkles and lines may deepen into folds in your fifties and sixties as, post-menopausally, there is much less oestrogen being produced. As well as wrinkling, skin can begin to sag and droop – and some women may notice a jowly appearance. In the fifties, skintone is likely to become increasingly uneven, with an increasing number of age- or 'sun-spots'.

how do we age?

According to experts, there are two kinds of skin ageing...

Intrinsic ageing This is the natural, biological ageing that occurs in the skin without sun damage – and we have little control over it. (Although a healthy diet, regular exercise, plenty of sleep and fresh air and tackling stress will certainly help.) All of the organs in our body – including skin – become intrinsically aged as the years tick by. Intrinsic ageing causes major changes in our complexions: at 80, for instance, our skin is 30 per cent less thick than at 18. In addition to the structural changes in the dermis and the epidermis, there are other changes that take place as we age: we sweat less as we get older, and there is decreased pigmentation – so older skin can be paler. There is also a loss of muscle tone and a relocation of the fat under the skin's surface, which accounts for the cheeks sinking in as they lose their padding, while little pockets of fat settle in the jowls.

Extrinsic ageing Extrinsic ageing, or photo-ageing, was until quite recently believed to be a fast-forwarding of intrinsic ageing. But differences between the two are now emerging. 'Without the damaging effects of the sun, intrinsic ageing only really starts to show from the age of 60 onwards,' says Dr Daniel Maes, vice-president of research and development for Estée Lauder. But exposure to UV light and pollution speeds up ageing, due to the production of free radicals on the surface of exposed skin, damaging the cells. Their attack on the collagen and elastin fibres results in a rough, dry skin texture, deep wrinkles, uneven pigmentation and broken veins. At the same time, new skin cells may be damaged as they form. By the time they get to the outside world, they're already weakened – leaving skin even more vulnerable to future external damage. A vicious circle that speeds up the wrinkling and crêpiness we think of as natural ageing – but which is mainly linked with our exposure to the sun, pollution and smoking.

don't fast-forward ageing

How we age is dependent on two factors: lifestyle – and genes. If your parents aged well, then you will probably go on looking good for your age, too. But how we live – even where we live – can also have a major impact on how we age. Here's how some lifestyle factors can add years – decades, even – to our faces.

Sunbaking: add 20 years. (What more do we have to say?)
Regular solarium use: add 20 years. (According to an increasing body of dermatologists, sunbeds are even more damaging to skin than direct sunlight, because they give out pure UVA rays – which penetrate deep into the skin, causing damage.)
Stress: add three years. (A major skin savager, especially as the associated behavioural symptoms – excessive alcohol and caffeine consumption, missed sleep and skipped meals – have detrimental side-effects. Try to reduce stress by finding new ways to relax and slow down.)
Big city living: add five years. (Don't think the only solution is to move to the country – try a skin cream rich in antioxidants, instead, to mop up the damage.)
Crash dieting: add ten years. (Yoyo dieting deprives skin of vital nutrients. If you lose weight quickly, your skin will stretch and sag.)

I've only ever had one wrinkle – and I'm sitting on it.

JEANNE CALMENT
(the world's oldest woman, before she died at the age of 122)

SKIN ENEMIES – AND HOW TO FIGHT THEM

Much of the damage these do is the result of free radical attack (see opposite).

THE PROBLEMS

Alcohol Drinking alcohol dehydrates the skin and interferes with circulation, robbing skin of moisture and vital nutrients. It can contribute to broken veins (see page 142), particularly over the nose and cheeks. Alcohol also depletes the body of vitamins and minerals essential for a healthy complexion.
The solution: cut down to a maximum of one or two glasses of good wine daily and ensure adequate intake of Essential Fatty Acids (see page 195).

Pollution Smog, dirt and the sun's rays bombard skin every day. And according to Toby Mathias, MD, former head of occupational dermatology at the US National Institute of Occupational Safety and Health, 'While there are strict regulations regarding the chemicals we breathe or ingest, little is done to restrict the toxins we touch and handle, or that skin comes into direct contact with.' Our skins are regularly assaulted by free radicals, triggered by everything from burning coal to household cleaning products.
The solution: creams featuring antioxidant ingredients can help neutralise the free radical damage triggered by smoking and chemicals.

Smoking Facialist Eve Lom – among many others – insists that she can spot a smoker at fifty paces. 'Their skins are pallid, grey and lined,' she explains. 'Smokers in their forties have wrinkling and sagging in their faces comparable to non-smokers who are in their sixties.' In fact, the *Journal of the American Medical Association* refers to this condition as 'smoker's face'; it's characterised by deep lines around the corners of the mouth and vertical lines in the upper lip – from the repeated action of drawing on a cigarette – and deep lines around the eyes, from squinting through a fug of smoke. (See page 66 – How to Win the War Against the Big Wrinkler.)

The skin also has an obvious greyish cast and tired appearance – due to a lack of oxygen supply. This oxygen starvation leads to dehydration, dryness, pallor – and wrinkles. As a person smokes, the toxic chemicals enter the body and stick to the skin – and around 4,000 chemical compounds are produced when tobacco burns. Other visible problems resulting from this can include staining, irritation, blackheads – even skin cancer.

The damage that smoking can do to the skin was clearly revealed in a recent study of identical twins where one smoked and the other didn't. Of the 25 sets of twins studied at St Thomas's Hospital in London, the smoking twin consistently had thinner skin than the non-smoking sibling – by as much as 40 per cent. Tobacco may wreak its havoc by constricting blood vessels, damaging gene repair or stimulating the release of enzymes that dissolve the skin's elastic components. Professor Tim Spector, director of the Twin Research Unit at St Thomas's, asserts that the chemicals in cigarettes put pressure on the body's metabolism, increasing production of damaging free radicals. 'With time, these speed up the ageing of the cells, breaking down collagen and elastin tissue in the skin. Blood supply to the top layer of the skin may also be restricted.'
The solution: as for other forms of pollution, creams featuring antioxidant ingredients can help – but also: stop smoking!

Sun The number one cause of skin damage is the sun. No wonder the face and hands are the first places to show signs of ageing; they are always exposed. Peter Pugliese, MD, a biomedical researcher who has been studying the skin's response to sunlight, believes that 90 per cent of the skin problems associated with ageing are the result of too much sun exposure. These include premature wrinkling, dry leathery skin, distended blood vessels, blotchy pigmentation and skin cancer. Holiday sunbathing is not the only menace, however. It is constant daily exposure to UVA that ultimately leads to long-term damage. 'Research has shown that even as little as 30 minutes of UV exposure twice a week during a typical London winter will result in long-lasting damage,' says Nicholas Lowe, clinical professor of dermatology at UCLA.
The solution: daily application of a moisturiser featuring an SPF15, together with antioxidant ingredients that fight the free radical damage.

why antioxidants are your best friend

THE SOLUTIONS

There are a couple of words that you will encounter time and again throughout *Feel Fab Forever*: free radicals. As far as ageing is concerned, they are public enemy number one. Our bodies create them naturally – particularly when exposed to sunlight or when we're stressed. Excessive exercise also sets off an avalanche of free radical production, due to an increased intake of oxygen. (Although we're talking running a marathon or mountain-biking up a fairly impressive peak, rather than a brisk daily walk.)

But in the course of modern life, we encounter many more free radicals – in smoke, toxins, chemicals and other pollutants in the air and in our food. What they do is trigger peroxidation – in less than the blink of an eye. (The skin generates free radicals in a millionth of a second if it's exposed to, say, cigarette smoke.) That peroxidation leads to oxidation – which in turn leads to cell breakdown. Cells, organs and tissues break down or decay, resulting in skin ageing and internal disease.

Like 'cellular terrorists', free radicals are highly unstable molecules which are deficient of a negative charge called an electron – so they rush around inside cells seeking that missing electron 'mate' in order to make them stable. During this process, however, they cause other molecules to become unstable – triggering a chain reaction that produces thousands more free radicals.

In the skin, free radicals attack the repair mechanisms, together with the DNA itself (the genetic material responsible for cell reproduction). Free radicals react with protein in the cell's collagen and lipid membrane, resulting in loss of elasticity, slackness, discoloration and wrinkles. The rate at which this damage shows up depends partly on how well skin can defend itself against these destructive free radicals. Young skin generally has sufficient enzymes and vitamins to enable it to neutralise free radicals. From as early as the mid-twenties, however, our natural defence mechanisms become depleted – particularly under emotional or physical stress, so the skin becomes unable to defend itself from attack, resulting in the visible signs of ageing.

The antidote? While the body manufactures some free radical neutralisers, science is still looking at ways of increasing that supply – and the best candidates so far are the antioxidant vitamins. For now, skin creams featuring antioxidants, eating a diet rich in vitamins A, C, E and also taking antioxidant supplements seems to be the wisest insurance policy, working to prevent (and even reverse) damage to the face and body. Which is why you'll be hearing a lot more about antioxidants throughout *Feel Fab Forever*.

MIRACLE CREAMS

> **"**The wrinkle is a serious disease. Do you know anyone who gets up every morning and worries about illness? But everybody worries regularly about wrinkles...**"**

Leading US dermatologist DR ALBERT KLIGMAN

• **STATISTIC: worldwide, women are expected to spend $2.86 billion a year on anti-ageing creams by the year 2009.**

As Dr Kligman observes above, millions of women all over the world are obsessed with their wrinkles. Eavesdrop on just about any group of fortysomething women at a glamorous party, or in the hairdresser's, and you'll overhear gossip about this miracle cream or that magic line eraser. There's nothing wrong with that: psychologists have established that when we look better (or just think we do), we feel better. So wrinkle patrol is about self-preservation in more ways than the obvious. But – crucially – women want to know what really works.

As we age, there are plenty of emotional and spiritual compensations for encroaching lines and wrinkles – wisdom, a more relaxed outlook on life, enrichment of our souls – but the simple truth is that most of us would like to delay the physical and visible signs of ageing for as long as possible. And we are prepared to spend billions in that quest.

In the search to satisfy us, the cosmetic companies have raised skincare research to the levels of rocket science – literally: one of the top-selling 'cult' creams in the US was developed by a former NASA scientist. But just consider this: if you're sending a rocket to Mars, you don't know what's out there, don't know whether you'll land successfully, what will happen when you arrive or whether you'll get back safely. Buying anti-ageing skincare is a similar journey into the unknown – though few cosmetic companies would ever admit the uncertainties or limitations of their products. More practically for the consumers – ie, all of us – the time and expense involved in finding the creams or lotions, serums or ampoules that really do improve our skins can be incredibly frustrating.

That's one reason we wrote this book: to share with you the secrets your best friend would tell you – if she knew. We cut through the hype, the myth, the blurb and the mystique – and also, for the first time, bring you first-hand experiences of the creams that really work: the results of the Tried & Tested surveys carried out on a total of over 2,500 women, working in panels of ten, who tested literally hundreds of creams.

BIG BEAUTY, BIG BUSINESS

The beauty industry is mega-business. Every year, it spends billions on research. And to recoup that outlay, it has to earn back billions from the sales of the skin creams that emerge from its high-tech labs. Skincare companies are literally at war to ensure that their product sells the most. And dazzling the consumer (and the journalist) with science is currently their favourite marketing approach.

Before deciding to green-light a launch, many of the leading skincare companies, who already run vast labs of their own, also have prototype products tested independently. This results in stacks of scientific papers, complete with statistically significant figures purporting to show how effective the product is. Those glowing figures are destined for the press and are also widely used in marketing and ad campaigns. Time was when beauty journalists would pretty well reproduce the press release; now they are starting to ask tough(er) questions. So the companies wheel out not only scientific papers but real live scientists to talk about the products. (Although delve a little deeper and you'll often find they or their labs or their research projects have been enriched in some way by the cosmetic companies.)

There's nothing intrinsically wrong in all this. The scientists aren't making up their figures and the companies aren't inventing their claims – although we have discovered some what you might call 'imaginative' research methodology and definitely some embellished interpretations of the results. But the real point is that these results may have very little impact where it counts – on our skins.

Every year, we wade through literally reams of weighty results given to us by skincare companies claiming that their hot anti-ager-of-the-moment delivers a benefit such as '50 per cent reduction in wrinkle depth'. Taken at face value, you'd imagine that the cream made your wrinkles half as deep. But as leading cosmetic dermatologist and researcher Professor Nicholas Lowe explained to us, that's just not the case: 'Very often, the units for the measurement are so small that those changes may not even be visible to the naked eye.'

Furthermore, what the ads almost certainly won't tell you is what the women were – or weren't – using on their skin before they started applying the product in question. In some studies we've looked at, the answer is: nothing at all. (Skincare companies frequently ask women to cease using any moisturiser for two weeks or so leading up to the tests.) Now, if you were to put anything on the skin at that point – even verruca cream – you would instantly get a measurable improvement simply because of the emollient effect of the ointment.

But would you ever guess that from the 'oh-wow-hold-the-front-page!' way those results are presented? Uh-uh…

is it a face cream – or is it a drug?

That's not to say that space-age skincare doesn't work. The great paradox – as we know from our own and our 2,500 testers' experience – is that, as well as the results which are overstated, there are some extremely impressive products out there which actually undersell what they can achieve. Some of the effective high-tech skin creams may be more similar to drugs than cosmetics, penetrating the skin to bring about really noticeable changes.

According to the official definition of the Food and Drugs Act of 1936, a drug is a substance that alters the structure or function of any part of the body. In the old days, the skin was seen very much as a one-way street. Today, scientists understand that a cream applied to the skin – or even the ingredients from a patch stuck on the surface – can penetrate deep inside. (This technology is being exploited by drug companies in the shape of skin patches or gels which deliver, for instance, HRT or nicotine.)

If a manufacturer claims that its product will give you a healthy glow, that product is regarded as a cosmetic. But if the packaging or the advertising were to state that the glow is achieved through, say, improved blood flow to the skin, the governments of both the UK and the US would require it to be tested – and then classified – as a drug.

'The game involves not what a product does, but what a company says it does,' according to Dr Albert Kligman. (He's the 'grand old man' of anti-ageing skincare, who coined the term 'cosmeceutical'.) If the companies made more extravagant claims, the products would have to be licensed as pharmaceutical drugs, not cosmetics – which would be prohibitively expensive and time-consuming. (It takes about a decade – and well over £10 million – to get a drug to market.) 'So companies are careful not to make any claims that would be considered drug claims,' says Dr Kligman. That's why there are some anti-ageing products out there that do more than they actually claim to.

now cut through the hype – and find out what really works

Ever since our first book, this is the category which has triggered most interest. With so much hype out there, it was impossible for women to find out what products really work to reduce lines, wrinkles and visible signs of ageing, in an area rife with scientific jargon and exaggerated claims. Our Tried & Tested Miracle Creams results are based on reports from over 1,500 age-conscious women of 35-plus, out of more than 2,500 who've been involved in our trials.

tried & tested MIRACLE CREAMS

These are the skin creams (night and day), the serums, lotions and potions which scored impressively in the most challenging category: 'miracle' skincare. Expensive and cheap, natural and high tech: we have tested hundreds of products in all price ranges, making this the most ambitious and wide-ranging survey of anti-ageing creams ever.

Each product was sent to ten women and tested until the jar/bottle was finished – several weeks, usually months. We asked panellists to try the product on one side of their face only, to see the difference (or not). Fascinatingly, results are sometimes so obvious after a few weeks that testers often ask permission to start using it on the other side, too.

We have included a handful of products which featured in our first book, as their high scores have never been exceeded in subsequent tests on our testers, who we now recruit through our website – www.beautybible.com.

Few testers report overnight miracles; results are generally seen with this type of product in anywhere from two weeks to two months. (Thirty days seems about average, although many testers note their complexion is 'energised' almost immediately.) Having started out cynical, we are now completely convinced that there are creams which really do help your skin to defy time.

beauty steal TIME DELAY REJUVENATING DAY CREAM SPF8
(exclusive to Boots)
Score: 8.71/10

In their wisdom, just as our last book, *The 21st Century Beauty Bible*, was published, Boots renamed this product – it was previously called Time Delay Repair Face & Neck. Aside from that – and subtly tweaking the fragrance – they reassure us the highly effective formulation has not been changed.

A no-nonsense cream at a truly outstanding price, this came in well ahead of the competition – and none of the creams we've tested since has outperformed it. Targeted at face and neck, the active ingredients include pro-retinol and a 'pro-lift' complex from white lupin extract, together with powerful antioxidants. There is a moderate SPF8 in there – fine for winter, but not for summer, we'd advise.

Comments: 'I thought age-delaying creams were a con – but this one has changed my mind' • 'I looked glowing – and was even asked if I was pregnant, several times!' • 'marked reduction in fine lines; my partner made nice comments' • 'totally transformed my skin's appearance – my face looks years younger than I am, and I'm 100 per cent sold on this' • 'my skin felt plumper, younger and looked fresher; loved this – it looks and feels expensive' • 'a few people mentioned how well I was looking' • 'definite improvement in tone'.

ESTÉE LAUDER RE-NUTRIV ULTIMATE LIFTING CRÈME
Score: 8.4/10

Ritzily packaged and with a sky-high price tag, this is truly in the realms of skin luxuries – a Mercedes-Benz of an anti-ageing cream, with active ingredients to turn back the clock that include green tea and resveratrol – from grapes – white birch extracts and creatine, an amino acid. Most of our testers concurred that the only downside to this cream is the cost.

Comments: 'This cream is definitely a miracle cream – it changed my skin from dry to glowing and although I didn't have deep lines, my fine lines have almost gone' • 'definite improvements in skintone and texture – gorgeous to use' • 'reduction in lines on neck, bright radiant glow to skin; my open pores are also diminished'.

ESTÉE LAUDER ADVANCED NIGHT REPAIR
Score: 8.4/10

A true beauty classic, and one of Lauder's top-selling products. This serum is designed to repair at night and to protect by day, with a very high dose of antioxidant ingredients. Several testers commented that, used in the daytime – with or without a moisturiser over the top – it made an excellent base for foundation. Advanced Night Repair also features a calming cola nut extract and other anti-inflammatory ingredients 'to help reduce environmentally caused irritation and longer-term damage'. (NB: Nigella Lawson uses it when she burns herself in the kitchen, because it's such an effective skin-calmer.) Several testers commented on improvements to the neck and all said they would buy it.

Comments: 'A joy to use this product, as I could see improvements after a couple of weeks; a little amount was needed so it went a long way' • 'loved the way my face glowed and looked fresher; did not seem to make a difference to deeper lines, but smaller ones were improved' • 'I think my skin looks more radiant, smoother and younger' • 'I feel I really do look better: I am more "ironed" on face and throat; after two months I started using it all over my face because the difference was too visible'.

ELEMIS PRO-COLLAGEN MARINE CREAM
Score: 8.4/10

This was the first serious anti-ageing cream from the respected 'spa' brand, incorporating ginkgo biloba, to boost circulation, seaweed extracts – the 'marine' element – and absolutes of rose and mimosa, combined together in a nourishing base that includes carrot seed extract, jojoba oil and shea butter.

Comments: 'This really is a miracle cream – and a little goes a long way, so, although it's expensive, it should last a long time' • 'people at work – men – seem to be giving me a second look and I feel much more confident after using it; I've seen a dramatic improvement' • 'I was very sceptical that any product claiming to reduce lines/wrinkles would work, but I've been proved wrong – I'm hooked!' • 'this will be on my Christmas list as a special treat' • 'please send me a bucketful of this cream'.

ELEMIS LIQUID RADIANCE CELL RENEWAL SYSTEM
Score: 8.35/10

Elemis's latest anti-ageing innovation enters the ranking just a teensy bit behind Pro-Collagen Marine Cream: they call it a 'skin detox', which helps to neutralise the damaging effects of free radicals, packing a mega-dose of no fewer than 15 antioxidants, plus other vitamins. A two-phase treatment programme, it's not designed to be used all the time but for 30 days in all, whenever the complexion needs a boost – making it, promise Elemis, 'more luminous and satin-like, while reducing pore size'.

Comments: 'Ten out of ten: before my skin was grey and dull – now even my husband commented on how my skin glowed and was fantastically bright, very soft, with a great reduction in fine lines; I can't praise it enough' • 'skin definitely looks younger' • 'divine smell, very lightweight, instantly absorbed milky lotion; after first week, skin definitely clearer, softer and pores refined, more even-toned – amazing!'

NEAL'S YARD FRANKINCENSE NOURISHING CREAM ✹ ✹
Score: 8.25/10

When this featured in the original edition of *Feel Fab Forever*, it flew off the shelves in such huge quantities that not only did Neal's Yard sell out, but as production was stepped up, it triggered a global shortage of blue glass! A natural, essential-oil-based rich cream by one of the world's pioneering aromatherapy beauty companies, it contains nourishing oils of wheatgerm, jojoba, almond and apricot kernel, together with frankincense and myrrh – renowned for their regenerating and moisturising properties. It can be used at night or as a day make-up base – and although this natural product was one of the highest-scoring products we tested, it is also a great 'beauty steal'.

Comments: 'The original feeling of plumpness has been replaced by a smooth uplift and youthful tightness to my features, yet skin still feels comfortable, has no dry patches or discomfort' • 'always felt my skin looked colourless and grey until I tested this product' • 'after two weeks, I felt able to go out without foundation – I've never been able to before' • 'no adverse reactions – a pleasant surprise because my skin can be sensitive' • 'very noticeable improvement in brightness and translucency – not as sluggish looking' • 'I cannot over-emphasise the healthy and "strong" feeling of my skin afterwards'.

PHILOSOPHY WHEN HOPE IS NOT ENOUGH SERUM
Score: 8.2/10

The 'sister' product to the original Hope In A Jar, this scored even higher marks with the ten women who trialled it. A light, fluid gel, it can be worn under moisturiser on drier skin, and harnesses amino peptide technology with skin-brightening vitamin C. None of our testers had a negative word.

Comments: 'Lives up to its promise – noticeable reduction in bigger grooves and wrinkles, as well as a moderate improvement in crêpiness' • 'brilliant stuff – my skin looks like I've had a facelift and several people have said that I'm looking well' • 'made my skin look like I live on a healthy diet of fruit and water – and I couldn't stop touching its baby-softness' • 'it took about two weeks to see the difference but it was worth the wait – I didn't even feel the need to wear make-up some days' • 'I love the pipette-style dispenser – very scientific, yet the smell is very holistic, herbal, floral and natural' • 'also claims to retard hair growth, which, amazingly, appeared true – upper hair regrowth on my top lip slowed down'.

what is a serum? (and do they work?)

Today, serums – pumps or vials of potent but lightweight anti-ageing ingredients, often a cocktail of antioxidants or alpha-hydroxy acids – have joined the clutter on our bathroom shelves. Some are designed to be used every day, others when skin is in the doldrums, generating everything from fresh new skin cells to a burst of brightness. But should they be used instead of a moisturiser – or as well? 'Serums are mostly designed to be used underneath a moisturiser,' make-up guru John Gustafson explains. 'These may not have enough moisturising ingredients to be used on their own.' Experiment: you may find that a serum is enough, on its own, at night – or you may want to 'layer' a moisturiser on top.

serum how~to

We have found this is the most effective way to apply serum: first, cleanse your face (and use alcohol-free toner, if you like that). Wait till skin is just dry, then apply a few drops of serum (a little tends to go a long way) and sweep over skin. We like to 'tap' serum into skin with patting movements, rather than massage it in, which stimulates circulation and gives the face a gorgeous glow. Remember: you can also use it under day moisturiser or night cream for an extra boost.

CULT CREAMS

Can any skin cream justify the price of a jacket – or, in some cases, a secondhand car? Is any mere moisturiser worth adding your name to a list of 1,600 women – the number who were wait-listed at Saks Fifth Avenue for Crème de la Mer, when it launched? Well, here are our thoughts on the matter.

In the last couple of years, there have been several break-the-bank face cream launches. One – a new launch in the Crème de la Mer line – even smashed through the $1,000 barrier. Yet in reality, all moisturisers and anti-ageing creams are basically a mix of oil and water. So how can manufacturers justify these stratospheric price tags? Let's hear what one insider has to say on the matter: according to the former UK MD of Lancôme, Peter Bloxham, 'The quality of the ingredients is a major factor in differentiating between prestige and mass market brands. There are cheap liposomes and expensive liposomes, cheap vitamins and expensive vitamins.' And, he adds, 'With a prestige brand, you're getting a level of research and development which mass market brands don't match.'

Karin Herzog's Vit-A-Kombi cream, for instance, was the creation of Nobel Institute epidemiologist Paul Herzog. The world-famous Crème de la Mer, a rich, sea-kelp moisturiser was developed by a brilliant aerospace physicist, Max Huber, as a treatment for his own face, severely burned while he was conducting chemical tests for NASA in the 1960s. After the cream healed his scars, Huber began selling it on a very limited basis – and after he died, in 1991, Crème de la Mer was sold to Estée Lauder.

Now, from all our experience, we know very well that women aren't stupid. They won't go without essentials just in order to get their hands on the latest whiz-bang skin cream. And we would never, in a million years, suggest to them that they should. But what we've seen is that women tend to buy according to their budget. So: if you live in the kind of house that has a swimming pool and you drive a Mercedes and holiday in St Barth's, then it probably won't cause any hardship to splash out £150 – or more – on a pot of face cream. What we would maintain, though – as evidenced by the results of our Miracle Cream Tried & Tested, on the previous pages – is that there are many others which perform well, at a fifth of the price (or less).

And in truth – though we'll probably make ourselves unpopular with some cosmetics companies here – we do think there's something wrong with a world in which face creams can cost as much as a secondhand car. Speaking entirely personally, we'd actually rather you sent the money to earthquake victims, or Friends of the Earth, or used it to pay for a holiday with your children/ grandchildren/best friend, storing up memories to keep you warm in your twilight years! Here endeth our rant.

But if you're still curious to know how cult creams performed, in our trials, just look at the results, opposite.

tried & tested CULT CREAMS

Are pricier creams worth the money? We asked our panels of testers to trial some of the most costly (on one side of their face only, for the sake of comparison). Their reports make fascinating reading. NB: we usually include only the highest-scoring products, but felt that it was worth reading what our testers had to say about some high-priced but lower-scoring 'cult' creams, too.

ESTÉE LAUDER RE-NUTRIV ULTIMATE LIFTING CRÈME
Score: 8.4/10

You can read the full (and rapturous) review of this product on page 16. In a nutshell, our testers felt this somewhat heart-stoppingly expensive anti-ageing cream – with all the bells and whistles Lauder's skincare scientists could find room for – really made a significant difference to their skins.

ELEMIS PRO-COLLAGEN MARINE CREAM
Score: 8.4/10

Again, you'll find the full rave review of Elemis cult anti-ageing star on page 17.

ELEMIS LIQUID RADIANCE CELL RENEWAL SYSTEM
Score: 8.35/10

Designed for occasional use when skin needs an energy boost. For more on this product, see page 17.

CRÈME DE LA MER MOISTURISING LOTION
Score: 8.1/10

A lightweight version of the costly cream (see right) which caused a waiting list when it launched in the US. When we actually analysed the results, the high score was due mostly to the lovely texture and smell and the fact it makes a great make-up base – but arguably the improvement didn't match the price tag.
Comments: 'Lovely cream, really perfect for combination and sensitive skins; calmed my skin down. The skin on the tested side was quite clearly smoother and healthier' • 'absorbs beautifully, ready for make-up' • 'feels wonderful after application but no long-term changes' • 'amazingly smooth and light yet very moisturising. Skin felt really soft and silky, with slightly more glow – but no redness'.

CELLEX-C HIGH POTENCY SERUM
Score: 7.12/10

Very mixed reviews for this serum, which delivers an intense burst of vitamin C to the skin: some testers found it irritated their sensitive skins. Fewer than half the testers said they would buy this in future.
Comments: 'The tested side is a lot softer and firmer; fine lines noticeably reduced and some reduction in bigger grooves' • 'my sensitive skin had no problem with this – makes skin appear younger' • 'definitely makes skin look younger; many people have said how well I look; crêpiness on my neck visibly reduced'.

KARIN HERZOG VIT-A-KOMBI 1
Score: 6.4/10

While some testers gave this 'oxygenating cream' a rave 10/10, others only awarded it two points – because it didn't sufficiently moisturise very dry skin.
Comments: 'An immediate lifting effect' • 'the glow has come back to my skin and it feels moist' • 'skin looks younger, brighter and firmer, with an even skintone; sun spots faded slightly' • 'less obvious crêpiness on the treated side of my neck'.

CRÈME DE LA MER
Score: 6.1/10

Several testers scored down this product (which kick-started the 'cult' cream frenzy), complaining it was complicated and time-consuming to apply: you warm it in the palm, then pat on. Others felt the results justified the fuss, but less than half would buy it.
Comments: 'A great reduction in the depth of frown lines' • 'a definite reduction in bigger wrinkles and softening of fine lines' • 'a big plus: I've used this on my cleavage and can't wait to wear low-cut necklines – it has really made a difference' • 'skin looked healthy and glowing after four weeks; a brown mark I had on my forehead seems a lot lighter; crêpiness on my cheeks has almost gone' • 'must I steal for this?'.

you and your skin – what's really going on?

On a good day, it may look like the calm velvety surface of a bowl of cream, but the skin is a living, breathing, constantly changing organ – the largest we have, composed of billions of cells floating in a salty, watery liquid. Half the water in our bodies – over 30 per cent – is found in our skin. Just like the rest of the body, bones and all, skin continuously renews itself. Every day, we lose about four per cent of our total number of skin cells; about 30lb of skin in a lifetime. The big question for older women is why skin ages. There are two main reasons: firstly, it simply doesn't renew itself as fast, and secondly, the support structure of collagen and elastin degenerates. Scientists are working on ways of overcoming the problems – but they're not quite there yet.

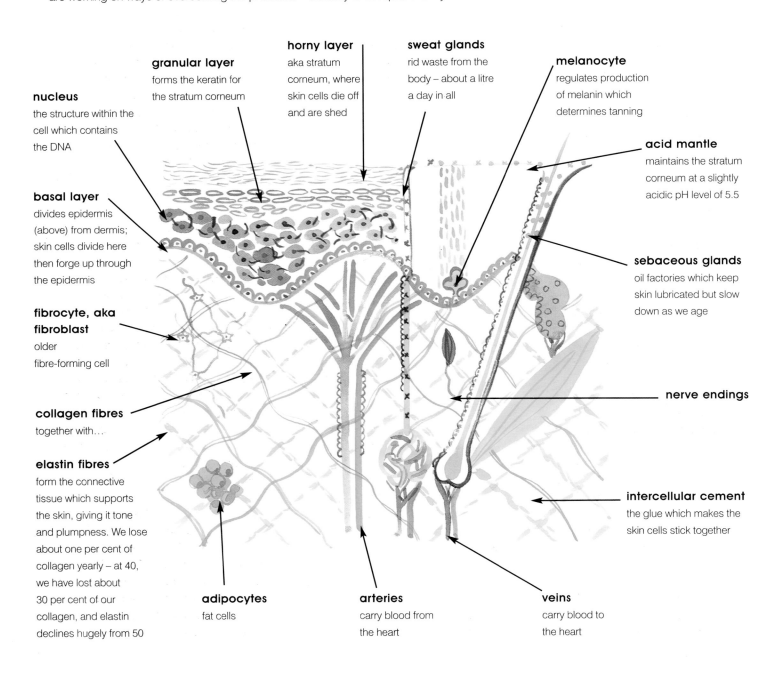

granular layer
forms the keratin for
the stratum corneum

horny layer
aka stratum
corneum, where
skin cells die off
and are shed

sweat glands
rid waste from the
body – about a litre
a day in all

melanocyte
regulates production
of melanin which
determines tanning

nucleus
the structure within the
cell which contains
the DNA

acid mantle
maintains the stratum
corneum at a slightly
acidic pH level of 5.5

basal layer
divides epidermis
(above) from dermis;
skin cells divide here
then forge up through
the epidermis

sebaceous glands
oil factories which keep
skin lubricated but slow
down as we age

**fibrocyte, aka
fibroblast**
older
fibre-forming cell

collagen fibres
together with…

nerve endings

elastin fibres
form the connective
tissue which supports
the skin, giving it tone
and plumpness. We lose
about one per cent of
collagen yearly – at 40,
we have lost about
30 per cent of our
collagen, and elastin
declines hugely from 50

intercellular cement
the glue which makes the
skin cells stick together

adipocytes
fat cells

arteries
carry blood from
the heart

veins
carry blood to
the heart

SMALL CHANGE, BIG DIFFERENCE

Over the years, we have made an observation: that skin changes, almost daily. Not that it veers from ultra-dry to ultra-oily, but there are just some days when it seems touchier, or thirstier, or shinier, than others. It's probably related to diet, and to the season of the year – one of life's great mysteries, but definitely worth paying attention to. Supermodel Linda Evangelista once told us that she touch-tests her skin on a daily basis – and that's not a bad idea; keep a lighter lotion for days when your skin feels naturally dewy, and a richer cream for when it's parched. Sometimes, when the air's moist, a serum is all skin needs – and these can be a great base for make-up, too. Many of the products that did well in our Tried & Testeds are actually available as a lotion and as a cream; it's no more expensive to buy both, because they'll each last twice as long. When skin is super-dry, you can also 'layer' on products: a facial oil under a night moisturiser, for instance.

skincare we love

We get to try everything. For free. It's one of the perks of this job. (But not always great news for our touchy skins.) Here are the products that we can't live without…

Jo loves… I have very sensitive skin and tend to stick to natural-as-possible products, as there are many synthetic . ingredients, which make my skin red and result in a rather unalluring 'facial dandruff'. Also, as chair of the Soil Association's Health Products Standards Committee, which helps create the guidelines for what is and isn't organic, in terms of skincare, I like to 'walk my talk'.

Cleanser: I'm a long-term fan of balms, and now use Vaishaly Cleansing Balm, from the top London facialist whose tips you can read on page 58, which has very high levels of organic ingredients. It melts make-up instantly and I love the lavender and geranium fragrance. (Vaishaly is anti using muslin cloths, but I love mine.)

Moisturiser: I'm a complete convert to the products naturopath Dr Andrew Weil has created for Origins, Mega-Mushroom Face Serum and

matching Face Cream, based on organic reishi and chaga mushrooms. The idea isn't to 'turn back the clock', but to help the skin function optimally. In summer, I slather on Estée Lauder DayWear Plus Multi-Protection Anti-Oxidant Moisturizer SPF15 Sheer Tint Release Formula, a 'self-adjusting' tinted moisturiser that's the perfect shade on everyone.

Night cream: Actually, I make this myself, from a recipe I created for *The Ultimate Natural Beauty Book*: it's super-rich, with beeswax and olive oil, and packed with anti-ageing, skin-preserving frankincense. (Well, anything that is effective enough to preserve Egyptian mummies for 3,000 years is clearly worth a shot.) Occasionally I layer this over a facial oil; a particular favourite is Vaishaly Night Nourisher for Normal/Dry skins, with its fab rose and geranium essential oil fragrance.

Sarah loves…
Like Jo, my skin is very dry and super-sensitive – so are my eyes, which can turn red and/or puffy and/or sore at just a drop of the wrong ingredient. So I tend to stick to products that I know will work for me.

Cleanser: Cleanse & Polish Hot Cloth Cleanser from Liz Earle's Naturally Active Skincare suits my skin brilliantly, is easy to use, well priced and takes off mascara (non-waterproof). For nights away, I occasionally resort to Shiseido Pureness cleansing sheets.

Mask: BKamins Chemist Bio-maple Diotamamus Earth Masque has well-nigh miraculous plumping qualities, and also Liz Earle's Brightening Treatment, which does just what it says – as well as sorting out the ages-old open pores on my chin.

Daytime: In the mornings, I love Aromatherapy Associates Renew Triple Rose Moisturiser. Like Jo, I really rate Mega-Mushroom Face Serum and Face Cream, which reduce any redness and sensitivity (because I spend so much time out in the elements with my horses, I can look like a bonfire). For droopy days, I swear by Shiseido Bio-Performance Super Lifting Formula. I don't worry so much about facial sun preps because I use Susan Posnick's mineral powder foundation Colorflo, which has a sun barrier (see page 74).

Night: At night I've more or less gone over totally to facial oils, such as Barefoot Botanicals Rosa Fina Intensive Radiance Face Oil and Aromatherapy Associates Renew Rose & Frankincense Facial Oil. I use Crème de la Mer's The Concentrate in one-week bursts as a treat. My long thin-skinned neck laps up Clarins Extra-Firming Neck Cream.

SIMPLE SKINCARE SHIFTS

Skin changes as we age. But many of us hang on to outdated beauty regimes because of habit, inertia – or simply the lovely smell of a particular moisturiser. But our skin's needs change with the years – and we need to adapt with them.

The twin skin shifts linked with ageing are reduced sebum production (for all but a few very oily-skinned women) – so skin is no longer as well lubricated – and thinning of the skin, which means moisture escapes more easily. Some women actually experience a surge in oiliness around menopause as hormonal changes kick in – but for the majority skin becomes progressively drier with the years. Changes to watch for are tightness, itching, dry patches, redness, flakiness, fine lines – or the fact that your make-up seems to be 'evaporating' after you've put it on.

It's vital not to get stuck in a skincare rut, believes skin and make-up pro John Gustafson. What worked for you at 20 almost certainly won't do the trick at 50. 'Every single time you go to replace a product, discuss your skincare routine with the consultant and see if it needs an update. And,' he says, 'you might want to change products when you get to the end of a jar or a tube, rather than simply sticking with what works. Otherwise, skin gets "lazy".'

Cleansing As oil production is slowed, an ultra-efficient cleanser may start to do its job too well, stripping away too much moisture. Most experts believe that around fortysomething, most women should leave soap – and even foaming cleansers – behind. 'Nobody over the age of 12 should be using soap on her face,' decrees Marcia Kilgore, of Manhattan's Bliss Spa. The appropriate choice is a richer lotion or cream formulation. Many of these can be rinsed away with water, so you needn't forgo that fresh feeling. (Avoid extremes of too-hot and icy cold water, however, as these can make skin more prone to spider veins.)

Cotton wool often leaves traces of cleanser behind, so top facialist Eve Lom's prescription is a muslin washcloth dipped in hot water and used to remove cleanser; repeat the action three times. 'When skin is warmed, use the cloth to rub gently away at patches of flaky skin, especially in the folds of the nose and chin.' Eve believes this is also the only daily exfoliation your skin needs. (See Exfoliation, right.)

Toning Alcohol-based toners are a definite no-no. (You might as well use paint stripper on a mature skin.) For freshness, try rosewater or orange flower water, look for the words 'gentle' or 'alcohol-free' on skin fresheners, or ask for a product which is alcohol-free and/or suitable for mature/ dry skins. Susan Harmsworth, of aromatherapy-based skincare line ESPA, suggests facial spritzers in place of toner – but look for mists with essential oils or hydrating ingredients as well as water. (These are also terrific instant cool downs for hot flushes. Try keeping yours in the fridge.)

Exfoliation This is a big 'buzzword', with dozens of new products hitting the shelves, designed to buff away the surface layers of skin. (For more on at-home peels and micro-dermabrasion kits – and why we're wary of them – see page 36.) The idea behind exfoliation is to slough away the dead surface layers which make skin appear dull, revealing brighter, newer, 'younger' skin underneath. This is achieved in several ways: manually – using an exfoliating scrub, or a washcloth – or chemically, with an enzyme- or fruit

massage magic

The biggest single thing you can do to boost your skin's radiance, we believe, is to massage it nightly – ideally, for two whole minutes, although even 30 seconds makes a difference. Don't move your fingers over the skin: move your face, with your fingers. Press hard with your fingers all around the eye orbital bone, and along the jaw (where most of us collect a great deal of stress). Press hard in the centre of your cheeks, and under the cheekbones, tracing the bones. This works to speed up blood flow (delivering a 'glow') and also drains the face, eliminating puffiness.

acid-based product, or a vitamin A product like Retin-A.

But – a big but – exfoliation should be carried out very gently on mature skins. Our own sensitive skins did not respond at all well when fruit acids were all the rage, a few years ago; if we used them more than once in a blue moon, our skins became inflamed. Until quite recently, we were both of the opinion that Eve Lom's method for cleansing – see left – was all the exfoliation that skin needed, but we have been converted by two very gentle facial scrubs, Liz Earle Naturally Active Gentle Face Exfoliator,

and Origins Modern Friction, which we each use when skin's looking a bit dingy. If you do use a manual scrub, make absolutely sure that it has no sharp exfoliant particles in it – such as crushed nut kernels – which may scratch the skin.

Protection Undoubtedly your greatest ally in the war against wrinkles is strict daily use of a reflective sunscreen with SPF15 or more – often now found in moisturisers – to protect your skin and possibly reverse existing damage. (More on sun, page 26.)

Antioxidants have also been found to

offer protection against free radical damage and a moisturiser with an SPF15 plus antioxidant ingredients is now widely accepted as your skin's best insurance policy. (Discover more about antioxidants on page 13.)

Everyday treatments All moisturisers combine water with oil, using ingredients that mimic the skin's natural sebum. Many women are happy simply to use a moisturiser that tops up the skin's water level and creates an almost imperceptible barrier trapping moisture in, where it can plump up fine lines and prevent a papery, dry look. We prefer to combine moisture with SPF protection (as we've explained). Whatever you choose, the rule of thumb is that mature skins need frequent application of moisturiser, morning and night. Don't neglect your neck and décolletage, use a special eye product for the eye zone, and avoid moisturising the folds of the nose, where excess moisturiser can contribute to the development of open pores. But when it comes to moisturiser, contrary to almost all our other advice: more is more, used sensibly. (See page 159 for advice on night creams, and turn to page 49 for details of skin replenishing facial oils.)

Masks and special treats If your skin isn't too sensitive and you like the occasional skin-brightening, mood-soothing effect of pampering yourself with a face mask, go ahead. The one caveat: choose moisturising masks, which don't set on the skin, rather than clay-based masks, which dry out – and mostly dry your skin out, too. Weekly or fortnightly is usually enough for most mature skins.

SHOPPING FOR SKINCARE

Our advice would be: don't buy a skin cream purely on the basis of a fancy graph. More important is to rely on your senses. Try the product before you buy it – on your hand, and preferably your face – to establish, firstly, how it feels on your skin and, secondly, whether it has the effect of making it feel and/or look smoother/softer/more hydrated. Trust your nose, too: do you like the fragrance? If possible, persuade the sales assistant to give you a sample so that you can try the product at home.

John Gustafson – who has completed the training programme of over 40 skincare companies – gave us this insight. 'Different companies have different policies on sampling anti-ageing products. When asked for samples, some companies have a strict policy: "Tell customers that because it's a long-term product, a mere sample won't give them enough time to see a result." Certainly, I'd agree

with that – but a sample is at least going to let them know if they like the texture, if they like the smell, or if they have a reaction to the product. So if a sales assistant says, "Oh, we don't give out samples of this product," say, "Would you mind if I brought in a little container and you gave some to me?" Then if they start saying, "I'm sorry but it's not hygienic and the product won't keep well like that," reply that you're willing to take that risk if they are.'

'I think it is significant that the real heavy-hitters in the beauty industry – for instance, La Prairie and Estée Lauder – are usually more than willing to sample their products, because they trust them implicitly. Yes, it is expensive to give out samples. But these companies are confident that if you use their product even for only two days a week for two weeks, you'll see sufficient results to want to come and buy them. And for the most part,' he concludes, 'you will.'

TAKE IT BACK!

You wouldn't think twice about taking a dress back if it fell apart after you'd worn it a couple of times. But most women never dream of returning a cosmetic that isn't working for them. Now, there are limits to what you can expect: you probably won't get very far in your quest for a refund if your complaint is that the skin cream which promised to work miracles in ten days hasn't made a blind bit of difference to your face. 'But if, for instance, a beauty consultant has sold you a moisturiser which she told you would be adequate for your dry skin and it's not, ask for a refund,' says John Gustafson. Also, you should definitely ask for a refund, adds John, if a product triggered an adverse reaction, even a minor one. Another good reason to take skincare or make-up back is if packaging is difficult to open, or delivers a wastefully large splodge of expensive moisturiser from the nozzle, because it has been badly designed.

Remember, your comments also give valuable feedback to cosmetics companies and help them to meet the consumer's needs in future. Except for items such as safety-sealed fragrances, returned skincare purchases are usually sent back to their individual manufacturers, who reimburse the stores. (One less reason to hesitate.) This is often the only way that companies get feedback from customers. A lot of problems, such as inconvenient dispensers, or hard-to-open jars, are identified in this way. After a particular product has been returned a lot, the manufacturers will often introduce changes, like redesigned packaging. Think of it as doing other women a service!

can you mix and match products?

At some stage when you're skincare shopping, you can be sure that a beauty consultant will try to sweet-talk you into buying an entire, matching regime – complete with heart-stopping price tag – from the company she represents. Well, don't fall for it. With refreshing honesty, Christina Carlino – founder of the Philosophy range – admits: 'I'm not a believer that you have to use everything from the same line. I'd love to say it was true, but it isn't anything we can prove or verify.'

Confirms John Gustafson, 'The reason people try to sell you the entire range is: that's their job. Most skincare lines do not work synergistically – that is, you won't get extra benefits from using the whole range together. Probably the best reason for buying products from one line is that you love the packaging.'

However, there are some products which definitely don't go together – and that's where the advice of a consultant may be extremely valuable. You'd be

absolutely nuts, we'd say, to buy a facial scrub and a home peel kit at the same time – quite simply, you'll be stripping off too many layers of skin. Our motto, when shopping, is: if in doubt, ask questions. But be prepared to walk away when the spiel goes into overdrive.

'It is very hard for women to get independent information,' John Gustafson acknowledges. So his advice is this…

● 'I always say: if it starts sounding like a chemistry lesson, leave. What I want is someone who'll say, "Look, Mrs Bloggins, if you take this product away now, by tomorrow you should find your skin is softer and smoother and by next week you'll find the fine lines are starting to soften." Practical, nitty-gritty explanations. What I don't want to hear is that it's an asymmetric carrier system with a time-release novasphere action. The question you need to ask is: "What am I going to see if I take your advice and buy the product?"'

● 'If you're going in for a moisturiser, tell the consultant that – and ask her to help you choose the right one for your skintype. If they then start trying to sell you a whole line of other things, simply be firm and say, "Today I just need a moisturiser, thanks".'

● 'Try to take the time to visit two or three counters and ask the same questions at each one.'

● 'Another good idea is to ask whether any of the consultants are beauty therapists; many are, and they may sometimes have a deeper understanding of the products. If the answer is "yes", then say to the assistant who is serving you: "I don't mean to insult you, but would you mind if I spoke with them? I have some questions that may be a bit technical." She shouldn't find that at all offensive – and should trust their products enough to be able to do it.'

Veteran supermodel **LINDA EVANGELISTA** is now fab at fortysomething, and still at the top of her profession. Some years ago, she gave us a piece of skincare advice we found really useful. 'I have a "wardrobe" of moisturisers,' Linda told us. 'In the morning, I don't just do things on automatic pilot: I really look at my skin, touch it, analyse what it needs. If I've been travelling or in the sun, I probably use a richer moisturiser. If I'm going to be outdoors working, I slather on a high-protection sunscreen. But some days my skin doesn't seem so "needy" – so I'll just use a lighter moisturiser.' Our experience is that skin does change – not just with the seasons, but from day to day and week to week, due to diet and hormonal cycles, among other factors. And it pays to tune into your complexion – and give it what it really needs.

SAFE SUN

When it comes to the links between suncare, skin cancer and ageing, there's so much confusion and misinformation that it's tempting to bury our heads in the sand (while leaving the rest of the body to fry). But in the war against skin ageing, sun protection is our greatest ally – and it's never too late – or too early – to start…

Lately, there has been a subtle shift in thinking about the sun. Yes, it still causes wrinkles. Yes, skin cancer statistics are soaring. But now, it is increasingly being recognised that the vitamin D production in the body triggered by sun exposure may also offer some health-protective benefits. Too little sun, and it seems that we're at added risk of osteoporosis, and perhaps colon, prostate and breast cancer; sunlight can also have a heart-protective effect, as well as its famous ability to alleviate tiredness, increase libido and alertness, and ease depression. According to the 'new thinking' on sun, we should all be making an effort to get outdoors, every day of the year, in order to keep our vitamin D levels topped up.

This is not a manifesto for reckless tanning, or a suggestion that you throw caution to the wind and fry, fry, fry. Nobody is advising that the deep mahogany tan that was so fashionable 30 years ago is A Good Thing. Apart from anything else, if you tan yourself the colour of hide, that's pretty much the texture of skin you can expect in later life: lined, wrinkled, leathery, with age spots galore. (Why do you think there's a sudden flurry of anti-age spot launches? Because the women who slathered on no-SPF oil, in the 1970s, are now getting the payback – in the form of hyperpigmentation.) Sunburn, too, is decidedly bad news: it does serious damage to skin's DNA, which in turn is linked with cellular changes that can lead to skin cancer. But between the tanaholic woman of the 70s and the sun-phobics of the 21st century, there is a happy medium.

In fact, according to Professor Anthony Quinn, a consultant dermatologist with the Imperial Cancer Research Fund, there is 'some evidence that you can actually reverse some of the damage sun does, even in later life. When patients in Australia with what's called actinic keratoses – pre-cancerous skin lesions – started to use effective sun protection, those lesions were reduced, even at a relatively late stage.'

We say: enjoy the sun – safely. Choose sun protection that you like to use – and use it. Take to the shade when possible (especially during the midday hours); you'll still tan, but slowly and steadily.

Slather on lots of antioxidant-rich after-sun, which helps neutralise some of the free radical damage triggered by UV exposure. Be sensible, yes. Paranoid? No.

The minimum daily protection you should be wearing is Sun Protection Factor 15 (SPF15), on face and body.
For experts we've spoken to, this is the 'magic' number. (Above SPF15, they say, numbers aren't truly representative: in fact, they're only a little more powerful.)

Get into the habit of wearing an SPF15 on your face.
Some dermatologists say you should do this 365 days a year, even when it's cloudy, in rainy Manchester or Montreal. We say: use common sense. If it's overcast, and you're barely seeing daylight, an SPF15 is probably superfluous to requirements. But if it's sunny? Or even bright? Go for it.

Wear an SPF on your lips, too.
Very wise: the lower lip is ultra-vulnerable to skin cancer, so lip sunscreen is a must, in summer. Most matte or satin lipsticks offer approximately an SPF15.

When shopping for sunscreen, always look for 'broad spectrum UVA/UVB protection.
Sunshine has different kinds of ultraviolet radiation: UVA and UVB. Both damage the DNA, so broad-spectrum protection is very important. (Boots offer a 'star rating' for UVA protection, with five stars the gold standard.)

Look for an SPF based on reflective ingredients, rather than chemical sunscreens.
Some scientists now believe that chemical sunscreens may transport solar radiation into the cells, unlike physical ones, which simply block it on the skin's surface. So we stick to physical ones, titanium dioxide and zinc oxide, which also seem to be more effective, according to research: new formulas are so fine that there's virtually no Mr Pastry look. Additionally, there are now antioxidant products (such as SkinCeuticals

CE Ferulic) designed to be applied topically alongside a sunprep for added protection.

Apply sunscreen before you go to the beach or sightseeing.
This is particularly important if you are pale or freckled. If you leave putting your sunscreen on until you've set up on the beach, you may already have been exposed for long enough to get sunburn.

Slap it on.
The key is to apply liberally – the equivalent of a shotglassful is needed to cover the whole adult body – and not to rub it in too hard, because you lose some protection.

If you are on the beach, reapply your sun protection frequently.
As soon as you're likely to be in the sun for long periods of time, you must reapply sunscreen frequently. This is because the sun breaks down the protective ingredients in the cream – reducing its effectiveness.

Use your common sense.
A sunscreen is useful – but it's only part of the picture. Think like Latin people. Avoid strong midday sunshine. Use your head – and put a hat on it! And never just lie in the sun. In reality, SPFs deliver only around a third or a quarter of the level of protection they promise; in lab conditions, a thick layer of cream is used, but we massage creams into the body, dramatically reducing protection. Our advice is to find a nice shady spot and relax there: you'll still get a tan (sunlight bounces off sand, stone and even grass), but you'll never burn.

Avoid sunbeds.
Don't go there. New evidence is emerging that they are far more harmful than previously thought – partly because, in a half-hour session, you get far more exposure than if you spent the same time

outdoors – and, in turn, that may be linked to an increased risk of skin cancer.

A fake tan gives no protection.
Although some fake tanners claim to offer a (low) level of sun protection, this is very short lived, and is only active immediately after first application.

suncare –
what we use

We don't believe in being paranoid about sun damage – the sun offers health benefits, as well as bringing risks. In England, Jo has been known to slather olive oil (which is packed with natural antioxidants) on her body, while using an SPF15 on her face – from Liz Earle, Estée Lauder DayWear, or Vaishaly Day Moisturiser SPF15. She does make a point, though, of never, ever sitting in the sun without a large hat.
Sarah will only use sunpreps with a physical barrier – titanium dioxide and/or zinc oxide. Brandwise, it's Liz Earle Naturally Active Suncare, Green People, Dr Hauschka or ZO1 (an Aussie brand).

NIGELLA LAWSON

We love the fact Nigella's no stick insect. Her glowing natural beauty and curves are a great advertisement for living life to the full. And, like Nigella, we think life's too short to live on celery and cottage cheese...

'In my 20s I was crippled by self-consciousness, but one of the best things about getting older is not being so concerned with how others view you. I think a lot of life is a struggle between vanity and laziness, and now I'm happier to give in to the laziness! But in reality, maintenance is required. Once upon a time, having my hair coloured was fun – "what colour today?" – but now, it's what colour do I not want to have, which is not so amusing. I have my brows threaded by Vaishaly Patel – who is a total genius – and occasionally, I'll have a facial with her, but generally, I am a very impatient person and when I'm lying on a massage table I just want to get up and flee. I always feel there are so many other things I could be getting on with. I feel very content with my life, but I do realise that I can't have everything. A wise friend said that you can have two lives, but not three: you can work and go out, or work and have children, or have children and go out, but you can't do all three. Actually, I don't want three lives; I love being at home, and the one thing I would like is a bit more time just to lie around with Charles (Saatchi) and the children.

'I read an interview with Liz Hurley in which she said, "You have to choose between the cookie jar and size 6 jeans," and she's right – you do have to decide which matters more: clothes or food. For me, it's definitely food. My father always told me two things: that men notice what you look like and women notice what you wear; and that a sticky-out tummy is very sexy on a woman! I make sure I dress to suit my shape, with fitted dresses and cashmere cropped cardigans. But more and more, I realise that how you feel about yourself really doesn't depend on your body, so much as what sort of mood you're in.

'I do try and eat for health – I eat blueberries every day, with hot porridge, and I love vegetables – if anything, too much; I can eat a pound and a half of broccoli and feel like I'm expecting quads. I find not picking is the best thing for not putting on weight. I take psyllium in water, every day, for my digestion – and I'm an aquaholic; I need lots of water and when I wake up in the morning there are probably six 330ml Evian bottles by the bed, which I've emptied in the night.

'I renounced exercise a few years ago but when I had a back operation and was completely out of action I was advised to take up Pilates; I now do half an hour a day, and it's made a huge difference. I like the fact Pilates doesn't make you hot and sweaty. I also think that walking is great exercise – and does my head a lot of good. If I could, I'd walk the children to school every day and just keep on walking. Cooking is another great way of clearing my head.

'I can't bear the feeling of going to bed with make-up on and I am still a huge fan of Eve Lom's cleanser, removed with a muslin cloth, to exfoliate the skin. But I've been converted to Vaishaly's night cream, which I like because it doesn't leave me shiny. I wear sunblock religiously and on holiday I look like a mad Englishwoman from a Merchant-Ivory film, in a big hat, with a shawl, and I swim in a hat and sunglasses. So that I don't look too white I mix Anthelios XL SPF 60 with a MAC Body Tint. And I wear a factor 20 Laura Mercier Tinted Moisturiser, all the year round, which looks much better than foundation.

'My mother was very disciplined; she used Boots Baby Lotion religiously and had hand creams on every surface, and I do feel her shadow reprimanding me, because my hands look like I've spent the last 45 years scrubbing floors. But my one good area is that I get Andrea Fullerton to do my nails once every three weeks. Otherwise, I read everything about health and beauty, am hugely inspired, go out and buy the latest cream or vitamin – and after about three days I go back to my lazy ways!'

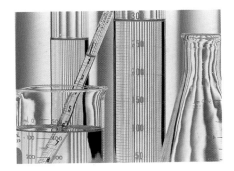

DRUGS FOR YOUR FACE

Women now have another choice in the anti-ageing skincare field, as dermatologists start to prescribe potent creams to hold back time.

RETIN-A

It is now well over a decade since news broke that a cream designed for treating acne could alleviate the fine lines and rough texture of sun-damaged skin. Derived from vitamin A, Retin-A (aka tretinoin) catapulted us into the age of the cosmeceutical, when changes effected by skincare are more than just short-lived plumping of fine lines with oil and water.

According to consultant dermatologist Dr Nick Lowe, director of the Cranley Clinic in London and clinical professor of dermatology at the UCLA School of Medicine, California, retinoid creams that contain prescription retinoid substances related to vitamin A have been proven to improve skin ageing, by increasing collagen formation and renewing the epidermis. 'The result,' he writes in his book *Away With Wrinkles*, 'is a brighter, healthier-looking and more supple skin with fewer fine lines and blotchy dark patches and a more resilient feel.'

Retin-A has been used since the 1960s for treating acne and has a long proven history of safety. However, there is some controversy over whether or not it increases sensitivity to the sun. Dr Lowe maintains not, although, like other experts, he recommends using it in conjunction with a broad spectrum moisturising sunscreen, applied every morning, for the best chance of improvement. Many physicians advise keeping exposure to sunlight – including sunlamps – to a minimum, however, while using Retin-A or related products.

The big downside is irritation. In the most publicised research project on Retin-A to date, at the University of Michigan, in the US, most of the patients developed serious enough skin irritation to warrant withholding the cream from them for a few days. In the end, three of the 40 patients in the trial withdrew from treatment. (Some patients using Retin-A for acne also stop for similar reasons.)

Irritation is especially high during the first two weeks, when redness, itching, slight burning and scaling are common. Because skin is thinned, water loss may be speeded up – and it may be easier for irritants to enter the skin, creating reactions to products that the complexion had got along with just fine in the past.

Dr Lowe says that side effects such as dryness, redness and flaking occur if Retin-A is used too frequently or at too high a strength. He recommends using creams, which are less drying than gels, at a lower strength (eg Retin-A 0.025 per cent) nightly, on alternate nights, or even every third night, to reverse skin ageing. He also recommends Retin-A as part of a combination treatment with chemical peels, microdermabrasion, Botox and fillers in more severely aged skin.

But would we put it anywhere near our faces? We would not.

what Retin-A did for me

AGE: 58
PROFESSION: HOUSEWIFE

'Like most women my age, I grew up not realising the dangers of lying in the sun, and though people think I look good for my age, I do have some wrinkles and crêpiness that are down to sun-worship. When I read about Retin-A, I was off to my doctor like lightning. He wrote a private prescription – then sent me off into the wide blue yonder. I certainly didn't get any instructions about how to use it, or information about side effects.

'The cream was to be used at night. I went home and slapped it on, expecting to wake up looking wonderful. But I soon realised that it was too strong to use every night, since it was making my face look quite red – like I'd been out in the sun; it was also itchy and irritated, so I cut down to every other night instead.

'Within a couple of months, my skin did look a little smoother and slightly "plumped up" – but the effects weren't very dramatic. I persevered for a while, but decided Retin-A was no better and no worse than other expensive skin creams. I still use it for a mini-treatment – if I want my skin to look brighter for a special event – but wasn't convinced enough to go on using it on a regular basis. On balance, my experience is that you have to treat Retin-A with caution.'

OTHER FORMS OF RETIN-A

In 1995 the US Food and Drug Administration sanctioned Retinova or Renova, a younger cousin of Retin-A, for use to reverse the effects of sun damage. Renova contains the same active ingredient in a more moisturising, cosmetic-like base. In the clinical trials, which involved more than 300 people between 30 and 50 over 48 weeks, physicians noted some signs of skin improvement in 78 per cent of subjects treated with Renova. Sixty-four per cent showed improvement in fine wrinkling, 65 per cent reduction in brown spots, and 51 per cent smoothing of surface roughness. But fascinatingly, in the control group, who were treated with a placebo skin cream plus a comprehensive skincare and sun-avoidance programme, 38 per cent showed improvement in fine wrinkles, 48 per cent reduction in brown spots, and 33 per cent smoothing of surface roughness. So you can get significant improvements by treating your skin well and protecting it against UV radiation.

The irritation level for Renova is said to be 'moderate', with potential for mild redness, itching and scaling, as with Retin-A. However, four per cent of patients in the study discontinued Renova because of adverse reactions. Be aware, too, that among women of colour, these products may cause pigmentation problems, such as lightening, mottling or darkening of the skin. Dr Lowe adds that Retinova/Renova is too greasy for some people and leads to whiteheads and acne.

A new type of retinoid goes by the name of Tazarotene, in cream or gel formulations. It's been approved as a skin rejuvenation cream in America and probably will soon be approved for use in Europe. Dr Lowe says that recent research shows that Tazarotene cream can reverse some of the effects of skin ageing much more quickly than Retin-A, but it can be slightly more irritating.

(And once again, we wouldn't dream of putting these products anywhere near our sensitive skins.)

what Retinova did for me

AGE: 46
PROFESSION: MANAGER FOR HAIR SALON GROUP

'I suppose, over my lifetime, I've had an average amount of sun exposure and I was beginning to notice lines and wrinkles. So about four years ago, I went on Retinova. I was prescribed it by a doctor in a cosmetic surgery clinic. He

HOW TO USE RETIN-A

It is very, very important that you use these products correctly to minimise the risk of adverse reactions such as excessive redness, flaking and irritation. As Dr Patricia Wexler, leading Manhattan dermatologist, told us: 'Just because a little Retin-A/Retinova may be a good thing, a lot is definitely not better.'

● Ask your doctor/dermatologist for written instructions, tailored to your needs, for a six-month programme.
● Ask where you should apply the product and only put it in those areas.
● Make sure you are given a low-strength product to start with, especially if you have sensitive skin.
● Always test a small area with the cream first; if it stings excessively or itches, contact your doctor.
● Apply it every other night for four weeks; if there is no redness or flaking, you can apply nightly. Clean the area first with a moisturising wash to reduce irritation; do not use soap or detergent, which will dry the skin out more.
● Do not get the cream into the eyes; if you do, rinse with running water and wash your hands afterwards.
● Use a sunscreen every day with an SPF (Sun Protection Factor) of 15. Ideally, the sunscreen should have a four- (****) or five- (*****) star UVA rating. Each morning after washing or showering, apply it to the sun-exposed skin of the face, neck and hands. In the summer, on outdoor days, or snow-skiing in winter, use a waterproof sunscreen with an SPF25–30. The sunscreen, again, should have four or five UVA stars. (Dr Nicholas Lowe suggests sunscreens by Garnier Ambre Solaire, Neutrogena, Nivea, Piz Buin, Soltan or Uvistat.)

NB *Retin-A is not recommended for pregnant women because of a risk that vitamin A derivatives may cause birth defects; it should also be avoided by women who are breast-feeding.*

was very careful to make sure that I knew exactly how much of the cream to use, and from that moment on I couldn't put my face in the sun except with a high SPF. Now I never venture outside without an SPF30.

'I was told that some people can expect mild side effects – in my case, it took the form of what felt like dozens and dozens of horrible tiny little spots under the surface of the skin, over the first few weeks of the treatment. You could hardly see them – but I could feel them. Apart from that, there was no redness or itching. I never really got to the point where I thought, "something's happening" – but I would say now that my skin isn't ageing at the same rate as people around me, and I'm sure that's down to the Retinova.

'I used the prescribed amount of cream – a pea-sized dollop – every other night, building up to every night after about a month; you use it instead of a night cream, because it's quite emollient. I stuck with that regime for about a year and then, when I felt I'd achieved the maximum benefits, cut back to a maintenance programme of two or three times a week. More isn't necessarily better.

'The real difference to my skin was that in the past I'd always felt I needed to wear foundation. After about a year on Retinova, I got to the point where I felt confident enough with my skin to go bare-faced: there was a new clarity and a kind of glow, as well as being smoother. It wasn't a massive, overnight improvement; it was very, very gradual – and nothing to make me go, "Golly, that's amazing." But I'm very happy with my skin and I've recommended Retinova to girlfriends. I don't think it's turned the clock back – but I'm fairly sure it's stopped it ticking forwards.'

NON-PRESCRIPTION ANTI-OXIDANT VITAMINS

In recent years, more and more skincare companies have been turning to members of the vitamin A ingredient family, and using them in anti-ageing formulations. These vitamin A derivatives – often retinols or retinyls (such as retinyl palmitate and retinyl linoleate) – have gained popularity because they offer some of the benefits of Retin-A or Retinova, without the irritation.

Other strong contenders are vitamins C and E, as we explain below.

VITAMIN C

There are two possible reasons for putting vitamin C on your skin: protection and treatment. As an antioxidant, vitamin C applied to the skin can help protect it, neutralising some of the damage done by free radicals caused by UV exposure and pollution.

But much higher concentrations of vitamin C – up to ten per cent – are also being squeezed into skincare. Dermatologists now believe that these larger, 'therapeutic' doses of topical vitamin C (L-Ascorbic acid, ascorbyl palmitate or magnesium ascorbyl phosphate) can help repair skin and encourage collagen growth and repair – thereby increasing skin firmness and helping to smooth out fine lines and wrinkles. In addition, vitamin C has been reported to inhibit our bodies' production of melanin – the stuff that produces not only a tan, but also freckles and sun spots. In the US, some doctors are also prescribing vitamin C after laser surgery, to quicken recovery.

You will probably never see – with a naked eye – any improvements to your skin from using creams which merely feature small doses of vitamin C as an antioxidant; they're just designed to prevent future damage. (See A-C-E protection, opposite.) But even as a treatment, in high concentrations, don't expect overnight miracles; Jeffrey Rapaport, MD – a Fort Lee, New Jersey, dermatologist – says: 'Vitamin C isn't a quick fix. It's a slow process, often taking six to nine months before you see results.' Skincare manufacturers, on the other hand, would like to persuade us that two months is the maximum it takes to see benefits.

And vitamin C has a couple of downsides. It can be very unstable and rendered ineffective by exposure to air. The leading cosmetics manufacturers claim, however, to have developed delivery systems which can get the vitamin into our skin intact – for instance with hermetically sealed ampoules or individual patches.

In high doses, vitamin C can also irritate and even burn sensitive skin, particularly when combined with other high-tech ingredients. If you use a prescription vitamin A cream like Retin-A or Retinova, warns Dr Patricia Wexler, use it at the opposite end of the day to your vitamin C cream.

VITAMIN E

Beauties often swear that simply breaking open a capsule of vitamin E and massaging it into their skin has a gloriously anti-ageing effect. (On the other hand, experts point out, vitamin E – particularly in the synthetic form – can cause contact sensitivity, so it doesn't suit everyone.) But scientists are still trying to unravel its mysteries and work out why vitamin E may be effective.

Like vitamin C, vitamin E is an antioxidant, helping to fight sun and smog damage when it's formulated into skin creams. (Look for it on the label as d-alpha tocopherol – the natural form – or tocopheryl acetate.) According to dermatologist Dr Nelson Lee Novick, MD, author of *You Can Look Younger At Any Age*, 'What we can say at the present time is that, at least in lab studies, vitamin E can block the sunburn in laboratory animals when applied to the skin – even up to eight hours after exposure. It is also able to decrease skin thickness and sensitivity after sun exposure, and to have direct sunscreening properties when applied before exposure.' So for now, vitamin E is particularly being deployed in sun protection, and after-suns.

A-C-E PROTECTION

Dermatologists have long believed that topical applications of carefully balanced doses of vitamins A, C and E – as well as other antioxidants like green tea, resveratrol (from grape skins) and pycnogenol (from pine bark) – may have an important effect in preventing skin damage, by 'mopping up' the harm done by UV light and pollution. Which is why almost any anti-ageing skin cream – or after-sun – now includes antioxidants in the formula, to 'neutralise' some of this free radical damage.

This hunch was confirmed almost a decade ago, with the publication of an eight-year French study – Su.Vi.Max (the Supplementation, Vitamin and Mineral Antioxidant trial), run by a non-profit group of independent French scientists and dermatologists. For the study, the skins of 160 women in Tours, Toulouse and Grenoble were looked at over 18 months. Half applied an antioxidant cream (formulated by none other than Estée Lauder); the others had a 'placebo' moisturiser (also Lauder-formulated) – and nobody was allowed to wear extra sun protection. Several tests were carried out to measure improvements.

It was a small sample (but statistically significant) and what the experts saw was a total surprise: not only did the topical antioxidants help protect the skin against ongoing damage from pollution and UV rays (resulting in a 23 per cent reduction in the formation of new lines and wrinkles), but in the group given the real antioxidant cream, the skin actually began to repair itself – resulting in a very, very small reduction in lines and wrinkles of an average of eight per cent.

'But if women were only going to do one thing for their skin, I would say, absolutely: use an antioxidant,' Dr Maes concludes. (And he's so convinced of the benefits that his ultimate career challenge is to produce a sun protection product which relies purely on antioxidants, to minimise sun damage.)

For ourselves, we are absolutely convinced of the benefits of antioxidants. That's why we take them internally (in the form of supplements), and slather them on to our skin, believing that (for now, at least), antioxidants are probably the best insurance policy we can invest in for our skins – and, indeed, our health.

THE BOTTOM LINE ON LINES

If you read the advertisements for some of the newest anti-ageing creams on the market, you'd think that they were the equivalent of Botox, in a jar. But do they work? Read on...

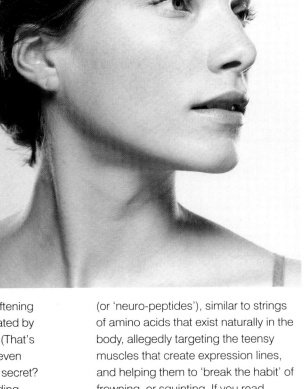

Oh, the fun that beauty marketing folk must have, dreaming up product and ingredient names. Lately, it seems, they've been working overtime. Suddenly, from out of nowhere, has come a new generation of anti-ageing cream: the line-relaxer. And most of them have names – or feature ingredients – that sound not a little like a certain well-known muscle-relaxing ingredient, Botox. Think: D-Contraxol (in Lancôme Résolution), or Protox, or Natralox. Why, Elizabeth Arden have even teamed up with Allergan, makers of the Botox muscle-paralysing injections, to launch a skin cream called Prevâge.

Five years ago, an anti-ageing cream was pretty much an anti-ageing cream. Now, it seems, in order to persuade women to splash out on these 'miracle creams', the marketing's been subtly reworked: creams must now 'relax lines', or 'smooth wrinkles' or 'freeze the muscles that cause frowns'. In other words, the implication is that what's in the jar can deliver pretty much the effects of a visit to a cosmeto-dermatologist, without the pain factor. Some of the spiel we're forced to read about these creams (in the line of beauty editor duty) has to

be seen to be believed. As one product trumpets, 'this revolutionary product relaxes facial muscles in a non-paralytic manner, softening deep expression lines generated by repeated facial movements.' (That's frowning, scowling and yes, even laughing, to you and me.) Its secret? A straight-from-the-lab-sounding peptide called Octamioxyl®. Givenchy's version is 'No Surgetics', while DDF's was initially called 'Faux-Tox' – until that proved a little too close for comfort to a certain line-relaxing jab, and they were encouraged to change the name to 'Wrinkle-Relax'.

We decided to put out dozens of these new creams, for testing, to our panellist teams. Each was assessed by ten women – and you can read about the highest-scoring products in the box on the right. But we've heard from many visitors to our website, www.beautybible.com, that you're intrigued to know about how these products are meant to work. Well, the active ingredients that are said to have the desired effect are mostly 'peptides'

(or 'neuro-peptides'), similar to strings of amino acids that exist naturally in the body, allegedly targeting the teensy muscles that create expression lines, and helping them to 'break the habit' of frowning, or squinting. If you read between the lines of the ads, many actually say they're strengthening the skin – which in turn (the manufacturers promise), makes it 'more resistant to the impact of dermo-creasing'. (That's expression lines, to you and me.)

Interestingly, many of these creams deliver a physical sensation – cooling or chilling the skin, so that you really feel that something is happening. Do read what our testers have to say – but also, bear this in mind, from Dr David Fenton, consultant dermatologist at St Thomas's Hospital in London: 'If they were really having an effect, relaxing the muscles, lifting the skin or causing it to contract, they would not be available over the counter but would need to be licensed. The effect may be more psychological.' According to Rand Rusher, of the Beverly Hills brand Leaf & Rusher, 'These creams may work on the tiny surface muscles – but I'd stake my career on the fact that they can't work on deeper expression lines.'

Actually, alongside this trend for line-relaxers, there is another new generation of products emerging to tackle our wrinkles – and in this case, we're definitely converts. 'Line fillers' (see overleaf) can be dabbed and smoothed into wrinkles and groooves to make them disappear in a flash. They don't bring about changes in the skin; they're purely cosmetic – working, rather like Polyfilla, to fill lines. Mostly, they're made of silicones and polymers (a sort of malleable plastic, in this case), which have a renowned skin-smoothing effect when applied to the skin's surface. They're also packed with light-diffusing pigments that 'bounce' light off the skin, 'blurring' the appearance of wrinkles. When Jo demonstrated one of these products (Prescriptives Invisible Line Smoother) on TV a few years ago, it created a nationwide stampede. Jo's fiftysomething 'guinea pig' professed herself so blown away by the results that the station's switchboard collapsed under the weight of calls – and Prescriptives had to airlift in back-up supplies from the US to meet demand.

They're definitely products where practice makes perfect: it's important to experiment with different techniques, to see whether the line-filler is best used under make-up or applied on top of foundation/powder, for a more flawless appearance. They may be a bit too much of a faff for everyday use – but definitely worth a go, we'd say, for special occasions, hot dates or when you're having your picture taken.

tried & tested LINE-RELAXING CREAMS

We'd love to have totally positive results to report in this category, but alas, our testers were for the most part disappointed with the dozens they tried. They were asked to look specifically for 'Botox-like' actions (which all of these creams promise) – but in the vast majority of cases, there were no significant (or any) differences, even after some months' use. But for a few individuals, there did seem to be some real effects – so remember, these scores are an average. The bottom line? These were the best of an underwhelming bunch.

beauty steal **SUPERDRUG OPTIMUM ADVANCE WRINKLE REDUCTION SERUM**
Score: 6.5/10
This highly affordable product has 'line-eliminating' ingredient Boxilift™ plus antioxidant vitamin C, green and white teas , and wheat proteins, for an instant tightening effect. The relatively low score reflects a couple of testers who saw absolutely no changes – whereas for several, it distinctly exceeded expectations.
Comments: 'Frown lines between my eyes seem less noticeable, and a friend complimented me on my skin condition – a first!' • 'I've had Botox between my brows and top lip before; though the result isn't as intense, this certainly does "lift"' • 'lines do seem a little less obvious on my forehead' • 'definitely gives a temporary "fix" – plumping up fine lines on forehead and from mouth to nose, but after a break of four days, lines seemed as visible as ever' • 'didn't do a thing'.

ELEMIS PRO-COLLAGEN WRINKLE SMOOTH
Score: 6/10
With Indian mulberry, malachite, montmorrilonite (a clay), and micro-algae, this new generation product gives an 'it's working' menthol-y tingle after the pen applicator targets your lines. But most of our testers failed to see the reduction in appearance lines by up to 68 per cent in 14 days that Elemis's own tests observed.
Comments: 'Forehead area plumper, and wrinkles reduced – like Botox' • 'deep lines don't look as deep – blurred' • ' my wrinkles haven't magically disappeared, but are definitely less prominent' • 'light-reflecting effect seems to reduce expression lines' • 'slight improvement in frown lines' • 'no difference at all'.

YSL LISSE EXPERT ADVANCED INTENSIVE ANTI-WRINKLE CRÈME
Score: 5.85/10
With bio-peptides – as in many 'wrinkle-relaxing' products – and a special application method, YSL describe this as a 'morpho-smoothing cream that adapts to each facial type, to effectively counteract all wrinkles'.
Comments: 'Very fine lines have disappeared and wrinkles are softer; my husband has even commented' • 'fine lines are slightly improved, but deep lines still deep' • 'none of the many I've tried give the line-free finish that Botox does. But this is one of the best at making lines appear better' • 'no visible difference'.

HANDLE WITH CARE

The beauty world likes to shout about its latest breakthroughs – and currently, home peels and microdermabrasion kits are all the rage. But we say: proceed with caution.

Ten years ago, it was AHA creams that were the hottest beauty news – derived from sugar cane, or milk, or wine. No self-respecting beauty company could afford not to have an AHA (alpha-hydroxy acid, also known as 'fruit acids') turn-back-the-clock cream in their skincare portfolio. And not surprisingly, AHA creams (and their 'sister' products, BHAs) had women rushing to the beauty counters. The idea was that these skin creams and serums would exfoliate skin through the use of fruit-derived acids, revealing fresher, newer, brighter skin beneath.

But the less alluring truth, as we – and many other women – discovered, was that these 'miracle' products often had a downside. Although we both experienced some (temporary) skin brightening, it came along with redness, scaliness and a kind of 'facial dandruff' – probably a sign of the speeded-up exfoliation process that the acids famously trigger. We – and all sorts of women we know – actually developed serious sensitivity problems which were triggered at the time we used these AHAs. (Maybe it was coincidence. We've no scientific proof of a link. But Jo knows that the very first time she used one, she woke up next morning with an angry red patch which she'd never had before, but which now flares up again whenever her skin is stressed. Or whenever she tries any other AHA-based product.)

So we're understandably a little cautious about the industry's latest thrust to encourage us to exfoliate our skins. Now, we're being encouraged to blitz away the top layers of our skin with at-home alternatives to microdermabrasion, based on equally potent ingredients which mimic the effects of a salon or surgery peel. And the trend's even trickled down to mass level. Everyone is jumping on this bandwagon, from the high street names right through to the big guns.

Now, in the right hands – which as far as we're concerned usually means the right doctor's surgery – these treatments can indeed be skin brightening, and help to 'roll back the years'. (For more about salon or clinical peels and dermabrasion – and how to find the right professional – see pages 144 and 147.) And it's true that the at-home use kits tend to feature lower levels of active ingredients than you'll find in a clinic or salon treatment. But we are still, frankly, anxious about home use versions. The problem isn't so much with the products themselves. It's that, as consumers, we have trouble adjusting to the idea that less is more – which certainly applies with home peels and microdermabrasion.

Used very, very gently and in accordance with manufacturer's instructions, you may get great results. But you need to follow those instructions to the letter. (And we know that the first thing most beauty-hounds do when they get a new product home is chuck the box and instruction leaflet.) If the instructions say leave it on for one minute, that's what you do – with a kitchen timer. Don't run away with the idea that two minutes, or five, is going to multiply the improvements the treatment offers. Ditto, if the how-to says 'rub gently': don't think that applying some extra pressure is going to turbo-charge the benefits. These products work by removing the surface layers of skin. Our philosophy is that these layers were put there for a reason: protection. If you do make the choice to use one of these products, be sure to shield skin during the day with an SPF15, minimum, for the following month, as it will be more vulnerable than usual.

Of course, we could have tested at-home peels and microdermabrasion kits for this book. But the truth is that we were anxious not to risk any harm to our testers' skins, so we decided not to. We wouldn't use them ourselves – and so it didn't seem fair to ask our testers to trial them. If you've bought one of these kits and would like to e-mail us with your own experiences – good or negative – we'd love to hear from you: just visit www.beautybible.com, and share your thoughts. For now, we remain cautious. (So don't say you weren't warned.)

tried & tested LINE FILLERS

These are the 'quick fix' alternative to Botox – perfect for the 'needle-phobic'. They work in two ways. First off, dabbed on to skin, they literally 'fill' wrinkles – just as Polyfilla fills a crack in your wall – plumping up lines with a combination of ingredients which usually includes silicone, for its amazing smoothing effect. (NB: when applied to the skin, silicone is completely inert and harmless – unlike when it's used as an injection, or an implant.) They also contain high levels of 'optical' pigments, which bounce light off the face – so that basically, your lines are blurred to the naked eye. (And – as a bonus – some of them actually incorporate anti-ageing skincare ingredients, too.) The technology's not completely perfect yet – these are the best of a not-very-high-scoring bunch – and frankly, they're probably too much bother for everyday use. But they're great for an important occasion like a job interview, wedding or party. We confidently predict that this category is going to be huge.

PRESCRIPTIVES MAGIC INVISIBLE LINE SMOOTHER
Score: 6.93/10

Prescriptives describe this as 'an intuitive gel', which fills in lines and deep wrinkles to re-create a supple, even surface. It's packed with optical diffusers which 'bounce' light off skin, and soften any unevenness. Several of our testers opted to use this as an all-over-face primer – which is an expensive method – but they loved the results!
Comments: 'Beautifully silky and soft, perfect for the under-eye area; skin looked younger and clearer; most lines disappeared; make-up went on well after' • 'my mother, who is 50, loved it' • 'perfect after a late night to perk up eye area – made skin look brighter and younger' • 'no stinging and felt very light on the skin' • 'invisible under foundation but skin felt a lot smoother; fine lines less noticeable' • 'never felt skin or eye area so silky' • 'very easy to apply; lines seemed to blur and soften' • 'make-up sat on it perfectly' • 'only needed a tiny bit – a friend commented how flawless my skin looked'.

LA PRAIRIE ROSE ILLUSION LINE FILLER
Score: 6.9/10

This is a skin treatment as well as an instant fix: alongside the silicone, light-deflecting polymers and optical diffusers, La Prairie have incorporated moisturising glycerine, marine collagen, vitamin E and their own exclusive Cellular Complex. And there's a bonus: the rose scent of this product wafts blissfully up the nostrils, as some testers commented. Again, some testers just couldn't resist using this as a primer.
Comments: 'The lines under my eyes and on my forehead seemed blurred; overall tone of my skin was firmer and plumper, skin appear more flawless and glowing; texture improved' • 'people said that I glowed; someone said my skin looked very peaches and cream' • 'you need less than the size of your little finger nail' • 'fine lines didn't disappear, but looked less obvious' • 'better than the primers and flash balms I've used in the past; it lifted my whole face' • 'skin felt springy, wrinkles seemed less prominent, lines smoother and finer, and it lifted the eye area' • 'I used this on one side of my face, which looked brighter and less tired – radiant' • 'my skin just got better during the day – more refined and glowing' • 'this was fantastic as a primer – my foundation just glided on, and it helped my eye make-up'.

CHRISTIAN DIOR CAPTURE R60/80 INTENSE DEEP WRINKLE FILLER
Score: 6.54/10

Dior tell us that this silicone-rich filler contains 'Bi-Skin', which plumps up the hollows of wrinkles, visibly tautening and smoothing even deep lines within an hour. Over time, a botanical extract (commiphora oil) is alleged to increase cell volume, 'pushing up' the bottom of the wrinkle – although our testers were asked to assess the immediate effects, rather than any long-term benefits. Some testers loved it, while others were decidedly underwhelmed.
Comments: 'Fine lines diminished and less visible' • 'looks very natural' • 'gave a nice, smooth texture, making any light foundation appear smoother and more radiant' • 'Did exactly what it said, filling deep lines; definitely something I'll spend my money on in future – in fact, my second tube is already in use'.

SKIN DOCS – IN A JAR

Once upon a time, we only thought of dermatologists in terms of skin problems: lumps, bumps, itching. But in the last couple of years, 'dermatologists' skincare' has become a hot anti-ageing trend. The thinking is that nobody knows more about complexions than a skin doc, who gets 'up close and personal' with pores, lines and wrinkles on a daily basis. And today, in the battle of the skincare brands, these doctors and dermatologists have become the new gurus.

Doctor-designed skincare falls into the category of 'cosmeceuticals': a cross between cosmetics and pharmaceuticals. The idea with these new 'doctor' creams is that the once-exclusive personal expertise that top derms offer by appointment is now available in a bottle.

Actually, we think it's a bit of a gimmick. In reality, every skin cream that you can buy is created by a skin expert – in the labs of the major beauty companies (like L'Oréal, or Estée Lauder, which we've visited, and where we've been hugely impressed at the gazillions poured into research and development each year).

LOOKING AFTER YOUR EYES

Regardless of what comes out of your mouth, your eyes speak the truth. They smile. They glare. They show stress. They cry. And they give the game away about your age.

The skin surrounding the eyes is the thinnest on the body, as fine as an eggshell and at least four times thinner than the skin on the soles of your feet. This means that the moisture evaporates easily – and precisely because eyes are so expressive, the skin around them forms wrinkles faster than elsewhere on the face. The eyelids themselves have some of the thinnest skin on the body – between a half and a quarter of the thickness of your cheek. Blood vessels are close to the surface. There is less elastin and only a thin band of collagen. What's more, eyelids get an exhausting workout, blinking between 12 and 20 times a minute. They even move while you sleep. And then there's the barrage of abuse that eyes are subjected to: contact lenses, mascara, eyeliner, marathon sessions at the computer, smoke-filled rooms and sunlight. No wonder our eyes start to show up signs of ageing sooner than anywhere else.

Depending on your habits, the first signs of ageing around the eyes can appear as early as your twenties or as late as your forties. Non-smokers who keep to the shade and wear sunglasses are, genes willing, going to have younger-looking eyes than their smoking, sun-worshipping peers. 'But the good news is that you can effect tremendous changes in the eye area,' says Debra Jaliman, MD, a dermatologist and clinical instructor at Mount Sinai School of Medicine in New York City. 'As easily as you can damage the eye skin, you can fix it. Everybody can improve its appearance, to some degree.'

While we are, in general, fans of simple skincare regimes rather than bathroom shelves cluttered with dozens of lotions and potions, there is definitely a case for using a separate eye cream from your regular moisturiser for the eye zone. 'It's important that products used near the eyes be appropriate for this sensitive area, where stinging and burning can happen all too easily,' says New York-based dermatologist Dr Karen Burke, MD, PhD. That's why some ingredients regularly used in facial moisturisers – like fragrance, certain emulsifiers and emollients – are eliminated from eye products. (Key words to look for, if you have sensitive eyes and aren't sure

which are the most effective way of shielding the eye area. An SPF15 sunscreen is also advisable. Here's the quandary, however: most sunscreens advise you to avoid the eye area, because of the very real potential for stinging. But dermatologist Joseph P Bark, MD, author of *Your Skin: An Owner's Guide* (see Directory), believes we should be using sunscreen around the eyes, regardless. The key is to find a suitable formulation: to minimise the potential for stinging, try different SPF15 moisturisers (on your hand), trying to identify those which go fairly matte after application, as these are less likely to travel into the eye itself. Many lightweight daily moisturisers now incorporate an SPF15 sunscreen (the magic figure); these are more suitable for the eye area than summer 'beach'-type sunscreens, which tend to be greasier. Or look out for specially designed eye products that contain sunscreens, which are starting to turn up within cosmetic ranges as the manufacturers respond to our angst about sun damage to the eye zone. The ideal regime is to use a basic, light moisturiser with sunscreen on the entire face – including the eye zone – during the day, and at night, try a specialised eye product.

There is a baffling number of options, featuring ingredients from high-tech liposomes to antioxidants via line-relaxing peptides – and whether targeting wrinkles, dark circles or puffiness, many eye cream manufacturers now tap into the botanical trend by using ingredients like rosemary, ginseng, green tea and rosewater.

So we asked our panellists – more than 2,500 testers, in all – to try out dozens of eye creams, over a period of several months. Here are their eye-opening conclusions…

whether a product will suit you, are 'hypo-allergenic', 'fragrance-free' and/or 'ophthalmologically tested' – which means that the product has been screened for ingredients that might trigger eye sensitivity.)

The skin around the eye area presents another problem in that it loses moisture easily but can't tolerate heavy products; this is because the oil glands in the eye area are fewer in number and smaller in size than those on the rest of the face. Use of too-rich cosmetics (or not removing make-up efficiently) can be a contributing cause to the development of milia, small sebaceous cysts which look rather like whiteheads under the eye, and can be unsightly. (See 'Getting Rid of Milia', page 136.)

Most importantly, the eye area should be protected from future damage. We are big fans of sunglasses with very wide arms,

tried & tested
ANTI-AGEING EYE TREATMENTS

One of the most common questions we're asked is which treatment product will actually make a visible difference to lines around the eye zone. The good news is that our testers were hugely impressed by some of the turn-back-the-clock eye treatments now available. They were asked to use them on one eye, for comparison – and as you'll see, some of the results were so dramatic that they had to 'balance' the effect, after a few weeks, by using it on both.

CLARINS SUPER RESTORATIVE TOTAL EYE CONCENTRATE
Score: 8.65/10

With soft-focus pigments for an instant brightening effect, this is packed with ingredients to 'lift' immediately, while targeting deeper lines and wrinkles. Our testers were thrilled by this latest innovation in Clarins's anti-ageing eye range, which contains shea butter, caffeine (to work on dark circles), circulation-boosting parsley, a special ceramide/peptide complex and Clarins Anti-Pollution Complex.

Comments: 'After four weeks, the difference was very noticeable; good hydration, and no problems with my sensitive skin' • 'perfect under make-up – it really did help it to stay in place' • 'loved the texture and the cool feeling; the effect on my lines and wrinkles makes it the best eye product I've ever used' • 'feels like it's quenching the thirsty skin around my eyes; the open pores and lines between my brows have diminished' • 'my fiancé noticed a more

youthful look in the eye area – praise indeed!' • 'large, button-style container makes it very easy to dispense' • 'After a few weeks, I saw a big improvement – a friend asked what I was using' • 'a few months ago my husband died – at 52 – and I spent most of the next few months in tears, but this product really helped to alleviate puffiness and brighten up my entire eye area – I've bought a second pot and recommended it to friends'.

CRÈME DE LA MER EYE BALM
Score: 8.05/10

This blow-the-budget choice, from the 'cult' Crème de la Mer range, contains the marine 'broth' found in every Crème product plus Brazilian malachite, an illuminating mineral that diffuses redness and "blurs" lines.

Comments: 'The amazing consistency glides easily over the skin and sinks in quickly, not greasy, but you can feel the moisture hours later' • 'some instant improvement – skin more elastic and softer round whole eye area; a good base for eye make-up; after six weeks, fine lines and wrinkles are less obvious' • 'a jar lasts a long, long time'.

CHANEL RECTIFIANCE INTENSE EYE
Score: 7.74/10

From Chanel's Rectifiance range – aimed primarily at women from 35 to 45 – this cream targets lines in '3-D', reducing length, width and depth of wrinkles, while giving a lifting effect. With collagen-boosting horsetail and a 'Micro-Protein extract' (from peas), plus comforting cornflower extract, and

special silky powders, it aims to create a 'line-blurring' effect immediately.

Comments: 'By week two there was such a dramatic improvement in crêpiness, fine lines – and dark circles – I had to use it on the other eye!' • 'I'd use this cream for the initial "brightening" qualities alone – I've stopped using my regular concealer/brightener. The fact that it improves the eye area is a bonus!' • 'I love this product and would advise anyone to try it' • 'I am always trying out new eye creams, but this is one of the more effective and lasts for ages'.

TRILOGY EYE CONTOUR CREAM
Score: 7.7/10

An excellent result for this totally natural product from a small but fast growing New Zealand beauty company, who are big on rosehip oil – a 'natural skin food', with powerful regenerating powers. This fragrance-free formula also has skin-toning eyebright, evening primrose oil and avocado, repairing carrot and vitamin E, all in a soothing, de-puffing aloe vera base.

Comments: 'It is noticeably easier to apply eyeshadow, now that my lids are smoother' • 'very pleasing to use – gentle on the eyes, like wrapping them in warm towels!' • 'my puffy eyes had all but vanished after one night – and it's a great quick fix treatment for tired eyes' • 'fine lines round my eyes are less visible and a few stressful weeks at work and a couple of very late nights don't appear to have taken their usual toll' • 'the natural, pure ingredients don't irritate my usually sensitive skin'.

ESTÉE LAUDER ADVANCED NIGHT REPAIR FOR EYES

Score: 7.7/10

Advanced Night Repair is a true beauty classic and this is its eye-treatment cousin, designed to rebuild the barrier of the super-thin skin around the eyes, also targeting puffiness and dark circles. Active ingredients include extracts from yeast, white birch, mushroom, algae – and the key antioxidant complex of mulberry, saxifrage, grape and skullcap.

Comments: 'Definitely improved bagginess after six weeks, wrinkles less prominent, lines smoother and finer, some improvement in dark circles and crêpiness' • 'did not irritate eyes' • 'fine lines blurred, touch of crêpiness disappeared – a miracle eye cream' • 'I noticed a difference within a week; fine lines went in under six weeks, and whole eye area was brighter and "lifted"'.

beauty steal **L'ORÉAL WRINKLE DE-CREASE EYES**

Score: 7.65/10

An affordable eye treatment that also claims to tackle the problem of fine lines through another patented ingredient – Boswelox™ – which minimises those wrinkle-causing mini-movements. Here's what our testers thought…

Comments: 'Light yet effective, absorbs easily and quickly, light pleasant fragrance; after six weeks fine lines seemed to disappear, wrinkles less prominent, eye area lifted, dark circles reduced – and I got compliments from friends' • 'within days, there was a noticeable improvement in lines' • 'put this on husband's deep lines and wrinkles, too – we have a baby and our eyes show how exhausted we are – this was a miracle worker' • 'reduced morning puffiness, and dark circles'

eye-care how-to

The last thing the delicate eye area tissue needs is any product – or action – that tugs, stretches or irritates. Elsewhere on the face, we have always felt that a bit of massage and stimulation is good for the complexion. But the eye area is so fragile and vulnerable that it needs constant TLC.

• Be gentle. Avoid paper tissues, which actually scratch the eye skin, and seek out soft and natural cotton wool. (We actually prefer organic cotton wool, which is now quite widely available; since cotton has a huge number of pesticides used on it, we would rather the residues didn't get anywhere near our eyes.) Q-Tips can be very useful for removing make-up from the base of the lashes without rubbing; Chanel teaches its cosmeticians to remove eye make-up with a remover-saturated cotton swab, vertically rolling from eyebrow to lashline until the make-up is removed. For under the eyes, horizontally roll another cotton swab from the outer corner to the bridge of the nose.

• You can also try the 'lash-rolling' trick, to avoid having to swipe cotton wool back and forth across the eye area to cleanse away make-up: apply your specially targeted eye make-up remover (most facial make-up removers just don't do the trick), wait a few seconds while it dissolves your mascara and then roll the residue very gently from your lashes, using your fingers or a cotton pad. In addition, avoid the use of waterproof mascara unless you are likely to get wet or to cry; the fact that it is harder to remove (even with special removers, in our experience) makes it likely that you will tug and pull the eye area more than you would to remove a non-waterproof formulation.

• Make sure you apply creams correctly. You don't need to apply a cream directly to the eyelid or underneath the eye; fine lines act as conduits, like a 'wick', drawing products towards the eye. (Which is also why so many women experience irritation with eye products.) Instead, apply creams and gels in minuscule dots on the orbital bone (circling the eye); all in all, you probably don't want to use anything more than the size of a grape seed. Use the orbital bone as a guide; the product will gradually work its way to the rim of the eye through the action of blinking.

• Don't rub the cream vigorously into the skin, whatever you do, or you're likely to create more of the very wrinkles you're trying to erase. Let the product do the work, not your fingers. Use a light tapping motion to apply it; you want to stimulate circulation, but not drag the skin. The bonus? The tapping motion will help drain fluid and puffiness from the eye area at the same time.

LIP SERVICE

The skin on your lips is different from the skin elsewhere on the body (as those of us who look in the mirror and see an ever-deepening network of lines spreading across our pout already understand). In fact, it isn't even skin at all, according to the experts.

As Michael S Kaminer, MD, one of America's most eminent dermatologists,

and Susan Preston-Martin of the University of South California showed that women who apply opaque lipstick more than once a day cut their risk of lip cancer by half. 'Lipstick pigment is a UV barrier,' says Dr Rino Cerio, consultant dermatologist at Barts and The London Hospital. (And the more richly pigmented the shade, the more effective it is.) If you

protection against future damage is vital. But what can we do to reverse the signs of ageing – those lines and fissures that worsen with the years? All of a sudden, our lips are being targeted with an avalanche of time-defying lip products, designed to smooth, soften or even plump up our pouts, and featuring high-tech anti-ageing ingredients like

Our best anti-ageing lip-care trick is to keep a lip balm in the pocket of each jacket or coat – so there's no excuse for not slicking it on, each time you step outside the door.

explains, 'It's a mucous membrane and, as such, is missing certain things like sweat glands, sebaceous glands and hair follicles.' Because the skin on lips is thinner and lower in melanin than the skin on the rest of the face, it needs a special protection squad to shield it against wind, sun and cold.

The good news is that lipstick may help do just that. Men are seven times more likely to develop lip cancer than women – because we wear lipstick, and they don't. A survey by Dr Janice Pogoda

don't want to wear lipstick, use a lip balm with special UV filters, offering a minimum SPF15; ideally, it should have a sticky, waxy look and feel, because this means it will stay on better. (Our favourite is Aveda Lip Saver.) Remember to apply both lipstick and lip balms regularly, because eating, drinking, talking and lip-licking all remove lip products fast. (Try to get out of the habit of lip-licking, incidentally, because repeated wetting and drying actually dehydrates lips.)

As with every zone of the body,

AHAs, vitamin E and vegetable waxes for softening.

But do they work? Dermatologists we spoke to tell us, for instance, that it's impossible to penetrate the lips with moisture, precisely because the 'skin' is different to that found elsewhere on our faces; all a cream can do is trap the moisture that's naturally there. So we asked our panels of testers to try anti-ageing lip products, over a period of months. Read their lips: here's the low-down on what worked.

tried & tested
ANTI-AGEING LIP PRODUCTS

LAVERA LAVERÉ LIP EXPERT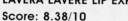
Score: 8.38/10

The winner in this category – by some distance – is actually a 100 per cent natural product, from a German range we like a lot. The fact it's natural seems relevant when you consider we basically 'eat' much of every lip product. The key ingredient in this firming cream is said to add volume, due to a natural 'plumping' ingredient called Septlift, and it has low-level SPF5 sun protection.

Comments: 'Within a couple of days two small vertical lines above my top lip had improved dramatically, and are much less noticeable' • 'this cream has kept my dry chapped lips more supple and moisturised' • 'lovely chocolate-y smell' • 'my other half commented on how smooth my lips felt ' • 'top lip looks plumper – almost "bee-stung" – in the morning after I apply it at night' • 'definitely stopped lipstick bleeding' • 'very economical – only need a tiny amount' • 'did wonders for my lips; I have a scar through my top lip and the damaged area was always peeling and rough; since using this product my lips are perfectly smooth and plump'.

PHILOSOPHY HOPE IN A JAR EYE & LIP CONTOUR TREATMENT
Score: 7.82/10

Another high-scoring anti-ager from Philosophy's 'Hope in a Jar' range, based on soybean extracts and a plant-derived ingredient called dipalmitoyl hydroxyproline, said to protect the skin's elastin, plus vitamins C and E, to guard against free radical damage. Usefully, this does double duty as an eye treatment.

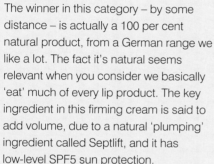

Comments: 'I was very sceptical but this works; a vertical wrinkle on my top lip and fine lines on bottom both vastly improved' • 'lips felt properly moisturised – not just a greasy film that sat on the surface; it's fabulous as an eye cream too!' • 'fine lines around the mouth are improved – there really is "hope" in this product' • 'I apply this if my lips look particularly crack-y or just old' • 'loved this product which left a bit of sheen to brighten the face'.

PRESCRIPTIVES LIP SPECIALIST
Score: 7.37/10

This little pot of lip wonder scored well as a lip balm in previous trials, and this time round our testers were asked to assess its anti-ageing, lip-plumping and line-diminishing powers. It's based on naturally derived oils – avocado, macadamia, olive, apricot, and shea butter – alongside petrochemical ingredients, known for their moisture-retaining action.

Comments: 'Plumped out lips' • 'has definitely smoothed the fine, feathery lines around my lips, making lipstick less prone to bleeding – it stays on longer, too, up to three hours; whole lip zone looks more youthful' • 'brilliant – lines are a bit less noticeable, and it's a fantastic lip conditioner – I used it in on two transatlantic flights, and suffered no dryness' • 'even in my youth I don't think my lips have ever looked this good'.

CLINIQUE REPAIRWEAR INTENSIVE LIP TREATMENT
Score: 7.35/10

This addition to Clinique's successful Repairwear range incorporates white birch extract, collagen-boosting soya protein, linoleic acid, moisture-attracting glycerine and more, in a glamorous silver tube. Many testers commented on the plumping effect, rather than line reduction.

Comments: 'As time went on, it improved the softness and plumpness of lips, and kept them from drying out' • 'my lips look plumper, especially in the morning (after wearing overnight); very rich but not greasy – divine!' • 'fine lines slightly lighter and lips softer' • 'smooth and creamy; after two weeks, fine lines less defined and lips feel plumper' • 'A huge improvement in my lips – fine lines are much fainter and my lips soft and kissable.'

DERMALOGICA MULTIVITAMIN POWER FIRM FOR EYE & LIP AREA
Score: 7.33/10

This silicone-jelly-like lip-firmer packs a power punch of stabilised vitamins A, C and E, antioxidant bioflavonoids, plus anti-inflammatory liquorice, camomile and green tea, and doubles as an eye treat.

Comments: 'My lips and the fine lines above them definitely look younger and smoother; lips stay moist for longer and retain that moisture' • 'big difference in fine lines and my lipstick doesn't bleed into lines any more' • 'my lips look a lot better and I feel I have a definite pout; fewer lines around the mouth and one hereditary line on the left hand side of my mouth (my mother and sister also have it) has much improved' • 'lips are smoother; I love gloss and this product gives it more staying power' • 'marvellous product – a small tube goes a long way, and it really delivers on its promises.'

NECKS

Even a great face can be brought down by a neck that is looking a little crêpey, wrinkled or saggy. Cosmetics may help. And failing that, we have advice on the perfect clothing cover-ups.

Our neck, like our hands, gives away our age in a flash. The skin of the neck tends to be dry and fine because it has only a small number of fat cells and meagre supplies of sebum (the skin's natural moisturiser) – making for a neck that becomes highly prone to crêpiness and dryness, getting increasingly less Nefertiti-like with the years. What's more, because we move our necks constantly, the collagen and elastin which keep the skin firm are loosened.

'Necks are very often neglected,' observes Christina Carlino – founder of the Philosophy range. What she recommends is incorporating your neck – and your décolletage – in your daily skincare regime, sweeping your cleanser in gravity-defying movements up the neck to remove the day's grime. 'Most importantly,' observes Christina, 'the neck can experience insidious sun damage.' Stephen Kurtin, MD, a New York dermatologist, agrees: 'The neck gets a lot of sun and is less able to tolerate it than other areas of the body.' So a broad-spectrum SPF15 moisturiser, applied religiously to neck and décolletage, is a must for shielding the skin – although it won't significantly reverse any accumulated damage.

Another age giveaway can be telltale brown stripes that appear on either side of the neck. These, explains Dr Karen Burke, are linked with perfume

usage: ingredients in some fragrances (specifically psoralens from bergamot oil – a common fragrance ingredient) stimulate the natural tanning ability of the skin, resulting in the stripes. Her advice is not to wear fragrance (which is also very drying, because of the alcohol content) on your neck if you are likely to be exposed to UV light. Instead, try lightly spritzing it on your clothes, or your wrists, which aren't vulnerable to this streaking.

For lined faces, cosmetic surgery is a viable option. But in the experience of women we know, neck-lifts are often disappointing. To be truly effective, the procedure would probably leave you with a zip-like scar at the back of the neck; as it is, the 'ringlet' lines on the neck (aka 'lines of Venus') – which are there from birth but worsen as we age – are hard to fix with surgery. Some women have experienced line-softening effects with chemical peels, but these aren't a universal rave with the women who've tried them, either. (As one woman interviewed for this book told us: 'Several of my friends have had their necks "done" – and all of them have been less than thrilled with the results.')

The good news, then, is that some of our testers were extremely impressed with the line-smoothing power of the neck creams they tested (see Tried & Tested Neck Creams,

opposite). Facial oils are another great age-defying secret (see page 49 for Aromatherapy Associates' prescriptions). However, our advice is that the very best way of defying crêpiness is to use neck lotions and potions not just once, not just twice, but several times daily, to keep the moisture level topped up and maintain the appearance of smoothness. And if you are really determined to maintain a soft and sinuous neck, you could try yoga. We have noted that women who regularly do yoga remain more swan-like and have more chiselled chins than women who don't – well into their eighth and ninth decades.

tried & tested NECK CREAMS

CLARINS EXTRA-FIRMING NECK CREAM
Score: 9.19/10

Active ingredients in this very high-scoring cream include ginseng, mallow extract and moisturising honey, plus antioxidant vitamin E and rice extracts. For optimum results, Clarins recommend exfoliating the neck once a week to remove any dead cells: for the scrubs we like, see page 23, or use a muslin cloth – or even a flannel.

Comments: 'Increasing improvement, especially in crêpey skin at the middle and front of the neck' • 'under my chin is firmer and less saggy' • 'neck looks loads younger and smoother' • 'loose skin tighter and less lined' • 'the bit under my jawline and chin is firmer, more defined' • 'delicious smell – a little goes a long way' • 'lines on my neck had disappeared by the end of the two month trial'.

CHANEL ULTRA CORRECTION ANTI-WRINKLE RESTRUCTURING LOTION
Score: 9/10

Light and non-oily, this lotion boasts an SPF10 – good news for necks, which are so vulnerable to sun damage. It's designed to work on dark spots and wrinkles, incorporating liquorice (to regulate hyperpigmentation), emollient canola oil and shea butter, a vitamin E derivative, and what Chanel call a 'Life Cycle Regenerator'. Chanel additionally prescribe a ritual massage to enhance the benefits of this cream, which our testers diligently followed.

Comments: 'My neck has lost its greyness and is not so crêpey-looking' • 'rich texture, smelled like heaven: massaging the skin makes me aware how much better

it seems – the best cream I've ever used' • 'my dermatologist said my skin was very moist – and smoother than usual' • 'skin looks plump, well-fed – "lifted" '.

GATINEAU DEFILIFT 3D THROAT AND DÉCOLLETÉ LIFT CREAM
Score: 7.88/10

Gatineau – a French beauty brand – are big on 'lifting': this rich but non-greasy cream contains four complexes they've labelled 'Peptilift' (made from almond, wheat and soy proteins), 'Fixlift' (polysaccharide-based), 'Densilift' (from soybeans) and 'Orgalift' (from corn protein). Ultra-nourishing, it also features camellia oil, soothing allantoin and vitamins A, E and F, and is designed to be used morning and evening.

Comments: 'My skin feels much firmer and smoother to the touch – I will keep using this till every last bit is gone' • 'As summer approached, I felt more confident about wearing lower-cut tops because my neck now looks the same age as my face – instead of five years younger' • 'lovely smell – really fresh and not too flowery or overpowering' • 'this product really works – an excellent pampering treat, and worth the money' • 'YES, YES, YES! That's all I can say; I am really pleased with the results of using this and will be buying it in future, once I've finished this jar.'

 beauty steal **LIZ EARLE NATURALLY ACTIVE SKIN REPAIR MOISTURISER** ❋
Score: 7.85/10

With the usual high level of active botanicals you'd expect from Liz Earle, this is also our 'best budget'

recommendation. It is actually a facial nourisher, but they were so confident of its performance as a neck cream that they submitted it for this category – and our testers loved it. Active natural ingredients in the mix include echinacea, borage oil, avocado, beta-carotene, hop extract and wheatgerm.

Comments: 'My neck, which tends to be crêpey, is smooth and soft – a significant difference' • 'smells divine, nice creamy texture – left my skin smoother and soft' • 'I'm raving about this – it actually does more than it says on the jar!' • 'cleavage in Christmas party frock – achieved with the help of a Wonderbra – wasn't as crêpey' • 'my neck looked less like plucked chicken skin – skin had a lovely sheen and healthy glow'.

JURLIQUE NECK SERUM ❋ ❋
Score: 7.55/10

This sinks-in-fast, lightweight gel is 100 per cent natural, with high quantities of organic ingredients, and Jurlique (one of our favourite natural companies) promise us that the soya on which it's based is not genetically engineered. Botanical actives include frankincense and myrrh, ginkgo flavonoids, vitamin C and oils of jojoba, rosehip, avocado and evening primrose.

Comments: 'My neck looks slightly younger, smoother, more hydrated and clearer' • 'definitely less crêpiness after just two weeks' • 'sinks in fast; lovely fresh and natural smell – lines are less visible' • 'skin on neck and décolletage noticeably smoother' • 'I'm amazed how much smoother my skin feels – definite improvement in fine lines'.

THE BIG COVER-UP

Trompe-l'oeil tricks are a godsend to the woman who feels her neck is looking more turkey-like with every passing season. (That includes us.) So we asked Betty Halbreich, author of the truly brilliant *Secrets of a Fashion Therapist*, who has styled some of Manhattan's best-dressed women – for her suggestions for clever cover-ups. As Betty told us, 'These all work – and help make a woman feel more comfortable in her skin.'

● 'The turtleneck (or polo neck) sweater and mock turtleneck remain the number one disguise for a wrinkled neck. The mock neckline has a clean, flatter look without creases, but these are harder to find than turtlenecks, so I often invert the overlap of the turtleneck, turning it inside. It is much smoother-looking, and lengthens the appearance of the neck. The problem most women have with both kinds of neckline is buying a sweater with a too-tight neckline, which causes bulges – and more wrinkles! So beware.'

● 'Jewellery is a wonderful foil. Chokers – whether real or faux – are wonderful, in pearls, diamonds, old or new. (But again, not too tight.) I use pearls – ropes of them – strung round the neck three or more times; the extra-large ones "fill up" the neck and look great. I also work with three or four strands of beads, twisted around the neck. Very feminine – and a good cover.'

● 'Collars can be helpful. The mandarin collar or Nehru stand-up collars are terrific; they should perch just under the jaw-line, where they look very good in profile. Any jacket with a stand-up collar seems to shadow the neck.'

● 'I'm the original scarf-lover. True, they can be hard to get the hang of, but, once conquered, they hide a multitude of wrinkles. A simple exercise: take a long oblong scarf or piece of soft fabric and wind it around the neck twice, very loosely. It then becomes a frame around the face. I find chiffon, soft-cut velvet, cashmere and any diaphanous fabric is easiest to manipulate. A scarf used kerchief-style, placed under a regular shirt collar and tied high helps the older neck.'

● 'I often use men's collars – nicely starched shirts – with the collars flipped up. Then slip a string of pearls or a thin gold chain around the neck, resting just above the breast-bone, to "break up" the line.'

● 'For evening, a long maribou scarf, four to six feet long, wound round the neck, is beautiful (think old Hollywood movie-star-style).'

● 'Last – and certainly not least – great make-up and a terrific haircut can work miracles and draw attention away from the neck. Hair can be feathered into the neck or cut below the jaw-bone to distract from neck problems. And most important of all is the way a woman holds herself, neck straight and standing tall, looking directly ahead when she enters a room. That's what people look at: attitude, posture, clothes – then the neck comes way down the list!'

when fatter is more flattering

Over 40, it's said, a woman must choose between her face and her backside: the thinner you are, the faster your face will appear to age. 'A thinner person will always appear older than someone who is plumper,' says Richard Fleming, MD, a plastic surgeon in Beverly Hills. Fat plumps out wrinkles and may mask other age-related changes, such as loss of bone mass in the jaw and cheek. Super-lean women wrinkle more noticeably and sag sooner because they have so little fat in their faces that every little breakdown is magnified on the skin's surface.

Changes start showing in the early forties, when women begin to notice what surgeons refer to as 'skin redundancy' – those creases and folds that can add years to your looks. This is due to the breakdown of various tissues of the face: everyone gets some muscle shrinkage, so the skin over the top sags. Second, weakened muscle tone causes some of the fat on the cheekbone to slide down, deepening the 'smile line' between nose and lips. Third, bone loss and the breakdown of supportive collagen reduce the underlying frame of the face – and by now, skin is too lax to shrink-to-fit. (Since collagen breakdown is accelerated by sun damage, tanning fans show these changes earlier.)

Worst off, according to experts, are women who abruptly lost large amounts of weight in their thirties or beyond; they will look older than if they had never lost the weight, because the extra skin will just hang. Yo-yo dieting is another culprit that can accelerate the development of jowls and folds.

NATURE V ROCKET SCIENCE

During our years as beauty editors, we've seen beauty go in two polar directions: at one end, the high-tech, rocket-science creams – and at the other, the more natural options, some of which are now even certified organic. Certainly, as we, and our testers, have discovered, there are some highly effective nature-based cosmetics on the market – if you know where to look.

As Dr Jurgen Klein – founder of the natural beauty brand Jurlique – points out, 'The skin is an absorbent organ. Everyone should think hard about what they put on their skin. If you wouldn't eat it, then it may not be such a good idea to slap it on your face or body.'

Homoeopath Lynne Crawford has found that many of her clients are suffering from toxic overload, which she believes can be linked back to beauty products. 'They go straight into the bloodstream and end up clogging up the liver and kidneys. Of course it will have an adverse effect on your health, as well as, eventually, your looks.'

Ironically, in the long term, the ingredients in some high-tech skincare might – just might – turn out to turbo-charge the ageing process, worries Dr Klein: 'When you assault the body with a lot of unfamiliar chemicals that it's not evolved to deal with, this activates the body's defences. We should use this immune system only when it's needed – not challenge it on a daily basis.'

In the same way, he feels, if the skin's immune system is being challenged regularly by an avalanche of unfamiliar chemicals, it may ultimately turn out to age more quickly than if you hadn't been using that potent anti-ageing cream. It's true to say that Dr Klein is regarded very much as a radical by the

" Everyone should think hard about what they put on their skin. If you wouldn't eat it, it may not be such a good idea to slap it on your face or body. "

skincare industry. But his observations certainly provide food for thought. Even Dr Daniel Maes believes that anything which creates an inflammatory reaction in the skin – such as a flare-up in

response to a new anti-ageing cream – actually damages skin.

Because we both eat organically, and live as natural a lifestyle as possible, we are drawn to skincare that reflects that. It just doesn't make sense, to us, to be analysing labels to ensure that what we put in our mouths isn't tainted by chemicals, yet at the same time slathering cocktails of them on to our skins. (Some of which, at least, sink right into the bloodstream.)

It's often hard, though, for beauty hounds to work out what is and isn't natural. So a couple of books ago, we came up with what we call our 'daisy' rating, to help readers identify which products in our books are more natural. If a product is 100 per cent natural, it gets two daisies. If it contains genuinely high levels of botanical ingredients, we award it one daisy. What we don't expect to find anywhere near the top of the ingredients list for those one-daisy products are synthetic or petroleum-based ingredients – and we do expect high levels of natural ingredients, like shea butter or cocoa butter. If you are interested in more natural anti-ageing products, look for the daisies. Only you can decide whether you want rocket science or to go down a more natural path. But we'll always do our best to inform you what's what.

tried & tested NATURAL MIRACLE CREAMS

If, like us, you are concerned to find more natural skin creams, then you'll want to know about these 'natural wonders', which have scored so well with our testers.

NEAL'S YARD FRANKINCENSE NOURISHING CREAM ✳ ✳
Score 8.25/10 – see page 17
Neal's Yard's products are not yet all totally natural, but more and more are now organically certified. This anti-ageing cream scored extremely impressive marks, well above many of the pricey and/or high-tech creams on the market, and has been a best seller ever since it featured in the first edition of *Feel Fab Forever*.

JURLIQUE HERBAL RECOVERY GEL ✳ ✳
Score: 7.62/10
A gel/serum-style product from a leading all-natural Australian beauty company (which grows its own plants organically). Jurlique have a growing reputation as a 'cult' brand offering high-performance ethical products, formulated without petrochemicals, preservatives and solvents. This gel features a high concentration of antioxidants from green tea, grape seeds and turmeric. It not only works as a 'miracle cream' in the longer term, but our testers were impressed by the short-term benefits of this product when used as an 'instant face waker'. Just over half said they'd buy it.

Comments: 'It certainly seemed to plump up the surface of the skin on application; skin also felt smoother and tauter with a shiny look' • 'I am allergic to many skin products but this one made my skin feel fantastic; a friend at work thought I looked ten years younger after using it' • 'after two weeks, texture and brightness had improved; it works like an instant pick-me-up' • 'lines around my eyes visibly reduced. My husband commented that my skin looked different' • 'this serum really is a dream to use and feels lovely; my foundation went on more smoothly and stayed on better than normal. Even my daughter said how nice my skin was – this is definitely a compliment!'

is your skincare genetically engineered?

The world of skincare is fantastically high-tech. For the most part, we wholeheartedly support the industry's research into how our skins age – and what we can do to minimise the signs. But there are certain scientific 'leaps' which we feel uncomfortable with. A few years ago, when we asked some of the leading skincare companies what the Next Big Thing in the development of anti-ageing skincare was likely to be, they answered: 'genetic engineering'.

There are two ways that skincare can be 'genetically engineered'. The first is through using ingredients that have been been genetically engineered, such as soya and maize derivatives. The second is through bio-engineering techniques: for instance, in the manufacturing of hyaluronic acid, some companies use bacteria, the DNA of which has been 'tweaked' to create these molecules.

Personally, we don't want to eat what the Prince of Wales once referred to as 'Frankenstein foods' – and we don't want 'Frankenstein face creams', either. We feel that there are risks involved in genetic engineering – for instance, in a worst-case scenario, the creation of bacteria or viruses which could be released into a world that does not have resistance to them. Genetic engineering may prove to be entirely safe and beneficial to humankind, but at the moment we – in common with many scientists and lay people worldwide – prefer to apply the precautionary principle. (Which translates as 'better safe than sorry'.)

Lately, there has been another industry innovation that we're cautious about, too: the introduction of nanoparticle technology (using tiny, tiny particles). According to one eminent toxicologist, Professor Vyvyan Howard, even otherwise safe ingredients (such as titanium dioxide) can become toxic when reduced to tiny particle size, and absorbed into the body. If you're worried about this, avoid skin creams which trumpet the fact they're made using nanoparticles. (Meanwhile, the manufacturers of more natural cosmetics – some 'winners' are listed above – pledge to avoid these novel technologies.)

ANTI-AGEING AROMATHERAPY FACIAL MASSAGE

Aromatherapy oils may be nature's greatest de-agers, restoring suppleness and vitality to even the tiredest skin. We love the effect they have on our weary complexions – and flagging spirits. So we asked leading aromatherapists, Aromatherapy Associates, (who were the late Princess of Wales's aromatherapists-of-choice), to give us this at-home facial massage, using essential oils. It's bliss...

'Aromatherapy massage and essential oils can be extremely beneficial as part of a holistic anti-ageing programme,' explains Aromatherapy Associates' Germaine Rich. 'They can be relaxing, detoxifying, stimulating and supportive to the immune system. They help support and balance the body's metabolic functions. And essential oils help balance the emotions, at the same time.' And depending on the oil – or combination of oils – that is chosen, they can also be tremendously beneficial for the skin. Beat that.

But if you've shied away from facial oils because you're worried they'll leave your face slick-shiny, be reassured. 'The oils are absorbed very rapidly into the skin – leaving it softer, smoother and nourished,' explains Germaine. As an alternative to a night cream, you might want to make up a facial oil using any of the seven anti-ageing essential oils listed, and apply a few drops nightly to the face. But be careful to keep the oils away from the eyes. 'Apply to the skin of the brow-bone and the lower eye socket bone,' advises Germaine. 'The oils will travel inwards to smooth and nourish the eye skin, but if applied too close to the eye, they may cause sensitivity.'

ANTI-AGEING ESSENTIAL OILS

Frankincense: An excellent skin tonic, particularly valuable for mature, wrinkled skins. Useful for helping to heal wounds. Working on the emotions, frankincense has an uplifting and clearing effect, giving a sense of rising above problems and clearing negativity.

Geranium: Brightens dull skin and balances combination skins; antiseptic and anti-inflammatory. Uplifting, it's one of the best all-round tonics for mind and body.

Lavender: Excellent first aid remedy for cuts, bites, bruises and burns. The most useful and popular of all essential oils, lavender can help counter depression, anxiety, tension, shock and emotional distress.

Neroli: Speeds up cell replacement so is extremely useful for rejuvenation, and in the treatment of scars and stretch marks. Distilled from orange blossom, neroli has a calming, strengthening and euphoric effect – and is an excellent tonic for emotional exhaustion, depression, insomnia, shock and stress.

Patchouli: Helps skin cell renewal, so rejuvenating for mature or prematurely aged skins, 'turkey neck' or on scar tissue; an effective antiseptic, it can be used on inflamed or infected conditions such as weeping eczema, dermatitis, ulcers. Relaxing yet reviving, patchouli is a warming and stimulating oil.

Rose otto (Damask rose): Excellent for all skintypes but particularly beneficial for sensitive, highly coloured or ageing skins; it is also an extremely effective antiseptic. Strengthens fragile capillaries and so is particularly useful for rosacea. A spiritually uplifting and protecting oil.

Sandalwood: A soothing, lubricating oil ideal for sensitive, dry or neglected skins. Nourishes and protects older, papery skin. Good for anxiety/insomnia caused by emotional distress.

THE BASE OILS

Before you apply them to the skin, essential oils should be diluted with 'base' or 'carrier' oils. There are a few exceptions to this rule: tea tree, lavender and frankincense are safe to apply neat. Use any of the following, or a combination of the oils. Experiment to find the blend that you prefer. 'Vegetable oils provide skin with nutrients, essential fatty acids – and have specific therapeutic properties,' explains Germaine. The following oils are widely available and particularly recommended in anti-ageing formulations.

Evening primrose oil   Regenerative and good for prematurely aged skins; using the contents of capsules – from health food stores – may be the most practical method.

Jojoba liquid wax   (more commonly known as jojoba oil) Penetrates well, leaving a protective, non-sticky, nourishing film; good for dry, sensitive skins and allergies.

Sweet almond oil   Light and nourishing, with vitamin E and high in vitamin A, it helps relieve itching, soreness, dryness and inflammation.

Wheatgerm oil   Featuring vitamin A and high in vitamin E; antioxidant. Good for dry, mature and prematurely aged skin and scar tissues.

For facial oils, use between a one and three per cent dilution, being sure to measure carefully. So to each 15ml of base oil, add three to nine drops of essential oils. 'Start with a one per cent dilution, then move up to three per cent when you are familiar and comfortable with the oils' effect.' Essential oils are potent, explains Germaine, and in too high a concentration may cause sensitivity. 'But even if you have very sensitive skin, you can use them: the most suitable oils for touchier complexions are sandalwood and rose.' Once you've mixed your facial oil, keep it in a glass bottle and out of direct sunlight, Germaine advises. Choose from any of the oils listed on the previous page – or blend two or three together, always staying within the dilution guidelines.

THE AROMATHERAPY MASSAGE

'To get maximum benefits, try to schedule the session so that it doesn't matter if your hair becomes oily,' says Germaine. 'Otherwise, tie the hair back from the face and remove clothes, so that the shoulders and décolletage can be treated. Cleanse and refresh the skin of the face and neck before you start.' She suggests doing the massage once a week (although facial oils can be used, without the massage, every night).

1 Rub one drop of frankincense essential oil over the palms. Start the massage on the head, to release tension.

2 Deeply massage scalp all over with fingertips to release tension; really get the skin moving over the scalp.

3 Place the pads of your spread-out fingers just on the hairline and make deep 'draining' movements from the hairline to the crown, starting at the forehead and temples and moving backwards through the hair. Do the same from the base of the skull, trailing fingers through to the ends of the hair. 'It gets the circulation going and releases tension,' explains Germaine. 'You can almost feel your scalp buzzing, straight away.' (If you prefer, wash hands before starting the actual massage.)

4 Pour about 5ml of blended oil (see box above) into the palm of the hands. Rub the hands together and apply the oil with both hands in long, sweeping movements, across the décolletage, round the shoulders, up the neck, across the cheeks, over the nose and the forehead. Cover the whole area to be treated, circling the eyes lightly with the ring fingers, being careful not to get the oil close to the eyes. Repeat the movements until oil is well spread and the skin is warmed.

5 With the fingers of the right hand, knead the upper left arm, shoulder and up the back of the neck to behind the ear. Repeat on the right side with left hand. 'We all carry a lot of tension in our shoulders – and that can show up on our faces,' explains Germaine, 'so this is a very important part of the massage.'

6 With the knuckles make circular, sweeping movements to the neck, shoulders, chest and upper arms. (If you are tense, this can be quite painful. That's normal.) Do one side at a time.

7 With the fatty pads of your thumbs under the chin, apply pressure up against the jaw-bone from the point of chin to the corner of the jaw-bone, moving the thumbs a short distance at a time. 'When you find an area that's sensitive or tender, just keep working on it gently, until it eases up.' Repeat the procedure from chin to jaw-hinge.

8 Place the pads of your fingers just on the jawline, gently touching (with the little fingers meeting). Press, then move the fingers along slightly. Press again. Keep moving the fingers to the edge of the jaw; go back to the beginning and start again. (For this – and the next two steps – be sure you aren't moving your fingers over the skin, but actually moving the skin and underlying muscle with the tiny circular movements.)

9 Using the pads of the fingers, which are now separated, make tiny, tiny circular pressures on the cheeks, in rows from the jaw-bone up to the top of the cheek-bone. Your little fingers should end up under the middle of each eye.

10 Using the pads of the fingers, apply small circular pressures in lines across the forehead, starting at the centre and finishing at the temples.

11 With the tips of your ring fingers, circle around the eyes on the socket-bones, inwards under the eyes towards the nose, up on to the eyebrows and outwards, to complete the circle. 'Do this ultra-lightly – absolutely no tugging,' says Germaine.

12 Place the thumbs just underneath the inner brow-bone and apply pressures upwards along the ridge of the eye socket, moving the thumbs slightly each time. Keep going till just about the mid-point of the brows. 'This is especially soothing if you suffer from headaches or eyestrain,' says Germaine.

13 Place the pads of the fingers on the lower ridge of the eye socket-bone, and press. Then move the fingers slightly outwards and press again. Repeat.

14 Rub hands together vigorously and then cup the closed hands over the eyes. Take several deep breaths and sigh out tension.

EVELYN LAUDER

We're inspired by Evelyn Lauder's work with Pink Ribbon, helping raise millions for breast cancer charities. We love her energy – and her photography, too. When she married Leonard Lauder – Estée's son – her mother-in-law said, 'I gained more than a daughter: I got a whirlwind.'

'What do you know as a 20-year-old? I'm far more confident in myself now because of the life experiences I've had. It all kind of goes into a mental computer so that when a crisis comes along, in relationships (or even medical emergencies), there's a sense of being able to do the right thing.

'My mother, Mimi Hausner, was a great role model for me. In her late 80s, she'd exercise every hour, getting out of her chair for a 15-minute walk so that by the evening she'd walked a mile. She also used to pedal on a stationary bicycle. She'd save up jokes to tell me, and loved to laugh – that is how I would like to be at that age.

'She was a devotee of the anti-sugar guru Gaylord Hauser and the first person I knew who believed in the benefits of eating fish. She taught me not to manipulate my skin too much. She never used soap on her face – and neither do I; it's terrifically dehydrating and I suffer from very dry skin. When travelling, one of my beauty tips is shampoo as a body cleanser – my favourites are Aveda Shampure or Estée Lauder Pleasures Bath & Shower Gel (which doubles as a great lingerie wash!).

'I actually have my skincare printed out on an Estée Lauder prescription pad! In the morning, after cleansing, I use Advanced Night Repair, followed by Perfectionist CP+, Idealist Skin Refinisher and Perfectionist Correcting Concentrate for lips. Then to keep my skin hydrated and comfortable, DayWear Plus Multi-Protection Anti-Oxidant SPF15, because sun protection is such an important part of anti-ageing. At night, I cleanse thoroughly – no soap! I'd never think of going to bed with my make-up on. Of course, I'm very lucky to be able to try new products from the Estée Lauder companies' brands – and I'm living proof that you can delay having certain procedures by good, diligent skin care as a lifetime habit.

'Small daily actions, added together, keep you healthy. I am as fit as I have ever been. I have a trainer who comes at 7am, three times a week. I do stretching, reaching, bending, the stationary bicycle for 15 minutes, followed by mat work with weights. I always walk up and down stairs at home and at work – I never take the elevator.

'I take a calcium supplement called Citracal + D, and Citracal + Magnesium; D and magnesium help metabolise calcium. I try to eat well: we only have wild fish, and we buy organic skimmed milk and yoghurt. I eat lots of vegetables and salads, with homemade low-fat oil and vinegar dressing, and drink bottled water.

'My work is really important to me. Corporate Fragrance Development reports to me and I work with the greatest talents in the business. Having been a teacher, I am still involved in training programmes.

'I've recently finished a recipe book called *In Great Taste: Fresh, Simple Recipes for Eating and Living Well*. It has healthy, low-fat – but scrumptious – ideas. All my royalties will benefit The Breast Cancer Research Foundation.

'My involvement with Pink Ribbon goes back to 1992, when Alexandra Penney, then editor-in-chief of *Self* magazine, and I co-created it as a symbol of breast health and a reminder to get a mammogram. I realised we should be giving away pink ribbons on counter to raise women's awareness. We've now given away over 60 million worldwide.

'After fragrances, photography gives me the most creative satisfaction. I started taking photos of our sons as they were growing, then photographing snow scenes for our Christmas cards and it became a real passion. I'm thrilled to have had several exhibitions and two books of my photography – *The Seasons Observed* and *An Eye For Beauty*.

'I think it's very important – and fun – to find out what form of self-expression pushes your buttons. The more you do, the more energy you have. When you're busy and connected with the world, you have a lot of fun and continue to grow as a person – but if you stop, you might as well be dead! I've still got places to go – and photographs to take.'

SKIN SUPPLEMENTS

Over the last two decades, there has been a steady stream of nutritional supplements that claim specifically to improve your skin, usually with a sideline in nails and hair. (Since they're all made of much the same substances, this makes sense.)

Skin supplements aren't cheap and they require persistence as much as investment, because you probably won't see any significant results for months, which puts off lots of women. Perhaps in consequence, many brands have been hyped to the hilt, only to fall forgotten by the wayside. (New ones come up like mushrooms, though.) However, the trailblazer Imedeen, based on a trademarked Biomarine Complex with added vitamins, is hugely successful. Indeed, there's now a range of Imedeen products for different ages and stages, plus an anti-ageing Expression Line Control skincare range, which some women we know swear by (again, not cheap, though).

If you can afford it, we think these supplements are worth trying. Jo has been 'unswervingly devoted' to Imedeen Time Perfection for the last 12 years. During that time, she's occasionally had her skin density assessed by Imedeen's high-tech screening equipment and seen with her own eyes that her skin is extremely thick and resilient for her age.

Sarah meanwhile swears by the American product Age Loss by Nature's Plus, an antioxidant supplement which contains GliSODin (see page 205), plus alpha-lipoic acid and n-acetyl cysteine, both vital for many body processes. Her hairdresser noticed that – as well as helping her skin tone and texture – it had improved the 'structure' of her hair. It's great for energy, too.

But don't just take our word for it. For our latest book, *The Handbag Beauty Bible*, our testers popped a dozen brands of beauty pills over three months. Although none earned praise from every tester, many women were surprised and delighted by the improvements they noticed. The winner was BioCare Hair & Nail Complex, which promoted glowing, plump, rosy skin as well as strong nails and glossy hair. One tester said: 'Loads of comments from men: my skin looks the best it has in years; hair's in great condition, nails looking fabulous. I can't afford not to buy these.'

Tied in second place were Imedeen Prime Renewal, designed for post-menopausal skins, and the budget-priced Healthspan Anti-Ageing Skin Nourishment Supplement, formulated with Dr David Harris of the London Clinic of Dermatology. Both delivered significant differences to skin, hair and nails over three months. One woman taking the Imedeen product found that her crow's-feet had almost gone and her neck was much smoother. 'Skin much brighter and more radiant, looks younger, slight improvement in fine lines,' found one tester taking the Healthspan supplement.

However, if you are on a budget, we don't think these products should be a priority. Wholesome fresh food, preferably organic, must come first, then a good multivitamin and mineral supplement, followed by an omega-3 essential fatty acid product. We're also keen on co-enzyme Q10, which is necessary for muscles (see page 205). Diet-wise, your skin will benefit not only from lots of oily fish, and as much fresh fruit and vegetables (topped with extra virgin olive oil) as you can pack in, but also what you leave out – too much coffee undoubtedly 'muddies' the complexion and, because it makes you more tense, can contribute to lines. White, green or jasmine tea, on the other hand, will pep up your brain and body, including your skin. Clinique, in tandem with nutritionists and other experts, assert that excess sugar can age your skin, by producing harmful waste substances that mean skin loses elasticity. So reduce or cut out added sugars and avoid processed foods, sweets and soft drinks. And eat more fibre (eg, fruit and veg), because this enables your body to handle sugar better.

If you're uncertain whether or not to try a beauty supplement, we'd suggest cleaning up your act first. Detox your diet, make certain you're managing stress levels as well as you can (yoga is great for exercise, relaxation and oxygenating your face, as well as keeping your jawline sharp) and get enough sleep. Add in the basic supplements and – we nearly forgot – make sure to have some fun! It's a potent anti-ager for mind, face and body. Try this regime for three months. You may find this is quite satisfactory, if not – you can consider one of these supplements.

THE NAMES TO WATCH

The hot tips for anti-ageing, from pharmacist Shabir Daya.

1. GliSODin: this bio-available and bio-active form of the antioxidant enzyme Superoxide Dismutase (SOD for short...) fights damaging free radicals throughout the body, helping to smooth existing lines and preventing the formation of new ones. It's found in the skin supplement Age Loss (which figures in our *Feel Fab Forever* capsule collection of nutritional supplements – for more details see www.beautybible.com). Some skincare companies may start to incorporate this into topical products, but it is expensive.

2. Oligomeric proanthocyanidins (OPCs): another vital antioxidant, OPCs are found in grape seed and pine bark – also wolfberry or Goji, which we love as juice. (Goji has been called a 'cellulite assassinator' by Dr Howard Murad). OPCs help repair collagen, protect against environmental toxins which damage skin, and act as a natural internal sunscreen, reducing radiation from the sun. Healthwise, OPCs are superstars.

3. Picrorhiza kurrooa (found as PicroLiv.): the most potent liver detoxifying herb available, much used in Ayurvedic medicine, where liver health is seen as the foundation of good skin. It also supports the immune system.

4. Holy basil: This Indian plant (aka tulsi) is prized for its adaptogenic qualities. A potent anti-inflammatory (which benefits skin as well as the rest of the body), it also supports the immune system and may help with stress, combined with breathing and aerobic exercise.

Never exceed recommended dose, and if you are taking any medication, do consult a health professional first.

flower power for face, body and soul

The way we feel in mind and body – both short- and long-term – is mirrored in our faces, according to London-based holistic facial therapist Joy Salem. ('No wonder my face looks like a map of the world,' commented fifty-ish novelist Elizabeth Buchan.) Joy prescribes an individual regime for each client using facial massage, manual lymphatic drainage plus Dr Bach's flower remedies to restore tone, flexibility and colour and bring both sparkle and calm to the face. Dr Edward Bach's flower remedies were some of the first to be used in the West at the beginning of the 20th century. He discovered that the extracts of various flowers were particularly effective at helping people deal with negative emotional states. We are both devotees of flower remedies so we asked Joy to give us the Dr Bach Flower Remedies which she felt would be most helpful to women at menopause. Take four drops in pure water at least four times daily, especially first and last thing, or as often as you feel the need.

Cherry Plum Helps keep extreme hormonal emotions under control.

Crab Apple Good when you're feeling hot and sticky during a hot flush, when your bed seems much too warm at night, or at any time when you are negatively obsessed with your looks.

Gentian For despondency accompanying bouts of sleeplessness caused by discomfort at night.

Hornbeam Good when you feel suddenly overwhelmed by lethargy and fatigue.

Impatiens Can restore calm and replace irritability with peace.

Larch Use when you feel unable to cope any longer and also when you feel self-conscious and that all eyes are on you.

Mimulus Helpful in allaying day-to-day fears; eases tension until hot flushes subside, and equally helpful for shy people who blush easily.

Olive Use when you feel irritable after losing sleep because of hot flushes.

Rescue Remedy Cream To counteract vaginal dryness and soreness during intercourse due to reduced levels of oestrogen.

Schleranthus For mood swings, indecision and volatility; helps restore emotional stability.

Star of Bethlehem For grief over lost youth and the feeling that part of you has died.

Sweet Chestnut Helps deal with the deep sorrow that can arise from the feeling that life from now on will be full of emptiness and that you have missed opportunities.

Walnut Very useful at any time of change in our lives; helps us to move forward and to adapt to upheaval.

Willow Use against over-reaction and over-sensitivity to insignificant matters which can often turn to self-pity and crying, particularly if you feel past your 'sell-by' date, or opportunities have passed you by, or that you are of no more use since your children have grown up and left.

NB Joy points out that if you are going through a really difficult time there is no substitute for consulting an experienced qualified practitioner in Dr Bach Flower Remedies.

FACIAL FITNESS

Most doctors work themselves into a sweat explaining why facial exercises can't work. But many women swear by the gravity-defying powers of facial aerobics, even using them as an alternative to going under the surgeon's knife. So we asked Eva Fraser, the bestselling queen of facial workouts, to share some of her easy-to-follow facial exercises to get you glowing and fix specific facial flaws. (Find them also in her latest book/DVD/video/audio cassette packages, *Eva Fraser's Facial Fitness.*)

EYELID EXERCISE

Look straight ahead into the mirror throughout this exercise.

1 Curve index (first) fingers under each eyebrow and gently push up – then hold against your brow-bone. Keep your fingers in that position.
2 Now close your eyes in five to ten very small downward movements. You should feel a gentle stretch in the upper lids.
3 Keep lids stretched downwards for a count of six.
4 Release the stretch slowly for three counts.
5 Open lids. Relax. Breathe deeply. Repeat three times.

TO ELIMINATE LINES ON THE BRIDGE OF THE NOSE

1 Place pads of middle fingers firmly on the top of the bridge of your nose, just below any lines or bumps.
2 Place your index fingers each side of the bridge of your nose. Hold firmly.
3 Gradually move the muscles under your finger-hold in the direction of the arrow in five tiny, slow upward movements.
4 Hold for a count of five, then slowly return in five movements.
5 Do this three times.
6 Stay relaxed, keep breathing and do not scowl!

NB The finger resistance must be held gently but firmly throughout.

TURKEY NECK ELIMINATOR

1 With a straight spine, look straight ahead and tilt head up.
2 Then gently jut out your chin. At the same time, draw lower lip over top lip. Do not smile with mouth corners up.
3 For extra resistance, place first lightly under chin.
4 Now press tongue firmly against lower teeth in a forward, upward thrust. Feel the movement under the chin.
5 Hold for a count of five.
6 Slowly release the pressure.
7 Stay relaxed and breathe. Repeat three times.

Women who do facial workouts should see great improvements in just six weeks, says Eva. (See below for what one client thought.) Here are her other anti-sag secrets…

- 'Sleep with one pillow, not two, to avoid a double chin.'

- 'If you must read in bed – and I advise clients not to – then lie with your head on a single pillow and hold the book above you. If you lie propped up with the book balanced on your tummy, it's just asking for a double chin.'

- 'If you work on a computer, bring it up to eye level, for the same reason.'

- 'Improve your posture; if you stand straight, your face is less likely to sag. Imagine that at all times you are being pulled up by a piece of string from the centre of the top of your head.'

- 'I'm a big fan of Frownies – which have been used by beautiful women for improving the lines on the forehead since 1898. They are small, skin-coloured adhesive papers that you stick on to the forehead so that you can't frown. Used regularly, they really do help frowns to disappear, making the forehead smoother.'

what Eva Fraser's facial exercises did for me

Age: 50-ish • Profession: interiors consultant

'I started doing facial exercises because I wanted to look as good as I feel – which is terribly well. My particular problems were the lines going from either side of my nose to the corners of my mouth and my jawline slackening. I have a superstitious fear of the surgeon's knife so I wanted to try anything else first – but with no expectation of miracles. I had heard about Eva Fraser's programme from a friend and it seemed absolutely logical to me that if you can work out your body and look different, then the same thing could happen to your face.

'I started off with the book; that was helpful, but I wanted individual attention and analysis, so I went to Eva's studio in London for a course of four private lessons.

'The first lesson takes one and a half hours, the next three are an hour long. During the first and second you learn all the basic movements, then the third and fourth you work the muscles against resistance – you have to hold on to each muscle at one end and work the other to make the muscle springier and shorter. You have to leave at least two weeks between lessons, so that the muscles are strong enough to go on to the next stage.

'There are exercises for every part of your face – brow, nose, forehead, the apple of your cheeks, around your eyes and mouth, jawline. Eva explains all the time which muscles she is working with and why. I understood immediately why it would work: for instance, if you do an exercise to tighten your cheek muscles, you can see it lifting the lower bit of your face.

'It takes at least 20 minutes a day for the first three months: you sit in front of the mirror with your own personalised set of drawings, trying to do things like wiggling one side of your nose up towards your outer eye in six movements. But you do feel your muscles getting stronger and you realise how few you use ordinarily. For the next three months, you do 20 minutes every other day, then you advance to about ten minutes on alternate days.

'Eva's programme is simple and sensible. The worst things about it are what you see in the mirror and the horrendous white cotton gloves which you have to wear to stop your fingers slipping when you do the exercises inside your mouth.

'After about two weeks, people started to say "you look awfully well" and I suddenly realised I was looking good and the only thing in my life that had changed was that I was now going to Eva. It has helped my face enormously. I don't know if it makes me look younger but it does retard the "Newton effect" – everything falling down. The exercises to lift my cheek muscles have made the lines from my nose to mouth enormously better, and my jawline is more defined. Also my skin glows much more and is much smoother, probably because the exercises increase blood flow to the skin.

'The course is very good value and, as a bonus, I hardly ever need to use night creams now – Eva says your skin will balance itself in three days, and she's right. I think external creams can give you a lift but they can't work as well as exercises like these. But facial exercises are like any other sort: if you give up, everything starts going right back, so you do have to keep on the maintenance programme.'

(See Directory for details of Eva's books, videos, DVDs and courses.)

FABULOUS FACIALS FOR OLDER FACES

We go behind the masks, steaming, sloughing and pampering to find out which facials are best for older faces.

Facials are a luxury. For some women, they're a luxury they 'can't live without', to brighten dull and dingy skin – or to plump it up before an important event. Right now, there's a beauty salon boom in facials for older women. In midlife, we're supposed to have more money – and (allegedly) more leisure – to indulge ourselves. And when we look in the mirror on a bad day and start to fret about lines that didn't seem to be there last week, a time-defying salon treatment can be extremely seductive. But not all facials are created equal. And not every mature skin will benefit. So here's what you should know before you decide to put yourself in a beauty therapist's hands.

First of all, remember that no once-in-a-while treatment can make a significant long-term impact – although it can whisk away drab-looking, dead skin cells, leaving your skin looking brighter and (depending on the ingredients) temporarily 'tighter', or 'lifted'. It's what you do to your skin on a daily basis – religiously cleansing, very lightly exfoliating (see page 22), moisturising and applying sun protection – which makes the long-term difference.

However, in a mature skincare regime, 'There is a place for facials,' believes Nelson Lee Novick, MD, associate clinical professor of dermatology at New York's Mount Sinai School of Medicine. 'If people want a nice, pampered experience and they have fairly normal skin, I don't have a problem with them having a facial.' But even people with normal skin are advised to wait six weeks between facials, warns Dr Novick – simply because too much of anything – like intense cleansing or even too-vigorous massage – can irritate the skin. Anyone with inflamed acne, rosacea (characterised by redness, pimples or enlarged blood vessels, see page 62) or skin conditions like eczema and psoriasis, should avoid facials, as they may aggravate the condition. If you're suffering an infection – such as impetigo or herpes – you should also forgo a facial, for the time being.

According to Mary Lupo, MD, associate clinical professor of dermatology at Tulane Medical School in New Orleans, 'I've seen patients with flat warts that were manipulated and actually spread on their face.'

Susan Harmsworth, spa consultant and founder of the aromatherapy-based beauty therapy and skincare range ESPA, says that women with sensitive skin – which is often a problem for menopausal women – should also be very cautious about facials. 'My advice, if you have sensitive skin, is to arrange for a "patch test" in the salon, before your facial. They can apply the products they're planning to use on your face to an out-of-the-way area behind your ear, to establish there is no reaction.' If a salon can't or won't accommodate this perfectly reasonable request, she says, go elsewhere.

The vast majority of mature skins, says Vaishaly Patel, should not be steamed – a procedure which is still integral to many facials. 'It can lead to

OUR FAVOURITE FACIALS

● **Vaishaly Patel** ('the new Jo Malone')
● **Amanda Lacey** (another rising skin guru)
● **Aromatherapy Associates Rose Facial**
● **Anne Sémonin** (mostly available in Paris, but also via Ewa Berkmann, in London)
● **Dr Hauschka facial** (which starts with your feet – because the state of your feet affects your face)
● **Organic Pharmacy facial** (with their divine rose-based anti-ageing products)
● **Jurlique facial** (another wonderful, all-natural experience)

acids – can also be used as chemical exfoliants, as an alternative to the 'grainy' kind of scrub; again, these should all be avoided by any woman with sensitive skin. (If in doubt, have the patch test, as recommended by Susan Harmsworth.)

One step that makes many of us particularly uncomfortable is 'extraction', or squeezing of the pores to remove blackheads and clean out clogged pores.

This should only ever be done to warmed skin, and manual squeezing, which is commonplace, makes dermatologists blanch. 'Sterilised implements are by far superior to the two-finger technique,' says Dr Lupo. 'If you squeeze in only two directions – with fingers – you can rupture the pore and send sebaceous material into the surrounding skin. By applying pressure with a "comedone extractor", the only way the stuff inside can go is up.'

Marcia Kilgore, meanwhile – who has an 18-month waiting list for her facials at her Bliss Spa in Manhattan – advises women also to ensure that the right type of mask will be used on the face. 'Mature skins almost always need a hydrating mask, except in rare cases of oily skin,' she explains.

Above all, the experts tell us, don't allow yourself to be bossed around (especially by a beautician who's probably young enough to be your daughter). So if, during any part of the treatment, you don't feel comfortable about what is being done to your face – or you feel claustrophobic – communicate that to the facialist and ask her to move right along to the next step. If you follow these guidelines, you should emerge glowing beautifully. Not looking (and feeling) like you're having a hot flush.

broken veins. Dry skin – and most mature skins are dry – needs to avoid extremes of hot and cold.' (Steaming can also be very uncomfortable for women who are prone to hot flushes.) Don't feel shy about asking whether a facial that you're booked in for includes steaming, and don't feel shy about telling the therapist that you'd like to skip that step, either.

Most facials consist of cleansing, exfoliation, massage, extraction, the application of a mask, and a finishing stroke of moisturiser before you go out into the world.

In our experience, the difference between a good facial and a great facial is often down to massage – something experts like Amanda Lacey and Vaishaly excel at. As Vaishaly

explains, 'massaging the face helps drain away the lymph, reducing puffiness – especially under the eyes – and boosting blood circulation.' (She prescribes a special massage technique for use at home with her signature skincare, and we can honestly say it makes a huge difference to how good our skins look, on a daily basis.) 'It gets the oxygen flowing, and helps kick-start dull-looking skin.'

If you use Retin-A or Retinova, make sure to tell the therapist beforehand; these skins should not be exfoliated as they have already been thinned by these prescription creams (see pages 30–31). Anyone with a tendency to broken capillaries should also ask for exfoliation to be skipped, according to Dr Lupo. AHAs – alpha-hydroxy fruit

tried & tested
NON-SURGICAL FACELIFTS

Non-surgical facelifts, using electrical tools to stimulate the skin, are often trumpeted as the alternative to the knife. And as quick-fix 'lunchtime' treatments boom, they attract quite a following.

In non-surgical facelifts, the skin gets a muscle-stimulating blast of infinitesimal pulsating currents of electricity, tuned to mimic those which naturally take place at cellular level. It's usually done through probes, moved over the face by a beautician or aesthetician to strengthen and tone the muscles. Muscles around the mouth are shortened, pulling up any deep furrows, while the 'corrugator' muscles (which create frown lines) are lengthened. The bonus is that the stimulation of the skin gives circulation a boost – putting back some of the glow that ageing takes away.

Some treatments use pads which stick to the face, while others have probes that are stroked over the skin. However it's distributed, the current is claimed to 'lift' the face, energise 'tired' cells and improve circulation.

In our experience, they are terrific before an important meeting or a glam evening out – but trying to fit in the prescribed series of regular frequent appointments could be tricky.

So can they make a difference? Two pairs of volunteers tested the two most widely available salon treatments, Guinot and CACI, and were impressed. Another brace tried the at-home Integra machine and reported good-ish results. But six turned it down because they couldn't face decoding the instructions – so we haven't included it.

CACI
Score: 8.5/10
Our testers went along for ten sessions each, to the Camomile Rooms in Canterbury, Kent, and to Good Looks, Blackheath, London.

TESTER 1 First treatment: 'It feels as if the therapist is using very soft pincers to iron out your face, painlessly. My left "older" side was done first, and my droppy left eye lined up exactly with my right eye for the first time in years. Also the line from nose to mouth was less deep than the other side.'

Fourth treatment: 'People are saying I look well; my face looks brighter, less tired and firmer, more like the one I remember a few years back – better definition on my cheekbones.'

After the course was completed: 'I'm impressed. It doesn't do the same as a facelift but made me look much brighter and was much more effective than a facial. I'm planning to keep it up.'

TESTER 2 First treatment: 'After cleansing, the wand-like probe moves gently over my face, concentrating on those horrible lines from nose to chin, saggy bits on my jaw and ropey bits down the centre of my neck. At the end of the hour, my jowls show no real difference but my face looks brighter.'

Fourth treatment: 'I saw a slight softening of the lines last session and feel a definite difference when I touch my "grooves". By the fourth and fifth treatment, I can see the change: my saggy jaw is definitely less saggy.'

After the course was completed: 'I am honestly rather thrilled. My jawline isn't completely smooth and firm but much better than it was. I'm sold on CACI and am booking up for more.'

GUINOT HYDRADERMIE LIFT
Score: 8.5/10
Our testers went for eight 45–50 minute treatments (twice weekly) to the Guinot Salon in Albemarle Street, London, and Essential Therapies in Sidmouth, Devon.

TESTER 1 First treatment: 'After lymphatic drainage to prime the face, the electro-lifting begins with a very low current. A bit uncomfy in sensitive areas. My skin looked very good after the first treatment, like a good facial.'

Fourth treatment: 'Breakthrough, when I could see the lower half of my face looking plumper and definitely more lifted. I glowed quite noticeably.'

After the course was completed: 'Delighted. There's a clear uplift especially in the lower half of my face; forehead furrow less deep, wrinkles greatly improved and my skin looks luminous. I've been using the Guinot products and I'm sure this helps. I will try to do a monthly maintenance session.'

TESTER 2 First treatment: 'Skin as soft as silk; can't see any real lifting, but face looks fresh and hydrated.'

Fourth treatment: 'Face looked firmer, skin tighter and more toned; the texture was fantastic – unbelievably beautiful, clear, soft and smooth.'

After the course was completed: 'The lines around my eyes and across my forehead are definitely smoother and jawline less saggy. Overall, so relaxing and brilliant – highly recommended.'

the magic of manual lymphatic drainage

Manual lymphatic drainage, a form of massage, can be wonderful for tired-looking faces. MLD, as it's known, was developed in the 1930s by a couple called Emil and Astrid Vodder. It's a very light, rhythmic form of massage that works on the superficial lymph system, just underneath the skin – you may hardly feel the movements and so wonder whether anything at all is going on!

Lymph is the clear fluid that oozes from a graze or a burn; it moves protein, water, white blood cells and electrolytes round the body. The more efficiently your lymph is flowing, the healthier your body – and the less puffy your face. Lymph also has a detoxing effect as it moves toxins to the lymph nodes, where they're pushed back into the bloodstream or out of the body, often via sweat in the armpit or groin.

In fact, some women report that MLD is a bit of an all-round wonder treatment: it not only gives the face a boost, but may have an effect on improving cellulite (see page 182) – and also, we've been told, can gradually fade scars and stretch marks. But there are some cautions: MLD may not be recommended in the case of active cancers, thrombosis, some cardiac problems or where there is a risk of embolism. Although therapists take a medical history before your first treatment, it's wise to mention if you have asthma, thrombosis, low blood pressure or thyroid problems.

SALON SAFETY

Don't take salons at face value, warns Barbara Simpson-Birks, a lecturer in beauty therapy and salon-owner, who is so concerned about the standards in some salons that she has established the Institut Distingué, to give a 'star' rating to beauty salons, covering staff, treatments, client-care, etc. This is her advice:

• 'Ask if the beauticians you will be seeing are qualified, how long they trained for (and what in); also ask how often they've carried out a particular treatment you're interested in. My experience is that good beauty therapists need to have been trained for at least two years – and practice makes perfect.'

• 'Check that the salon is adequately insured for public liability; many will display their certificate of insurance – usually for £1,000,000 up – on the walls; if not, you are perfectly within your rights to ask to see it.'

• 'Assess the overall hygiene of the salon. Are the floors clean? Is each customer given fresh towels? Ideally, there should be evidence of some form of sterilisation, for tweezers, cuticle clippers, etc. In the case of electrolysis, a new needle should be used for each client – so ask, to make sure. If there is a steaming machine, ask how often the water is changed (at least once daily is ideal, to prevent bacterial growth).'

• 'The staff themselves should look clean, tidy and presentable. Personally, I'm even happier if I see them wearing a uniform or protective white gown.'

lie back and relax

Eve Lom, top London facialist, prescribes facials every six to seven weeks – and believes they're not only good for skins, but for stress levels. 'A facial is a wonderful opportunity to take time for yourself to relax,' she says. To enhance the relaxing experience, she suggests using the facial to take time to meditate (she's a long-term devotee of transcendental meditation), or just to breathe deeply and rhythmically, from the abdomen. (See page 162 for the optimum breathing technique.) 'For many of us, it isn't practical to meditate daily, and we go through life not breathing to full capacity. A facial gives you time out to breathe perfectly for an hour or so.' And oxygenate your skin – from the inside out.

SKIN S.O.S.

Age spots, rosacea and sensitivity – resulting in redness and flare-ups – are skin woes that can potentially trouble women more as the years roll by. More than fine lines and wrinkles ever can, they often lead to feelings of vulnerability and anxiety. So when your skin's sending out an S.O.S., here are the solutions...

ROSACEA – AND WHAT TO DO ABOUT IT

The red patches of acne rosacea, which most often occur on cheeks and nose, can cause great emotional distress. There are four different phases, says leading cosmetic dermatologist Professor Nicholas Lowe: first, flushing and/or blushing; then acne-like pustules and papules (small, raised red lumps); third, spider veins; finally, red, lumpy, bulbous enlargement of the nose. In rosacea keratitis, pustules and acne-like rashes can affect eyes and eyelids.

Integrated medicine expert Dr Mosaraf Ali believes diet is key to treatment. 'Drink plenty of pure still water between meals,' he advises. 'Eat lots of cooling fruit and vegetables such as melons, summer berries, cucumbers, spring onions, courgettes. Avoid hot spices, such as curries and chilli, ginger and garlic, also yeast-containing products (eg, bread, pizza, Marmite, canned soups, etc). Eat soda bread and occasionally rye bread. Drink very little alcohol and avoid coffee and excess salt.'

Sometimes, cosmetics can make rosacea worse. We believe that rosacea can be a sign of skin rebelling against the constant changing of skin creams and cosmetics, all loaded with different chemicals to which the skin is unaccustomed. So, if you suffer from rosacea, limit the number of new creams, lotions and make-up items you introduce, and carefully monitor what differences you notice in your skin. Dr Andrew Weil, American holistic health expert, believes that skin inflammation ('the fire within') is incredibly common and suggests opting for the simplest, most natural products you can find. Keep a food/drink diary and also record products used so that you can pinpoint any links.

Drug therapy includes antibiotics (usually tetracycline, which is safe for most people, even over long periods) or Rosex gel, Dr Lowe's preferred treatment. As a last resort, Dr Lowe puts patients (not women of childbearing age) on a very low dose of the drug Roaccutane.

Any redness, flushing and spider veins left after treatment can be removed by laser. Kathryn Marsden also suggests taking vitamins B_1 and $_2$, and soothing skin with Dr Bach Rescue Remedy Cream.

Nutritional therapy, naturopathy and traditional Chinese medicine may help.

AGE SPOTS – AND WHAT TO DO ABOUT THEM

Hyperpigmentation, which includes sun spots, age and brown/liver spots, is a major skin woe for women. Basically, it is an overproduction of melanin, usually from cumulative overexposure to the sun. Melasma is another type of hyperpigmentation, usually triggered by pregnancy, oral contraceptives, or HRT.

Facially, this can range from a freckle to diffuse, all-over discoloration. Sun spots also appear on hands, décolletage and tops of feet. Darker-skinned people are more susceptible than fair ones. Some attempted treatments have been drastic: according to Barbara Salamone of US skincare brand Bioelements, harmful ingredients like mercury have been used in skin bleaching products, with women literally poisoning themselves. And until it was banned here, mainstream beauty brands in the UK offered creams based on hydroquinone – a harsh bleaching agent. As Dr Daniel Maes of Estée Lauder says bluntly, 'It kills the skin cells.' Nevertheless, companies still manufacture hydroquinone creams for sale in the US, and mainland Europe. Prescription hydroquinone creams are permitted by the US Food and Drug Administration in concentrations of up to four per cent – although they are now reviewing that figure, following studies suggesting carcinogenicity in rats.

Today, skin experts are excited about other, gentler fading agents, such as kojic acid and extract of white mulberry, which may help lighten pigmented areas. However, we recommend patch testing every age-spot lightening cream on your forearm, and waiting 24 hours to see if there is redness, itching, burning or irritation, before applying to your face.

Confusingly, products labelled 'whitening' or 'brightening' are now widely available; however, they aren't intended to lighten skin, but to enhance translucency and luminosity. Most contain vitamin C derivatives or, in some cases, extracts from sheep or cow placentas! So, make sure you get the right products.

Whether or not you choose to use a specific age-spot lightening cream – and you can read the results of our Tried & Tested, right – it's important to remember that the best way to stop age-spots getting worse (and, with luck, prevent new ones) is to make a serious daily commitment to using an SPF with broad spectrum sunscreen ingredients, outdoors and in. Remember: skin that has been lightened becomes 'photosensitised', ie, more susceptible to UV rays. If it's exposed to the sun, it produces even more melanin – and you could end up worse off than you started.

Professor Nicholas Lowe maintains that this applies indoors too; 'Even if the sunlight is coming through a glass windowpane, your skin will respond to it and start to go darker if you don't apply a sunscreen every day.'

Retin-A and Retinova can both help to fade age spots, and – more drastically – so can skin peels, laser resurfacing and Intense Pulsed Light treatments (see pages 65 and 147–8). But remember, whatever technique you resort to, sun spots will return – unless you stay away from the sun.

Meanwhile, we also urge a little self-acceptance. We like the philosophy of Bioelements' Barbara Salamone. 'Love those sun freckles,' she says. 'Love the skin you're in.'

tried & tested
ANTI-AGE SPOT TREATMENTS

After the disappointment of line relaxers, we're pleased to report moderately better results from the tough category of age-spot-fading creams. However – unlike most of the categories where results are incredibly consistent (reassuring us that our system really works!), these age-spot-faders showed amazing benefits for some testers while others found almost no difference. No 'natural' products scored well and there are certainly no 'beauty steals' among these close scores.

LANCÔME ABSOLUE PROGRESSIVE CURE
Score: 7.83/10

Lancôme call this an 'Absolute Intensive Replenishing Programme', designed as a four-week booster to stimulate skin's turnover; active ingredients include magnesium gluconate, fruit acids, chestnut, wild yam, soya and sea algae, among others. With a serum-like consistency, it's luxuriously textured – and luxuriously priced.

Comments: 'After two weeks the brown spot on my cheek was definitely fading and my skin felt really soft and looked good without any make-up' • 'after four weeks, pigmentation was slightly paler and less noticeable, which has lasted; skin looks great – luminous, and in fantastic condition' • 'skin looks refreshed, smoothed, "plumped out"; comments include "you're looking healthy" and "have you been away?".

CLINIQUE TURNAROUND CONCENTRATE VISIBLE SKIN RENEWER
Score: 7.35/10

This lightweight serum features light-reflective pigments for instant flawlessness. With salicylic acid, creatine and extracts from yeast, chestnut and clary sage (to enhance skin's barrier function), it speeds up cell turnover, for brightness and smoothness.

Comments: 'My face looks more even toned and textured; broken capillaries seem less noticeable' • 'leaves my skin silky like a primer – great base for make-up' • 'no real difference in age spots, but skin does look glowing – so I'm buying the Turnaround mask too' • 'skin looks fresh and dewy and it does seem to be delivering a result'.

ESTÉE LAUDER RE-NUTRIV INTENSIVE AGE SPOT CORRECTOR
Score: 7.25/10

Lauder say this concentrated serum/gel features 'a never-before spot-targeted complex', to correct existing age spots and prevent future dark spots from appearing. Unlike the treatments above, this product is meant to be used exclusively on dark spots.

Comments: 'Though it did not fade age spots completely, it made an improvement – and left skin very soft' • 'I have been surprised by the improvement – especially to an age spot on my face, which is not only paler in colour but is much improved in terms of texture and "prominence"' • 'my facial age spots have been a pain for a long time. Using this product, in combination with sunscreen, there is a definite lightening compared with an untreated spot. Very luxurious to use – and it works too!'.

SENSITIVE SKIN – AND WHAT TO DO ABOUT IT

Sixty-three per cent of all women report having sensitive skin. For many of us, the problem becomes worse as we get older because the skin's ability to keep the outside world out and the inside world in is increasingly reduced. Three factors influence this: tiny cracks appear on the surface which, literally, open the door to irritants; skin thins – due to sun damage and/or ageing; and dryness, a natural side-effect of ageing, compounds the problem.

Sensitive skin is most reactive when a woman is aged about 45–50, says Dr Daniel Maes, because skin is thinner and there are also the hormonal challenges of menopause to cope with. This touchy skin scenario isn't helped by the fact that, as we get older, we tend to use more products and increasingly heavy formulations to make up for what our skin's losing: ultra-rich night creams, heavy-duty exfoliants, fruit acids, strong cleansers, as well as a wide range of spot-targeted cosmetics for everything from necks to heels, designed to fight the ravages of time.

Although we believe more is more when it comes to moisturising, surveys reveal that by midlife, the average American woman is using 15–20 different products – containing as many as 200 different chemicals – on her skin every single day. The average British woman probably isn't too far behind. And as Manhattan dermatologist Dr Debra Jaliman, MD, observes: 'When skin encounters so many chemicals, the chance of developing a reaction is increased.'

Sensitivity is linked to a disruption of the skin's 'barrier function' – the primary job performed by the dead cells and lipids (fatty, moisturising, natural ingredients in the skin) which constitute the outermost 'barrier' layer of skin. Harsh cleansing, too much exfoliation, or not enough moisturiser during a brutal winter can all affect the barrier. Minute cracks develop that are not usually visible to the eye, but are big enough to allow hostile irritants to penetrate down into the dermis.

Unfortunately, scientists now believe that sensitive skin actually ages faster. When your skin is faced with an irritant, two things happen to it. The first is the onset of immediate – and visible – itching, burning, stinging and redness. The second may be invisible until it is too late. Trying to defend itself, the body releases substances that destroy collagen and elastin, the vital proteins which support the skin. The new wrinkle-busting 'resurfacing' treatments used by dermatologists and some anti-ageing skincare products (which work by triggering inflammation) can also contribute to sensitivity, leaving skin even more vulnerable to pollutants such as UV rays and smoking.

The silver lining to this cloud is that, in Dr Maes's experience, skin sensitivity often calms down of its own accord after the menopause. In the meantime, avoid aggressive skincare, limit exposure to potential irritants, concentrate on protecting the skin from future damage – and consider exercising caution when it comes to anti-ageing products.

SENSITIVE SKIN *checklist*

● **Keep it simple: use a minimum of products and avoid those that weaken the skin's barrier function, ie, exfoliants, peels and AHA creams.**

● **Stay out of the sun – minimising the risk of an irritating interaction between chemicals in skin products and the sun.**

● **Look for products that are labelled fragrance-free, or hypo-allergenic – although this is no guarantee that they won't trigger a reaction.**

● **Protect the skin with an SPF15 reflective sunscreen (look for the words titanium dioxide high up the ingredients list).**

● **If you are really sensitive, patch-test new products before using them on your face – either on your forearm or behind your ear, where any adverse reaction won't show; be alert for itching, stinging, redness or a feeling of heat. (You can do this using an in-store tester, rather than invest in the cream itself.)**

● **Never change your entire skincare regime all at once; introduce products one by one, so that you can establish what you're reacting to.**

● **If you boost your overall health – through eating well and exercising – you may find that skin becomes more tolerant as your overall immunity improves.**

FACIAL HAIR – AND WHAT TO DO ABOUT IT

Do you live in dread of turning into a bearded old lady? Well, so do we. One of life's cruel tricks is to send facial fluff production haywire around menopause. Even women who've never been bothered before can find hairs start sprouting more noticeably – particularly on the upper lip. Then there are those single, wiry hairs which make a break for freedom.

The reason? 'Hairs usually have a hormonally controlled, natural growing cycle, with a cut-out mechanism,' says leading dermatologist Dr Andrew Markey. 'But at menopause, the cut-out mechanism in some hairs fails to kick in, so they go on getting longer.' (Annoyingly, excess facial hair in women can go in tandem with thinning scalp hair.) Single stray hairs can be plucked with a pair of tweezers. (We swear by Tweezerman's.) If you're too short-sighted to spot the hairs, make a pact with your nearest and dearest friend, or a trusted beauty therapist, to tell you if you're sprouting.

OPTIONS FOR REMOVING FACIAL HAIR:
Bleaching Jolen Cream Bleach is the DIY favourite; however, excessive use of bleaching products containing hydrogen peroxide can irritate sensitive skin.

Depilatories Notorious for itches and odours but new formulations have reduced problems by adding soothing ingredients and masking the chemical smell. These may still be perilous for those with truly sensitive skin – so do a patch-test and be sure to use a product specially targeted at facial hair, for the recommended time only. You will stay smoother for around two weeks.

Waxing Salon or home waxing will keep you smoother longer; fine hairs appear in around two weeks, thicker growth in four to six weeks. But remember, you need around 5mm–1cm regrowth before you can wax again.

Threading Two intertwined threads roll across the skin catching hair and pulling from the root. Can be painful! And only available at a few beauty salons. Same regrowth as plucking.

Electrolysis Fine needles conduct a very low electric diathermy current to destroy hair. There's a high pain factor and since up to 30 per cent of hairs are dormant at any one time and won't be affected by the treatment, you will need a series of treatments. If you have recently waxed or tweezed, it takes longer. Make sure you consult a qualified electrolysist; if electrolysis is done badly, it may create scarring. Destroying the follicle by galvanic tweezer removal is another form of electrolysis, as is transdermal electrolysis, which uses a probe and an ionised gel to transmit the current via the skin to the hair follicles. It is claimed to avoid swelling, bruising, scabbing or scarring, but as yet is only in limited distribution. All forms of electrical hair removal can leave red marks which may last for some days.

Epil-Pro A new and very successful technique where tweezers grab the hair as thousands of sound waves pass through it in a fraction of a second. Pain, irritation and damage to surrounding tissues are minimal.

Laser hair removal/Intense Pulsed Light Although, strictly speaking, they are categorised differently, these both zap hairs with specific frequencies of light, damaging or destroying the hair follicle to eliminate future growth. Systems you may encounter include the Ruby Laser, PhotoDerm and SoftLight (the first laser to get FDA approval in the USA for hair removal). The best results with most systems are in women with dark, coarse hair against pale skin; grey, white, ginger and fine, downy hairs respond poorly because there is not enough pigment for the laser to focus on. Black and Asian women are generally advised not to have laser treatment as it could affect their pigmentation, although the manufacturers of SoftLight claim that it can be used on all skin and hair colours. Although these treatments claim 'permanent hair removal', future treatments may be required because at any one time up to 30 per cent of hairs are in the 'resting' phase.

Proceed with caution, and make sure that the clinic/therapist you use is highly experienced, clean – and, preferably, comes via personal recommendation. As Professor Nicholas Lowe says, 'You can set up a laser hair removal clinic with one day's training, and there are virtually no studies of long-term effects.'

Always follow manufacturer's instructions for at-home treatment. If you are anxious, consult your doctor and ask for referral to an appropriate dermatologist.

HOW TO WIN THE WAR AGAINST THE BIG WRINKLER

Most smokers know there's nothing good to be said about the habit. It can make the smoker (and other people) ill – very ill. It's very expensive. And when it comes to beauty, it's public enemy number one, causing almost as many wrinkles as the sun.

FACTS TO TELL YOUR SMOKING MIND

- Smoking increases the likelihood of your getting lung cancer, breast cancer, pneumonia, stomach cancer, oesophageal cancer (gullet), myeloid leukaemia, atherosclerosis (clogging of the arteries) and osteoporosis.
- The death toll globally due to cigarettes is greater than that in both world wars, estimate experts.
- Five women in the UK die every hour from smoking-related diseases – that's one woman every 12 minutes, 42,500 every year.
- Women who smoke 20 cigarettes a day could be quadrupling their risk of breast cancer.
- Lung cancer is set to overtake breast cancer as the biggest cancer killer of women.

Problem is that, although most smokers really want to give up, nicotine is a highly addictive substance – just like cocaine or heroin. Most people become physically dependent on nicotine within a few weeks of starting smoking. Nicotine hits your brain very rapidly (within seven seconds) and because it leaves the body more quickly, smokers reinforce the habit with tens, and more often hundreds, of puffs every day.

Nicotine makes smokers psychologically as well as physically dependent. It's a friend against the world, pepping you up or calming you down. And, totally illogically, it gives insecure people the illusion of self-confidence. 'My cigarette was my emotional breastplate against a frightening world – even though I knew it was really just a handful of chopped up, dried plants in a paper wrapper,' one ex-smoker told us.

The key to giving up, according to experts, is to understand that your mind thinks about smoking on two levels – which can be totally contradictory. Although the conscious mind can know and respect all the bad things about smoking, the powerful pre-conscious mind – the one targeted by tobacco advertisers – can override all your best intentions. With the help of advertisements and, of course, other smokers' examples – from parents long ago to friends and role models now – it can reassure you smoking is just fine. Of course you need it – to relax, keep thin, be social. Of course you will give it up. But not just yet.

Kicking the habit is seldom easy but it is possible. (Sarah used to smoke three to four packs a day, but stopped puffing more than 25 years ago. What's more, she didn't put on weight.)

Remember, however seductive it may feel, smoking is the biggest enemy ever to health, anti-wrinkling and wellbeing. Here's how to wage war on the weed.

THE QUIT CAMPAIGN

1 Set the date, make it the number one priority in your life. Pick a mid-cycle date if you can – PMS seems to exacerbate withdrawal symptoms.

2 Rehearse the arguments for giving up, write them down as emotionally as you can, then tape them on a cassette recorder so you can play it back when you're feeling tempted. Be honest about your feelings about cigarettes – then ask yourself whether they make sense.

3 Make a list of the benefits you can expect, eg, helping your skin, stopping a smoker's cough, spending less on dry cleaning, having fresh breath, getting on better with non-smoking friends, not having to dive out first thing in the morning or last thing at night for emergency supplies. Estimate how much it will save you and list how you will spend that money.

4 Keep a smoking diary so you can identify your personal cues for a puff (eg, coffee time, talking on the phone, after a meal, having an argument, in a bar) and then avoid them if possible, when you first give up. (Later, you can challenge yourself by exposing yourself to cue situations.)

5 If you can't avoid cues, plan diversions or activities which are incompatible with smoking, such as drinking fruit juice (cigarettes taste vile afterwards), taking exercise, or confining yourself to no-smoking zones.

6 Give your fingers something to fiddle with, eg, worry beads, tapestry or executive toys.

7 Tell friends, family, work colleagues. Ask them for positive feedback when you get to the end of each smoke-free day, week, month.

8 Consider joining a support group such as Nicotine Anonymous (www.nicotine-anonymous.org) where you can share the experience with fellow addicts.

9 Ask your doctor, health practitioner or pharmacist about nicotine replacement therapy (patches, gum, inhalator or nasal spray). It can't give motivation but it can aid giving up. But remember, it's still nicotine, so don't continue longer than you need.

10 Explore smoking cessation therapy, eg, hypnotherapy, cognitive behavioural therapy, acupuncture.

Last thing on the evening before, get rid of all your cigarettes, ashtrays and any smoking trophies such as lighters. (Use your global match book collection to light soothing scented candles.)

tip

'If you're going through a particularly stressful period when you're quitting cigarettes, take a herbal stress remedy such as Bach Flower Remedies Rescue Remedy,' advises Robert Brynin, director of the British-based National Health Association, a non-profit medical research company that runs stop-smoking clinics countrywide.

GIVING UP

1 On the day, quit completely. Chances of success go up ten times if you don't smoke at all on the first day.

2 Drink plenty of fluids to get rid of the toxins, particularly pure water and fruit juices.

3 Remember you're giving up one day at a time. You only have to get through to midnight. If you're tempted, tell yourself that if you want to smoke tomorrow, you can chain smoke a whole pack. Then replay your tape.

4 If you do lapse, don't beat yourself up about it. Treat it as a lesson to be learnt: ask yourself: 'Why did I do it? What was going on in my mind? What can I do differently?' Tell yourself that one cigarette doesn't mean you have to be a smoker again. Get rid of all the evidence, air the room, change your clothes and play your tape.

5 At the end of every smoke-free day, revel in the fact that you've kicked it a day at a time and you're on your way to a clean bill of health, a fatter purse and a smoother, fresher-looking face.

THE GOOD NEWS ABOUT GIVING UP SMOKING

• After 48 hours, your taste buds and sense of smell will be working much more keenly – food, wine, your favourite scent will take on a new delight.

• After 72 hours, you will breathe more easily – wheezes will evaporate – and your energy levels will zoom upwards.

• After two to 12 weeks, your circulation will improve and walking and running will require less effort.

• After a year, your chances of heart disease will go down by half.

• After ten years, your risk of suffering from (potentially fatal) lung cancer will be reduced by between 30 and 50 per cent.

GLOSSARY

For advanced readers only! If you just want to find out which products our testers judged the best, keep turning the page. But every week, it seems, we hear about baffling new 'wonder' ingredients. Making sense of it all requires more than a heartfelt wish to get rid of wrinkles: it sometimes feels as if you need a science degree. (And a sense of humour.) For label-hounds and anyone as fascinated as we are by what makes today's skincare more effective than ever, here's a rundown of the key ingredients to be found in today's 'wonder creams'.

AHAs Alpha-hydroxy acids, aka 'fruit acids': these were once the anti-ageing ingredients *du jour* in state-of-the-art skincare – but many brands have dropped them, except in bodycare, because in many women (including us!) they triggered sensitivity. (Fact: body skin is thicker, and so less vulnerable.) They work to brighten the complexion by loosening the bonds in the skin, helping to get rid of the flaky 'dead' top layer and speeding up cell renewal. The 'family' of AHAs includes citric, malic, glycolic and tartaric acid, which can also be used in combination.

Antioxidants See page 204 for the lowdown on these important weapons against ageing.

BHAs (also known as beta-hydroxy acids), the 'first cousins' to AHAs. Some dermatologists claim they're gentler than AHAs, but again, we've seen their popularity wane because of sensitivity issues.

Ceramides These lipids – which are made in a lab to a natural blueprint (and sometimes genetically engineered) help stabilise skin structure by retaining moisture in the skin – making them a valuable anti-ageing ingredient.

Collagen If only skincare was as simple as slapping on collagen to top up your skin's natural supply. Alas, it doesn't work like that: using a collagen cream certainly won't do anything to boost your skin's own levels – but it is an efficient humectant (it actually attracts water to the skin), making it a highly effective moisturising ingredient.

Elastin Like collagen, elastin is a vital part of the skin's connective tissue network – but, again, putting elastin in a moisturiser won't top up the skin's reserves. It does create a good barrier for locking in vital moisture, though.

Enzymes In washing powder and contact lens solutions, enzymes are used to break down dirt and oil – but now the beauty industry has woken up to what enzymes can do for skin: they help to brighten as well as to protect vital collagen and elastin. Some skincare now incorporates botanically derived enzymes – for instance, papain from papaya and bromelain from pineapple – which exfoliate, and so help to restore the skin's 'glow'. Other creams are formulated with 'enzyme activators', designed to quench the production of other, natural 'bad-guy' enzymes in the skin, such as collagenase and elastase – which damage collagen and elastin. Look for enzymes in everything from brightening creams to cellulite treatments.

Glucosamine Taken as a food supplement, this is known to have a beneficial effect on joints, as it boosts collagen production. Now cropping up in skincare, too, for its power to even out skintone and increase collagen synthesis.

Humectants Valuable ingredients in moisturisers or facial sprays, which attract moisture from the air to the surface of the skin. Humectants that are commonly used include hyaluronic acid, glycerine, sorbitol, squalene and urea. (Yes, you did read that last one right.)

Liposomes High-tech skincare 'rockets' which are launched into the epidermis to deliver their moisturising cargo deeper than would otherwise be possible, so helping to fill in the gaps in the 'intercellular cement' (the glue between the skin cells!).

Lycopene Now quite widely used, this exceptionally strong antioxidant free radical scavenger (extracted from tomatoes, pink grapefruit, red guava, watermelon and the skin of red grapes) was first 'spotted' by European pharmacists, who discovered that Hungarian girls achieved radiant skin by rubbing tomato pulp on their faces and bodies.

Nanospheres A fancy name for incredibly minute, rounded particles. For more on nanotechnology (and some of our concerns arising from it), see page 48.

pH A term often seen on packaging, denoting acid balance. Your skin is naturally acid, with a pH between 4.5 and 5.5. The correct balance can be disturbed by the use of mass-produced soaps (which are mostly strongly alkaline in content) and cosmetics which are not acid balanced, potentially triggering irritation. If you see the term 'pH-balanced' on the packaging of a product, it often denotes that it's designed for sensitive skins.

Peptides These are 'buzz ingredients': combinations of amino acids that link together to form the building blocks of protein, which makes up a big proportion of our skin, hair and nails; peptides are thought to be able to boost collagen synthesis, and can be skin-firming; they are increasingly widely used. Some peptides promise to deliver 'curare-like' substances to minimise facial muscle contractions, claiming to be 'alternatives to Botox' – but in reality, they can only work on the tiny surface muscles, rather than the deeper, expression-line muscles beneath.

Optical diffusing ingredients These are hot, hot, hot! Why? Because they are brilliant at 'tricking' the onlooker, as they sit on the skin's surface diffusing and scattering light. The result is a 'halo' effect that blurs the appearance of fine lines and wrinkles, helping to even out skintone. Because you can see instant improvements with optical diffusing pigments (even if it is an illusion), many products now integrate these with functional ingredients that take a longer time to begin working. Yves Saint Laurent's Touche Eclat concealer helped pioneer this technology, which is now increasingly widespread.

Pollution protection Many botanical and marine extracts – in addition to the better-known antioxidant vitamins A, C and E – can help to protect skin and hair from pollutants, ozone, pesticides and even cigarette smoke. As the world becomes more industrialised, many of us are as concerned about shielding skin from pollution as we are about protecting it from sunlight, hence the growing popularity of 'pollution complexes' in our lotions and potions.

Mitochondrial optimisation Phew, what a mouthful! Actually, this isn't an ingredient – it's a process, but one which skin scientists are becoming pretty excited about. Mitochondria are the 'energy powerhouses' of our cells, and new skincare technology coming down the line promises to boost cellular energy (improving radiance), protect the mitochondrial DNA, and extend cell life. Watch this space.

Proanthocyanidins (grapeseed extract, pine bark extract, bilberry extract). These are super-potent antioxidants, which help protect against inflammation. Applied topically to the skin, they are powerful neutralisers of free radicals, turning up (as we predicted) in more and more creams.

Pycnogenol This is another mega-antioxidant, from maritime pine bark extract. It can also strengthen capillaries.

Retinyls/retinols Ingredients derived from vitamin A are now widely used in anti-ageing products (see pages 30–31 for more information); they can be helpful in enhancing skin radiance and maintaining the complexion's overall smoothness.

Salicylic acid A 'beta-hydroxy acid' (BHA) which was first synthetically produced as long ago as 1860, as a treatment to reduce aches and pains, later used as a wart-removing cream – and which, since the 1980s, has been incorporated into anti-ageing skincare.

Tea (black, green and white tea). The key ingredient in tea is polyphenolic acid, which acts on the skin as a powerful free radical scavenger – meaning that tea is yet another ingredient in the growing armoury of antioxidants being used in high-tech skincare. Preliminary studies have shown that topical and ingested doses of either green or black tea extracts protect against sunburn and skin cancer induced by sunlight; scientists are currently trying to identify the specific mechanisms that provide this protection. Green tea also acts as a skin-calming ingredient, which is why you may find it teamed with others that have a potentially irritating effect, to 'balance' the formulation. White tea has been researched by several major universities and is said to be the most potent antioxidant of the three.

THE MAKE-UP FACELIFT

" More women should explore what make-up can do for them before taking a leap into the world of cosmetic surgery. Get a makeover, have some fun with colour, learn some techniques that can make you look well-groomed and colour coordinated. You can spend a few pounds on make-up and a great haircut – and maybe save yourself thousands on a facelift. *"*

DR ANDREW MARKEY, MD, FRCP, dermatological and cosmetic surgeon
and honorary consultant at St John's Institute, St Thomas's Hospital

FOUNDATION COURSE

We asked the world's leading make-up artists for their secrets for a flawless finish – because great-looking skin doesn't just have to be the preserve of fresh-faced teenagers.

When it comes to make-up guidelines for older faces, most make-up artists come up with three words: less is more. 'Foundation isn't plaster,' as the late, great make-up artist Kevyn Aucoin observed. 'It can't be used to fill in lines and wrinkles. In fact, if you try to apply foundation, concealer and powder over laughter lines in the hope of camouflaging them, the opposite happens. You draw attention to them.'

However, the good news is that foundation and powder can 'lift' older skin in a few seconds. 'If you're looking for one product that makes a huge difference to older women, it's foundation,' says Trish McEvoy. 'Skintone naturally becomes more uneven as we age. Perfectly applied, foundation smooths the complexion, so making it look younger and fresher again.'

STEP-BY-STEP GUIDE TO FLAWLESS FOUNDATION

Great faces, the professionals all agree, start with the 'perfect canvas'. So here are the insider secrets on how to create a flawless base...

1 Wash your hands. Never apply make-up with dirty hands; you spread grime – and germs – over your face.

2 Moisturise, then ideally wait ten minutes or more before applying foundation, or you'll find that it disappears very quickly. (The exception is if you use an oil-free foundation formulation, which can go straight over moisturiser without slipping.)

3 The golden rule with foundation is: get exactly the right colour and apply it where you need it most. (See page 72, 'Finding Your Perfect Match'.) You might think you need it all over, from hairline to jawline. 'That's never true,' according to Laura Mercier. 'Older skins only need foundation where there are shadows, darkness or broken veins. That may include: the innermost corner of the eye on the "nose-bone" (which most women overlook), the inner half-circle under the eye, on broken veins either side of the nose, and just under the corners of the mouth, which can be shadowy in some women. These are the key places that foundation can make the face look instantly younger. The rule is: what is dark, make light.' (Where you do not usually need to apply foundation is to the laugh lines at the outer corner of the eyes and upper cheek. 'The reason for applying foundation or concealer is to disguise discoloration – and the laugh lines usually aren't discoloured,' observes Laura.) Mary Greenwell's advice for disguising dark circles, meanwhile, is to lighten them – but not to obscure them completely. 'I find that if you totally disguise them, it takes the character out of the face – and it can look like a mask.'

4 Trish McEvoy believes in using a Q-Tip to dot the foundation on the skin. (She makes special longstemmed versions, which can reach easily to the bottom of a foundation bottle). This makes it easier to get the foundation exactly where you need it, and to apply just the right amount; if you tip foundation from the bottle on to your fingers, it's easy to get too much foundation – and then be tempted to rub it all into your skin.

5 Blend foundation into skin using fingers or a damp, squeezed cosmetic sponge (available at make-up supply stores and from many beauty counters) – whichever suits you best. (Many make-up artists actually like to work with their fingers, warming the make-up as they go.) 'If you use a sponge, work the foundation well into it before you put the sponge to your face, to ensure it goes on evenly,' advises Laura Mercier. Also apply foundation to the eyelids. 'Veins and blueness show up here as

we age,' observes Trish McEvoy. Use foundation to create as smooth a base as possible for eyeshadow, then set the foundation with powder.

6 If you need extra coverage in some places, you can either layer on a little extra foundation where required – or use concealer. 'When applying make-up, think 'layers'',' says Laura Mercier. 'You don't want one thick layer of foundation, but you can build it up where you need extra help.' Many make-up artists use a brush to apply concealer, then pat with a finger, warming the concealer on the skin and almost pressing it into the complexion. 'If you smear concealer on with your finger, you can wipe the foundation right off, at the same time,' points out Trish McEvoy.

7 Make sure the foundation is beautifully blended so that you can't see where your skin starts and the foundation ends. 'The biggest mistake, as we age, is not blending enough,' observes Mary Greenwell. 'You have to do your make-up in the best possible light – I prefer daylight, facing a window – and blend, blend, blend. And a magnifying mirror is a must, if you can't see well.' (Actually, we suggest making up in the coldest, most northerly light that's available to you. If you look good there, you'll look good everywhere.)

Remember: once you've powdered, there's no more opportunity for blending.

8 Most make-up artists we know advise applying powder with a velour powder puff, rather than a brush – which can overload the face and settle chalkily into fine lines. Many make-up artists' lines – from MAC to Trish McEvoy, Bobbi Brown to Vincent Longo – make velour puffs, which you can also find at beauty

supply stores. These are not to be confused with old-fashioned swansdown puffs, which will deliver way too much powder – as do the big, fluffy powder brushes that you'll find in many make-up lines. Mary Greenwell, however, is one of the make-up artists who likes to apply powder with a brush – but she gets round the potential problem of overdoing it by using a small, 2cm (3/4inch) brush (hers is by Shu Uemura). 'This is small enough to make it easy to avoid getting it in any crinkles, thereby highlighting them.' If using a brush, always sweep powder lightly downwards on the face, never upwards – or you'll accentuate pores and hairs. (The same applies to blusher and foundation.)

9 Use loose powder, in preference to pressed powder, for morning make-up. (You can carry pressed powder with you for daytime touch-ups.) 'Press the edge of your puff into your loose powder,' advises Bobbi Brown. Thwack the puff once or twice on a hard surface – like the edge of a washbasin, or the palm of your hand – to shake off any excess. 'Then press the powder into your foundation, again using the edge of the puff.'

10 Make-up artists all agree that excess powder – which tends to settle into lines – is extremely ageing. 'So if there's too much powder on the skin after applying with the velour puff, I use a bigger, fluffy brush to whisk away the excess,' explains Bobbi Brown. (NB: sometimes Trish McEvoy avoids the use of powder altogether on older skins. 'Experiment with just pressing the puff itself on to your foundation to absorb the extra oil,' she advises. 'You may find that's all you need to do to blot the shine.')

FINDING YOUR PERFECT MATCH

Most of us were raised in an era when you learned to test make-up on your hand. But hands are usually darker than our faces, because they get more UV exposure than almost anywhere else. So the best place to test foundation is on the jawline and the lowest part of your cheek. The perfect shade will 'disappear' into your skin, so that you almost can't see that it's there.

'Carry a mirror with you so that you can do the natural-light foundation test,' advises Bobbi Brown. 'Apply a couple of possible shades of foundation than your foundation. For broken veins, choose a shade that exactly matches your foundation – or layer on foundation, in very thin layers, until you've achieved the level of coverage you want.

There are always fewer concealer colours to choose from than foundations. If you can't find the perfect colour, Vincent Longo recommends blending two shades together on the back of your hand with a stiff brush, to get the right shade, then dabbing that on to the skin.

What most of us want to avoid, says Vincent, is foundation with even a hint of pink in it, 'especially if you're prone to flushing'. Most foundation ranges today feature shades based on so-called 'yellow pigments', which are extremely natural looking. If you're not sure, ask at the counter to see only the yellow-toned foundations – and focus on finding the shade from those that works best for you.

Bobbi is not a fan of translucent powders, preferring instead a shade perfectly matched to your foundation. (Most lines offer these options.) 'It's a myth that translucent powder is invisible; I find translucent powder makes a woman look pasty – and can be chalky on the skin.'

> ## Attitude is more important to beauty than cosmetics ever can be. When you are at peace with who you are, you are beautiful. Work on the inside, as well as the outside.
>
> **BOBBI BROWN**

to the jawline in a downward stripe and leave them for a few seconds before blending. Then go to the nearest source of daylight to see how they look.' Artificial lights distort colours so that a shade which looked perfect in a marble beauty hall may be quite wrong when you get it home.

Don't rush your selection. The skin's natural chemistry can actually make the foundation change colour after a minute or two.

When choosing a concealer for under-eye circles, Bobbi Brown advises selecting a shade very slightly lighter

small change, big difference

You want to avoid a too-matte look, after a certain age. Dusty, dry-looking skin has an ageing effect. So, to that end, companies are now creating specific foundations which incorporate 'light-reflective pigments' to bounce light off the face, giving a texture that is dewy – which mimics how young skin looks. So although on this page we talk about powder, you might want to see whether your foundation looks more flattering if you don't powder. Try it. You may find your foundation 'disappears' too quickly for your liking – or you may love the youth-enhancing effect.

more secrets of flawlessness

• 'You should spend twice as long on your foundation as any other element of your make-up. If you're giving it less time than that, you're skimping,' says Mary Greenwell. 'It makes such a huge difference that it's worth the extra time and effort.'

• If your skintone is still fairly even, in summer you can get away with tinted moisturiser for a light, natural coverage. But if you need a dab of concealer to cover flaws, apply it before the tinted moisturiser, for a natural look.

• Many women are self-conscious about freckles and sun/age spots – and want to even them out. When it comes to freckles, says Mary Greenwell, 'you have to accept that if you're going to cover them totally, it's going to look like a mask. So I'd advise a foundation that's midway between the colour of your freckles and the colour of your complexion, to play them down a bit – with concealer (or Estée Lauder's Maximum Cover), on the bigger age spots. The best way to apply concealer to an age spot is with a 3mm (1/8in) brush. Dab it on to the affected area, then set with powder, applied with a velvet powder puff. The rule is: always start with a little product, then build up. It's easier to add than take away. Alternatively, use a cream-to-powder formulation, which is halfway between a foundation and a concealer, in terms of texture and coverage.' (Most leading beauty houses now make these foundations, which are also extremely convenient to carry around in a handbag. They go on smoothly, like foundation, then dry swiftly to a lightly powdered finish.)

• 'If you overdo foundation, lightly whisk off the excess with a very slightly damp cosmetic sponge,' advises Laura Mercier.

• 'As you touch up make-up during the day, don't over-powder – or make-up will look "caked",' cautions Vincent Longo.

• One of the cleverest tricks we know for a younger-looking complexion comes from Trish McEvoy. To soften the appearance of laugh lines around the eye, she applies a dab of Trish McEvoy Liner Refiner there. (This is a portable wand of moisturiser, but you could experiment with a dab of eye cream.) 'It re-creates the dewiness that young skins have, and counteracts the natural paperiness that women tend to have round their laugh lines, which is accentuated by powder,' she says.

There is something to be said for acceptance. As make-up artist Pablo Manzoni points out, 'Look at Jeanne Moreau. She was a sex symbol with bags under her eyes. People just thought she looked like she was having a terrific time in the bedroom.' (And she probably was.)

FACE-SHAPING TRICKS

Most of the make-up artists we spoke to are agreed that face-shaping – using contouring powder to create shadows and re-shape features – is tricky, tricky stuff. Jenny Jordan, for instance, is sometimes asked by clients to help them re-shape a bumpy nose. 'And I have to say to them: what'll happen if you want to blow it? All the shading will come off on your Kleenex.' Embarrassing stuff.

For round cheeks, however, movie star make-up artist Gary Liddiard has a tip for creating contours that's worth a try. He suggests using two foundations – your usual shade for the whole face and then just a shade darker, for blending on the cheek under the bone to the jawline. (Be sure to blend, blend, blend at the jaw itself.) 'The new foundations are so easy to blend that the contouring is basically undetectable. If you then use blusher as you normally do, no one will know – but everyone will notice.'

If you have a thin face, meanwhile, Stephen Glass suggests using an under-make-up primer beneath your foundation, in a pale or white shade. (Chanel, Prescriptives and MAC are among the many companies who now offer these.) 'It makes the face glow and stand out more,' he explains. 'And be careful of blusher placement,' he adds. 'Blusher must go on the cheekbones, never underneath, or the cheeks will look hollow.' His last tip? 'Earrings make a tremendous difference to the impact a thin face has – but steer clear of anything too big, or they may swamp your face.'

camouflage make-up for rosacea and other problems

So popular is Laura Mercier's make-up range with rosacea sufferers that she was recently invited to speak at a conference on the subject, and her postbag bulges with letters from grateful women. The product they rave about is Laura's Secret Camouflage Concealer, which is also a favourite with Hollywood stars. The reason, Laura explains, 'is that Camouflage has a very high level of pigmentation, so you get excellent coverage without having to put it on thickly'. The technique, she explains, is to dab the finger in Secret Camouflage, and apply to the affected area, building coverage layer by layer until the characteristic redness is completely disguised. 'Then set with a light covering of powder.'

Another product which gets top marks from make-up artists for its truly incredible covering powers is Estée Lauder Maximum Cover. Be warned: if you apply it straight from the tube, it goes on way too thick. The technique, explains Stephen Glass, 'is to invest in a small plastic spatula. Then squeeze around three pinhead-sized dots of Maximum Cover on to the spatula. Dip your ring finger in the foundation, then wipe your finger on the edge of the spatula. You'll be left with just a tiny amount of Maximum Cover on your finger – but because it covers so densely that's still enough to disguise some broken veins or an age spot. If you need more, do exactly the same again – and repeat until you've covered all the areas where you need the extra help.' (He recommends Maximum Cover only for areas affected by broken veins, dark circles, rosacea, birthmarks and port wine stains or age spots, not as a general foundation.)

NB If you have a birthmark, vitiligo (uneven pigmentation) or scarring (including burn scars), you might want to know about the British Red Cross's cosmetic camouflage programme. It's available on referral from your doctor only. The consultations offered – with specially trained volunteers who are all experienced therapists – are free, and most of the special creams (which are waterproof and contain a sunscreen) are available on prescription. Further information is available from the beauty care officer at local Red Cross branches in the UK.

Advice is also available from the British Association of Skin Camouflage (BASC). The BASC will supply the name of your nearest member, who – for a modest fee – will discuss individual requirements and recommend products from the Dermablend, Dermacolour, Covermark, Veil and Keromask ranges. These are available on prescription and/or over the counter at Boots.

Stephen Glass also highly rates the Doreen Savage Trust in Fife; Doreen herself has a port wine stain down the side of her face and provides information and help for people with birthmarks.

THE BEST ANTI-AGEING FOUNDATIONS WE'VE FOUND

The advent of 'light-reflecting' pigments – which work to create an optical illusion 'soft-focus' effect – is a real boon to older faces. Moisturising ingredients can also make a difference, time-releasing moisture into the skin to prevent it looking dry, as the day wears on. They're now being incorporated into foundations and powders. The two of us tried all the leading 'anti-ageing' and 'time-defying' foundations for this book. Our favourites are Estée Lauder Futurist Age-Resisting Make-up, Clarins Extra-Firming Foundation, and Guerlain Issima Anti-Aging Silky-Smooth Foundation. We also like Chanel's Double Perfection Compact (elegant enough for public nose-powdering!), while Jo swears by Giorgio Armani Hydra Glow Foundation's amazing 'soft focus' effect. Sarah loves Susan Posnick's Colorflo, a superfine sweat-proof powder with SPF26, which gives a foundation finish as it warms on your skin. But what turns the clock back more than anything, we found, is using a shade that matches our skintone perfectly.

" I apply make-up sparingly and quickly. I play with bronzing powders and tinted moisturisers. It's important to be natural – but worked-at natural, which takes a lot of time! A face that's not overly made up looks younger.

CATHERINE DENEUVE

THE ESSENTIAL TOOLKIT

Do you still put on blusher with the stubby brush that comes with the compact? Fiddle with those tiny eyeshadow applicators in an attempt to shade your eyes? Age-defying make-up relies on perfect application – and that means using the right tools. 'We need a bigger toolkit as we get older, because it makes for a more natural finish,' observes Barbara Daly. So we asked her to select the ultimate toolkit for the older face.

1 A lash comb. 'One of the most ageing make-up mistakes is clumpy lashes.'

2 An eyelash curler. 'They really do make a difference to older eyes.' (So we really do promise to learn how to use them this time, Barbara.)

3 An old, soft toothbrush. 'This is dual-purpose: it's brilliant for grooming brows into place – and for cleaning your lash-comb.'

4 A nice, fat blusher brush with a dome-shaped head. 'You don't want a spindly little one because that can make blusher go on in stripes.'

5 Although some make-up artists prefer velvet powder puffs, Barbara likes to apply powder with a brush. 'It should have a wide-ish head but not be as fat and fluffy as a blusher brush, so you can apply powder just where you want it.' (NB: if you do prefer to apply your powder with a puff – as many make-up artists suggest – a powder brush is still useful for whisking away the excess.)

6 An eyeshadow blender brush. 'The right size and shape will help you apply shadow to the socket and soften any hard lines.'

7 A slanted eyebrow brush. Stiff bristles are less likely to smudge, spread or smear pigment where you don't want it.

8 A smaller eyeshadow brush, for applying colour to the brow-bone.

9 Two retractable lip brushes – 'one for lip colour and one for applying concealer perfectly on broken veins and shadows. Then you can pat the concealer with your finger, warming it and pressing it into the skin.'

10 A soft, more pointed eyeliner brush, if you like to use eyeliner. (You can wet this and dip it in shadow for a more dramatic effect.)

brush notes

Invest in real hair brushes, rather than synthetic hair – in most cases, these tend to be stiff and not to pick up colour so well. However, if you prefer synthetic brushes for ethical reasons, we recommend those from Origins, and the Good Karma brushes by Urban Decay.

Good brushes are the key to a polished, professional look, but they're often too big to fit neatly into a compact make-up bag. The solution is either to opt for the travel size next time you buy one – many ranges, like Bobbi Brown, Trish McEvoy and

Shu Uemura offer short-handled or long-handled options – or adapt what you've already got.

'I always cut down the handles on my brushes,' says Jenny Jordan. 'They fit into my kit more easily and they're better for fiddly application.'

BLUSHING BEAUTY

Women of a certain age should 'think pink'. Blusher can restore youth to a fading complexion, soften lines, blur sags – and give the skin a fresh (girlish) glow. But it's a fine line between healthily blushed and hotly flushed.

The great cosmetics legend Estée Lauder was evangelical about blusher. She used to keep a blusher compact in her handbag and apply it to the faces of women she met, to show them how 'glow' could transform them with the flick of a wrist. And it's true. As Bobbi Brown says, 'Nothing makes a woman look prettier than a shot of blush. And there is no faster "up" if you're flagging in the middle of an afternoon. It can instantly take ten years off you by making you look healthier.'

But where you apply your blusher today may not be where you wore it ten years ago. Natural changes in the shape of the face with age demand a shift in make-up application techniques. Until we're about 35, we can wear blusher high on the cheekbone. But because one of the first signs of an ageing face is the loss of fatty tissue and the formation of natural hollows, in most cases it becomes more flattering to place blusher towards the centre of the face and on the apple of the cheek, to soften it.

BLUSHER HOW-TO

In general, we prefer cream blushers these days – with their easy, glide-on formulations and sheer textures. But if you still prefer powder, here's the perfect technique to follow…

1 Switching to a smaller blusher brush – a 2.5cm (1in) blusher brush, rather than a big fat version – makes for better control.

2 Dip the blusher brush in your chosen colour, then tap the handle of the brush smartly on a hard surface – like the edge of a table or a basin – several times, to ensure that you only have a whisper of colour left. ('Never blow on a brush,' warns Trish McEvoy, 'it just blows on germs.')

3 Where you put your blush depends on how plump your face still is. If you have developed hollows or sunkenness under the cheekbone, concentrate the blusher on the apples of your cheek. 'This gives a more youthful look,' says Mary Greenwell. 'To find the "apple" of your cheek, smile in an exaggerated way. The fatty area that sticks out is the apple. Using light, circular movements, apply just the very lightest dusting of blusher to the apples. With the same brush, blend, blend, blend at the edges until there are absolutely no harsh lines.' (If you overdo it, she advises, you can apply a touch of pressed powder with your velvet puff, to tone the colour down.)

4 If your face still has fullness you can apply blusher on the cheekbone as well as the apples. Again, make sure that your blusher brush only has the lightest amount of colour, by tapping the handle of the brush first. Then, advises Laura Mercier, 'Start at the ears and make an inward movement with the brush, as if you were going to draw an oval with it on the entire cheek. Break the oval, when you get to the apple of the cheek. Continue to make these ultralight broken-oval strokes until you have achieved the right depth of colour.' Then clean the last traces of blusher off the brush by drawing with it on a Kleenex, and use the brush to blur any edges, so that you can't see where it begins and ends. (Sweeping blusher in from the ears, explains Laura – rather than following cheekbones outwards – avoids putting too much pigment on the middle of the cheek.) 'Lastly, gently brush the cheek hairs down so they are lying in their usual direction.'

5 Trish McEvoy likes to whisk the lightest dusting of blusher around the temples and hairline, creating the lightest halo of warmth around the face. But again, the watchwords are 'softly, softly'.

NB To avoid the painted-lady effect, try applying blusher as the final step in a make-up – so that you can judge exactly how much you need, and not overdo it.

BLUSHER NOTES

• For emergencies: if you're out and about without a blusher and feel washed out, reach for your lipstick, put a tiny dab on your finger – and apply to your cheeks. 'This works best with sheer lipsticks, which don't have too much pigment,' says Laura Mercier.

• If you have broken veins or high colour, Vincent Longo's advice is to 'avoid blusher that has any red in it – go for tawny or honey shades instead, which create a peachy effect'.

• 'Don't be scared to wear blusher if you have a tendency to hot flushes,' says Laura Mercier. 'If you tone down the redness of your face with foundation, concealer and powder, you can add blush to look healthy and alive. But choose a tawny shade with a touch of brown in it, rather than fleshy pink or anything with blue undertones.'

cream versus powder blush

Many make-up artists suggest cream blusher for older faces. 'Cream blush is terrific if you're the sort of woman who feels she needs some help in the morning before facing the milkman or the postman, as it blends so beautifully on bare skin,' says Vincent Longo. 'It goes into the skin so it doesn't sit on the surface and look powdery, which is an advantage for older skins. And it's especially good in summer. Powder blusher can look dusty in intense light.' Cream blusher is, however, best applied over moisturiser on bare skin, or over foundation before powdering, otherwise it's hard to blend evenly.

THE BRUSH BATH

According to Bobbi Brown, it's essential to wash brushes at least every two months to get rid of skin-irritating oil, bacteria and mildew – and to ensure that colour glides on smoothly. To clean blusher, powder and eye brushes, gently swish (don't soak) bristles in sudsy water. (Use a mild shampoo, rather than soap.) Rinse immediately, squeeze out the water and rearrange the bristles in their normal shape. Then lay a towel on a flat surface with an edge and leave the brushes to dry with their heads hanging over the edge. For lip brushes, wipe bristles with a tissue, then dip them into a cup of non-oily eye make-up remover and tissue off the residue.

thinking pinker

Pink isn't just flattering as a blush shade – it also flatters older faces if you use it in the home. Sister Parish, who was America's favourite interior decorator, insisted that 'pink makes the rich look healthy'. Joan Crawford, too, couldn't get enough of pink: her three Manhattan apartments all had pink walls, pink lamps with flesh-toned shades, pink headboards and pink monograms on the sheets. Even Dorothy Parker – she of the wicked pen, who was so quick to skewer vanity in others – had a pink room in her Pennsylvania house that became a favourite because she felt its warm glow made her look younger. Which is worth seriously considering next time you're redecorating.

climbing out of a make-up rut

Old habits die hard. Especially when it comes to make-up. But one way that women inadvertently add years is by allowing themselves to be 'freeze-framed' with a particular look. Observes John Gustafson, 'I think it's really sad to see an older woman who doesn't look her age – but her make-up does.

'I often meet women who are wearing the same make-up as they were when they were 20 years old. And all you see is the make-up. That was when that woman felt comfortable – so she stopped experimenting.'

Because our complexions change, tending to become drier and paler every year, too, make-up kits need to be adjusted to these new needs. The solution is to turn to insiders for help. John Gustafson goes so far as to suggest that 'you should get a department-store makeover – usually free, at make-up counters – at least twice, preferably four times a year. Mostly, you'll learn something. You might not like the results, but you should have acquired some new techniques to help you in future.'

But don't just sit there passively. Ask questions and in particular badger for how-to advice. New colours and textures call for new techniques, so ask about the equipment you'll need to re-create the look at home. Your best beauty investment is the right tools and brushes for the job: Q-Tips and fingers just won't achieve the desired effect. So when you're next in a beauty hall, why not ask a make-up artist or counter consultant how you should be using these tools? (It really is all in the wrist action.)

'When it comes to makeovers, don't go in as a "blank canvas",' adds John. 'Wear your usual make-up, so the consultant gets an idea of the way you usually like to look, rather than projecting their own ideas on to you. And if you just want an update, rather than a whole new look, suggest that they work by adding colour to the make-up you usually wear – a sweep of one of the new colours on the lid, a touch of shimmer on the brow, but basically not straying too far from the make-up you feel comfortable with.'

He also has advice on how to wean yourself off a lipstick colour you're clinging to like a family heirloom. 'If you'd like to wear a brighter lipstick which you think would suit you but it's outside your usual "comfort zone", pick a bolder colour that appeals. Then wear one coat of your usual lipstick, with a coat of the new one on top. After a few days, when you get used to that, add another coat of the new shade, until you're sure it suits you. Then you can move on to wearing the new shade on its own. And hey, presto – you've a new look.'

when less isn't more...

There's one exception to the 'less is more' rule, says Bobbi Brown. 'If you've never worn make-up, it's never too late to start. We tend to get washed-out looking as we age,' she observes. 'Make-up makes up for that.'

Happy is the woman who never makes a make-up mistake. Happy – and rare. As we age and complexions become washed out, it's tempting to reach for the paintbox in the hope that it will instantly 'lift' the face. But if you make the wrong colour choices, what actually happens is that strangers and loved ones will see your make-up – not the 'you' underneath. 'Older women do need colour,' believes Bobbi Brown, 'but it's all about adding soft, flattering shades.'

'cool' colours are equally complexion-perkifying.)

To help show you how 'warm' or 'cool' shades can work best for you, we have put cool shades down the top of this page and warm shades below. Hold them up to your face. Look in the mirror and hold the book up in front of your face, then move the page so that first the warm, then the cool part, is just below mouth-level. It's amazing to see the difference: one will make you look vibrant and healthy – and the other, washed-out.

If you still can't tell, then the sales pros at most make-up counters are able

leave bright, funky colours to the teenagers. 'Don't get lured into wearing bright colours,' counsels Barbara Daly. 'Bright eye colour can be very ageing.' Barbara's advice is to keep the palette neutral, sticking to smoky greys and browns. 'You can always use a touch of gold, pale pink or even lavender on the brow-bone. But don't go bold on the lid or in the socket.' Avoid burgundy, she warns, because it can bring out redness in bloodshot eyes. (Ditto pink on the brow if you are prone to red-eye.) 'In the same way, if you have a tendency to redness, examine brown eyeshadows

cool

THE COLOUR CODE

When it comes to choosing colours, though, it's a minefield. Hard-and-fast rules are difficult to come by. But some companies have set out to render make-up shopping mistake-proof, dividing the colours they offer into groups of shades most likely to suit, often by dividing us into 'warm' and 'cool' skintones.

The trouble is, according to leading international make-up pro Sharon Dowsett, that 'most women don't know whether they're cool or warm'. So Sharon has developed the simplest of tests. Take an actual peach, and a soft pink rose flower – choose a pink that reminds you of sugared almonds, without any fleshy tones – preferably the colour of the pink in the 'cool' list, on the right of this page. 'Then look into the mirror – and hold up the peach. If you're a "warm", you'll look better with that peach next to your cheek. If you're a "cool", the pink rose will "lift" your face.' (That said, there are, however, some rare fortunates – Jo happens to be one – for whom both 'warm' and

to tell, at a glance, which grouping you fall into. You can then train your eye to spot the 'warm' and 'cool' shades in each colour family. 'There are even some "cool" browns,' explains John Gustafson. 'You can usually spot them, because in a sea of brown colours, they stand out as looking different. They're the ones that will suit "cool" skins.' ('Cool' browns are the taupey ones with blue/mauve undertones, rather than the bronzey red 'warm' browns.)

Prescriptives, helpfully, is one company that assists the warm/cool shopper; they pioneered 'skintone analysis' some years back, subdividing women into four categories – red, blue/red, yellow/orange and red/orange – then organising the cosmetic carousel so that you can pick the kind of colours you like – and the exact, most flattering tone is preselected for you.

Whichever brand you choose, and whether you're 'warm' or 'cool', it pays to listen to this wisdom, from some leading pros. For foolproof eyes, stick to a palette of neutral, natural tones, and

carefully for any gingery notes, which will have a similar effect.'

Whatever you do, forget the old advice about matching your eyeshadow to your eyes. If you have brown eyes, try emphasising them with grey shadows; if they're blue or grey, go for browns.

And for lips? Says Bobbi Brown: 'Steer clear of nudes – but don't go to the other extreme with fuchsia, either. You want colours that are softened – like soft rose, soft plum, soft apricot – but which are definitely there.'

There are also organisations like Color Me Beautiful, specifically set up to help pinpoint the elements of the spectrum – in cosmetics and fashion – most likely to flatter individuals. But do these colour consultations work? We are not convinced. Where they may score, however, is by helping to rescue women from a 'colour rut'. If you've habitually bought virtually the same lipstick shade for years, a 'colour consultation' may be worth a shot. But better, we feel, to try a department store makeover – or three – first.

warm

MULTICULTURAL MAKE-UP

All skins are not alike: Oriental, Asian and black skins have distinct advantages when it comes to ageing. In Asian and black skins, extra melanin production makes skin much more resistant to sun damage – whereas in Japan, according to make-up artist Noriko Okubo, 'Sun protection is a must throughout life, because Japanese women like to maintain a very pale complexion. As a result, they don't suffer the wrinkling and crêpiness that Western women do.' Nevertheless, every woman everywhere faces beauty challenges. So we asked experts in Oriental, Asian and black make-up for some special tips...

ORIENTAL

According to Noriko, Oriental faces age in one of two ways. 'Either they get plump – with marked sagging from jaw to neck – or become thinner, leading to hollow eyelids, cheeks and temples. Colour fades from all faces, giving a tired, "quiet" look, and circles under the eyes can become more prominent.'

● It's possible, says Noriko, to 'correct' downward-drooping lines. 'You can't erase them altogether, but you can minimise the sagging look by using upward strokes to finish the eyebrows, eye corners and lips.'

● To make skin and features look more 'luminous', Noriko advises emphasising the definition of eyebrows, lips and eyes. 'But keep to a natural palette and avoid strong reds or dark black,' says Noriko, 'otherwise you can actually draw

attention to wrinkles and sagging.'

● 'Hollow temples make eyes look closer-set,' explains Noriko, 'and lines between eyebrows or at the corners of the mouth create a stern look. For a serene, peaceful look, direct eyebrow and lip lines outwards.'

● For specific guidelines on how to shade Oriental eyes, see page 85.

● Sagging on the cheeks or the tip of the chin can create a plump, heavy look, so Noriko advises using two shades of base. 'First apply a base perfectly matched to the face, wherever you need coverage. Then use a concealer that is very slightly lighter on hollow areas such as temples, eyelids and under-eye. Be sure to camouflage the dark circles around the hollow of the upper eyelid, which can be very draining.' And of course – the make-up artists' mantra – blend, blend, blend...

ASIAN

According to Ruby Hammer, whose family come from Bangladesh, 'Although Asian skins are resilient to sun damage – and stay wonderfully wrinkle free in many cases – the real challenge is dark circles under the eyes.' Her suggestions for minimising/ concealing the problem are:

● 'Tap, tap, tap away puffiness

before you apply make-up; it really decongests the area. I also recommend a de-puffing cream, like Estée Lauder's Uncircle, which is also designed to get rid of darkness. Alternatively, rub an ice cube in your hands, then apply your cooled fingers to the area. You can even wrap an ice cube in a couple of tissues or some clingfilm and lightly run it around the puffy, dark area, without risking broken blood vessels.'

● 'Keeping the eyes themselves bright and sparkly – with a product such as D.R. Harris's Eye Drops, to get rid of redness – will distract from the circles.'

● 'Take the time to find a concealer that really matches your skintone, and use it on dark shadows and scars, which also go very dark. Many concealers are too pink or too light and just emphasise the problem in a different way. Aveda do a great pecan shade that's good for many dark skins, and Nars have good shades for dark skin – or you can get 'custom-blended' foundation at the Prescriptives counter, and they'll give you a matching concealer. Cosmetics A La Carte also have a good range of dark colours.'

● 'Colour can really "lift" a face, and Asian skins can get away with bold tones – but make sure that your foundation is always perfectly matched to the skin on the jawline, and save the bright make-up shades for your lips,

'The specific problem of black skin is an increase in ashiness – a grey cast to the skin,' says Edith. 'You need a better moisturiser – ie, a richer formulation – and perhaps to use an AHA-based product to exfoliate skin, at least once or twice a week, if not every night, to make it look brighter.'

'Although black skin stays relatively unlined, the last thing you want is for make-up to settle in any folds or creases. I always recommend a lightweight, oil-free formulation, which won't accentuate problems by settling into the lines. That way, you can avoid the use of powder – which again draws attention to fine lines and wrinkles.'

'Black skin can be very sensitive – more so as it ages,' explains Edith. 'And a pimple can turn into a black scar. You need a good concealer, perfectly matched to your skintone.' (She recommends Fashion Fair's Cover Tone, a maximum cover concealer.)

'To brighten the face, go for bold lipstick – plums, browns, oranges, purples. Dark skins can get away with these intense colours. But keep eyeshadows muted, otherwise you'll look overdone. A touch of purple or cranberry blusher can give a healthy glow, too – but use a very light hand. As with all make-up, less is more.'

'If brows are greying, use a dark charcoal pencil or a dark brown – not a true black – to colour them in, otherwise the look is too intense.'

'Remember: if you have healthy skin, you'll need less make-up – which will give you a younger look. Don't think of make-up as a kind of camouflage; it's important to work to improve the "canvas" – your skin – underneath.'

eyes or nails. The foundation and blusher have to look natural, and it's better to emphasise just one feature strongly – eyes or lips, not both, to avoid looking overdone.'

'Asian women love nail polish. But they also love to cook, and it's hell on the hands. Take the time to do a proper manicure, or have it regularly done professionally, because chipped nail polish looks so awful. Use base and top coat, and take time. Otherwise it'll be chipped before you've done the washing-up, and spoil your whole look.'

BLACK

Although black skins have the highest level of melanin – and so are least vulnerable to the sun – Edith Poyer, assistant director of product development for leading black cosmetics brand Fashion Fair, says it's a myth that black skins don't need protection. 'Under her make-up, every woman should be wearing a moisturiser with antioxidants and SPF in the formulation to shield her skin from the environment,' she says.

LIPS INC

The world's top make-up artists share inside-track info on choosing and applying the perfect, age-defying lipstick.

We love shopping for lipstick. (Not least because you don't have to get undressed to try it on.) But ageing lips present challenges: feathery lines – which make lipstick 'bleed' – and dryness. As we age, the skin's barrier function becomes less efficient, meaning moisture escapes more easily. Lips are already super-vulnerable to dryness, because they start out with just three layers of skin, compared with 15 or so elsewhere. What's more, over time, lips get thinner – because they lose fat – and paler in colour.

The good news is that lipstick – perfectly applied, in a flattering colour – can miraculously create the illusion of fuller, younger lips. The perfect lipstick also gives the face an instant 'lift', taking years off in a flash. But in our experience, there are certain basic rules that apply to older lips.

This is no longer a competition to see who can wear the most daring and outrageous lip colour; instead, it's time to find a shade that gives your complexion an immediate boost. The simplest trick? Hold a selection of colours up in front of your lips – and without even having to try a shade on your lips, you'll see which ones make your complexion look brighter and your eyes sparkle. Then you can try the most flattering colour on the lips themselves, and see if it stays true on your lips – an important factor because as we age the body's chemistry can cause lipsticks to change colour on the skin. (That's why it's so important to wear a lipstick before you buy it.)

Another problem, we've found, is that lip colour disappears – seemingly into the ether – soon after application. We're not fans of most long-lasting formulations (neither are most make-up artists); they can turn lips as parched as the Sahara.

Instead, try our secrets for making lip colour stay put longer.

TO FROST OR NOT TO FROST?

Super-frosted shades are not great on older lips because they can draw attention to lines and ridges. However, make-up artists are agreed that a sweep of light shimmer – or a 'dot' of a lightly frosted lipstick, blended into the middle of the bottom lip only – can be extremely flattering.

HOW TO MAKE YOUR LIPSTICK STAY PUT

We really suggest steering clear of lipsticks which claim to be 'long lasting'. In our experience, while they do deliver enduring colour, the formulations are also super-drying and leave lips parched. There are other ways to make your lipstick last longer. Vincent Longo outlines the lips with a lip pencil, then draws all over the lips with the same colour. 'This creates an "undercoat" for your lipstick, which will last much longer.' (Vincent is also a fan of the special lip bases designed to help lipstick last longer; brands to look for include Estée Lauder Prime FX, Guerlain and BeneFit.)

Using a lip brush to apply your lipstick, rather than slicking it on from the tube, always makes it last longer. (We advise buying a retractable lip brush, or one with its own cap, to stop it getting gungey.)

If you like to use gloss (as we do) you need to be careful where you apply it. Says Laura Mercier: 'Confine this slippery substance to the middle of the lips. By applying all over the mouth, you'll cause the colour to "bleed" into fine lines.'

products we love

We're lip gloss fanatics. Our fave raves are Dr Hauschka Lip Gloss and Aveda Lip Glaze, which are (almost) good enough to eat. Sarah adores our own luscious Prescriptives Custom Blend Beauty Bible Pink Lip Gloss, which truly does suit everyone. (Available from the Prescriptives counter at Harrods; £2 from each sale goes to our fave charity, Changing Faces, for people with facial disfigurements.) Hot second is Dior's Kisskiss in Praline.

plump up the volume

Recently, a whole new category has emerged: the lip-plumping lipstick/gloss or base. Many contain a local-irritant ingredient (though not harmful, it does make lips tingle). This stimulates blood flow and increases lip volume. Additionally, optical pigments bounce back light, creating the illusion of fullness. Do they work? Our testers for *The Handbag Beauty Bible* had these comments about their favourites:

• **Lancôme Primordiale Lèvres** 'Definitely made the lip outline stand out more – very Liz Hurley!'
• **Estée Lauder Prime FX Lip Amplifying Base** 'My lips were genuinely fuller.'
• **L'Oréal Paris Glam' Shine** 'Lips shiny, fuller, softer – very kissable!'

for a brighter smile

Some lipsticks will have the effect of making teeth look whiter than other colour choices, Barbara Daly tells us. 'What you want to create is contrast,' she suggests. 'Be careful with any colours with yellow or orange – including corals and brown-based shades. Pinks, reds and burgundies are often the best choices.'

LIPSTICK HOW-TO

• If your lips are prone to chapping or flaking, try this tip from New York make-up artist, Darac: slather on a thick coat of Kiehl's Lip Balm. Leave for five minutes, then buff with a baby's ultra-soft toothbrush. The flakes will be gently whisked away, leaving lips smoother and 'prepped' for lipstick application.
• Make-up artists always apply foundation all over the lips before applying lipstick. Laura Mercier takes that one step further: when she's making up the rest of the face, Laura then lightly applies powder on top – using a velvet powder puff – before outlining with lip liner and adding lipstick and/or gloss.
• As we age, lips get 'blurry' and lose definition. That's where a lip pencil can be so valuable, outlining the lips and putting definition back.

Trish McEvoy has a secret for creating the optical illusion of a fuller pout. 'Using a lip-coloured pencil, draw just *outside* your natural lip line, using light, feathery strokes as you follow the line. (At the *corners* of your lips, however, make sure that the drawn line meets your own lip line perfectly – to avoid a "clown" effect.) When you're using the pencil to outline the cupid's bow – just above the middle of the top lip – draw in two soft "mountain peaks". Here, you can afford to go a little further away from the natural lip line. The effect is to make lips look plumper.'

• To avoid a harsh line when using a lip-liner, blunt the pencil slightly before using it on your lips, by drawing backwards and forwards several times on the back of your hand.
• When you've drawn on your lip line, use the pad of your middle finger to blur it very slightly. (Don't rub hard, though, or it'll smudge.)

If you still find that the line you draw looks too obvious, Bobbi Brown suggests applying your lipstick *first*, then lip-liner over the top. 'It's sometimes easier to define lips this way,' Bobbi explains. 'The liner and the lipstick wear off together, so you're never left with an obvious outline around your mouth.'

• If shaky hands make it difficult for you to apply lip-liner smoothly, hold the pencil near the pointed end, for maximum control.
• Don't try to match your lip-liner to your lipstick. Instead, every make-up artist we know advises picking a lip-liner that's closest to your own natural lip colour. That way, when your lipstick fades (or you've chewed it off), the line that's left looks natural – not unnaturally red, orange, burgundy or fuchsia.
• Puckered lips can create an uneven surface that lipstick often 'skips', making for uneven application. If this happens to you, stretch out your lips between your second and third fingers when you're applying colour.

Eyes tend to present the biggest make-up challenge as we age: make-up just doesn't seem to work the way it used to, mainly because it settles into fine lines and wrinkles. 'But that's no reason to avoid it,' insists Vincent Longo. 'On the contrary, I think women of "a certain age" get a real looks boost from wearing glamorous eye make-up.'

GETTING YOUR EYES RIGHT

Clever eye make-up can emphasise your eyes in the most flattering way. The first thing you need to do is learn to understand your eye shape. This makes perfect eye-shading easier. Once you've worked out your eye type from the five basic shapes opposite, follow the guidelines. By using eyeshadow with care, you can modify the shape of your whole eye area and control emphasis. The time to practise this, however, is a rainy Saturday afternoon – not when you're heading off for a party.

Most eye-shading requires just three colours: a light 'base' colour – usually ivory, vanilla or almond; a medium tone; and a dark shade for eyelining and perhaps emphasising the outer corner of the upper lid. Choose muted colours in the same tonal family – and remember, as with all make-up, the rule is blend, blend, blend.

FIRST AID

● For puffy eyes, brush medium-toned eyeshadow over that part of the lid, to make it recede.

● For under-eye circles, the trick is to keep the focus above the eye – so don't put on any make-up under the eye except concealer, patted on very lightly.

MORE TIPS FOR GETTING YOUR EYES RIGHT

● Most make-up artists advise steering clear of frosted shadows, except on the brow-bone, 'which is rarely wrinkled', says John Gustafson. But the new, gently shimmering shades can open out eyes and be more flattering than matte. To see if a shimmer shadow will flatter you, says John Gustafson, apply a smear of shadow to the back of the hand. 'Then turn your hand sideways; the shimmeriness should go flat and more matte-looking. If it does, then it's suitable for older skins. If it stays shimmery whichever way you hold it to the light, don't buy it.'

● After dipping your brush in the eyeshadow pan, always tap the handle of the brush smartly on a hard surface to get rid of specks of excess shadow, which may shed on to your cheeks and spoil your foundation.

● Trish McEvoy's trick is to apply eye make-up before base – so if you make mistakes, they're easy to remove with a Q-Tip dipped in eye make-up remover.

● There should never be any harsh demarcation lines with eyeshadow. An extra eyeshadow contour brush can 'blur' any harsh edges, but never rub with your finger in the hope that you can blend or soften colours. If you need to soften colour further, take a powder puff dipped in face powder (then 'thwacked', as usual), and press it on your eyelid to tone down colour.

● This is the time to wean yourself off liquid liner, which becomes increasingly hard to apply – thanks to wobblier older hands and crêpier lids. Make-up artists advise switching to a dark, powder shadow, applied with an eyeliner brush. Stephen Glass advises, 'If you like a more intense line, use a wetted eyeliner brush dipped in powder shadow – giving a much softer effect than liquid liner.' Or use a pencil, then 'set' and also soften the line with a matching powder shadow. A real trick is to work the liner carefully into the very base of the lashes, creating the illusion of much longer lashes when you then apply mascara.

If you follow these step-by-step guidelines and still can't seem to get your eyeshadow to work the way you want it to, consider one of the new cream-to-powder shadows. These glide on to the eyelid and then set to a powder finish, giving you a 'window' of about 30 seconds for perfect blending with your fingertip. (We have had very good results with Revlon ColorStay Eyecolour, which comes in a range of wearable, neutral shades.) They are also great for weekends or casual days, when you don't want to wear full make-up but would like a little extra eye definition.

Eye shapes and shadows – how-to

For all eye shapes, 'prime' the eye zone first with foundation and/or powder (see pages 70–71).

Deep-set eyes The goal here is to bring your eyelids out. Apply a light shade all over the lid, from brow to eye. Vincent Longo suggests using a slightly darker shadow along the lash-line from the centre to the outer corner, but not in the crease. This makes lashes look thicker and smokier, focusing attention on the eye, not on the recessive lid.

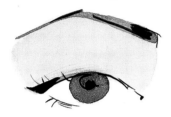

Almond This classic shape is easy to make up. Try applying a pale colour across the entire upper lid, from lashline to brow (if your eyelid is wrinkle-free you could try a whisper of shimmer). For extra emphasis, New York City make-up artist Trish McEvoy then takes a darker colour and creates a soft, horizontal 'V' around the outer corner, just to outline the eyes. The line should end on both top and bottom lids at the pupil. 'I like to keep almond eyes looking fresh and simple,' says Trish.

Round You can use the same technique as for almond eyes. Alternatively, Vincent Longo suggests applying dark shadow on only the outer third of the lower eye area, which creates the optical illusion of 'stretching' the eye. For added drama and to 'lift' the eye, extend the dark shadow about 1cm (1/2in) past the outer corner, in an upward direction, towards the temple.

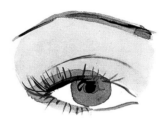

Droopy eye 1 (This same technique works brilliantly on Asian eyes, too.)
Trish McEvoy showed us a terrific trick for applying eye colour that is especially useful if you have droopy eyelids: when you apply eye colour/mascara to your top lid, hold your mirror at a 45-degree angle below eye level and tilt your head back so that you can see the entire lid and socket; the 'crease' disappears (even on very hooded eyes), so that it's easier to apply eye colour, liner and mascara. 'That way you can see the socket-bone. Often, if you have a droopy eyelid, the socket is invisible – but at this angle, it magically reappears on every woman.' For the bottom lid/lashes, hold the mirror slightly above eye level and tilt your head downward slightly, giving you the perfect view of the area you are making up.
'Clever shading can combat hooded eyelids,' continues Trish. 'Apply a light-coloured shadow to the lower eye area, and to the brow-bone, for emphasis,' she advises. 'Then, using a contour eyeshadow brush, use a mid-toned shade to shade the entire crease, in an arc. Don't apply eyeliner, because that will make the eyelid recede again. But do add a coat of mascara to both top and bottom lashes.' Then, when you open your eyes – and stare into a mirror straight ahead – your 'hooded' lid should be less obvious, thanks to the optical illusion you have just created with the help of your eyeshadow.

Droopy eye 2 If your eye droops at the outer edge, over the corner of the eye, follow the same instructions as above. In addition, line the lower eyelid with a fine eyeliner brush dipped in dark shadow, extending the line slightly beyond the corner of the eye, in an 'up' direction. (But don't line the top eyelid.)

BRILLIANT BROWS

As we age, experts advise that it's vital to take into account brow shape – and what it does for a face that may be undergoing subtle changes.

As London's 'brow queen' Vaishaly Patel observes, 'You can have beautiful skin and a beautiful face – but if your eyebrows are wrong, you just won't look right.' And the simple fact is that, as we age, women face new brow challenges: thinning brows (as a side effect of natural ageing, over-plucking or sometimes an accident) – and greying ones, which make us look washed out – and plain older.

Eliza Petrescu – Vaishaly's Manhattan equivalent – believes the right brow shape can take ten years off a woman's age, by counterbalancing the natural 'droopiness' that affects lids as gravity kicks in. 'I curved Vanessa Redgrave's brows more, because at a certain time in life, you need to have more of an arch, to create the illusion of an instant eye-lift,' she says.

So here's how to create the perfect, groomed brow…

★ Consider calling in a professional. Having your brows shaped by a pro can create a 'blueprint' for the perfect brow, making it easier to maintain the line at home.

★ Buy good tweezers, which allow you to grasp each hair firmly and avoid unnecessary tugging. Like most make-up artists, we are big fans of Tweezerman – and we particularly like the ergonomic, easy-grip version designed by Laura Mercier.

★ Don't be brave. If you've a low 'ouch' threshold, Prescriptives' make-up artist Darac suggests using a toothache analgesic (eg, Ambosol gel, from good pharmacies). Apply a few minutes before plucking, to numb the area slightly.

★ Head for daylight. If your eyesight's not too good, use a magnifying mirror. (NB: we swear that the ultimate place for brow-tweezing is in a parked car, during daytime.)

★ Try drawing in your brow, first. Use a brow pencil to draw on your ideal shape – then pluck everything that falls outside that line. (Blondes find this especially useful, using a taupe pencil.) But be particularly careful when tweezing the narrowest outer part of the brow; look at where the root of the hair is – and exactly where that hair lies – to make sure that you won't be creating a gap by tweezing it.

top tip

We suggest that you try tweezing first thing in the morning, before you shower. That way, any redness of puffiness has a chance to subside before you put on make-up.

★ Don't rush. Start by removing just the hairs above the nose. Your brow should start directly above the inner corner of your eye and extend as far as possible at the outer edge, to create the longest arch. Do a few hairs on one eye, then swap, to get a balanced look as you go along. Pull the skin taut, if you like, to minimise discomfort.

★ Accent the natural arch. The highest point of the arch underneath your eyebrows should line up with the outer edge of your iris. Tweeze any stray hairs that fall under that arch. And according to Laura Mercier, it's a myth that women shouldn't tweeze above the brows. She says: 'I discovered that tweezing away some hairs at the top of my thick brows made my forehead look less heavy.' So go carefully, plucking a few hairs at a time – and standing back to analyse your reflection.

★ Swipe the area with a cotton bud, dipped in tea tree oil, after tweezing, to prevent infection.

★ Keep up the good work, with weekly – preferably twice-weekly – maintenance sessions. But be aware that continual plucking will eventually make the hairs grow more and more slowly, until they stop growing altogether. That's why it's so important not to over-tweeze.

BROW ZING

One of the commonest make-up mistakes we see on older women is brows that look drawn on. 'People shouldn't see your eyebrows coming before they see you,' points out Valerie Sarnelle, whose same-name salon in Hollywood is in many stars' little black books.

For can't-tell-them-from-real brows, the options are: pencil, shadow (brow powders or eyeshadow) or pencil and shadow.

If you are simply enhancing the colour of your natural brows, eyeshadow alone is best. If, however, you are replacing any gaps in brows, we prefer pencil with shadow on top. NB Before you start, always brush brows downwards and then across with a small brush – an old, clean toothbrush is perfect, or an old mascara wand, cleaned up.

getting the colour right

- Our brows are not all one colour naturally – so consider using two slightly different shades of pencil, plus shadow, for the most realistic effect.
- Advice for grey-haired women from Mary Greenwell: steer clear of blue-grey or charcoal grey, which will look harsh; experiment with a soft taupe instead.
- Be very careful to avoid brow pencils with the slightest hint of red – even if your hair colour happens to be red. 'That ginger brow look is extremely fake,' says Mary. 'The make-up rule is: you should look like you've done something to your lips and your eyes – but not your skin or your brows.'
- If your hair's going white – or you've gone blonder, to disguise grey – make sure you're not using a too-intense brow colour. 'Too-dark brows can make you look like you're scowling,' says Mary Greenwell. Try going slightly lighter – to a light taupe, a shade that's usually 'specially for blondes'. This can soften the face.
- Some women with thinning brows believe semi-permanent make-up – literally, tattooing brows on to skin – can be the answer to their prayers. But we have never seen an example of this that didn't look unreal in both colour and shape. Far better to experiment with pencil and/or powder, we believe.

pencil how-to

Most brow pencils give an effect that is way too obvious for most faces. But if you like pencil, test the texture on the back of your hand: it should be soft, and glide easily. Pencils are used either to enhance colour – in which case you're only trying to colour the hairs, *not* the skin – or to 'replace' lost hairs, drawing in the missing hairs on to the skin. After using pencil, gently use the brush again, to soften the line.

Even if you prefer a brow pencil, you will get a more realistic effect if you go over the lines afterwards with a toning powder shadow.

shadow how-to

You need the right tool: a small, hard brush (see The Essential Toolkit, page 75), angled at the tip. Dip it in the colour and tap the handle of the brush smartly on the side of a basin, or on your wrist, to shake off excess.

Start at the thickest point in the brow and work outwards, using light, feathery short strokes – trying once again to get the colour on to the hairs, rather than the skin. At the outer edge, if your brows are naturally pale (or nonexistent), you can apply colour to the skin to alter slightly your natural brow-line so that it flatters your face shape. You can also buy special brow powders from BeneFit, Chanel and Laura Mercier.

Comb the brows through afterwards again with a brow-brush to sleek them. If your brows are unruly, you can groom them in place with a brow gel – Laura Mercier makes one, and there's one in the Estée Lauder's excellent Artist's Brow Stylist Mobile Essentials kit. Or spritz a tiny bit of hairspray on to a brow brush and comb them into place.

Mascara is a true make-up miracle-worker – and it's the one make-up essential that most women would take to a desert island. However, while mascara can help turn back the clock, it can also advance it: tarantulas clinging to top and bottom lids are extremely ageing. (Much as we adored Barbara Cartland.) So, here are the secrets of age-defying mascara application.

MASCARA MAGIC

- 'Emphasising the lashes gives amazing, instant definition to the face – especially if your lashes have lost their colour. Even if you don't wear any other eye make-up, opt for mascara,' says Mary Greenwell.
- Consider switching from black mascara to brown, says Barbara Daly. 'It gives a softer, more flattering look,' she explains.
- The perfect way to apply mascara is to work it well into the roots first, 'then "shimmy" up the lashes using minute side-to-side movements,' advises Trish McEvoy.
- If you want to apply two coats, the trick for avoiding clumpiness is to make sure you don't let the first coat dry before you apply the second.
- Barbara Daly advises all over-forties to invest in a lash comb, which will help comb out any clumps if you do get them. An old mascara wand, carefully cleansed (using lashings of eye make-up remover) will do the same job.
- Avoid clumpiness by changing your mascara at least every three months. In addition, 'Always wipe your mascara wand on a tissue, before you apply it to your lashes,' advises Trish McEvoy. 'It gets rid of blobs and excess.'
- Never 'pump' the mascara wand in and out of the tube – this forces air into the tube and makes the mascara dry out, fast-forwarding blobbiness.
- Lashes should be kept in optimum condition. Bobbi Brown finds waterproof mascaras dry out lashes – so recommends them only for sweatily hot days, weepy movies or emotionally charged encounters!
- If your lids have become droopy, use a light touch with your mascara – or do the outer lashes only. A thick, dark veil of mascara only makes the eye area look heavier.
- All the make-up artists we spoke to swear by the eye-opening effects of eyelash curlers – in fact, believes Ruby Hammer, 'if you use them regularly, they can actually give your lashes a permanent curl'. (Her favourites are Tweezerman, which have nonstick silicone pads. Avoid all-metal curlers, as these can snap lashes.)
- Eyelash curlers always have to be used before mascara. Hold the curler from underneath; place it so that your upper lashes are in the gap between the two rims. Then squeeze for about five to ten seconds. Roll the curler slightly up and away as you remove it.
For special occasions, consider false eyelashes. You can either buy them in strips, or in little clusters, packaged with their own rubber glue that ensures painless removal (with a little tugging). Stephen Glass recommends Eylure Naturalites Underlashes – used as top lashes. For a natural effect, cut them to fit before glueing them into place: 'I apply eyeliner first, as a guideline, and then again after the lashes are in place, to disguise the glue.' Agrees Vincent Longo, 'They're useful as a boost – lashes often get more sparse as you age – and they're a must for special events. It isn't expensive to have false lashes applied in a salon, and they add a real elegance to any special evening.' (A salon session is also a good way of learning the secrets of truly professional eyelash application.) Alternatively, Eylure make One by One 'semi-permanent' lash clusters, which are particularly good for adding emphasis to the outer corner; at a pinch, they can even be left in place for a couple of days. (However, at any sign of sensitivity, remove the lashes – eye health is more important than lash length.)

mascaras we love

We used to look for mascaras that pumped up the volume or dramatically lengthened lashes. Not any more. What looks best at this age, we find, is a mascara that gives very natural results. Jo loves Lancôme Définicils, and Max Factor Masterpiece, both of which colour and separate lashes beautifully – and realistically. Sarah favours Clinique Long Pretty Lashes Mascara and Dr Hauschka Mascara in black, with rose oil to condition.

EVENING MAKE-UP

The art of after-dark make-up – for when the lights go down and the band strikes up.

Transforming your make-up for night is not a question of simply piling on extra layers. In fact, Barbara Daly's sage advice is: 'Don't stray too far from the make-up shades you wear for day. You want to look sophisticated – not like an entirely different person.' So we asked Barbara for her guidelines for after-dark make-up.

● 'You must always use the best possible light to make up in. By day, that's a mirror in front of a window. At night, if it's dark, I take the lampshade off a bright bedside lamp and make up in front of that. And I always use a magnifying mirror. The close-up view of the face is terrifying, to start with – but as the eyesight goes, a magnifying mirror becomes absolutely necessary.'

● 'Evening make-up isn't necessarily about using more products – it's about taking more time to put make-up on. If you've got plenty of time, do the whole works – and do it well. Otherwise, do only those elements of the make-up that you have time to do beautifully. It might mean that you use fewer items – but you'll look better because they'll be more expertly applied. You can look a million dollars with immaculate skin, mascara and lipstick.'

● 'Don't put too much coverage on the skin. You are not going to do yourself any favours by slapping make-up on all over. Sometimes women think that because it's evening light, they can get away with more base – but it's not true. Keep your base light – and keep it where you need it most. Use very fine layers of concealer to cover problem areas, rather than thick foundation.'

● 'I am an advocate of loose powder for day and for evening. But slip a pressed powder compact in your bag for light touch-ups. Use it sparingly; if you keep powdering, it will look caked – and ageing.'

● 'This is the time when you can get away with a *touch* more blush. But I mean a whisper.' (You can also dust blush very, very lightly around the hairline, Barbara suggests.)

● 'I like creamy or shimmery highlights in the evening. Put them anywhere the skin normally shines a little: the brow-bone, a touch on the lids, cheekbones, the middle of the bottom lip – but avoid any areas with fine lines or wrinkles. You want just enough to make you gleam – not to make you look sweaty.' (Experiment with a sheer liquid highlighter that glides over the skin.) 'If you are unsure whether your facial skin can take shimmer, try using a lightly shimmering powder on your shoulders and décolletage – in a gold or a glimmering rose – instead,' Barbara suggests.

● 'I am a big fan of lip gloss for evening – a sheeny product, on the middle of the bottom lip. But put it over a lip-liner and lipstick, as it tends to disappear easily. Otherwise, be prepared to touch it up regularly.'

● 'You can use slightly smokier eye colours in the evening – but don't be tempted to stray from your usual palette.'

CARMEN DELL'OREFICE

Born in 1931, Carmen dell'Orefice is often called the oldest supermodel. She still works constantly. We love her elegance and earthiness, her sense of fun and her un-precious portmanteau mind, which allows her to segue effortlessly from discussing consciousness to cosmetics.

'What makes me happy? Waking up every morning…the littlest things…everything! Almost nothing makes me unhappy, except injustice, war and killing – but you can't live continually in that space. I've been sad and had problems I couldn't solve, but I don't linger on them to the point it becomes self-destructive.

'I was born just after the Depression. I lived alone with my Hungarian mother, who was out all day working so I always had jobs to do when I got back from school. I still like to be self-reliant. I can spend a spare day mending and fixing. I sew, I can wallpaper and do upholstery, I'm a pretty good carpenter and I know about AC/DC currents. It tickles my soul to know that in an emergency I can do almost everything.

'You have to know yourself and figure out how you want to live every second of your life. My three marriages didn't go the way I expected them to, but they were all a success because they helped me understand myself. Of course I still have romance in my life: am I not breathing?!

'I started modelling at 13 and I loved the adventure of it – still do! I keep my energy topped up by resting in between jobs, with no agenda on my mind. Thinking in your sleep is a wonderful way to sort problems. I discovered if I went to sleep with the question, my unconscious would work it out.

'You can't be lazy with your skin: I practically go to bed with sunblock on. When I go out I always wear a little concealer, mascara and lipstick – it makes me feel good, and my doorman…! I try to make up in daylight so I don't end up looking like a hooker. You just need to accentuate your best feature. At night I make up again fresh. I use a Bufpuff very, very lightly once or twice a week to keep my face really clean.

'I can't live without Elizabeth Arden Eight Hour Cream and Christian Dior Crème Abricot for cuticles – and on my lipline and the corners of my eyes. I also use Bag Balm [a salve created in Vermont in 1899 to soften cows' udders, www.bagbalm.com] on my skin at night to seal in the moisture the skin loses.

'I let the grey come into my hair when I was 43. I liked it so much that I frosted the rest of my dark hair to give it some texture. As you get older, your skin loses its vibrancy, so doing aerobic exercise like housework – bending down and letting the blood get to your head – is essential.

'I do a yoga-based stretch, which comes from ballet moves. I had a scholarship with Ballets Russes as a kid but I got rheumatic fever and had to give up. This routine forces you to breathe more deeply and pay attention to your breath.

'I love Italian food: I eat a steak a week, lots of fish and veg. My metabolism is slowing down now. I haven't gained weight but because I've lost an inch in height, my waistline has put on an inch and a half in two years.

'Listen: life is maintenance. Put your money in your mouth early. Even when times were very thin financially I had the best periodontal care science could offer. I've had my cataracts removed by laser. I've never had a face-lift but I've had 35 years of silicone injections. I'm on a weekly oestrogen patch as part of a research programme. It keeps me nicely balanced.

'I take two grams of vitamin C every day and vitamin E, plus Centrum Silver, which has all the trace minerals in it. When I'm really tired I occasionally get a vitamin B shot.

'I can only work on myself. That's my job in life. I aim for simplicity and joy in every day, being true to my word, being on time and to put my few discretionary dollars where it's meaningful.

'I'm very grateful for my lot. I truly have walked between the raindrops. I love to photograph rainbows – and flowers and people. I am afraid I will forget the wonderfulness otherwise. My life is so full I just can't hold it close enough.'

FABULOUS FRAGRANCE WEARING – FOR EVER

Fragrance can turbocharge our pleasure in life. But a favourite scent won't always suit you for ever – so here are the secrets that ensure you smell fabulous for a lifetime.

One day we may wake up – and our signature perfume won't smell the same any more. Our hormones can play tricks with our favourite fragrances, altering the way they interact with the skin. (That's why pregnant women are often nauseated by a fragrance they'd always loved.) Worryingly, though, our fragrance may change character without us even realising it – because we may also experience a gradual dwindling of our ability to smell, a natural process that begins in our fifties and can really become noticeable from 60-plus.

Jilly Fraysse, a fragrance expert who has worked at exclusive London perfume boutiques L'Artisan Parfumeur and Les Senteurs, has time and again seen customers experiencing this phenomenon. 'Whenever hormones go into overdrive – or into decline – it can interfere with fragrance-wearing,' explains Jilly. The first time she noticed the strange, chemical interaction between fragrance and menopausal skin was on her own mother-in-law. 'All her life she'd worn Arpège, because her husband bought it for her when they were engaged. But at about 50, it started to smell literally cheesy on her. And the worst thing of all was that she was unaware of it.' When Jilly herself hit the menopause, she found herself unable to wear Joy – a lifelong favourite – because it made her nauseous. The white floral,

jasmine-based scents tend to pose most problems, in Jilly's experience. 'Fruity and citrussy fragrances are usually "safer". But the silver lining to the cloud is that all this is usually temporary,' she says. 'Once the change of life is over, you can probably go back to wearing an old favourite without any problems.'

If your fave scent 'goes off' on the skin, all is not lost. 'You don't have to wear it on your skin,' says Jilly. Her alternatives: spritz it on to hems, cuffs and collars, or on to a cotton wool ball to be tucked into your bra. 'Be careful it isn't going to stain, if you're going to use it on fabric; spray it on to a white Kleenex, and if it doesn't leave a mark, it's safe on pale clothing.' She also suggests a voile of fragrance: 'Spray it into the air and walk through it, subtly perfuming your hair and your clothes.'

Meanwhile – since our noses may be less sensitive – how can we tell whether we've overdone it? 'Nobody needs more than a single spritz either side of the neck, and one on the wrists and/or the back of the knees,' she advises.

Jilly's trick: spray fragrance on the outside of the wrists, rather than the inner pulse-points, 'because it subtly diffuses outwards when it's warmed by the body. And then,' she adds, 'there's the famous advice: wear fragrance wherever you want to be kissed.'

PS Our all-time favourite scent? Guerlain's Mitsouko. Rich, velvety – and irresistible.

MAKE-UP TIPS FOR THE VISUALLY IMPAIRED

One of our favourite and most talented make-up artists, Jenny Jordan (who has her own eyebrow and make-up clinic in Belsize Park, London), has spent many years pinpointing the key problem areas for visually impaired women when they set out to apply make-up. 'Many of them shy away from wearing make-up because it seems too difficult, yet it can give every woman a terrific confidence boost,' she says. Having a professional consultation first is the best idea, she advises – department store makeovers are often free, or, if you're feeling flush, book in with someone like Jenny, who has lots of experience with the particular concerns.

● Use a good magnifying mirror – big enough to use but small enough to carry around in your bag.

● Keep your make-up simple.

● Try using cream-to-powder foundation, which is easier to apply than liquid foundation. Use a fresh sponge after five applications of foundation.

● If you have fairly good skin, use tinted moisturiser instead of foundation – it's easier to apply.

● Smile, then brush a soft shade of blusher on to the apples of your cheeks, using a soft, rounded blusher brush (or a ball of cotton wool approximately the size of a golf ball).

● You only need to put lipstick on the top lip and then rub your lips together.

● Try lip gloss, instead of lipstick.

● Cream eyeshadow – applied directly with your finger – is easier to manage than powder shadow.

● Have your eyelashes professionally dyed and then use colourless mascara (Max Factor, for instance), instead of trying to cope with a coloured wand. Applying five strokes of colourless mascara to the top and bottom lashes (moving from the inner corner to the outer corner of the eye) should give sufficient effect.

● Put Vaseline around your nails before you paint them; if you make a mistake and the polish gets on your finger, you can wipe it off without staining. Mistakes are less visible with clear or natural pink polish.

● Use eye make-up and nail polish remover in pad form. You have more control with them than liquids or creams.

● Two-in-one cleanser-and-toner formulations save mixing up the bottles (and using toner before cleanser).

● Tidy your eyebrows by brushing them with a toothbrush, then stroking through with a dab of Vaseline, to keep them neat.

QUESTIONS TO ASK WHEN SHOPPING FOR MAKE-UP

Jenny also has these guidelines to follow when you're at the cosmetics counter. 'Don't be shy about asking for help,' she says. 'In my experience, beauty consultants are just delighted to give advice to the visually impaired – but you can help steer them in the right direction with these questions…'

Foundation 'Please can you find me a cream-to-powder foundation that matches my skintone perfectly in daylight. And show me how many strokes of foundation I will need to make up my face.'

Blusher 'I want a blusher that gives me a healthy glow but also looks natural in the daytime. Please show me how many strokes of colour are enough. I would also like a soft, rounded powder brush to apply my blusher with.'

Lipstick 'Please pick me a long-lasting lipstick and/or a lip gloss that brightens up my face.'

Eyeshadow 'I would like a cream eyeshadow that I can apply easily with my finger and which suits my colouring.'

Look Good, Feel Better is the beauty industry's way of 'giving back' – funding a programme of workshops for women undergoing cancer therapy that's now operating in several countries.

Volunteer professional beauty therapists and make-up artists teach ways with wigs and scarves – and a 12-stage programme for skincare and make-up. Among Look Good, Feel Better's supporters is make-up legend Barbara Daly, who says: 'I think what they're doing is absolutely sensational – giving women self-confidence-boosting care at a time in their lives when they need it most. Because if you look good, you do feel better.' Liz Collinge has also worked with cancer patients, teaching them how to face special beauty challenges. So we asked Barbara and Liz for their look-good-feel-better tips for women undergoing cancer treatment.

'One of the common side effects of

additional depth – it gives you a guide while you're sticking on the lashes. Single lashes are another option if yours are simply sparse.

'Cancer treatment may make you appear very flushed – but don't be tempted to cover your whole face with foundation. Stand back and analyse where you need extra camouflage. First, apply your regular foundation but only where you really need it. Then if you're still too flushed, apply concealer – or try mixing it in on the back of your hand with a dot of one of those green under-make-up bases. Mixing the two makes for more natural results; the green concealer on its own is very draining,' says Barbara.

'If you're pale and washed out, don't think that a darker foundation is the answer – it will just look unnatural. Instead, choose a colour that matches your natural skintone, then add colour with blusher, or a slightly rosy-toned

LOOK GOOD, FEEL BETTER

chemotherapy is brow-loss, or lash-loss,' says Barbara. 'The solution is to draw brows on to the skin with ultra-fine strokes using a pencil or brow make-up – preferably using two shades, since our natural brows are virtually never one colour. If your pencil has a brush at the end, use that to brush through the colour afterwards – otherwise, use an old soft toothbrush to soften the effect. I'd steer clear of tattooed eyebrows, because they can look false – and most women's brows do grow back, after treatment.'

'It looks more natural if you draw on the brows with the side of the pencil, rather than the tip,' adds Liz. 'If the

lashes have gone, I like to outline the eyes with a medium-to-dark eyeshadow, using a sponge applicator rather than a brush, for a more natural look. Avoid eyeliner pencils, which can give too sharp a line.'

'Lashes, if you have them, can be boosted by using a lash-thickening mascara. But if you've lost your lashes, I wouldn't use false lashes unless you're quite good with them,' warns Barbara. 'However, if you do have the knack, there are plenty of natural-looking lashes around and you don't have to look like Twiggy, circa 1968. Draw on a line with eyeliner, first – it will not only give

under-make-up base. Alternatively, lightly dust on a slightly pink-toned powder during the day if your complexion needs a boost,' Barbara suggests.

'Try dusting just the tiniest touch of blusher around the temples, the hairline, on to the nose and chin if you're looking pale,' says Liz.

'Dry skin and lips can be a problem,' Barbara points out. 'Step up your moisturiser and keep a lip balm handy.'

And lastly, says Barbara: 'Lipstick is great medicine – so don't think twice about buying yourself a wardrobe of inexpensive new lipsticks as a way to cheer yourself up, fast!'

FABULOUS HAIR

It's simple: if our hair looks great, we feel great – but bad hair days make for bad days. After 40, roller-coaster hormones and the onset of grey make for new hair challenges. The flipside is that these changes give us the opportunity to reinvent ourselves – with style and glamour. So we asked the world's leading hair experts – in cutting, colouring, styling (and even hair loss) – for their advice to ensure that hair looks and feels fabulous – forever. Here's everything you need to know to make every day a good hair day.

hair shapes for older faces

Trading hairdressers is almost as much of a 'sister act' as swapping builders – or lovers. Many women feel that if their hairstyle is great, they can take on the world – if it's not, it's time to slink home with a paper bag on your head and wait until it grows again. Our expert line-up of world-famous hairdressers – John Barrett, John Frieda and Charles Worthington – all agree that the bottom-line key to a good cut is that it should complement your face shape. You don't know your face shape? And your hairdresser doesn't seem to either? OK, here goes…

how to find your face shape

Tie your hair back off your face and wear something with a low neck. Stand or sit in front of a mirror, a little less than an arm's distance away. Grasp a lip-liner pencil (or anything like that, for instance a coloured eyeliner pencil) in your writing hand, close one eye and trace the outline of your face, round the hairline, jawline and back to the hairline, on the surface of the glass. Now add in your ears, neck and the outline of your head around the top and sides. There you have it. (Yes, it will come off with window cleaner!)

the experts' tips for cuts to suit your face shape

If you have a basically oval face (like the one on the left), you can wear almost any shape and cut, agree our experts. Since few of us can lay claim to that 'beautopia' shape, here are tips for styles to flatter different face shapes. We have taken the most common shapes. (Although not every woman will have exactly one outline; some are a variation of one or more.)

NB: one of the most common problems with older faces is that they tend to get thinner – make sure always to balance this with softness and fullness rather than hard lines.

ROUND
Aim for:
- A slightly domed, pointy look at top of head to elongate head shape.
- A fringe cut on an angle, blending in slightly longer than the temple to create shadows under cheekbones.
- A sleek, rather than full, look at sides.
- Hair feathered at bottom on to neck to disguise a plump or short neck.

Plus: use make-up to elongate eyebrows and eyes; miss out on blusher, but try highlighter on top of cheekbones and under brows; try lighter brighter lips.

I know haircuts can be traumatic for some women, but not for me. Hair grows back – and if you don't like it, you can always change it. Personally, I like short hair – it's me.

ISABELLA ROSSELLINI

OBLONG

Aim for:

● A soft top of head.

● A slightly asymmetrical fringe, which graduates, blending and continuing the line into the body of your hair.

● Fullness behind the ears to widen your face; this will also help if you have a long distance between nose and chin, or a long upper lip.

● A medium-length layered bob.

TRIANGLE

Aim for:

● Fullness at top on sides to balance head shape.

● A soft, slightly asymmetrical fringe to disguise hairline and shorten face.

Plus: accentuate eyes; wear earrings to draw attention away from jaw.

(See also square and oblong.)

LONG JAWLINE

Aim for:

● Hair cut on an angle from chin to shoulder to soften line.

Avoid:

● Long straight hair or a short, eg, ear-length, bob which will make the jawline look even longer.

Plus: biggish earrings to distract eye from jawline.

SQUARE

Aim for:

● A slightly domed, narrow look at top of head to elongate head shape.

● A slightly asymmetrical fringe.

● Short hair worn behind ears feathered down on neck to give length.

● Longer hair with fullness at top to balance jawline, soften outline and edges of hair and avoid hard lines.

Plus: accentuate and lengthen brows and eyes, and use earrings to take attention from square jawline.

INVERTED TRIANGLE

Aim for:

● Gentle curves on the top of the head.

● A fringe which is longer in the middle and shorter at temples.

● A one-length bob to just below the ears.

PROMINENT NOSE

Aim for:

● A gentle curve at back of head to balance nose.

Avoid:

● The Mrs Thatcher look, which will make it worse.

long VERSUS *short*
THE DEBATE

Once upon a time, the rule was: hit 40, buy a twinset, lop off your hair. But today – so long as your hair's healthy and shiny – the rule-book's been torn up.

Nicky Clarke – one of the world's most expensive hairdressers, and a man who once turned down Marie Helvin's request to take her hair shorter, insists: 'I've got dozens of older clients with fabulous long hair. If it's in good condition, then who says it's got to go? The look might need adjusting a little – for instance, having it slightly layered, rather than just long and straight, or blown dry more regularly, or putting it up now and again so it has an air of elegance about it – but it's just ageist to lay down the law about long hair.'

Hollywood actress René Russo couldn't agree more. In fact, the suggestion that women ought to cut their hair in middle age has René

Remember hair will always 'lift' about 1cm (½in) shorter when it's dry – so if you want, for instance, a chin-length bob, it must be cut about 1cm (½in) longer.

insisting: 'It makes me want to grow it down to my toes, just to say go **** yourself.' Novelist Jackie Collins – who wouldn't dream of cutting off her trademark tresses – shares René's sentiments. 'Long hair's much sexier – I wear my hair up to keep it out of the way when I'm working, and down when I'm playing.'

Still, if you long to stay long, the one thing that you don't want is to get freeze-framed with an outdated signature look. You know it's time to re-think your long hairstyle if you dust off your 20-year-old graduation photo or your wedding snaps to see that, basically, your hairstyle was fossilised right there and then. If you're using your hair as some kind of security blanket to hide behind (à la Old English sheepdog), it's probably also time for an update.

But if you want to avoid the 'timewarp' trap of long hair, the solutions are simple: have a few layers put in, texturise the ends with wax (creating a softer impression) – or learn how to put it up. 'For evening, there's nothing more elegant than a chignon,' insists Hugh, of

Hugh & Stephen (who spends half the day 'up-do-ing' royals, aristocrats and stars of everything at his Pimlico salon). 'Long hair's much more versatile than short hair – which is why women love it.' *(See page 102 for step-by-step instructions on how to put your hair up.)*

For longer-haired women who want to wear their hair down but off the face, John Barrett – who works out of Bergdorf Goodman, in New York – still believes that 'a thin black grosgrain head-band' is most chic. Donna Karan prefers to scoop her hair up into a mid-height pony-tail, 'which works like an instant face-lift,' she enthuses. Certainly, long hair lets you play around with the images you present to the world: you can put it up and feel professional for work, or let it down (literally!) when it gets to Friday night. Alternatively you can loosely pin it up, so that – sexily – you can un-pin it in front of your partner.

But the downside, of course, is that long hair is old hair. Philip Kingsley, a leading international trichologist (who, insiders say, helps keep fiftysomething Jerry Hall's bleached-to-high-heaven

HOW SHORT CAN YOU GO?

An urchin cut works brilliantly on Sharon Stone – but you need to make sure that a very short cut won't give you a pinhead. Before you commit to a cut, try scraping your hair right off your face and looking at yourself in a full-length glass, checking out your reflection from the sides as well as straight on. But according to John Frieda, a simple measurement can also tell you whether you can go for an Audrey Hepburn gamine look.

- Look straight ahead into a mirror, chin absolutely straight – not tipped up or down at all.
- Use your finger to follow a line on your neck, directly down from your earlobe. Stop when your finger is perfectly in line with the tip of your chin – or the lowest part of the chin, if yours happens to be double.
- Measure the distance using a tape measure or a ruler.

'If the distance is more than 5.5cm (2^1/$_4$in),' says John Frieda, 'then short hair probably won't suit you and you'll need extra length, or extra layers cut into the neck, to help soften the look. If that distance is less than 5.5cm (2^1/$_4$ in), short hair should flatter you.'

ponytail shiny as a racehorse's), points out that hair which has reached a length of 45cm (18in) is actually around three years old. 'During that time, not only will it have been environmentally damaged – by hairdryers, for instance – but the chances are, if you're over 40, it's coloured, too, so it may have taken a beating. And as you get older, the hair shaft actually becomes a little thinner in diameter – which makes it more likely to break.' Acknowledges John Frieda, 'If hair is fine or tatty, there's no point hanging on to it – it'll look better and have more oomph if it's short.'

The first, essential step to being a post-40 Rapunzel, believes Nicky Clarke,

is to have it regularly trimmed. 'Every six to eight weeks is a must to keep it looking good. Women run away with the idea that because it doesn't need trimming to keep its *shape*, they can leave it longer between cuts.' Then split ends become a problem.

Condition is also crucial. One reason why long hair was always a no-no for the over-40s is that hair conditioners didn't even exist until a couple of decades ago – so long hair was simply tatty hair. But the good news is that high-tech haircare – which enables us to keep our hair in glorious, gleaming condition, even when it's way past our shoulders – has now green-lighted long hair for the

over-40s. 'If you give hair plenty of TLC, there's no reason you shouldn't keep it – or grow it – long,' insists Philip Kingsley. Jane Seymour, for instance, gets away with almost waist-length hair because it's always alluringly super-shiny.

Nicky Clarke points out that 'long hair is also prone to the effects of static – it gathers a lot of electricity, especially in winter, which makes hair look flat and flyaway.' Leave-in conditioners help combat the problem.

Keeping hair well moisturised, explains Kingsley, also prevents premature breakage. Poor condition is often outwardly apparent when it's too late – when strands are already split and breaking off. So prevention is better than cure. And every expert we spoke to advised occasional deep-conditioning treatments as the ultimate maintenance option for long hair. 'Use them at least once a month – preferably once a week,' advises Nicky Clarke. (NB: masks that did well in our book *The Handbag Beauty Bible* include Lancôme Hair Nutrition Extra Rich Conditioning Mask, TIGI Self-Absorbed Mega-Vitamin Conditioner and Redken All Soft Heavy Cream.)

Over-drying – with a too-hot hairdryer – is bad news for long hair, however. Experiment with leaving hair to dry naturally until it's 80 per cent dry – or use your dryer on a lower setting, while you gently ruffle it – and try silicone-based serums, which help protect long hair from heat damage. Long hair's worst enemy, believes Kingsley, 'is Granny's prescribed 100 brush-strokes a night'. He prefers wide-toothed combs to brushes, which tug at hair.

For some women, giving up long hair is even harder than giving up chocolate, sex or men. So why do it? With just a little TLC, you can stay a glamorous Rapunzel for ever.

PUMP UP THE VOLUME

Few of us go through life with a permanently thick and bouncy head of hair. Whether your hair always tends to be fine, thin and flat, or is just going through a bad phase, there are techniques which can improve the look by adding volume, curves and shape.

We asked former British Hairdresser of the Year Charles Worthington – known for his expertise in creating big hair – for his advice on how to make more of what you've got.

'If your hair is usually bouncy but suddenly becomes flat, do look at whether you're taking care of yourself properly,' recommends Charles. 'I always know when regular clients are not eating well, or just not looking after themselves; their hair loses spring and bounce in the roots, and starts looking dull and lacklustre. And you must have exercise: cardiovascular exercise sends the blood rushing round your body, it feeds the hair follicle and everything just works better.'

Although some hairdressers say thinner hair is better short, Charles says just on the shoulders can be a good longer length because it will kick out when it hits your shoulders and you can also put it up easily. It's vital not to let the hair drag itself down, he adds, so go for long layers to create shape, volume and curves. Both Charles and John Frieda agree that short layers, like shampoos and sets, are ageing (could someone please tell Her Majesty?). Have your

fluff it up

John Frieda has an amazing tip for volumising hair: rub the hair between your fingers, almost like rubbing butter into flour to make pastry. With wet hair, spray on your thickening product then get it to the point where it's almost dry, he says, and really rub it together – it fluffs out each individual cuticle. 'You can do it on dry hair when you want it to be really full: it's something I've often used in the studio for fashion shoots,' he says. (We tried it; it's extraordinary.)

style trimmed regularly, every five to seven weeks, depending on how fast it grows (remember that also will vary from season to season).

'For the fullest head of hair possible, use a regime of specially tailored products: shampoo, conditioner, styling spray and finally a fixing product,' says Charles. The key words to look for are 'volumising' and/or 'thickening'. Go for a good range; you get what you pay for. There may be a case for sticking to one brand because the products are formulated to work well together. Useful ingredients are panthenol, keratin-amino acids and brown sea algae (which you'll find in Charles's own range).

Hair condition will change with the seasons; for instance, as the central heating goes on, the scalp gets drier and you may need to shift to more moisturising products. If you're going grey, the hair texture changes and becomes dryer and more wiry, so it needs more nourishment and moisture.

Wash thin, fine hair every day if possible: 'It goes out of shape more easily than a thick mop; any warm atmosphere will make it limp and simply sleeping on it tends to crush the style.' But, as with make-up, less – overall – is more. 'Always use conditioner but use it sparingly or you risk making hair lank and droopy,' Charles recommends. You may find that volumising shampoos and conditioners seem to work better if you use them in the bath rather than the shower: 'The problem with power showers is that they can deliver such a jet of water that they strip the product out of the hair, whereas a bath tends to leave a residue.'

roller culture

Perms used to be the only big hair solution until Velcro rollers came along – and perms slunk out of the back door. A good thing too, according to all the hairdressers and colourists we talked to. Without exception, they rolled their eyes in horror at the damage wreaked by perms. Susan Baldwin of John Frieda says: 'They make hair dry, dull and basically dead-looking.'

Rollers are a godsend for fine, thin or flat hair but can be a mystery to the uninitiated. To decode The Big Roller Mystery, here are Charles Worthington's top tips:

● Go for easy-to-use Velcro self-grip rollers, secured with an extra Kirbigrip if you like.

● Put them into warm hair, then wait until the hair is cold before taking them out and styling. Warm hair is malleable; it 'sets' when cold.

● Roller size: hair needs to go round a roller a minimum of one and a half times. So start by measuring the length of hair on the different parts of your head that you want to lift. You need rollers with a diameter which is two thirds the length of the hair; eg, if your hair on the top is 7.5cm (3in) long, choose a roller that is 5cm (2in) in circumference – a good medium size to start with, by the way.

● You will probably need about 20 rollers in all. How many you need of each sort is usually a case of roll it and see: but start with at least six of each type.

● Putting in the roller: take a square section of hair, a little bit wider than the length of the roller. Put rollers in from the front top of your head and work back and down.

● Dry with a diffuser on a hand-dryer on a cool temperature to set the hair, or use a portable hood-dryer.

● When the hair is cold, take the rollers out, working from the bottom up.

● With your head upside down, spray a little fixing product on to the roots, before running your fingers or a brush through hair.

Heated rollers can be useful when you're in a hurry. Spray a little old-fashioned fixing spray (rather than a styling product) near roots. Only trial and error will tell you how long you need to leave the rollers in – so practise. If you're getting too curly, try letting them cool down a bit and only leave them in for a moment.

BACK IT UP

Fine hair is bound to droop a bit over the day, especially if you're hot, busy or hurried. It may sound a bit 1960s, but a little back-combing or back-brushing is marvellous for maintaining a style. Both techniques have a bad name for damaging hair but the trick is to do it very gently, says Charles. 'Hold the section of hair gently between finger and thumb, letting some strands escape, and tease the hair. If you hold the hair too tightly, you create too much tension. A natural bristle brush is the gentlest for back-combing hair and will fluff out a shape and give a little more volume with the least amount of tangles. To create volume just at the roots, back-comb them; then when you come to brush out the back-combing, use a brush with flexible bristles. Be gentle and don't pull at the hair shaft. If you want a lot of volume and staying power, turn your head upside down and spray with a styling or fixing product before back-combing.'

fringe benefits

If you have a furrowed or lined forehead, try a fringe before you try a brow-lift! John Frieda says that a fringe over the brow can be extremely de-ageing for older women, can soften a face, hiding a bad hairline and – if strategically styled – minimise facial flaws. 'Steer clear of heavy fringes, though,' he advises, 'as this look is too severe for women of practically any age. Go for something light and feathery.' (Think what a veil can do for a face. Well, a fringe achieves much the same glamorising, line-softening effect.)

MORE HAIR WISDOM FROM JOHN BARRETT

• Commit to a hairdresser you trust – one who does the hair of other women of your age, whose style you admire.

• Regularly look at photos of yourself and realistically analyse the pros and cons of your hair length with a good friend, as well as your hairdresser. Sometimes you can see yourself more objectively in a photo than a mirror.

• Talk to your hairdresser honestly and with an open mind. Most hairdressers will be as honest in giving you feedback as you are in seeking it. Repeat back what you've agreed to – to make sure communication is clear. Good communication is a two-way street and very necessary for something as important as your haircut, colour and styling.

• For bad hair days, pull hair back wet – or use light conditioner to dress the hair, then pull it back with a very thin or a very wide head-band.

• Time emergency? Shampoo and blow-dry your fringe only. This can work with headbands, ponytails or simple, natural styles.

• Don't overcondition. Most people do – and it's just like overwatering houseplants, or orchids. Overconditioning leads to problems like build-up, and limp or hard-to-style hair. Use conditioner sparingly and focus on the ends.

PUT IT UP

Piling your hair on top is not only an answer for a bad hair day, it can give you a whole new look – which is wonderful fun if nothing else. And a put-up job is incredibly useful if you've left your cut two weeks (or more) too late.

There are two main looks: sleek and smooth – think Audrey Hepburn in *Breakfast at Tiffany's* – or soft and frothy. You can put up all sorts of different lengths of hair, although the optimum length is just on your shoulders with long layers through your hair. Don't worry if hair is shorter – you can still get a lovely, casually elegant look by twisting it up and fanning out the ends (fix them in place with fixing spray). It doesn't even matter if the grips show – just look for ones with a pretty detail at the ends.

the steps

1 Divide the hair into four sections, back, top and two sides, using butterfly clips.

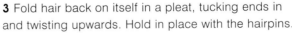 **2** Starting with back section: if hair is long, brush horizontally to one side, then put a line of grips all the way from nape to top of section, criss-crossing them if you can, to anchor the hair.

3 Fold hair back on itself in a pleat, tucking ends in and twisting upwards. Hold in place with the hairpins.

 4 If hair is short, don't worry about tucking the ends in at the top, just fan them out casually and spray.

5 Now dress the sides. With the sides and the top you need to look at the overall proportion of your face and dress your hair to suit that (see the section on face shapes, pages 96-97). Either comb the sides back smoothly and pin into the pleat or let some or all of the hair drop casually down and around your face; use a heated roller or tongs to give shape if necessary.

6 Move on to the top: arrange fringe and hairline then back-comb or brush the rest if you wish, arrange gracefully over the sides, and smooth some back into the pleat; if your hair is short on top, either leave the top section as you would normally or pin some of it to the top of the pleat. Again secure with pretty pins if you have some wild bits.

7 As a final touch on this or any other style, try Charles's tip and 'polish' the surface of the hair with a serum product. Put a little tiny dab of serum – about the size of a five-pence piece or a dime – into your palm, then use a big floppy make-up brush to pick up some of the serum and brush it on to your hair. This also works brilliantly with long straight hair, giving it a glossy, almost glass-like finish.

the rules

● Always practise before trying to do this for an important event; allow hairdressing rehearsal time to play around, see what's easiest for you to do and what looks best.

● If possible, have your hair put up in a salon so you can see what the hairdresser does and she/he can give you some individual tips.

● The key to putting your hair up is to do it in sections: section off the back and start with that, then do the sides, then the top.

● A three-way mirror is very helpful.

● As well as styling and fixing products, you will need: matte Kirbigrips – if you're worried they'll show, look for ones with pretty details at the ends like a single tiny flower or rhinestone for evenings; small hairpins – bend one end into a fish tail beforehand so that they will stick there without sliding out.

● Rollers are not vital but hair that has been lifted in rollers is much easier to work with.

MORE HAIR WISDOM FROM JOHN FRIEDA

● 'Always have a (free) consultation before booking an appointment with a new hairdresser. The relationship is all-important – you've got to feel comfortable. Ideally, you should visit two or three salons – and compare.'

● 'Don't be embarrassed to take pictures to give your hairdresser an idea of the look you want. It helps put you and your hairdresser on the same wavelength.'

● 'If you have a haircut you hate, wait a week before you rush off somewhere else, so you're more rational. The eye takes time to adjust – after a week, you'll know if it's really bad.'

● 'To achieve body, blow-dry roots in the opposite direction to how your hair naturally grows. The secret is to imagine that your head is a giant roller, and – with a blow-dryer in one hand – run your fingers through your hair, literally winding it around the head in one direction. Then, after a minute or so, switch hands; put the dryer in the other hand and wind it round the scalp the other way. Carry on alternating like this, and, as the hair gets closer to being dry, switch over to a bristle brush or a Mason Pearson, instead of your fingers, for final sleeking and styling. Because the roots are being lifted and dried in opposite directions, the result is great body.'

Banana reconditioning treatment

Mash one ripe peeled banana with one tablespoon of sunflower oil and a half teaspoon of fresh lime juice. Mix well then apply generously to dry, well-combed hair. Leave for 30 minutes before shampooing as usual.

Why it works: potassium in banana helps scalp health; natural sebum-like sunflower oil conditions dry scalp and hair; lime juice helps adjust scalp's acid/alkali balance and smooths cuticles to increase shine.

Lime juice perm reviver

Mix a teaspoon of lime juice with 300ml (1/2pt) cold water; rinse through the hair before washing.

Why it works: lime juice contains citric acid and oils which contract the cortex of each hair strand to tighten curls without stripping natural oils.

Rum and egg conditioner

Mix together an egg yolk, a half teaspoonful of vitamin C powder and two teaspoons of dark rum. Apply to dry hair, leave for ten minutes then wash with a mild shampoo.

Why it works: lecithin in the egg yolk revives hair, while rum stimulates the scalp, and vitamin C helps adjust the scalp's acid/alkali balance, encouraging shine.

French dressing for tangly hair

Mix one measure of vinegar to three of sunflower oil; work through hair and leave for five minutes before shampooing and conditioning as usual.

Why it works: acetic acid in vinegar encourages cuticles to lie flat and the oil moisturises the hair.

Tomato sauce colour corrector

Chlorine in swimming pools often makes

KITCHEN MAGIC

Your fridge and store-cupboard can yield as many goodies for your hair as for every other part of your face and body. Eat as many fruits as you can – but also mush them up and mulch them in!

Daniel Field, the leading London hairdresser whose organic range is a celebrity favourite, gave us the recipes on this page to feed your hair.

lightened hair khaki-ish. Apply a generous dollop of tomato sauce to well-combed, dry hair, massaging well. Leave for 30 minutes, then shampoo.

Why it works: the pink tones in the sauce neutralise the khaki.

Lemonade detangler

Chemically treated hair can tangle easily. For a quick fix, pour some lemonade into a clean plant spray and spritz liberally over dry hair then leave for five minutes before shampooing and conditioning as usual.

Why it works: citric acid closes the cuticle layers and contracts the hair cortex back to its pre-damaged state.

Corn oil for split ends and static prevention

Put a small amount of corn oil on to the palms of your hands and smooth down

over dry hair, right to the tips. Shampoo as usual.

Why it works: the corn oil will protect the ends of the hair from the impact of the washing and drying.

Mango winter restorer

Chop a peeled ripe mango roughly into a clean bowl. Add a tablespoon of walnut oil and a squeeze of lemon juice. Mix well with a fork or blender until reasonably smooth. Wrap a bath towel round your neck before applying the mixture evenly all over dry, well-combed hair. Massage well into scalp and hair. After 30 minutes, rinse thoroughly – then shampoo as normal.

Why it works: the combination of minerals, vitamins and trace elements in the mango, plus concentrated scalp massage, stimulates scalp and follicles.

Léonor Greyl's tips for hair health

Madame Greyl is France's healthy hair guru; her Paris treatment centre is a mecca for stars, including (it's rumoured) Catherine Deneuve and Princess Caroline of Monaco. So we asked her to give us her tips for head-turning hair...

• 'If you've chosen a great quality shampoo and you're washing your hair quickly, you're wasting your money. Most women don't shampoo for long enough. Always comb the hair before you wet it, then put a blob of shampoo in the palm of your hand and add a little water, to dilute it. Apply evenly to the scalp and run your fingers through the hair. Gently work it into the scalp for ten minutes – then rinse for at least another five. Finish with a cold rinse, which is good for circulation.'

• 'Never use a fine-toothed comb on your hair; always use the widest-toothed comb you can find. Only use a brush when actually styling, to minimise wear and tear.'

• 'Visit a salon at least twice a year, spring and autumn, for a deep treatment "facial for your hair".'

• 'See a nutritionist for hair problems. Hair needs feeding from the inside out as well as outside in.'

• 'Wash your brushes and combs once a week in a mild shampoo.'

• 'Always take two or three hours out of a busy schedule each week to make time for yourself: a massage, an exercise class, a walk. Hair health is a reflection of inner health and if you're under pressure, it shows up in your hair almost immediately.'

AT-HOME SCALP MASSAGE

Madame Greyl's prescription includes regular scalp massages. 'Women store a huge amount of tension in the scalp,' she explains. 'Sometimes, when I'm massaging a woman's head, the scalp is literally immovable – as if it's glued down – because the scalp muscles are so tense. Which, in turn, restricts blood and nutrient flow to follicles.' What we should aim for, through regular massage, is a scalp which moves easily over the bones of the skull.

• Ideally, she says, you should use borage oil (also known as starflower oil) for the massage; wheatgerm oil is also effective. (Both easily wash out again.) 'But if you prefer, you can also massage the scalp without using oil.'

• If you're using oil, part the hair in five or six places on the scalp, using a wide-toothed comb. Break open five or six capsules of borage or starflower oil, or drip wheatgerm oil from a dropper, and apply along the partings.

• Lean forwards to boost circulation.

• Now bunch up the fingers of each hand and massage the temples, to release tension. Do this for at least a minute and try to feel the day's tensions ebb away.

• Then place the pads of the fingers of each hand on the front of your head, just behind the hairline, placed so that your little fingers are almost touching. Massage in strong, circular movements. You should be moving the scalp, not letting your fingers skim over the surface. Do this for a minute or so.

• Move your fingers back an inch or so, and repeat. After a minute, re-position the fingers, another inch back. Keep doing this until you reach the crown, and continue, massaging the back of the head down to the nape. Use all of your fingers and thumbs, applying even pressure.

• In all, devote a full three to five minutes to the head massage. (If it gets uncomfortable to lean forward for all that time, or you have neck problems, you can do the head massage in a sitting position; make a point of keeping your shoulders relaxed.)

• 'You should aim to do the massage three times a week,' believes Madame Greyl, who insists she has seen amazing improvements in hair health among women who pay attention to their scalps in this way.

PLUMPING UP YOUR LOCKS

Léonor's spécialité de la maison is helping women with thinning hair. 'You need to feed the scalp,' insists Mme Greyl, who tailor-makes health-boosting, gloss-restoring hair masks for clients – using ingredients like wheatgerm, silk, camomile, mimosa and borage oil – then prescribes an individual programme of products to maximise hair health back home.

THINNING HAIR – STILL A MYSTERY AFTER ALL THESE YEARS

Hair loss isn't a men-only problem. One of the less engaging facts about getting older is that a significant number of women also experience thinning hair. Two out of every three men are bald or balding by 50, and as many as 36 per cent of all women between 40 and 49 are affected by some degree of hair thinning or loss. And alopecia, as it's called medically, tends to be an extremely traumatic event for women – because we see losing hair as losing part of our femininity.

Female pattern hair loss (alopecia androgenetica) and moult, or increased hair shedding (chronic telogen effluvium), account for by far the majority of all hair-loss complaints in women – up to 95 per cent, in fact, before menopause. Unlike men, who tend to lose a lot of hair in particular areas, like the temples and crown – 'male-pattern baldness' – women are more likely to thin diffusely from behind the front hairline to the crown. Alopecia areata (patchy hair loss) affects about 0.1 per cent of women. (The very rare scarring alopecias, caused by conditions such as lupus, may affect about 0.01 per cent, but there are no precise figures.)

CHANGING HAIRLINES

Doctors are seeing increasing numbers of women patients with hair loss but it's not certain if this is to due to more cases, or more women seeking help. It's very difficult to treat because there is no single cause, according to Dr Sara Riley, GP and medical adviser to the Hair Management Academy, a not for profit organisation which gives evidence-based advice in this charlatan-ridden area (www.hairmanagementacademy.com). Menopausal women, in general, suffer increasing hair loss, probably because of dihydrotestosterone (DHT), a naturally produced sidekick of the male hormone testosterone. Before menopause, oestrogens – the female hormones – help protect women against the action of DHT but that protection fades at and after menopause.

Thyroid problems are one of the few known health-related causes of hair loss: thyroid malfunction accounts for less than two per cent of hair loss problems in women under 45, but, for reasons that are still unclear, this seems to increase as women approach and go through menopause. Thyroid disease is treatable but it is widely underdiagnosed in this country and many doctors treat it poorly. If you gain weight without eating more, are tired, lethargic, and suffering hair fall, do discuss the possibility of thyroid malfunction with your doctor, ask for comprehensive tests, and also consider consulting a qualified naturopath. Also see *Your Thyroid and How To keep It Healthy* by Dr Barry Durrant-Peatfield.

GENES OR MOULT?

If you have one of the following…
● more hairs falling when shampooing and combing;
● less thickness of hair when you draw it back into a pony-tail;
● short hairs along your front hairline;
…but your parting is no wider and your hair looks the same to friends, then you're probably suffering from increased shedding rather than a genetic condition. (Beware that you don't think your parting is wider because the hair is grey.)

Unlike a genetic condition, a moult will correct itself eventually, usually within two to three months; if it goes on much beyond that, consult your family doctor, who will probably refer you to a consultant dermatologist for investigation.

THE STRESS CONNECTION

What is now clear to hair-loss experts is that stress not only exacerbates male- and female-pattern baldness, but is also a direct cause of increased shedding or hair 'moults'. Stress events may cause hair loss but you may not always link cause and effect because the moult may not start until ten to 12 weeks later. Dr Rushton says the most likely causes of non-genetic hair loss are:

● **Pregnancy:** 50 per cent of women have postnatal hair loss, which usually regrows without intervention.

● **Menopause:** the reduction in oestrogen (female hormone) levels and a relative increase in male hormones (see DHT, opposite) may cause some hair loss, which usually then grows back if the hormonal imbalance is put right.

● **Hormone replacement therapy (HRT):** this has been reported, in some cases, to trigger hair loss similar to genetic hair loss; however these changes can be prevented with a well chosen HRT (ie, one that does not contain an androgenic progestin).

● **Emotional shocks:** acute stressors, from divorce to job loss, may affect hair.

● **Physical stressors:** eg, a car accident, the aftermath of a heart attack, surgery.

● **Shallow breathing:** hyperventilation, as it's called medically, can affect all your body systems.

● **Not enough rest and sleep.**

● **Drug therapy:** chemotherapy and radiotherapy for cancer, cortisone, sedatives, tranquillisers and barbiturates, amphetamines, antibiotics.

● **Immunisations:** there is some evidence that immunisation in children may trigger temporary hair loss and this may also extend to some pre-travel immunisation.

● **Yo-yo dieting.**

● **Poor diet and/or nutritional deficiencies:** particularly iron, lysine, B_{12} and zinc.

● **Smoking:** it robs the body of nutrients.

● **Eating disorders:** for example, anorexia.

● **Misuse of hair:** perming, colouring, using curling tongs or heated rollers, too much brushing with a sharp bristled brush and blow-drying at too high a temperature; these may all cause hair loss due to hair breakage.

● **Central heating.**

● **Pollution.**

● **Dandruff-like conditions:** these may affect the rate of hair shedding.

● **Inadequate or infrequent shampooing:** it's important not to reduce shampooing if you have hair loss.

HAIR SUPPLEMENTS

Naturopath Jan de Vries recommends MaxiHair by Nature's Best, which contains a wide spread of nutrients, alongside Urticalcin homoeopathic calcium by Bioforce. Trichologist Dr Hugh Rushton, who believes that iron absorption is a major problem in hair loss, has formulated NutriHair for Nature's Best, which includes iron and vitamin C to help iron absorption. Pharmacist Shabir Daya suggests Superior Hair by FoodScience of Vermont, a complete hair support formula for men and women.

From starting a supplement, the average time before you'll notice a reduction in hair shedding is 16 weeks; since hair grows about 1cm/^{1}/2in a month, seeing more volume may take months. So don't give up!

DRUG TREATMENTS

There are few hair loss drugs available – and most experts agree their performance is fairly disappointing, and there are potential side effects. However, some people with thinning hair may think a small improvement is better than nothing – and worth the risks.

The treatment for genetic hair loss in women is usually a combination of anti-androgen (ie, an anti-male hormone) medication plus a topical drug – but this regime must of course be prescribed and monitored constantly by a medical expert.

According to Dr Sara Riley, medical adviser to the Hair Management Academy, women with thinning hair who need contraception may be helped by the anti-androgen contraceptive pill called Dianette. However, this has been linked to liver toxicity, so all the risks and benefits must be thoroughly discussed. Another anti-androgen drug, spironolactone (originally designed as a diuretic) may stabilise hair loss and has shown some improvement in 35 per cent of women. However, there are potentially serious risks and side effects.

The anti-baldness prescription drug, finasteride (Propecia), which has been approved in America, is not suitable for women of childbearing age because it could theoretically cause birth defects (in two per cent of men, it can cause temporary loss of libido and impotence while the drug is taken). However, post-menopausal women (who have had no periods for two years) may be prescribed the drug. The downside is that no one is absolutely certain how effective

finasteride is – or on whom. Finasteride was actually formulated as a drug therapy for prostate problems – and it was then discovered that it helped some cases of male-pattern baldness. It works by blocking the enzyme (5-alpha reductase) which converts testosterone, the male hormone, to DHT, the villain behind hair loss.

However the snag is that there are two types of this enzyme involved; either Type 1 or Type 2 may be the dominant form of the enzyme in the scalp and hair follicle. Finasteride, however, only works on Type 2, the type predominantly involved in the prostate. As things stand at the moment, scientists simply don't know how many men's balding pates are controlled by Type 2 – and certainly not how many women's hair loss problems.

In addition, a prescription lotion, minoxidil (marketed as Regaine in the UK, Rogaine in the US), has been shown to stop hair loss in 60 per cent of women who used it, but only 19 per cent reported moderate hair regrowth and 41 per cent said there was no regrowth at all. Some experts recommend a combination of minoxidil, an anti-androgenic drug, plus balanced nutritional support. The bottom line, though, is management, not cure.

other options

If thinning hair is a problem, you may want to check out specific hair-restoring and thickening products by respected brands including Phytologie's Phytocyane (in tandem with Phytologie's dietary supplement, Phytophanère), plus the ranges from Léonor Greyl in Paris and from Jan Adams at Romanda Healthcare in London.
The American skincare company Nioxin, who believe that the key is scalp health, have an impressive range of three stage Thinning Hair Systems, including chemically enhanced locks. Their products also contain ingredients to block the action of DHT on the scalp.
One important bit of advice: the chlorine in tap water is a strong chemical, which you really don't want to leave on your scalp. So always give your hair a final rinse with distilled or filtered water, or apply a product such as Nioxin's Scalp Treatment.

feed your hair

Healthy hair responds to what you eat in the same way as your skin and the whole of the rest of your body.

Non-genetic hair loss, say experts, is much worse in women who are deficient in iron (vegetarians may need to supplement with chelated iron), and those who have low levels of the B group of vitamins, including folic acid and B_{12}, and also zinc.

About nine out of ten women between the ages of 16 and 50 are deficient in iron, and one third of women between 51 and 64, despite the fact they're not menstruating. (According to London-based trichologist Dr Hugh Rushton, the problem is that many women these days prefer not to eat red meat.) A test for serum ferritin levels (not the haemoglobin level used to assess anaemia) can detect this type of iron deficiency. Dr Sara Riley says a normal level is not enough: it needs to be in the upper part of normal, with a reading above 70 millimols per litre to allow the hair to have its growth potential.

However, if iron stores are replenished to a certain 'trigger point' then hair growth should start again (if it's moult and not genetic). 'The growing stage of the follicles is lengthened so there are more hairs in the growing stage' says Dr Rushton. But, he cautions, the whole process can take six to nine months – so you have to be patient.

For iron to be absorbed by the body, you need vitamin C and lysine, an amino acid mostly found in meat. If you don't eat red meat, or very little, you might consider a supplement (eg, Florisene by Lamberts, for hair loss due to anaemia).

Meanwhile, look after your digestion with plenty of fresh vegetables and fruit and the foods in our chart below. Lots of pure still water is also vital – a sluggish digestive system can lead to dull, limp, oily hair. For more advice, consult a naturopath or a doctor with expertise in nutrition, or a nutritionist.

hair food

Eat lots of:
Fresh vegetables, salads and non-citrus fruit
Live natural yoghurt
Cold-pressed oils (olive, sunflower, sesame, flax)
Pulses (peas, beans, lentils)
Whole grains (brown rice, oats, buckwheat, millet, spelt)
Seeds (sunflower, pumpkin, sesame and linseeds)
Almonds, figs and dates
Plus fresh oily fish, if you're not a vegetarian (salmon, mackerel, tuna, sardines, trout, herring, pilchards)

Drink lots of: Water

Try to cut down on:
Cow's milk products
Caffeine (coffee, tea, chocolate, cola)
Sugar and salt

DANDRUFF-BUSTING

Good news first: true dandruff – a combination of flaking skin cells, a yeast called *Pityrosporum ovale* and overactivity by the sebaceous glands – tends to die out as you get older. After 50, as the sebaceous gland activity dies down, dandruff should be just a memory.

But the bad news is that you may experience the scaly drifts of 'shoulder snow' after 50 and the cause is likely to be a form of eczema or seborrhoeic dermatitis, triggered by dairy food, sugar and chocolate, also yeasty foods.

Here's how to tell the difference and what to do:

Step 1: Wash hair thoroughly every day with a mild medium-to-expensive shampoo (not a cheap one), which leaves your hair feeling clean and shiny. Soak your hair, apply a good blob of shampoo, rub into the scalp well, then rinse very thoroughly. If you can only wash your hair every other day, repeat the process. Put conditioner on ends only. Try this for four weeks and see if it makes a difference. If it doesn't, move on to…

Step 2: If you have flaking, with or without itching or oiliness, you may have real dandruff. Try an anti-dandruff shampoo containing either octopirox (piroctone olamine) or zinc pyrithione (zinc omadine) for three to four weeks.

If, however, you have red patches on your scalp or eyebrows, or down the folds running from nose to mouth, possibly with some itching, you probably have a mild form of eczema (also known as seborrhoeic dermatitis). In that case, try cutting out all dairy products for a month, particularly cheese and milk, also chocolate, sugar and yeast. (See below, too.)

Step 3: If there is still no improvement, ask your family doctor to refer you to a specialist – either a dermatologist or a trichologist.

MORE ABOUT SEBORRHOEIC DERMATITIS

According to Dr Mosaraf Ali of the Integrated Medical Centre in London, seborrhoeic dermatitis is an inflammatory condition of the skin, which appears wherever there are hair follicles. On the face and earlobes, it comes up as a rash, which may be itchy, red and swollen. As well as the dietary measures suggested above, Dr Ali recommends taking a product called Exspore for one month and rubbing one tablespoonful of chickpea powder blended to a paste with a little cold or warm skimmed milk. Scrub this on the face, concentrating on the affected areas for a few moments,

then wash your face with warm water. This is best done at bedtime. The skin will be quite dry, he says, but just leave it like that overnight. Aru Cream is useful, too: apply to the affected areas twice daily. You can treat dandruff-like seborrhoeic dermatitis in the same way, according to Dr Ali. Additionally, he suggested that sufferers use Bioflame Oil, extracted from wild red tropical flowers known as Flame of the Forest. Apply one to two tablespoonfuls of this oil to the scalp, massage gently until fully absorbed. Remove with Biomargosa Shampoo (see Directory).

(see page 108)

haircare we love

JO: I have a sensitive scalp, definitely aggravated by sodium lauryl and laureth sulphate. I now use Essential Care Shampoo, which is certified organic by the Soil Association, and gets hair beautifully, gently clean. As I plan to stay blonde, I am slavishly devoted to regular hair masks, to counter any damage. Favourites include ESPA Pink Hair & Scalp Mud, and John Frieda Miraculous Recovery Strengthening Triple Crème Masque. If I'm in LA or he's in London, I book in with 'the King of Shiny Hair', Philip B, a true miracle-worker who likes to massage oils into the hair (and heat them, for extra penetration). I always feel afterwards that I can almost see my face in the reflection from my hair!

SARAH: My hair is colour treated and, as I spend so much time outdoors, invariably dry. Current favourites are The Organic Pharmacy's totally natural Jasmine High Gloss Shampoo and Rose Intensive Conditioner. Also an American anti-ageing range called L'anza, which combines high tech and plants. I gave my scalp a course of Nioxin (see page 108), which made my hair look fab but – inexplicably – straight. Cut and colourwise I am totally faithful to Andreas and Stephen at John Frieda in London (where Jo goes, too, so we often meet up there).

WIG WISDOM

The good news for anyone who's lost, losing or about to lose their hair is that both real hair and synthetic wigs are now highly advanced – and there are also now specialised hair extension systems, which look completely fabulous.

The big story today is the development of hair extension systems – not the 'glamour' brands (see overleaf), but those developed specifically for people with hair loss due to causes ranging from chemotherapy to spontaneous alopecia, genetic hair loss and even trichotillomania (compulsive hair pulling). White Cliffs Hair Studio, with branches in London and Hollywood, has pioneered the only product passed by the FDA in America for oncology patients. They also do a range of other options. Also based in London, hair expert Lucinda Ellery has developed her own Volumiser system, for people with 40 per cent hair loss or more, with Medi-connections for people with less severe problems. The results are gorgeous and only the closest observers would see anything apart from a lovely head of hair.

Realistically, however, many more people will still opt for wigs. Hairdresser Andrew Collinge advises that, if possible, 'The best time to buy a wig [or have extensions] is before you need it – for instance, if you are scheduled to have chemotherapy or are suffering hair loss which might accelerate.' That way, he explains, the salon staff can see your natural colour and style and direct you to the closest match.

Some women, says Andrew, see hair loss as an opportunity for a radical makeover: 'but most want to stay in the "comfort zone", as close as possible to their former look, because that way nobody but their nearest and dearest

need know that anything has changed.'

Partings are traditionally the trickiest thing to get right (though much better nowadays). So, as a rule of thumb, remember that if you can't see the parting, it's much more difficult to tell that the crowning glory is an add-on. If you know you're embarking on chemotherapy, Andrew's advice is to get your hair cut in a shorter style, or one that disguises your parting, then choose a wig that re-creates that shorter hairstyle. If you've already lost your hair before you decide to invest in a wig or extensions, take along a selection of photographs so that the salon can see how you want to look.

You might also want to consider taking your regular hairdresser along to a wig fitting, for expert advice. 'Most women don't think of it – but hairdressers are usually delighted to be of help,' says Andrew. 'If you've put your hair in the hands of your hairdresser in the past, he/she is probably the best person to advise you.' What's more, your hairdresser can 'customise' your hairstyle.

Andrew recommends synthetic wigs, for their wash-and-wearability. 'Synthetic wigs no longer look like "dolly hair",' he explains. 'They're very realistic. And the price means that it's easier to afford two. You wouldn't wear a blouse day in, day out. Well, wigs need cleaning, too. But the synthetic type spring back into shape and don't need restyling.' If a woman is too sick to travel to a wig department for a fitting, her family can

take along photographs or a lock of hair, and the staff will find the best match.

The other option is a real hair wig, which means that bespoke wig-makers can re-create your hair's appearance right down to the last streak. But maintenance can be a problem, unless you're flush enough to be able to afford two bespoke wigs. (Real hair wigs can 'drop', just like real hair, when they're washed – and may need professional restyling.) In many cases, they need to be mailed back to the maker for restyling – so you'll need to muddle through in the meantime with scarves. Also, warns Andrew: 'Real hair wigs only have a limited lifespan – probably about a year.' A question to ask is whether or not the wig is made with European hair – the priciest option – or Chinese hair, which has been bleached to a lighter shade.

Nobody should feel nervous about visiting a wigmaker, in-store wig department or extensions salon. 'You may feel like the only woman in the world with this problem – but you're not and the staff are there to help you feel better about yourself again,' says Andrew.

THE ART OF THE SCARF

We are both keen supporters of Look Good, Feel Better, a programme which has dramatically boosted the self-esteem of thousands of women undergoing cancer treatment, through workshops at hospitals in the US and UK where they learn how to use make-up, scarves and wigs. Charles Worthington has produced a wonderful leaflet on how to cope with hair loss from cancer and its treatment (see Look Good, Feel Better in the Directory for how to get hold of a copy). Here are some of the tips and ideas it features.

GET AN EXTENSION

If you have fine hair, there is always the option of extensions. Carly Simon – she of the apparently lustrous mane – is said to be a fan of extensions, as are Tina Turner and Pamela Stephenson. There are two kinds: a temporary clip-in, clip-out extension, and a more permanent type with a plastic base which is bonded to the hair near the roots, using heat; this bond is snapped when you want to have the extensions out – and the hair shouldn't be damaged.

These can both be colour-matched to provide low- or highlights, and then cut and styled with your own hair, in-salon. 'They can be quite effective volume-boosters for fine-haired women. But they aren't so appropriate if you're actually thinning on top,' explains John Frieda. 'The base of the hair extension needs to be hidden under layers of hair – and then it can look very realistic. But extensions are also quite high maintenance: they grow out, along with your hair, so every few weeks you have to have the extensions replaced. A lot of women do it, though – and love the result.' However, John advises that it's important to locate a salon which specialises in extensions, to ensure they really know what they're doing. If your hair salon doesn't do extensions – and most don't – they should know (through the hairdressing grapevine) of a salon which is more experienced at this volume-boosting technique. But our advice is that it's certainly worth making an effort to find the right person (White Cliffs Hair Studio, for instance – see Directory).

• Headwraps and turbans offer a stylish and comfortable alternative to wearing a wig. Be daring and choose bright colours – they will lift your spirits. Cotton-knit turbans are great, as they don't slip. They help with the problem of heat loss from the scalp and also catch any falling hair. It is a good idea to wear them around the house, particularly when cooking, as wigs tend to make the scalp sweat. Cotton turbans also make a great base for tying a scarf. They keep it from slipping and help to give an appearance of fullness.

• When choosing scarves – those of 65–70cm (26–28 in) square are best – opt for cotton rather than polyester or silk, which can slip.

• A soft shoulder-pad placed on top of your head will give height and a more natural look.

• If you practise the basic tying techniques shown here, you will soon be confident enough to develop your own individual styles.

• Hats, of course, are another good way of disguising hair loss. Look for those with special gussets which are designed to hold the hat snugly on the head without slipping off. If you buy a straw hat, make sure the weave is close, so the scalp is properly protected from the burning rays of the sun.

• By combining headwraps with hats or berets, you can achieve a stylish effect and ensure your scalp is totally covered.

BASIC HEADWRAP 1

1 Lay scarf flat, wrong side up. Fold into triangle, leaving one point slightly longer than the other.

2 Drape scarf over your head with points in the back. Pull scarf down in front, about 5–7cm (2–3in) above your eyebrows.

3 Tie the scarf ends in a half-knot behind your head, with flap anchored beneath the knot.

4 Tie the scarf ends into a square knot.

BASIC HEADWRAP 2

1 Follow steps for Basic Headwrap 1. Using both hands, spread lower flap under a half-knot, as close to the back of your ears as possible.

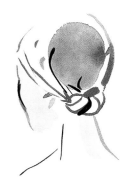

2 Carefully bring flap up over knot.

3 Or use this basis to play with interesting knots/bows.

BASIC SIDE TWIST

• Tie Headwrap 1, placing knot over one ear, instead of at the back of the head, letting the scarf ends hang loose.

CONTRASTING SIDE TWIST

• Tie Headwrap 2. Twist a second oblong scarf. Knot and twist over headwrap, above ear.

tip

Sleeping on a satin-like pillowcase will minimise tugging of hair at the scalp and wearing a soft stretch cap at night will keep your head warm.

GREY MATTERS: THE ULTIMATE GUIDE TO HAIRCOLOURING

Whether you've a few grey hairs, salt-and-pepper streaks or all-over white, there's an effective answer – and often many options, both salon and DIY. (Plus the choice of staying silver – but sensational.)

As life's landmarks go, the morning we notice our first grey hair isn't one that has most of us singing hallelujah from the rooftops. But today we can choose to play up the silver fox style – and look fabulous. Or colour it, and nobody (but our colourist) need know.

If you get it right, that is. According to the experts, that's really not so hard – provided you follow a few simple guidelines. The world's leading haircolouring experts are agreed: don't be tempted to make dramatic changes and stray too far from your natural, pre-grey haircolouring. Every woman has a 'buffer zone' of 'safe' shades – two or three either side, just lighter or just darker than her natural colour.

Be conscious, too, that nobody's hair is naturally all one colour. Consider having highlights or lowlights for a super-realistic effect. As Louis Licari (Manhattan's 'King of Colour') explains, 'A few lights are as good as a mini-lift for ageing women. If you put highlights above the temple, it automatically makes eyes lift upwards.'

For most of us, grey hair arrives just as we hit life's prime, when Nature plays a cruel trick and stops the production of melanin, the substance which gives hair its natural colour. Fifty per cent of the population is grey by the age of 50. Studies have shown that more women are going grey – and sooner than ever before – as a result of pernicious anaemia (often linked to dieting), hormone treatments (including the pill), and our frantic, stressful lives.

When grey hair sets in, it can make you appear washed-out and pale. According to Louis Licari, 'When hair loses its colour, it loses its richness and lustre. And when this happens it tends to make skin colour look faded, too.'

We can all think of women who go grey gracefully, and look utterly chic. 'But they are the exceptions,' insists top London hairdresser, Nicky Clarke. 'And they tend to be fabulous, striking women, who'd look great whatever their hair colour.' Your skintone will determine how good you'd look if you decide to stick with grey. The sallow-skinned rarely find a silver frame flattering – nor do natural redheads, whose hair tends to turn a pale apricot when white mixes in. Classic silver-haired beauties tend to cluster at opposite ends of the skin spectrum: women with almost ebony colouring, or pale 'English rose' complexions. If you don't fall into those categories – or you just don't want grey hair, period – the fixes are quick and convincing.

Covering up the grey restores not only the colour and rejuvenates the face – it makes hair glossy again. Hair texture actually changes as it goes grey; it may be wirier, coarser and/or dry. (Or even curlier.) 'Grey hair absorbs the light and looks flat,' says Jo Hansford, whose London salon is a mecca for the not-so-glad-to-be-grey. 'Put back the colour and the light picks up on it and automatically makes the hair appear healthier.' The good news is that today's high-tech colourants offer natural results – and boost hair health, to boot. So let us steer you through the colour maze.

MAKE-UP FOR GREY HAIR

When you go grey, more colourful make-up is essential,' explains Bobbi Brown. 'Grey or white hair drains colour from the face, so you need the lift of make-up colour – soft shades, but not washed out.' Bobbi's recommendations:
LIPSTICK: rose, red, apricot, peach (but not brown).
BLUSH: rose tones, pastels.
IF YOU HAVE BROWN EYES: use a grey or brown shadow palette.
IF YOU HAVE BLUE EYES: use a shadow trio of grey, slate and navy.

your product options?

A FEW GREY HAIRS

On dark blonde or fair hair, you could try highlights – lighter streaks which disguise the grey; up to three different tones may be used for natural-looking results. Highlights should be done by a pro. As there's no obvious regrowth at the roots, they only need to be touched up every eight to 12 weeks. On darkish hair, deep blondes and redheads, try streaks of colour which tone down the grey only, bringing it back to your original shade; again, a good colourist is essential. 'Sometimes we use the grey hair as a third colour, creating a tortoiseshell effect,' explains Jo Hansford (whose clients include the Duchess of Cornwall).

Another option – which you could try at home – is a 'vegetable rinse', which is basically henna, so don't be deceived by the appealingly natural-sounding name. All the hairdressers we spoke to caution women against using henna like the plague. 'Henna coats the hair in a colour that won't wash off and is impervious to other colours – so you can't change your mind,' says Christophe Robin, the Parisian haircolourist who looks after colour for Catherine Deneuve and Kristin Scott Thomas.

Another 'starter' option is to use colour shampoos and colour conditioners. Susan Baldwin isn't a fan of the shampoos – 'they're unpredictable,' she says – but she does like colour conditioners, which don't contain any peroxide or ammonia, and are very gentle. However, she adds, they will only give around 20 per cent coverage of grey, so you shouldn't expect to see miracles after you've applied one. But according to Susan, 'They can still be a good way of very slowly building up colour, gradually – helping you to decide whether you like a particular colour and want to go for a similar, semi-permanent colour. But beware of the warmer shades, as they can look a bit brassy.'

UP TO 20 PER CENT GREY

Hide with one of the new generation colour glossers or colour glazes, which offer sheer coverage, or semi-permanent colour, in the same shade as your natural hair. Semi-permanent colours like these fade gradually, without noticeable regrowth – and also last six to eight washes. Jo Hansford explains: 'I never say, "This will last X weeks" when I'm colouring women's hair, because if you wash your hair frequently, it'll need colouring more often.' Vegetable colour and semi-permanents are relatively low-maintenance options which coat the outer layer of hair with colour, rather than penetrating the hair shaft, which requires the use of stronger chemicals. Because they blend with the colour of grey hair, rather than cover your hair colour totally, the effects are very realistic.

UP TO 50 PER CENT GREY

Cover with a longer-lasting semi-permanent colour, which stays for up to 24 washes, and gradually fades, meaning there is less obvious regrowth than with a permanent dye. (These are also sometimes known as demi-permanent or tone-on-tone colours.) There is no ammonia, so the colour molecules do not penetrate as deep as in permanent hair colours. However, longer-lasting semi-permanent colour does contain between one and two per cent peroxide (the ingredient that opens the hair's cuticle, allowing colour molecules to enter the strand's cortex) – which is why the colour lasts longer than regular semi-permanents.

UP TO 100 PER CENT GREY

Replace colour completely with a permanent dye; these are chemically based and so penetrate the hair shaft. Jo suggests adding professional highlights or lowlights first, to break up the colour and make it more natural-looking. Remember, roots will need retouching about every four to six weeks – but not always the whole head.

FADE TO GREY AGAIN

So you've been covering up your grey for a while – but now you've decided you want to go back to natural again? According to Beth Minardi, of Manhattan's Minardi Salon, 'If you've been dyeing your hair, silver should evolve gradually. It's a matter of trimming off the old dye job, putting in lowlights, perhaps highlighting the regrowth – minimising the application of tint until there's less and less colour and more and more white.'

YOUR COLOUR OPTIONS

John Barrett says that whatever your hair colour, you should take your cue from the base colour you are now – not the colour that you think you were 15 years ago, or when you were a teenager.

BLONDE

Don't go too blonde; think of adding some lowlights or you may look too pale-all-over. Blondes tend to go too light and ashy. They should have some golden tones mixed in to keep the colour warm and natural. As Louis Licari says, 'Your hair colour should give a contrast to your skintone so it defines your face.'

MEDIUM BROWN

According to Louis Licari, if this is your natural hair colour, then 'You should go no lighter than light brown or light auburn.' 'Paper-bag brown' should have highlights, or lowlights. And try ash browns, rather than reds, which are very hard for the complexion to take.

BRUNETTES

Lighten up two or three shades from the colour that you were naturally – but preferably with extra highlights, for a more realistic effect. And according to Louis Licari, 'Go no darker than chocolate brown or auburn.'

Explains Jo Hansford, 'When you go grey, the skin softens down and becomes paler. If you're greying and go back to your original brunette, the contrast may be too severe: you can end up looking like a witch.' Too-dark hair also emphasises wrinkles, undereye circles and sagging skin – another good reason to go slightly lighter. (If you need proof, 'Tie a black ribbon around a lemon,' suggests James Viera, senior vice president for L'Oréal, 'then try doing the same with a white ribbon. You'll see that the surface looks far smoother.'

REDHEADS

According to Louis Licari, covering up grey hair with red colour is a tough one for greying women to carry off; that's partly because red can have the effect of turbocharging any ruddiness in your complexion. 'You definitely need the right skintone and eyes for it to work,' he explains, adding that the pale colouring and freckled complexions of Sigourney Weaver and Susan Sarandon, for example – natural to many redheads – make them an exception to the don't-go-red rule.

Certainly, if you are determined to make a strong statement like covering grey with red, then Louis advises: 'See a professional.'

Secret: **Don't ever be tempted to pluck a grey hair. 'Pulling won't kill the hair or make it grow back with its old colour,' explains Philip Kingsley. 'Plucking only distorts the hair follicle, making regrowth more wiry and obvious.'**

TESTING TIME

Today's home hair colourants are safe, effective and (mostly) foolproof. But disasters still sometimes occur because people don't follow instructions on the pack. Take time to complete both of the recommended tests. To avoid having to re-mix ingredients, do the two tests at the same time – 48 hours before colouring – to allow for signs of allergy, ie, itching, stinging, burning or redness. Be sure to have a patch test if you are having colour done in a salon, too.

A strand test

This is a colour test on a hair strand. The strand test should give you a good idea of the final colour result you will get, as well as the condition of the hair after colouring. Snip a small strip of hair (about 5mm/1/4in wide) from an easily hidden area, such as the nape of your neck; apply the colour mixture. Be sure to note how much processing time was required to achieve the desired results.

A patch test (aka skin test)

This is conducted by applying a small amount of the mixed colour to a hidden area of your skin, usually the inside of the forearm, to determine if you're allergic to any of the components; watch for redness, stinging, itching or burning. Manufacturers recommend a skin test should be carried out every time a colour is used. Don't assume because you've used a colour safely in the past that you have the green light to go ahead without a patch test this time round. People have been known to use a product without any problems for many years and then develop a reaction.

HAIRCOLOURING – A RISKY BUSINESS?

As many women tell us, the use of hair dyes can trigger irritation – or even contact dermatitis – with symptoms ranging from mild itchiness to blisters and, in some, hair loss.

But according to Marilyn Sherlock, consultant trichologist and member of the Academy of Expert Witnesses (who has frequently been called to give evidence in connection with hairdressing litigation), almost all hair-dye-linked problems arise from misuse – not because of the formulations themselves. Her advice is always to do a patch test first – whether you're having your hair coloured in a salon, or doing it at home. (Allergies are more common with single-process colour;

less so with the cap method of highlights or lowlights.) She also advises: 'Follow the instructions very carefully and time application; a lot of problems come from not reading the box – or leaving the colourant on the hair for too long.'

If you are experiencing scalp irritation and re-colour your hair frequently – say every three weeks – try leaving six weeks between treatments and touching up the hairline with Bobbi Brown Natural Brow Shaper (see p.119) to see if this helps. In addition, if you happen to have any cuts, sore spots or scratches on your scalp, it's wise to ensure that they are covered with a layer of Vaseline, to avoid possible penetration of the dye directly into the bloodstream.

AT-HOME HAIRCOLOURING

If Martha Stewart were to colour her hair at home, here's what she'd be telling you. The following rules apply to both permanent and semi-permanent colouring.

First of all...

• Read the instructions – preferably twice – before you start. (Do your skin and strand tests if advised on the packaging – see page 117.)

• At the start of your colouring session, coat the frame of your face with Vaseline, to stop the haircolour 'taking' on the skin around your hairline.

• Put an (un-precious) towel around your shoulders, for protection.

• Take off all your jewellery so that you don't make holes in the plastic gloves.

• If the gloves provided with the kit are too loose, grip them on with a wide rubber band at your wrist. (If that's too tight, try sticky tape instead.) Otherwise, in our experience, the gloves tend to slip.

• Use a timer or an alarm clock to tell you when the time's up. It's all too easy to lose track of the passing minutes when you're immersed in a favourite TV show/book/phone call to a friend.

Then for semi-permanent haircolour...

• After protecting your hands and shoulders, dampen and towel-dry hair. Then open the applicator bottle, shake and apply.

• Work the colour into the hair, starting at the temples, but avoid actually rubbing into the scalp.

• Once applied, pile hair loosely on top of your head.

• Set a timer – even if the colour is designed to stop developing automatically.

• When the timer rings, rinse with water. Be thorough and keep rinsing until the water runs clear.

• Shampoo, style and/or blow-dry.

For permanent haircolour...

• Read the instructions very carefully, and do strand and patch tests some 48 hours before (see page 117).

• Mix, following the instructions carefully. Snip off the top of the developing solution bottle, open the bottle and pour in the colourant. Cover and shake.

• Having wrapped yourself in gloves and towels (and splatter-proofed your bathroom), apply haircolour evenly to all sections of dry, undampened hair.

• Time the process exactly, according to manufacturer's instructions.

• When the timer rings, dampen hair and work the mixture in, saturating the roots but being careful not to rub the colour into the scalp.

• Immediately rinse, shampoo and condition. (Many permanent dyes feature a conditioner in the kit; use this.)

• Style and/or blow-dry as usual.

home haircolouring timetable

Louis Licari – the haircolouring guru responsible for the colour of stars like Susan Sarandon – advises women to plan ahead if they want to achieve the best home haircolouring results. Here is his countdown to perfect colour – with maximum shine.

Seven days before

Treat hair with a deep-conditioner or hair mask; this strengthens the hair but allows enough time for the product to be fully rinsed out, ensuring that your haircolour will 'take' evenly.

On the day

Don't shampoo just before colouring. (The natural oils that are secreted by your scalp will protect and hydrate it during the haircolouring process.)

The days after

Deep-condition with a hair mask once a week, beginning seven days after colouring. When it comes to day-to-day haircare, preserve your colour with shampoos and conditioners that have been specifically created for colour-treated hair.
NB: Louis Licari – like John Barrett and many other top hairdressers around the world – swears by the gloss-restoring Phytologie range of shampoos.

MORE HAIRCOLOURING SECRETS

- Try on a selection of wigs in a department store to see how the different colours flatter you. (Or not.)

- Should you visit a salon or try home colouring? According to Manhattan colourist Brad Johns, 'Home and salon products contain the same formulas. In a salon you pay for expertise.'

- Ask friends for recommendations of colourists. Your regular salon may not specialise in haircolouring and you may get better results at one that does.

- If you can't afford salon colour on a regular visit, aim for a salon visit at least once a year for advice on the choice of tints to use at home.

- Standing at the home haircolouring fixture in a store is baffling. (We know, we've done it.) It is so hard to tell from the model's picture on a box what the results will be like. If in doubt when choosing permanent colour, go for one shade lighter; it will be easier to remedy than if it's too dark.

- Dramatic colour switches require far more maintenance as roots show faster. If you want to stray further from what nature gave you (once upon a time), be prepared to spend extra time and money on touch-ups. Whereas picking a shade close to your natural colour will at least give the impression your colour is lasting longer.

- Be aware that active ingredients in dandruff shampoos may cause semi-permanent haircolour to fade more rapidly.

- If you live in a hard water area and colour your hair, use a deep-cleansing or 'clarifying' shampoo every few washes; when minerals build up on your hair, colouring (and perming agents) don't work as well.

- To extend the life of your semi-permanent haircolour, try a colour-enhancing conditioner between colour treatments. Pick a shade as close as possible to your coloured hair; a too-dark conditioner may 'stain' a shade that's lighter.

- After roots begin to show, you need to do a touch-up application. But don't apply colour to your whole head, as this will make the ends brittle and dry, creating 'stripes' in the hair as the colour is overloaded. Most packs include instructions for touch-ups; the difference is that you apply colour to roots only, working through to the ends for just a few minutes at the end of the treatment.

- If a home haircolouring treatment goes wrong, don't panic; check for a hotline number in the box. They may be able to tell you which shade will 'correct' the problem. With a semi-permanent colour, frequent use of a clarifying shampoo will speed up the rate at which it washes out again. But if a permanent colour has gone wrong, it's best to go to your salon, explain what's happened – and get them to put things right. Most salon professionals are highly experienced in fixing home haircolouring disasters.

- Consider a make-up makeover when you've had your haircolour done. Your old lipstick, blusher and eyeshadows may look wrong if you've had a haircolour overhaul.

magic wands

On behalf of grey-haired women everywhere, thank you, Bobbi Brown! Our favourite make-up artist – who has her own hair coloured regularly, to cover grey – has brought out a must-have product for women troubled by re-growth. Natural Brow Shaper will delight women who used the earlier generation of high-fashion 'hair mascaras' (from brands like Dior, Rimmel, etc), as it can be used for instant hair touch-ups between salon visits. Sarah, who lives hours from London and John Frieda's salon, is particularly grateful. (Before Bobbi invented the Brow Shaper, she was known to use an eyeliner pencil to cover up grey, when she had a regrowth S.O.S.!)

JENNIFER GUERRINI-MARALDI

We're inspired by Jennifer's joie de vivre, wonderful style (she's fashion editor of *Country Life* – but twinsets and pearls are not her mode) and by the fact this Australian-born beauty is a shining example of how sun protection and beauty care can keep a woman looking fabulous.

'Growing up in the harsh Melbourne sunlight with an outdoor lifestyle was the most fun – but not the best start in life for perfect skin. It was essential from an early age to take care of face and body. A strict rule, when we were growing up, was that no one went outside in summer without a hat. All the sunblock in the world will never be as effective as a hat. In fact, you need both. I always a wear a moisturiser with a high SPF. I love Decléor sun products.

'My mother, Noelle Heathcote, is known for her flawless English rose complexion: she never, never lay in the sun. Her strict beauty routine always intrigued me. I often sat on the edge of her dressing table watching my mother cleanse, moisturise and apply her make-up – the height of 1950s and 60s glamour! I'm sure I drove her mad with questions. I remember her telling me that as a teenage girl, during and after the war, there were no luxuries like cosmetics – so she used Vaseline on her lips and eyes to get a healthy shine.

'The training stuck with me and I'm addicted to the latest creams and cosmetics. I believe the big cosmetic houses produce the best of the latest beauty treats, because they pour so many millions into development. One longterm favourite is Clarins Eye Gel. But I do also swear by Eve Lom's Cleansing Cream and I love Jan Marini's products.

'On the question of facelifts, I'm definitely anti. I would never put myself through surgery, under anaesthetic, for reasons of vanity. And I hate that unnatural look. I swear by regular sessions with facialist Annette Cuddy in Chelsea. She uses a non-surgical facelift called Bio-Ultimate.

'I believe there are several key ingredients for looking good: fresh fruit and vegetables, exercise and plenty of sleep. (Obvious, and we're probably sick of being told them – but true.) But in my life these aren't always practical. Yes, I squeeze a few grapefruits or an orange in the morning, and I love vegetables and salad. It's the other things I also love

– dessert and champagne – which counterbalance my intentions! But as long as I exercise regularly, it all works. I hate gyms so a personal trainer taught me how to speed walk properly and I go round Hyde Park in London for 40 to 60 minutes three times a week, carrying 1kg weights.

'I love glamour and am married to an Italian who assumes women should always look glamorous. I think every woman should change her image every ten years. I call this "the decade dump". As the face matures, you need a different haircut (long hair can look wonderful as long as it's well groomed), different make-up – and a change of style of what you wear. The decade dump focuses the mind on a youthful image. Keep it simple: the rules are neat, shiny hair, natural make-up and plain, well-cut clothes, with not too much jewellery in the daytime. Feet are hugely overlooked: pedicures are a must every month in the summer.

'Time is always a problem. I tend to burn the candle at both ends, but make up for it by being a good cat-napper.

'But the most important ingredient for feeling and looking good is happiness. Growing up beside the sea was an idyllic childhood: free as a bird, breathing the purest air imaginable. While twenty years in England have been kind to the skin – it's the best climate for a beautiful complexion – I missed the sea. So my husband and I have found the perfect, stress-busting hideaway on the cliffs of Cornwall, overlooking beautiful beaches. We all need to switch off from our (increasingly) hectic lives, for the sake of good looks and wellbeing. If anything will contribute to feeling fabulous for ever, it's going to be the return to the seaside and rejuvenating walks on the wild, wide open beaches. Just being by the sea again. Full circle from childhood.

'I never think about age. I'm too busy. Every hour of the week is accounted for, so no time to ponder the inevitable. And I plan to go on working my whole life. Retire? Never.'

After trekking upwards of 50,000 miles by the age of 40, feet understandably begin to show signs of wear and tear. Here are the secrets of putting the spring back in your step.

FEET, DON'T FAIL US NOW

Blame our love of footwear, if you like, for the fact that women's feet age faster than men's. The glamorous, sexy shoes we love aren't designed for our natural wide-in-the-front, slim-at-the-heel shape – making foot faults commonplace: hammertoes, bunions and corns are all the result of crowded-toe conditions. Skin also changes with age; already the least lubricated on our body, skin on the feet becomes even drier – and prone to cracking and infection.

Of course, most of us tend to ignore our feet – until they start to hurt. According to the 'Pedicure King', Bastien Gonzalez – who jets between London, Dubai, Manhattan and Paris, lavishing TLC on famous feet with his 'medical pedicures' – prevention is better than cure. 'But it's never too late

to start getting feet healthy,' insists Bastien. Ideally, he believes, we should see a chiropodist or podiatrist every ten to 12 weeks for upkeep – more often if we have problems such as corns. The toenails will be trimmed (guarding against ingrown toenails), any buildup of hard skin can be whisked away, and the chiropodist can warn you of any incipient problems – which can then be treated.

The state of your feet also shows on your face: pinched feet equal a pinched expression. And since walking is nature's greatest anti-ageing exercise, happy feet are crucial to wellbeing. Caring for your feet with the same amount of TLC you'd lavish on your hands or your face can help you stay one jump ahead of foot problems.

note: **Twice as many women as men develop osteoarthritis. Be aware that signs of this disease can show up in the feet first; the initial symptoms are stiffness and pain in the joints; continued use of the joint then makes it stiffen up until it refuses to move at all. Make an appointment with your doctor for a diagnosis and treatment; regular visits to a chiropodist or podiatrist afterwards will enable them to monitor the development of the disease and stop or reduce any deformity that may occur as a result of osteoarthritis.**

FOOTNOTES

Just like our waistlines, feet can actually develop a kind of 'middle-aged spread': after years of being on the receiving end of pounding weight, the arch of the foot, which acts like a natural shock absorber, may begin to fall. As that arch flattens, the foot is pushed forwards and outwards – and may actually become a whole size larger by the age of 45. Foot insiders recommend, then, that we should have an annual foot measurement – to track any changes. (Keeping a healthy weight helps, too: remember that every pound may exert three times its weight whenever your foot hits the floor.)

• As well as an annual measuring session in a shoe shop, you can determine your own foot length to make sure you're buying the right size of shoe. Stand barefoot on a piece of thin cardboard with the heel of your foot perfectly at one edge of the cardboard. Mark the place reached by the longest toe – for many people, this is the second toe, not the big toe. Cut a thin strip of cardboard from the edge to the point of the longest toe. When you insert this into a shoe, there should be 7–14mm (3/8–5/8in) between the end of the cardboard and the heel of the shoe.

• The biggest favour that we can do our feet, according to the experts, is to whisk away hard skin – preferably every other day –with a foot file. Use the foot file on dry feet, before a bath or using a special foot scrub on wet feet. (We swear by Diamancel foot files; they're expensive – but worth the investment in foot happiness.) You can use a foot file on feet that have been in the bath or shower, but not if you've indulged in a long soak and feet have become

'spongey', as it's easy to remove too much skin. However, go lightly: Bastien advises that if you rub too hard, it just compacts the layers of skin, creating rather than easing build-up. In fact, some experts advise filing with an emery board daily – plus creaming, as below.

• Bastien's advice is that feet should also be creamed – with a special foot cream – at least once (preferably twice) a day. 'Use a special moisturiser, targeted at feet. Your regular body moisturiser isn't rich enough for the soles of the feet, which get steadily drier after the age of 40,' he explains. (Bastien makes his own fabulous deluxe cream.) You should really work the fatty pad on the ball of the foot, he says, which will help maintain the thickness of the padding – helping feet to stay comfy. (The only exception to the daily foot-creaming rule is if you have sweaty feet, in which case, you'll only make them clammier.)

• By the age of 60, the padding under our feet starts to thin – making walking painful. Padded insoles can make up for that loss of natural cushioning.

• Poor circulation is another challenge as we age. Because feet are the furthest point from the heart, they can get short-changed when it comes to blood supply. But regular exercise – think walking, again – will boost blood flow to the feet, beating chills as well as helping any infections and cuts to heal faster.

• Soaking feet for 15 minutes in a roomy plastic basin is another swift soother (see page 124 for suggestions of aromatherapy oils to use). If your feet feel particularly hot and prickly, add two drops of peppermint oil. Add a handful of dried milk for a moisturising soak.

• Change your shoes every day and vary your heel height to keep the muscles in your feet and calves flexible. (In women who habitually wear high heels, for instance, the calf muscles may actually shorten so they can't put their heels to the ground.) Try to go barefoot often, too.

• If you like to wear open sandals, slather your feet with an SPF in the mornings; feet are perfectly angled to pick up damaging UV rays, fast-forwarding ageing.

• Foot experts tell us that having corns removed by a professional chiropodist is far preferable to corn plasters, which don't discriminate between the skin of a corn and normal skin – so they may damage the surrounding tissue. (This could be particularly problematic for anyone with poor circulation, delicate skin or for diabetics.)

• Never buy shoes in the morning, when the feet are still rested; in the afternoon, you'll get a better fit.

• When out walking, take first-aid supplies – like plasters or antiseptic cream – with you, in case of accidents. If your toes chafe together, try a dab of Vaseline between them.

• That age-old advice – to put your feet up – really is the best way to combat swollen ankles and achy feet. Our tip is to lie comfortably on the floor or your bed with your feet propped at a 45-degree angle for ten minutes, so that extra fluid can drain away.

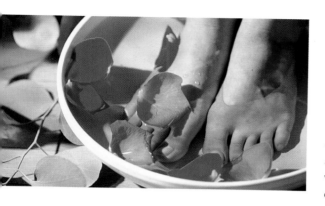

THE AROMA ZONE

Aromatherapy Associates gave us these aromatherapy suggestions for feet that have notched up plenty of miles. They prescribe regular foot baths, particularly for tired (or less-than-fragrant) feet and puffy ankles. Add up to 12 drops of cypress oil to warm water for smelly feet, and the same quantity of peppermint or lavender in cool water, on hot days. For cracked and super-dry feet, Aromatherapy Associates suggest concocting a special foot oil, made up of 90 per cent almond oil and 10 per cent wheatgerm oil, with 30 drops of healing frankincense oil per 50ml (2fl oz) of the base oil. Then massage it into feet on a nightly basis.

get fit feet fast

Exercising your feet will keep them flexible and strong (as well as beautiful), and will help you maintain your balance over the years to come. The Foot Health Council (an organisation founded to promote foot care) suggest these exercises for fabulously fit feet forever…

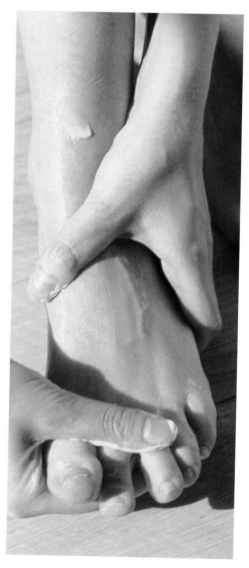

• Stand, feet slightly apart, and raise yourself slowly up, then down, with the weight on the toes. (If you have balance problems, hold on to a chair while you're doing this.)

• Stand on the bottom step of a staircase, toes extending over the edge. Bend the toes as if gripping the edge. Hold while counting to two, then flex the toes upwards and hold again to a count of two. Repeat several times, then reverse the way you're standing – this time dropping and raising the heels over the edge of the stair.

• Sit or lie with feet outstretched; arch one foot at a time and slowly sketch wide circles, first in one direction, then in the other. Repeat several times.

• Lie flat on the floor with the soles of your feet against the wall. Spread your toes wide as they grasp the surface and 'climb' the wall. (This is good for fighting cramp.)

• In addition, the Foot Health Council suggests standing and walking on tiptoe, as often as possible.

• We also like these suggestions from Gary Null and Dr Howard Robins, authors of *How to Keep Your Feet and Legs Healthy for a Lifetime*. To strengthen and increase the flexibility of your toes, try picking up pencils or marbles from the floor. Another exercise (to strengthen toes, feet and legs) is to draw the letters of the alphabet on the ground with the toes. Then do it again in the air. Write each letter in capitals, or joined-up writing, whatever – and do it several times a day. Then every muscle in your feet will get a terrific workout.

DIABETIC ALERT

Foot infections heal slowly in diabetics, so be very cautious about pedicures. In a salon, inform the staff you are diabetic; they will make sure not to use metal implements which may cut. In the same way, be especially careful using nail clippers, scissors, foot files or orange sticks if you are doing an at-home pedicure. Daily use of a tea tree oil-based foot lotion or a neat lavender oil massaged into your feet may help keep infections at bay.

AGEING FOOTCARE CHECKLIST

For healthy feet, do this at-home foot check-up once a month

Examine your nails for...
• ingrown toenails
• fungal infection
• nail thickening

Examine the skin on your feet for...
• athlete's foot
• corns and calluses
• skin lesions or any changes in any moles (ie, changes in colour, growth, itching, raised edges or bleeding)

Examine the skin on your legs for...
• varicose veins
• eczema
• skin lesions or mole changes

Check your footwear has...
• shock-absorbing soles
• uppers that are large enough to accommodate deformities, ie, bunions and/or hammertoes
• the right shoe size, as feet can change shape (shoes should grip the back of your foot, rather than flap)

MATURE PEDICURE

If you can't get to a salon for regular pedicures, try this at-home treatment for older feet, to help prevent the build-up of hard skin or the development of ingrown toenails.

1 Soak the feet for five minutes in a bowl of warm-to-hot water, to soften skin and nails. (Add a couple of drops of tea tree oil, if you like, as an antibacterial agent.)

2 Trim the toenails straight across and, to smooth them, buff lightly with a nail buffer (available through pharmacies or nail salons) or a big emery board (recommended by experts). The buffing shouldn't be abrasive; leave anything more aggressive to a chiropodist. NB: ideally, toenails should be softly rounded at the edges. Unfortunately, it's awkward to get the right angle to cut them correctly. The at-home cut to aim for is straight across; lightly file down any sharp edges; don't clip the corners to round them, as this can lead to ingrown toenails.

3 Rub in cuticle remover and, ultra-gently, push back cuticles with an orange stick around which you've wrapped cotton wool, candy-floss-style.

4 Exfoliate and moisturise the skin with an exfoliant cream, to remove dry, dead and flaky skin cells.

5 Gently remove hard skin with a foot file (or big emery board), especially around the heels and on the ball of the foot.

6 Massage a light moisturiser all over the feet, making sure it's a non-greasy one.

7 If you like to wear polish, clean nails with soapy water and dry thoroughly before applying base coat, two coats of polish and a top coat.

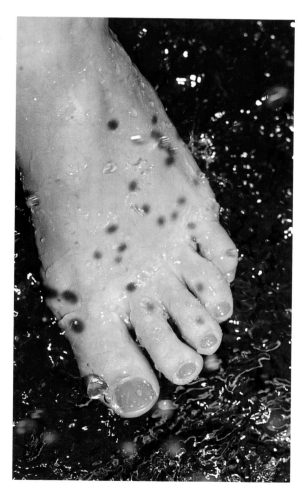

HOLDING BACK THE HANDS OF TIME

Gentlemen may never reveal a woman's age – but our hands will often give it away for us. However, happily it is possible to turn back the clock – with rejuvenating hand and nail care.

Hands go through hell. We subject them to daily dunkings in water, expose them to acidic household cleaners, endlessly handle pieces of paper (which strip vital oils from skin) – and forget that they're as vulnerable to sun damage as our faces. So even if our complexions get their daily slathering of UV protection, hands are left to the mercy of the elements, leading to 'age spots' – which form as the melanin (skin pigment) in unprotected skin reacts to sunlight.

Compared with the face, the hands have thinner skin, less fat to camouflage wrinkles and veins, and fewer oil glands and hair follicles – the structures which moisturise naturally and generate new skin. All of that adds up to accelerated ageing. But if we treat hands regularly with lots of TLC, they will reward us well into our dotage.

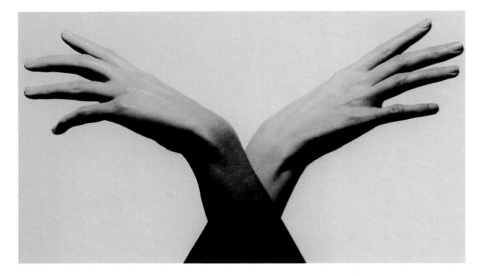

AGE-DEFYING MANICURE

After a certain age, 'nail guru' Robyn Opie – whose Chelsea Nail Studio, in London, is in many smart women's little black book – believes that nails should go a little shorter. 'The most flattering shape is square with rounded edges,' she says. 'That's also the least vulnerable to breaking. Also beautiful are slightly oval nails that follow the natural nail line.'

Colour should be chosen to flatter, too. 'Women who are self-conscious of their hands often choose an opaque nude or biscuity shade, which makes pale-skinned hands look green or grey. Stronger colours – or "pale brights" – are much more flattering. If you want to go pale, choose a strong sheer colour, like a pale pink or a sheer white.' (Some of the funkier colours – like gold, or a pretty pale blue – look good on hands of any age.) Robyn also gives the thumbs-up to the French manicure, where nails are clear rose and tips are painted white – but only if nails are nipped shorter. (Leave the talons to Barbra Streisand, please.)

1 Remove nail polish; use an acetone-free polish remover, which is less drying. (The label should say 'acetone-free' or 'gentle'.)

2 File and shape nails, filing in one direction only, from the sides to the centre. Use a padded emery board, now widely available from pharmacies and beauty supply stores, which is kinder to nails than old-fashioned metal files or 'sandpaper' boards. NB: Kathryn Marsden – who gives us the Nail Food suggestions on page 128 – recommends to people with fragile nails that they should always file the nails before removing polish, to lessen the risk of breaking. So if you think your nails are vulnerable to breakage, swap steps 1 and 2.

3 Soak nails in a small dish: add a few drops of jojoba or almond oil to warm water, or create an 'oil bath' of slightly warmed olive oil on its own.

4 Apply an exfoliant to your hands and slough away dull, dead skin. (Or use a handful of fine salt, mixed with some of the oil from your soak.)

5 Wipe hands and apply a moisturising face mask to the entire 'glove' area. Rest your hands on a towel while the mask gets to work. Remove mask according to the instructions.

6 Cuticles will be softened by the mask and oil treatment, ready for pushing back. (Use a special cuticle remover, if you prefer.) Push them back with a rubber-tipped hoof stick or orange stick wrapped in cotton wool.

7 Scrub nails gently with a nail brush and clean, warm water. (Or swipe away the last traces of cream/mask with a pad soaked in facial astringent.)

8 Buff nails, using the soft side of a nail buffer from The Body Shop (or the old-fashioned chamois kind, available from some pharmacies). Rub gently to polish nails naturally and never allow nails to get hot while buffing.

9 Apply rich hand cream. Wipe over nails with a cotton pad soaked in soapy water, to remove the cream before polishing.

10 Apply base coat (to prevent staining by nail enamel), two coats of enamel and a protective top coat. (To prolong the life of your manicure, reapply top coat each day.)

MORE HAND TIPS

• To start on a nail-improvement programme, we suggest that you invest in a manicure at the best salon available to you and watch and ask questions. If regular weekly manicures aren't within your budget or agenda, aim for at least four a year, for maintenance – and use them as a learning experience.

• Dermatologist Dr Fredric Brandt (dubbed 'the Baron of Botox', and now with his own signature cosmeceutical line), advises patients that fake tan can help camouflage obvious veins on the backs of hands.

• One of the biggest favours we can do hands is to keep hand cream by every set of taps in the house, on the desk and in the car. (Manicurist Mara Caskin suggests keeping hand cream by a radiator. 'It feels better and absorbs faster,' she maintains.)

• Ideally, look for a hand cream with an SPF15 for daily use; research has found that age spots will actually fade somewhat if hands are no longer exposed to UV light.

• Most of us want hand creams that sink in fast. But Robyn Opie warns that, in fact, these can have a drying effect on hands, because the alcohol in the formulation – which has a cooling action and makes the cream 'disappear' into hands fast – is actually dehydrating. 'So choose a rich, nourishing formulation that's a little stickier or greasier. It won't sink in quite so quickly, but your hands will love it.'

• Never submerge hands in water; even when you are in the bath, try to keep them above the waterline. (Soaking nails will also shorten the life of your manicure.)

• Robyn Opie suggests rubbing left-over night cream into your hands.

• We both suffer from fragile, flaky nails and have found the best way to prevent breaks is to make sure that nails are never left 'naked', except during a manicure itself. Testers for *The Handbag Beauty Bible* got excellent strengthening results from OPI Nail Envy, used as a base, topcoat or on its own for a clear manicure, and Jo also likes Sally Hansen Age Correct No Chip Top and Base Coat. Sarah digs her nails into Liz Earle's Superbalm, rubs in Dr Hauschka's Neem Nail Oil and takes silica capsules daily.

• Robyn Opie recommends carrying out this deep treatment at least once a week. 'Before you wash the dishes or do any hand washing, slather oil all over your hands – anything from olive oil to hazelnut oil or almond oil. Then put a layer of Vaseline on top of the oil to seal it in. Put on a pair of disposable plastic gloves and slip your hands inside your rubber gloves while you do the dishes. The warmth of the water turbocharges the treatment, and, once you have washed away the gunk, your hands will be super-smooth and silky.'

• Our tip is always to remember to take your own chosen polish to the salon when you have a professional manicure. Otherwise you (a) have to buy theirs, or (b) accept your manicure won't last as long, because you can't touch it up back home.

NAIL FOOD

Nutrition has a terrific impact on nail strength; good growth depends on a healthy diet to nourish new cells developing from the base. Nutritionist Kathryn Marsden is a walking advertisement for her own philosophy of nail nutrition. 'Mine are so strong, my husband insists I could undo screws with them,' she says.

As well as emphasising the importance of the best possible diet, Kathryn's vote goes to Essential Fatty Acids (EFAs). 'Evening primrose oil really does seem to have a significant effect on nails. My prescription is four to six capsules of Efamol Evening Primrose oil per day, or two capsules of mega-GLA by BioCare. In addition, you should be taking a good multimineral tablet with B_2, B_3 and zinc in it.' The white spots we see on nails signal a lack of zinc – not calcium, as is often thought.

Kathryn's other secret nail-booster is to buff regularly using a Body Shop nail buffer. 'One side of the buffer is gentle enough to be used *over* polish, without causing damage to a manicure; the friction stimulates blood flow. I keep several buffers around the house, where I can be reminded to use them during the day.' (Do be careful with most other buffers, which should only be used sparingly, if ever, on weak nails because they remove layers of nail, weakening them further over time.)

NAIL CLINIC

To Kathryn's diet prescription, Robyn Opie adds: 'Exercising regularly and taking time to de-stress has a hugely positive impact on nail health.' However, our experience is that even lifelong tough nails take a pounding around menopause, with cracks and splits occurring right down the nail – and a healthy lifestyle alone can't always fix the problems. So we asked Robyn for her solutions to the common challenges to older nails…

Soft and peeling nails 'Nails bend and flake because they're too moist. Nail hardeners work by reducing excess moisture – but I only recommend them for a seven-day burst, or they start to overdry the nails, making them brittle. For long-term improvements, massage the nail bed and the cuticle daily with oil, which will give you strong but flexible nails that resist breaking. Almond or hazelnut oil is perfect; add a drop of lavender oil to make it smell pretty.'

Dry, brittle nails 'If nails snap, rather than flake, it's because they're dehydrated. Over-exposure to water and sunshine (if nails are unprotected) can dry out nails. Brittle nails will also respond to daily oil treatments.'

Ridges 'For longitudinal ridges, very lightly buff nails on a regular basis to smooth them. Then use a ridge-filling base coat to create a smooth base for polish.' (Ridges can sometimes be the result of a damaged nail bed, caused by a yeast infection, or from cuticles that have been cut or damaged; they can also be a sign of zinc deficiency.)

Lengthways splits 'Sometimes, nails start to split down a ridge, all the way down to the base of the nail. An acrylic nail will mend the split and allow the nail to grow out; at the same time, feeding the nail bed via oil massages will encourage healthy future growth.'

Dull, colourless nails 'A healthy nail is a pink nail. Dull, colourless nails may be a sign of a circulation problem. If you squeeze a nail, it will go white; if it takes more than three seconds for the pinkness to reappear, that's another sign of poor circulation. Daily nail massage will help – as will physical exercise.' (NB: smoking can stain nails brownish-yellow – another good reason to give up.)

Uneven skintone 'A big age giveaway is patchiness and dullness, as the skin starts to become more transparent. The fix: exfoliate skin regularly. Face masks, used on the hands, also brighten skin. And I've seen amazing, albeit temporary results from electrical non-surgical facelift machines, used on the hands; they tighten the skin and improve circulation.'

SEE YOUR DOCTOR IF YOU HAVE…

…thickening, crumbling or opaque nails; this may indicate a fungal infection.

…pitting, spotting and thickening – classic signs of nail psoriasis.

…darkening of the nail: a brown or black streak that begins at the base of the nail and extends to the tip could be a sign of melanoma (skin cancer), requiring urgent attention. Some antibiotics, such as tetracycline, may turn nails dark grey; this should fade once the drug is out of your system and the nail grows out.

And if nail problems continue for months rather than weeks, ask your GP for blood tests to determine any nutritional deficits.

high-tech hands

Cosmetic surgery for hands is fast growing in popularity. According to Professor Nicholas Lowe, age spots (aka sun spots) on hands can now be removed by laser. Medical peels – using AHAs – are also being used to fade dark spots; they remove surface layers – revealing brighter skin underneath. Some doctors prescribe Retin-A to improve skin on prematurely aged hands, while others are now carrying out vein removal operations (like those for varicose veins on legs) to take out the prominent veins that make some women self-conscious (see You're So Vein, page 142). Because hands tend to get thinner as we age, some doctors have experimented with extracting fat from, for example, the buttocks, and injecting it into the hands – but this bruises badly and provides only short-term plumping. As with any cosmetic surgery procedure, these should never be undertaken lightly – no matter how self-conscious you are about your handshake.

HAND WORKOUT

Exercising the hands regularly will help keep them youthful and supple. (Doctors actually prescribe knitting for arthritic hands.) Follow these simple exercises, to keep hands in tip-top condition.

- Stand upright with your hands by your sides. Raise them slowly, moving the hands back and forth from the wrist. Hold arms out at shoulder level. Then lower them, flexing the hands in the same way.

- Sit or stand with your arms by your sides. Turn the whole arm and hand so that the palms are facing backwards. Clench the fists and – with your arms straight – push them back as far as you can, several times.

- Lace your fingers in a prayer position, then turn them inside out so that palms are facing out, meanwhile straightening and pushing arms in front of you at chest level. Hold for 30 seconds and release. Repeat.

- To keep fingers flexible, stretch and separate your fingers. When you feel a good stretch, hold for five minutes. Follow with a thumb workout: hold your right hand outstretched, away from your body. With your left hand, very gently pull your right thumb back towards your body. Hold for five seconds. Switch hands. (These exercises will also help prevent RSI – Repetitive Strain Injury – so if you use a keyboard, take regular exercise breaks and give them this workout.)

- Look for squidgy 'stress balls' that offer a double-whammy: they exercise the muscles of the hands as well as helping to bust stress.

- To encourage nails to grow more quickly, improve circulation to fingertips and hands by drumming them on the table as if you were playing the piano.

- Or, better still, why not try piano lessons? According to a spokesman at the Royal Academy of Music, although the optimum age to begin piano lessons is between seven and ten, 'It's never too late to take up piano – which definitely promotes suppleness and strength. People can successfully play through their seventies and eighties, with great flexibility.' It may be too late to become a concert pianist. But belated piano-playing may mean that in future years we can still get the lid off a crusted-up honey jar.

tried & tested HAND CREAMS

Our hands instantly give away our age, so, over a period of months, our testers tried dozens of anti-ageing hand creams with a slew of time-defying features such as anti-wrinkle and anti-age-spot technology, alongside the moisturising, smoothing properties we expect in a hand cream. Some incorporate an SPF, to guard against the ageing effects of UV light.

ORIGINS MAKE A DIFFERENCE REJUVENATING HAND TREATMENT
Score: 8.31/10

This joint first place treatment from Origins includes 'Rose of Jericho' (a desert plant), plus trehalose (from corn sugar), sea algae, skullcap and meadowfoam seed oil. Almost every tester rhapsodised about its softening qualities and the improvement to nails and cuticles, but only three testers saw a difference in age spots.

Comments: 'Startlingly effective; you only need a 5p-sized dollop and within seconds, it's like you've pulled on silk gloves; also it's stopped my eczema, which is a miracle' • 'completely lovely smell: improved smoothness/softness in seconds – slight reduction in age spots over three weeks' • 'immediately softened and enriched skin so hands looked better' • 'my dry hands looked soft and cared for straight away' • 'perfect consistency, not runny, greasy or sticky' • 'nails shinier and cuticles more groomed' • 'I loved this cream – it's very pampering and a little goes a very long way, so, although it seems expensive, it's worth it' • 'this is the first

brilliant hand cream I've found which incorporates such amazing cuticle and nail effects, particularly after gardening and washing-up' .

LA PRAIRIE CELLULAR HAND CREAM
Score: 8.31/10

The ultra-luxe La Prairie body range harnesses marine ingredients for their moisturising, nutritive and protective powers: sea lettuce, green and red algae, sea fennel, sea minerals, antioxidant sea parsley – even seawater, as well as firming AHAs from heather and apple, plus age-spot fading mulberry, skullcap and liquorice. Testers were less impressed by the promised anti-age-spot properties than other aspects of this cream.

Comments: 'Very definite improvement: all dryness was combated by the cream, and hands feel soft and silky' • 'I garden without gloves – so my hands get very dry from the soil, and scrubbing them with soap after. Applying this cream felt like a huge relief' • 'after six weeks, there's a build-up of firmness, radiance and glow' • 'a marked improvement – miraculous for a nurse who washes her hands at least 40 times a day' • 'the skin on the backs of my hands – formerly dry and red – is now shiny and smooth' • 'age spots a little less noticeable'.

SISLEY SISLEŸA GLOBAL ANTI-AGE HAND CREAM
Score: 8.22/10

Among those-in-the-beauty-know, Sisley has a 'cult' status, up there with Crème de la Mer. Our testers certainly loved this

silky-textured deluxe treatment, with an anti-age-spot action (from nasturtium petals and apple seed), repairing shea butter, vitamin A and E, plus a useful SPF10. (Not quite as high as we'd like to see in creams for the exposed hand area, but much better than nothing.)

Comments: 'From the first application I could see a difference; after six weeks, dryness completely gone, age spots less obvious (though not gone completely) and the ridges on my hard nails are less obvious' • 'the colour of my hands and wrists is much better – they don't look so grey; nails seem a little stronger' • 'age spots less pronounced; hands a lot smoother and "energised" • 'worth using for the gorgeous smell alone' • 'my hands are scrawny and veiny, which I hate; after using this, they look more luminous, plumped-up and smooth – really loved this cream'.

CRÈME DE LA MER THE HAND TREATMENT
Score: 8.2/10

The spiel for this luxuriously priced, silky-smooth cream declares the use of 'Deconstructed Waters, to deliver a Skin Lightening Complex along with marine proteins and botanicals that improve skin colour and clarity'. In other words, it's designed to fade age spots, with consistent use. Crème de la Mer – which became part of the Estée Lauder empire, some years ago – prescribe a special massage application technique, to boost the ingredients' effectiveness.

Comments: 'Instantly my hands felt as if

they'd been massaged for an hour, with a dewy, gorgeous glow; skintone is now more uniform and luminous, and nails are so much stronger – this stuff is addictive' • a dramatic effect on wrinkles, age spots faded – and also softened the skin on my elbows' • 'a slight improvement in age spots' • 'I have lovely soft hands, which definitely look younger, to me; the dry pads on my fingers have gone – and it has also helped heal a scar on the side of my thumb, caused by a burn from the iron – I loved this product' • 'massaging it in last thing at night has a calming effect; I absolutely loved this product'.

beauty steal **CHAMPNEYS OVERNIGHT SENSATION HAND TREATMENT**
Score: 8.08/10

This was definitely the most affordable of the treatments that scored exceptionally with our testers, from a range which has been formulated with the input of experienced therapists from the Champneys spa empire. Champneys promise that this cream, which is rich in vitamin E, shea butter, jojoba oil, liquorice and panthenol, will 'transform dry, tired and ageing hands overnight', leaving them feeling soft and supple. It has an almost solid consistency, which then melts in contact with the skin.

Comments: 'After a month my hands look and feel younger; I used to have dry skin on my hands but this has changed them for good' • 'when I wake up in the morning my hands are very soft and silky; they look less dehydrated, and more youthful' • 'my hands are softer and more even in skintone' • 'the best hand cream I have ever used – it totally delivers and my hands look better than they have done for years; I feel quite evangelical about it.'

AHAVA SOURCE LIGHTENING HAND TREATMENT
Score: 8.08/10

This SPF 12 cream, with a complex of Dead Sea minerals (like all products in this range) to lighten and brighten hands, is just a little more expensive than the Champneys Overnight Sensation cream with which it tied.

Comments: 'Age spots on back of hands appear reduced; improvement in skin softness, texture – slight colour imperfections evened out' • 'absorbs so quickly and doesn't leave a greasy residue; over the weeks, my gardener's mitts have improved steadily' • 'one age spot on my right hand is not as noticeable' • 'the wrinkly, saggy look is replaced by much younger-looking skin; also the first winter I've got through without split skin on my fingers' • 'hands look and feel 100 times more lovely'.

DIOR AGE SPOT CORRECTION HAND CREAM SPF15
Score: 7.9/10

From a targeted range containing Dior's 'D-30 Complex', this aims at melanin-producing cells deep in the skin, using an enzyme to inhibit their activity. Not every tester found it corrected age spots, though. But we applaud the inclusion of an SPF15.

Comments: 'Lovely to use; the moisturising effect lasts a long time – I had to hide it from my husband, who kept pinching it' • 'didn't really treat age spots, but the light-reflecting properties did make them less noticeable' • 'absorbed surprisingly quickly for such a rich cream' • 'brown spots did fade slightly' • 'skin texture smoother, hands softer – and after six weeks, age spots very slightly lightened' • 'great for use in the office as no greasy residue on the keyboard; palms are considerably softer

and wrists less wrinkly-looking' • 'very obvious which hand I've been using this on; my age spots are far less noticeable, and my left hand no longer has fine lines – so I will balance them out by applying to my right hand, as well!'

GUERLAIN SUPER AQUA-SERUM HAND CRÈME OPTIMUM HYDRATION SPF15
Score: 7.9/10

Guerlain would like us to think of this as a regenerative 'glove', for use as often as possible. The rather flowery bumf they supply trumpets the fact that it 'works in the same way as the sap of the Atlas Blue Cedar, re-creating a state of ideal hydration'! Certainly, it boasts a characteristically pretty Guerlain fragrance – and also delivers an SPF15 and anti-UV protection. Although it's said to target age spots, only one of our testers experienced results on that front. They did, though, almost universally comment on its power to strengthen and improve nails.

Comments: 'Madonna and I are the same age and my body has been likened to hers – well, my hands, actually! Awful, old-looking – but after using this product, all I can say is: "Madonna, eat your heart out!" Beautiful smell, got rid of age spots, moisturises all day' • 'if ever there was a product to make you feel special, this is it; if I could have given my skin a drink of water, this is what it would be like: super-fast, and leaves my hands feeling like they have silk gloves on' • 'the first application of this just blew me away; it did more in one layer than all the cheap ones I've used; my nails have started growing, ragnails have healed, and I have started wearing rings, to show my hands off again' • 'my nails have actually grown to a decent length again'.

EYES

Even if you've had perfect vision all your life, there's a moment somewhere in your forties when you realise your vision is changing. The print in newspapers seems to be getting smaller. Or your arms are getting shorter…

Presbyopia – middle-aged eye spread – is the first sign of ageing eyes for most of us. What happens is that because the lens of the eye, like the whole of your body, begins to lose elasticity, it loses its ability to adjust (accommodate, in medical terminology) to objects near to your eye. So reading, especially small newsprint, becomes increasingly difficult. Long-distance vision, however, can be unaffected. (Sarah has presbyopia but 20/20 vision otherwise.) Reading glasses are the easy answer – but remembering where you've put them can be a problem.

Although little can be done about presbyopia, there is evidence that some other ageing eye problems, including cataracts (opacity of the lens resulting in blurred vision), age-related macular degeneration (AMD, the leading cause of irreversible blindness in elderly people which affects the central and most important part of the retina) and glaucoma, can be prevented – or helped – by good nutrition. The chief culprit once again appears to be oxidative stress, the process where free radical molecules cause damage to the cells (see page 13). An increasing number of studies shows that both cataracts and AMD are helped by an antioxidant-rich diet and supplementation.

In one American study, women who had religiously taken vitamin C in daily doses ranging from 400mg to 1g for at least a decade were 77 per cent less likely to develop cataracts than others who had relatively little vitamin C in their diets. Vitamin E has also been shown to help in the prevention of cataracts. Another study found that the highest dietary intake of two carotenoid antioxidants – lutein and zeaxanthin, found naturally in spinach, kale and corn – was linked to a 57 per cent lower risk of AMD.

Supplementation may also have a therapeutic effect on eye disorders and AMD in particular. A product called Brite Eyes with Lutein by LifeTime Vitamins contains the exact formula used with significant success in the Age Related Eye Disorder Study (AREDS). Brite Eyes also contains anxioxidants, including bilberry and beta-carotene.

Glaucoma (where vision is impaired because of abnormally high pressure on the eye) may also be helped by supplementation with antioxidants, ginkgo biloba extract plus fish oil. Research is ongoing in these areas, worldwide – so watch this space.

There is also an increasing number of high-tech options for vision problems. Consult your family doctor and optometrist for details.

LOOKING BETTER

Whatever comes out of your mouth, your eyes speak the truth about how you feel. And they give the game away about your age.

The skin surrounding the eyes is the thinnest on the body, so the moisture evaporates easily – and precisely because eyes are so expressive, the skin around them forms wrinkles faster than elsewhere on the face. Then there's the barrage of abuse that eyes are subjected to: contact lenses, mascara, eyeliner, marathon sessions at the computer, smoke-filled rooms and sunlight.

'But the good news is that everybody can improve eye appearance, to some degree,' says US dermatologist Debra Jaliman.

Although we're generally fans of the simplest possible skincare, there is definitely a case for using a special eye zone product, particularly if you have sensitive eyes. We love Green People's Eye Gel and Eye Cream. (Key words to look for, if you have sensitive eyes and aren't sure whether a product will suit you, are 'hypo-allergenic', 'fragrance-free' and/or 'ophthalmologically tested'). (See 'Getting Rid of Milia', page 136.)

how to protect your eyes

● Eat an antioxidant-rich diet, with lots of fresh foods and oil-rich fish if you're not a vegetarian; consider antioxidant supplements.

● Exercise regularly to reduce stress and consequent eye pressure.

● Don't smoke – it robs the body of nutrients, is a major risk factor for eye diseases and makes your eyes look red and feel gritty.

● Protect your eyes from UV rays with big sunglasses, particularly when the sun's rays are strongest between 10am and 3pm. Unprotected 35-year-old eyes can have the vision problems of a 50-year-old.

● Have regular eye checks, yearly if you wear glasses or contact lenses. Check out symptoms such as increased dryness, redness, itching, burning or watering.

● Be aware that some medications, eg, antidepressants, steroids, blood pressure lowering drugs, antihistamines and some antibiotics may affect your eye health.

UNPACK YOUR EYE BAGS

Some mornings we wake up with eye bags we could put our shopping in. Here are our favourite low-tech de-baggers:

• Exercise. Eye bags are due to fluid retention; bags are usually worse in the morning because fluid collects overnight. Any load-bearing exercise where gravity is pulling the fluid down, eg, jogging or bouncing on a mini-trampoline, even running up and down stairs, makes bags disappear swiftly south.

• Apply ice, or 'frozen' teaspoons. Wrap a cube of ice in clingfilm, smooth round and over your bags – supermodel Linda Evangelista's favourite trick – or do the same with teaspoons (stainless steel rather than family silver) chilled in the freezer.

• Lie down with slices of cucumber or raw potato over your eyes.

• With your middle fingers, tap the under-eye area lightly and swiftly, moving from the inner to outer corner of your eye and back, for a minute or two.

• Track your bags: are they worse when you've eaten certain foods, eg, wheat or salty foods, after you drink alcohol, or in smoky rooms? If so, you could be sensitive to that substance. Try avoiding it and see if that makes a difference.

• Try switching brands of products you use daily, eg, eye make-up remover, contact lens solution or mascara, in case you are sensitive to one of those.

• Try substituting an eye gel for your regular skin cream, night and morning; the lighter gel on the eye zone may help puffiness.

• If you still want to use a cream at night, make sure it stays out of your eyes by using a very thin layer; pat along the bony ridge beneath your eye, not right under the lashes, then lightly dot cream along brow-bone, under the brow.

what to do about dry eyes

Postmenopausal women are especially susceptible to the syndrome of dry eyes. According to Michael S Berlin, MD, director of the Glaucoma Institute of Beverly Hills at Cedars-Sinai Medical Center, that's because a reduction in oestrogen production can go hand-in-hand with a reduction in tear production. If your eyes sting, burn or feel scratchy, it may help to humidify your home and work environments – and to wear sunglasses outdoors. You can also buy artificial tears – Hypromellose – which can be used safely to 'top up' your own tear level. Pharmacist Shabir Daya of Victoria Health recommends taking Essential Oil Formula capsules, which contain omega-3, 6 and 9, and using VisiClear Eye Drops to soothe and lubricate.

Don't be tempted to turn to over-the-counter eye drops to combat any redness, however. While these are OK for special occasions, eyes can become dependent on them very quickly. In a study at Baylor College of Medicine in Houston, scientists found that patients with unexplained conjunctivitis – redness, swelling and tearing – had been overusing eye drops which are meant to be used for three consecutive days at most. (If eyes still hurt after that, see a doctor.) Patients had used the drops daily for between three and 20 years. Once the patients stopped the drops, the condition cleared up, usually within a month.

THROW AWAY YOUR SPECS

Some people believe that glasses make our eyes lazy – and what we really need isn't a new pair of Armani frames, but an eye workout.

THE BATES METHOD

There's no question that glasses are a godsend for millions with less-than-perfect sight. But they may encourage wearers' eyes to become lazy. The less frequently you give your eyes a workout – even by just going without your glasses whenever you safely can – the less they may achieve without the aid of lenses.

The good news is that this downward spiral can possibly be stopped – even reversed – with the Bates Method, a technique which keeps eyes strong and healthy. About a century ago, Dr William H Bates cupped his eyes in the palms of his hands to help himself relax at the end of an exhausting day. Just a few minutes later, he found his eyes no longer ached and he felt infinitely zippier. From this simple start, he devised a regime which combines relaxation exercises with stimulation exercises. Techniques include regular blinking, swaying the body with the eyes closed ('sunning'), twice-daily splashing of the eyes with cold water several times, focusing exercises, 'shifting' – or rapidly moving your gaze around – and palming. All is revealed in his bestselling *Better Eyesight without Glasses* and we explain a couple of simple exercises here.

Bates exercises can be practised simply at home, but are best first taught by a recommended teacher (see Directory). One famous Bates Method devotee was the author Aldous Huxley, whose sight condemned him to milk-bottle glasses at 45. Within a couple of months of starting Bates, he was able to read without glasses.

The following relaxation exercises will give you some idea of what the Bates Method can offer you; they also work as terrific de-stressors, even for those with 20/20 vision. Do them without glasses or contacts. Breathe calmly and deeply and don't strain or try to overachieve.

(NB: eye problems can accompany various illnesses, such as diabetes or glaucoma; experts suggest that you should be screened for these before undertaking any vision improvement programme.)

Palming A method for resting your eyes in what Bates called 'perfect blackness', free of visual demands. Rub your hands briskly together for about 20 seconds until you feel heat and tingling. Then cup your hands and place your palms over your closed eyes without actually touching them or applying any pressure. Rest your fingers lightly on your forehead and concentrate on your breathing. Without straining or opening your eyes, see the blackness before you.

Blinking Many people with refractive sight problems don't blink enough. Deliberate blinking – which also helps fight dry eyes – is simple: make dozens of delicate butterfly blinks for 10–20 seconds, several times a day, gently turning your head from left to right, and back again. Frequent blinking momentarily rests the eyes, stretches the eye muscles, massages the eyeballs and exercises the pupils by continuously dilating and contracting.

what the Bates method did for me

AGE: 45
PROFESSION: MANUFACTURER'S AGENT

'At 39, my sight started to deteriorate. I realised I was seeing things in a blur and went along to be fitted for glasses. The optician diagnosed an astigmatism (I had had a squint as a child) and myopia. He prescribed glasses and I very quickly couldn't see without them. In 1996 an article about the Bates Method inspired me to find a local teacher. I started with five minutes' practice daily and built up to ten. As well as palming, blinking and sunning, I was given exercises such as looking for a different colour for each day so you see with your brain as well as your eyes. You pick out all the red around you: letter boxes, hats, flowers, etc. It was my 'goal' to be able to read the writing on a Cointreau bottle label about four feet away on the kitchen table. About nine days in, after palming, I saw the word 'Cointreau' perfectly clearly for one micro-second. After six or seven sessions, I took my glasses off and have never needed them again. I do my practice for 20 minutes twice a day, before and after work. The Bates Method has changed my life. Nobody tells you that there is an alternative to glasses. For me, this is nothing less than a miracle.'

THROUGH THE PINHOLE

Another option to turn eyes into regular little Arnold Schwarzeneggers is pinhole or Trayner glasses (available from many health-food shops) which you wear, instead of your usual prescription, for just 15 minutes daily during everyday activities such as using the computer, reading or watching TV. Hundreds of tiny pinholes force the eyes' ciliary muscles both to relax and to exercise, building up flexibility and strength and reminding eyes how to focus on their own without tight muscular control – helping to avoid headaches and visual stress. It takes a week to get used to them.

Manufacturers say they may also reduce the heart rate – a well-known stress indicator – by up to four per cent during ten-minute test periods.

SUPPLEMENTARY STORY

We know that antioxidants are powerful helpers for our eyesight. Jo Fairley has her own theories about the link between diet and vision.

How Jo threw away her glasses...

'Ever since childhood, I have had an astigmatism – one eye doesn't focus on exactly the same point as the other. I wore specs off and on through childhood and for almost 20 years as an adult. About three years ago, I noticed that things became blurred when I wore my glasses – basically all the time. The reason, a somewhat bemused optician told me, was that my eyes had actually improved considerably – odd, because, generally, an astigmatism is for life. He told me firmly that the improvement could not be diet related but I have my own theory. I eat a very healthy fruit, veg and whole grains diet, but I also noticed that the improvement coincided with beginning to take blue-green algae, which is extremely high in beta-carotene, the 'eyesight vitamin'. If I run out of the algae and forget to stock up, it becomes harder to read number plates or the digital numbers on the video recorder. Now I have virtually stopped wearing my glasses, my eyes have become steadily stronger; I can sit in front of a VDU for long stretches without strain. Yet when I wore glasses, taking them off for a few minutes and trying to read or look at the screen made my eyes hurt.

'Based on my own experience, my advice would be that, unless you're in actual physical danger through not wearing them – for instance, driving – then it's worth giving specs a rest whenever you can.'

what pinhole glasses did for me

AGE: 55

PROFESSION: ESTATE AGENT

'I have worn glasses for distance most of my life. In my late forties, I started to have problems reading and focusing. I didn't want to wear bifocals so I decided to look for other ways of treating my sight problems. I found Trayner Pinhole Glasses at a health exhibition and the people on the stand explained they are helpful for all kinds of health problems. I started wearing these lightweight glasses for 20 minutes a day, plus an hour before I went to bed, watching TV or reading. You're aware of the holes for about five minutes but then your eyes adjust and they simply fade away so you see normally. When I first started wearing them, I still had to take my reading glasses around with me in case the lighting was bad or the print small. After three months, I noticed a significant improvement in both long and near sight. My eyes were so much better I barely wore my glasses at all. At an eye check four years later, my optician told me my astigmatism had gone and my vision was back to 20/20. I said, 'It must be the pinhole glasses'; he said, 'That's ridiculous.' But I know the glasses work; I just think the optical world is threatened by alternative sight improvement techniques.

'When I first got a computer, I suffered burning, redness and irritation. So now I keep a pair of Trayner glasses beside the computer for the odd symptom of eye strain and I can work for two or three hours without any problems. My one message would be: stick with it. Even if you don't experience any improvements at first, persist because they can really change your life.'

GETTING RID OF MILIA

Milia are tiny oil-filled cysts just under the upper layer of the skin, usually found near the eyes or on the cheeks, most often on oily or acne-prone skins. But they can develop around the eye area whatever your skin type. 'When you wear glasses, sweat builds up in the area where your frames rest,' explains Wilma F Bergfeld, MD, of the Cleveland Clinic Foundation. 'The excess oil gets under your skin and forms milia.' Prevent this by wiping the area under your glasses frames with a soft cloth and occasionally clean your glasses with an astringent cleanser or soap. If the milia don't disappear, don't attempt to pick or remove them yourself. Visit a doctor or dermatologist who will probably 'nick' the top with a sterile scalpel or electric needle. Skin peels can also be effective.

choosing glamorous spec frames

Despite advances in contact lens manufacture – and leaps in laser surgery – more than half of all people with sight problems choose to wear specs. Then, of course, there are sunglasses – the positively glamorous side of specs – where we can all indulge the Jackie O in our souls, and at the same time protect our eyes against damaging UV light, which may cause inflammation of the cornea, cataracts and degeneration of the macula – the most important part of the retina for vision. Even on a moderately cloudy day, up to 80 per cent of UV light can still reach the eye.

Specs can be a great accessory – enhancing good points, minimising less attractive ones, and balancing face shapes. The trouble is that, until recently, guidelines on how to choose a new pair have been limited to vision criteria only – perish the thought that you might want to consider how they look. As spec wearers ourselves – Jo for an astigmatism (in the past) and Sarah for presbyopia – we have taken a keen interest in putting these guidelines into practice.

The choice of sizes and shapes nowadays is enormous. Materials are mainly plastic or, today's fave, metal: usually titanium and stainless steel. Not only do these look elegant, but metal is durable and should last for two to three years, by which time most people want a new pair anyway. Or *pairs*: many women choose to have two or more sets, discreet for day, more flamboyant for evenings. But beware of rimless specs: although they suit most faces, they are more fragile because the lenses are unsupported.

Today's frames are smaller as well as lighter. But unless you're remorselessly trendy – and very young-looking – very small frames tend to be unflattering for older faces. Aim for medium- or larger-size frames which camouflage the eye area and its bags and wrinkles. Large-framed sunglasses effectively prevent UV light getting to the vulnerable skin of the eye area.

It's worth finding an optician who will give you a personal consultation. Also, take time to look around and see that you're getting the best deal, price-wise.

The guidelines for choosing the most flattering frames are straightforward. Gather up several pairs, and consult with assistants at the stores before making your final decision:

• Avoid frames the same shape as your face; if you don't know your face shape, find out with the technique on page 96.

Oval face Can wear just about any size and shape frame: for fun, try angular or rounded 'aviator' shapes or small, round wire frames.

Round face Go for shapes that will slim down your features, eg, cat's eye, above, rectangular or square.

Square face Look for light, thin frames in an oval shape.

Long face Opt for wide frames, not too small, to counteract the length and narrowness of your face. Steer clear of small, square styles.

• Make sure your eye is in the centre of each frame.

• Close-set eyes will appear more wide apart with lightweight, thin, small frames and a narrow bridge.

• The top bar should follow or echo the line of your eyebrows.

• Owners of one and a half, or even double chins, should look for (non-extreme) cat's eye or oval frames which are higher at the temple and so distract from the chin.

• Try toning the frame colour to your hair: silver, gold, grey, tortoiseshell, etc. If you want to go superfunky, try combinations such as turquoise or red with salt and pepper hair; olive, bronze or antique gold with fair or red hair; shiny black with olive or dark skintones.

• Ensure frame sits comfortably on your nose; small – but not major – adjustments can be made.

• Shorten long noses with a lower bridge; for short noses, choose a higher bridge in a light colour.

• If you suffer from headaches under strip lighting, you may want to try having your reading glasses tinted to cut the brightness.

SUNGLASSES

• Always choose sunglasses which give 100 per cent UVA and UVB absorption; this is an especially important consideration as you get older, because it helps protect against radiation reaching the lens and possibly causing inflammation of the cornea or cataracts.

• For very hot climates, also look for infra-red protection to keep your eyes cool and comfortable.

• Buy plastic (eg, acrylic or polycarbonate) lenses, if possible; these don't break as easily as glass and are less permeable to UV rays. If you do decide to buy glass, opt for toughened or laminated.

KNOW THE JARGON

Photochromic lenses change tint with light intensity so are good for driving or whenever the amount of light may vary, eg, with time of day or where you are.

Polarised lenses reduce glare from light that bounces off flat surfaces, eg, roads, water or snow.

Fixed tint lenses (made from plastic) are good for very light-sensitive people or those who have had cataracts.

Do you need sunglasses even when it's cloudy?

Yes, yes and yes! For the same reason you should wear sunscreen even when it's overcast: there is still plenty of harmful UV light getting through. Good sunglasses are much, much more than a fashion accessory: they help to keep your eyes healthy. According to Dr Hugh R Taylor of Johns Hopkins University, USA: 'When it comes to eyes, the more protection you have against UV radiation the better, especially against UVB radiation.' Wraparound or large-frame glasses are best, as they block more light, not only giving you protection against vision damage but also helping to stop wrinkles forming around the eye zone and keeping eyes cool and comfortable.

TOOTH TALK

A wide smile with gleaming teeth is one of the most attractive assets for anyone. But teeth often get relegated to 'poor relation' status, possibly because they may seem less important or obvious than smooth skin or glossy hair. But taking care of your teeth, gums and mouth and finding a good dentist is essential.

Meticulous daily dental care is vital always, but particularly as we get older. The big thing to avoid is the build-up of plaque, the layer (mainly composed of bacteria) on the surface of teeth which leads to disease of both teeth and gums, and to dental caries (tooth decay). You can prevent plaque by brushing and flossing teeth regularly and thoroughly, and having regular checkups with the dentist and hygienist. The same care can prevent gum disease, caused by bacterial infection, which increases in frequency as we age, causing receding gums and sometimes even loss of teeth.

Although hormones have never been definitively proved to be linked to gum disease, some dentists notice that the state of women's mouths alters cyclically, which suggests a hormonal connection (see 'Beating Bad Breath', opposite). So it may be worth considering scheduling dental checkups mid-cycle, if possible, and also taking extra care of teeth, gums and mouth around menopause.

London-based dentist, David Klaff, president of the British Academy of Aesthetic Dentists, helped us compile these top tooth tips for keeping your pearly whites gleaming with health.

TOP TOOTH TIPS

● Consult your dentist to set up an examination and hygiene programme about every three to six months routinely, depending on your individual needs.

● Change your toothbrush every month; ask your dentist about the most suitable design for you and the best brushing technique. Rotary electric brushes currently seem to show excellent results for controlling plaque, removing food debris and stimulating the gums (please remember to change the head every month.)

● Clean your teeth when you get out of bed in the morning to remove debris.

● Floss your teeth regularly at night.

● Consider also using a water-jet/water-pick at night (available via your dentist or at a pharmacy) to flush out debris.

● Eat well: nutritional deficiency may cause gum disease by reducing resistance.

● Eliminate unnecessary acidity in the mouth, caused by sugar, citrus fruit and stress; it increases the risk of tooth decay and gum disease by allowing harmful bacteria to flourish.

● Drink lots of water – particularly if you like citrus fruit or orange or grapefruit juice. (Remember that other fruits and vegetables give you vitamin C too.)

● Take positive steps to relax and combat stress: many dentists believe that stress also causes an acid environment in the mouth.

● Opt for gentle, non-stinging mouth sprays. (Look for plant-based natural sprays, like Janina Programme Opale Spray Cleanser; see Directory.)

● Don't smoke: as well as causing yellowing teeth and bad breath, smoking prevents healing and contributes to disease by restricting blood supply.

beating bad breath

Bad breath, or halitosis, is a confidence downer of the first order. Dr Mervyn Druian, of London Cosmetic Dentistry and a spokesman for the British Dental Association, says bad breath is not just a one-off social discomfort: it can cause marital break-ups and even spell the end of promising careers.

Fortunately, however, it's relatively simple to treat. There are plenty of at-home measures you can follow, but if the problem persists, do consult your dentist. Very, very rarely bad breath could indicate a disease condition, such as diabetes, liver or kidney disease or a cancer. So don't ever let it go on for weeks or months.

Why it happens

Some 90 per cent of stale-smelling breath is due to the millions of bacteria living – and dying – in your mouth. The dead bugs form the whiffy sulphurous gases. Bleeding gums cause an unattractive combination of dead and dying blood cells to add to the bugs. The bug population also shoots up when there's infection or inflammation. Saliva, your mouth's waste-disposal operator (also a very efficient antiseptic), just can't cope, so the dead cells hang around creating problems.

Bacteria also get trapped in the dark folds at the back of the tongue where oxygen (which knocks out the sulphur compounds) can't reach easily.

Other causes of bad breath include: broken or cracked fillings which can trap food particles, sinusitis or rhinitis which can cause a bug-laden drip from the back of your nose into your mouth during the night, smoking (a major cause of very unpleasant breath), poor digestion, plus any activity that dries up saliva and allows decaying bugs to make a takeover bid for your mouth. So beware of dieting, only eating one meal a day, not drinking enough water or drinking too much caffeine, and medications including anti-allergy drugs, diuretics, tranquillisers, blood pressure lowering drugs and any drugs containing sulphur. Basically, anything that makes you feel as if a gerbil has slumbered in your mouth overnight may make it smell that way too.

Hormonal cycles from puberty through to menopause affect breath (and possibly gum disease, see opposite), creating more sulphurous compounds for a couple of days before menstruation, around ovulation and during menopause (because of a slightly drier mouth and an increased likelihood of bleeding gums due to stress).

Consulting your dentist and following the guidelines below should keep the problem at bay.

Is it you?

Check your breath in any one of the following ways:

• Lick the soft part of your wrist, using the farthest back part of your tongue, wait a few seconds then sniff.
• Rub a piece of tissue or gauze at the back of the tongue, then smell it.
• Draw a piece of dental floss back and forward several times between your top back teeth, then give that the sniff test.
• Dentists may also use a device called a halimeter. If the result gives you a nasty moment, don't despair, there is a range of simple remedies.

What to do

The top tooth tips on the previous page will go a long way to solving any long-term problem, but for an instant fix, try the following:

• Brush carefully on the outside and inside of your teeth and gums, then sluice with a specific antiseptic rinse: try RetarDENT toothpaste, and RetarDEX rinse (made by Rowpar Pharmaceuticals); or Janina Ultrawhite Toothpaste and oral spray (which is brilliant for travelling).
NB: avoid rinses with alcohol; they may provide an instant fix, but the alcohol will then dry the mouth, making bad breath more likely.
• Floss thoroughly.
• Use a special tongue cleaner, which you can buy at a pharmacy, or use an upside-down spoon, rubbed back and forth across the tongue at the back of the mouth.
• Chew on a sugarless dental gum.
• Stop smoking.

WHAT'S THE ALTERNATIVE?
Natural helpers

• Try an infusion of myrrh; or make your own peppermint, rosemary, fenugreek or sage infusions with one dessertspoon of fresh or dried herbs infused in a cup of boiling water and strained.
• Chew on cinnamon, or liquorice root, star anise, cloves, fresh parsley, apple or carrot.
• Plant-based 'green drinks' may also help: try a tablespoon of liquidised alfalfa or wheat-grass juice twice daily, added to water or fruit juice.
• Use digestive enzymes (eg, those made by Udo Erasmus) and/or chlorophyll; if tooth decay or gum disease are suspected, use goldenseal tincture (Eclectic Institute) with Co-Q10 100mg (LifeTime Vitamins) and Gengigel.

WHAT YOUR DENTIST CAN DO FOR YOU

Scaling and polishing

Make a regular three- or six-monthly appointment with the dental hygienist to remove plaque and surface stains, and give teeth a brightening polish. Ultrasonic scalers are generally available; the latest technology is the air-abrader – an 'airgun' which fires a flow of abrasive powder at the teeth at high speed, giving excellent results in stain removal.

Bleaching

Whitening teeth professionally with either carbamide peroxide or hydrogen peroxide is one of the fastest-growing dentistry treatments in the UK. However, professional bleaching has been the subject of a long-running controversy. Originally there was a possible carcinogenic risk (not substantiated), but now the problem is essentially a trade dispute over the use of branded bleaching systems.

You can buy over-the-counter systems for home use, but these contain minuscule levels of peroxide and, say dentists, will have little effect.

Before you go ahead with tooth-bleaching, your dentist must establish that your teeth are sound and healthy. Bleaching can improve the hue and brightness of teeth by 60–70 per cent. Stains from antiobiotic tetracycline treatment in early youth are less likely to go, and bleaching won't touch the big white patches on teeth resulting from demineralisation; the only way to remove those is with micro-abrasion (polishing with a mild, safe form of hydrochloric acid). The bleach may also penetrate down the sides of any existing white fillings and cause sensitivity. Fillings may need to be replaced after bleaching.

Some dentists use a bright white light to activate the bleach; others the speedier argon 'laser' which looks set to become the tooth-bleaching choice of the future. The Zoom2 power system takes just 45 minutes to achieve a six-to-eight shade improvement and, because of its new formulation, greatly reduces any post-whitening sensitivity.

Crowns

The traditional way of repairing a broken or unsightly tooth. The tooth is ground down to a peg and a replica fitted over the top. Top dentists are now working in porcelains so strong that internal metal supports are no longer necessary, with the result that crowns look translucent and perfectly lifelike. With healthy gums, a porcelain crown will last 20 years.

Bonding

Sticking tooth-coloured material to an existing tooth is an alternative to crowning. The tooth is etched using a weak acid, to create a rough surface on the tooth to which composite or porcelain inlays (which fit entirely within the confines of the prepared tooth) or onlays (which fit over the prepared tooth and cover all or most of the biting surface) are attached (see 'Veneers', below). Bonding is far easier than other means of fixing. It's particularly helpful for filling gaps between widely spaced front teeth. But it's much shorter lasting – about five years.

Veneers

The 'vogue' solution for perfecting a smile, favoured by the A-list. Veneers can correct a multitude of problems, including crowded teeth, discoloration, worn-down teeth, gaps and gummy smiles. A very thin layer of porcelain, rather like a false fingernail, is bonded to the tooth. Veneers now are so thin that they can be applied without removing any of the tooth. Disadvantages are that veneers can chip and, in rare cases, may fall off, usually because of poor technique. Since teeth darken with age, veneers will need to be done at intervals to match other teeth. Always ask to see samples of the dentist's work and ask about the quality of the ceramicist who creates the porcelain. The most skilful are said to be in America.

Implants

Titanium screw implants have revolutionised the replacement of lost teeth. Until recently their use was limited to places in the mouth where there was sufficient bone to screw in the implants. Now, however, advanced surgical techniques mean that surgeons can graft the patient's own bone from another part of the body into the mouth as a 'bed' for the implant.

Amalgams

Removing amalgam fillings and replacing them with composite (plastic and ceramic) or porcelain fillings will give you an all-white yawn instead of a mouth like an ironmonger's. For larger fillings, where shrinkage is a big problem, the dentist takes an impression and the filling is made in the laboratory and pre-shrunk before use. These fillings are also stronger and can be excellently colour-matched, but are more expensive.

Mercury is a powerful neurotoxin which has been shown to escape from fillings and to lodge in tissues, and many dentists have stopped using it. However, the dental governing bodies in America and Great Britain, among other countries, maintain it's perfectly safe and there is no link between ill health (apart from temporary and minor problems) and mercury fillings. Many women we know are delighted to have had their mercury fillings removed. At the very least, their mouths taste fresher; at most, all sorts of chronic symptoms such as headaches, joint aches, skin conditions, fatigue and non-specific ill health improve. Amalgam fillings also cause cracks and fractures in teeth. The downside is that tooth-coloured fillings, although becoming more durable, cannot yet match the 15-year-plus lifespan of the amalgam filling, and require more skilful fitting. NB: because mercury vapour may be released as the fillings are removed, they must be replaced by a dentist who is experienced and takes due precautions.

Bite problems

Problems with your bite can cause a range of symptoms, including headaches (especially in the temples), migraine, poor sleeping patterns, neck/shoulder pain, dizziness, tingling fingertips, tinnitus, facial pain and worn-down teeth. The cause is an imbalance between the head/neck musculature and the teeth. Treatment involves a full examination, then a muscle scan to identify the source of the problem, followed by expert therapy to relax the muscles and restore harmony between teeth and muscles. It can be a long job, involving an orthotic insert.

Orthodontics

A trained orthodontist can correct the alignment of teeth, adjust the relationship of teeth and jaw, improve the shape of the jaw and correct congenital anomalies such as cleft lip and palate. In extreme cases, the upper and lower jaw are so out of alignment that surgery is also necessary.

The latest ceramic technology means that fixed braces can be tooth-coloured, rather than silver. Treatment may take 18 months to two years.

what veneers did for me

AGE: 40. PROFESSION: ADVERTISING SALES EXECUTIVE

'My teeth had always looked disproportionately small and had yellowed a lot. Veneers offered an affordable way of getting them fixed. At my initial consultation with the cosmetic dentist, computer imagery superimposed an image of eight new teeth on to a picture of me, allowing me to see how I could look. The dentist first took a putty "cast" of my teeth, then smoothed them under local anaesthetic and filed some away before a temporary plate was cemented into place while the veneers were being prepared. I was walking around after about three hours, feeling a bit achey but otherwise fine. The plate felt like a set of false teeth, and what was left of my teeth felt very sensitive to hot and cold. My second visit – to have the veneers permanently cemented into place – took about two hours. The main discomfort, aside from more local anaesthetics, is having to keep your teeth totally dry so the cement will stick. The moment you're told you can't have a drink you just long for one. They had to tug the plate off first and the new teeth had to be scraped and smoothed a bit; my mouth felt a bit gritty while that was going on. They felt enormous at first, but now they feel like they've always been there. Friends said they knew something was different, but couldn't work out what it was. All those years when I could have had smile-worthy teeth.'

REJUVENATING SURGERY

YOU'RE SO VEIN... We have a love-hate relationship with our veins. We love them when they're invisible, pumping blood healthily from A to B, but often become extremely self-conscious about them when they start to show. Today, you can zap them, collapse them – even have some veins completely removed. So if you're feeling vain about the appearance of yours, here are the latest options...

SPIDER VEINS ON THE FACE AND LEGS
(aka telangiectasia, dermal flares or broken veins)

THE CAUSES: In fact, the veins aren't 'broken' at all – they simply become more obvious as skin thins with the years. Some women are genetically predisposed to them, especially the pale and fine-skinned. Aggravating factors include hormonal changes due to pregnancy/menopause, the pill, HRT, injury, sunburn and alcohol. 'Spider veins are very common in women from twenty up,' says our 'vein expert', Mr John Scurr. Spider veins can also be painful; the pain is often cyclical and related to periods.

THE FIXES

Electrolysis: Using a similar needle technique to hair removal, an electrical current is passed into the skin to cauterise the vein so the blood is absorbed into the body. This treatment is available through beauty salons but, advises Mr Scurr, 'you need to be very sure that the beautician knows what she's doing and has the back-up to deal with potential problems, such as infection.'
Micro-sclerotherapy: This uses an ultra-fine needle to inject a

'sclerosing' solution – a detergent substance – into the vein. (In the US, saline solution is commonly used.) The solution irritates the vein lining, causing the sides to stick together so that the top, just under the skin, is no longer filled with blood and visible.

The introduction of foam sclerotherapy has improved the result. The solution injected (Polydocanol) remains the same but it is made into a foam which clears a larger area, produces a more long lasting effect and is particularly valuable for treating the venous blushes (flares). Sclerotherapy leaves no scab or obvious mark. Sometimes results are instant, but there may be up to a three-month wait for veins to clear. In some cases, blood slowly leaks back into the veins so they become apparent again. The length of the session – and the number – will depend on the extent of the problem.
Laser treatment: Lasers can be used for removal of spider veins on the legs or face. It is vital that they are used properly, by a qualified surgeon, and, even then, Mr Scurr is

cautious; laser treatment can leave some scarring, as it burns the skin and can create blistering. Mr Scurr prefers PhotoDerm pulsed light therapy – one of the 'new generation' laser-type technologies – which uses a high-intensity light filtered to a very narrow wavelength to heat and destroy the blood vessels. (Different surgeons have different laser preferences, however.) PhotoDerm works best where there is greatest contrast, ie, red veins against pale skin. The light, delivered in pulsating flashes, feels like a rubber band snapping at the skin. Afterwards you may look as though you have a slight sunburn in treated areas; if you're unlucky, you might peel. But as the redness fades, so do the underlying flares. Repeated treatments may be necessary.

'To get the best results, avoid exposure to the sun for three months before treatment. But,' Mr Scurr adds, 'spider veins are like weeds in the garden. If you're predisposed towards them, you're likely to get another crop, at some stage in the future.'

VARICOSE VEINS ON THE LEGS

THE CAUSES

These dilated superficial veins, which occur when veins in the legs aren't able to return blood efficiently to the heart, can range from a minor bulge to a bunch-of-grapes effect. Veins have a series of one-way valves, which direct blood flow towards the heart. If the valves work poorly, blood stagnates in the veins, so they become swollen and twisted. Anyone who spends a lot of time standing around is vulnerable, as are pregnant women. Over the years, there is a loss of tone in the valves and veins, leading to a higher incidence of varicose veins. Sufferers may complain of symptoms including aching, tingling, tired legs with irritation, cramp or pain on standing. There are potential dangers in ignoring obvious varicose veins. Over time, the skin around the ankle may start to discolour, and may actually break down, causing an ulcer; these are difficult to heal and very unpleasant.

THE FIXES

Before treatment, a clinical examination, with an ultrasound scan, to measure blood flow.

Support hose: surgical support stockings or tights may control minor varicose veins.

Drug treatment: recent drugs that have become available, such as Paroven in the UK or Daflon in France, constrict the muscle and improve tone in the vein wall, giving a constricting effect – but only while you are taking the drug.

Ultrasound-guided foam sclerotherapy (see opposite): this is the same treatment as for spider veins, but under ultrasound control. It won't replace surgery in all cases, but is very useful because it makes the same solutions into a foam, so a large volume can be given, with more complete results. It can also follow surgery (see below) for large varicose veins.

Surgery: often the best solution for advanced veins – the earlier the better. After a light general anaesthetic, incisions are made in the groin (sometimes behind the knee), to stop the blood supply to the legs during surgery, and the veins are hooked out through the cuts. Ultrasound guide foam sclerotherapy may then be used. Post-operatively, after 12 hours in bandages, compression stockings are worn day and night, then removed at night, for ten days in all.

Infection is extremely rare but if wounds become red and angry, tell your doctor immediately.

Laser: VNUS Closure and EVLT (Endo Venous Laser Treatment) can be used to remove the main superficial vein giving rise to varicosities. Less bruising is likely in the thighs, but further treatment will be required, and complications are quite common.

SELF-HELP

• Regular exercise is excellent prevention. Walking is ideal .
• Avoid sitting for long periods of time. Walk around every hour for a few minutes.
• While sitting, lift your legs and point and flex feet to stimulate calf muscles and help circulation.

THE ALTERNATIVES

Over time, naturopath Jan de Vries believes that a combination of diet, exercise and prescribed homoeopathic remedies (hyperisan, urticalcin and aesculus hipp, or horse chestnut) can be effective, plus avoiding alcohol, nicotine and salt, and, for some, twice-yearly courses of vitamin E. Dr Joseph Pizzorno suggests it can be beneficial to eat liberal amounts of cherries, blackberries, bilberries and other dark berries, which contain high levels of bioflavonoids, together with garlic, onions, ginger and cayenne.

Mr Scurr recommends Zinopin Daily, a supplement with maritime pine bark and ginger, which supports the circulation and reduces ankle swelling.

Pharmacist Shabir Daya suggests VeinFactors by Futurebiotics, which contains a range of plant extracts plus natural bio-accelerators to help absorption.

essential steps in choosing a surgeon

Just because this is often called 'cosmetic' surgery, don't forget that all surgery – to any part of your face, scalp or body – is an invasive procedure which carries risks, some potentially life-threatening. It is also very expensive – very little cosmetic surgery is available on health services or on medical insurance – but just because surgeons charge a lot, that doesn't mean that they are necessarily any good. It is vital that you take time and care choosing the person you're putting in charge of your looks – and your life. Most important of all, according to Rajiv Grover who drew up these guidelines for the British Association of Aesthetic Plastic Surgeons (of which he is a Council member), is to have a good relationship with your surgeon and to be thorough in your questioning – but not aggressive.

We recommend that before you finally decide on surgery, you try the other non-surgical lifestyle options we write about in this book.

FINDING A SURGEON

Beware of glossy advertising and free consultations. Reputable surgeons will rarely need to advertise and will almost always charge a fee for the preliminary consultation.

Ask for recommendations from friends or consult your family doctor (beware, though, that many won't know either the best person to go to or the best procedures).

Be wary of travelling overseas for surgery unless you are completely certain of the arrangements for follow-up, and the management of any problems that may arise.

Also be aware that it is difficult to verify qualifications of surgeons overseas, and if there are problems after surgery you may have no form of redress in a foreign healthcare system.

BEFORE THE CONSULTATION

Check the surgeon's qualifications: He/she should have passed the exam FRCS (Plast), the only specialist examination in plastic surgery. Some older surgeons may not have done this, as it was not introduced until 1988.

He/she should be a member of the British Association of Aesthetic Plastic Surgeons (BAAPS) and should be listed on the GMC Specialist Register for Plastic Surgery.

DURING THE CONSULTATION

It is crucial that you understand the procedure, so make sure the surgeon explains what it involves clearly and in terms you can understand. Ask for written information to take away.

Also make sure you have a clear picture of the likely outcome, so that you have a realistic idea of whether it can achieve what you are looking for.

Ask the surgeon for a comprehensive written list of the possible risks, bearing in mind that no procedure is 100 per cent risk free. Also, ask for details of the expected recovery time and about the possiblity that you might need to be absent from work.

The surgeon must be experienced in performing the procedure you are contemplating, so don't feel shy about asking when they started, how many such operations they carry out each month and how many they have done in total.

Also ask if there have been any problems, which have led to legal action by patients.

Make sure you get written details of precise costs and whether these cover follow-up visits, and for how long. Most reputable surgeons include post-op checks for six to 12 months, or as long as they consider necessary.

VERY IMPORTANT You must choose someone you trust and feel a rapport with. Remember, you are putting your life in their hands.

AFTER THE CONSULTATION

Do not be rushed into making a decision or paying a deposit. Remember, this is a serious commitment.

Unless the circumstances are exceptional, avoid having surgery immediately after a major stress event such as the break-up of a relationship, arrival of children, bereavement, moving house or changing job.

FINALLY Don't be afraid to say no.

non-surgical techniques

A new generation of minimally invasive devices and techniques has emerged: these soften lines and wrinkles, plump up facial contours and minimise skin conditions such as acne, rosacea and pigmentation. Wendy Lewis, an international image enhancement coach and authority on cosmetic surgery, gave us her expert views on the best techniques.

ALTERNATIVES TO SURGERY

Today, the trend is for smaller cosmetic procedures at a younger age, to produce subtle changes that delay the need for more drastic nips and tucks. Another option is to combine several procedures which act synergistically, such as a light laser with a filler. Botox®, for instance, complements almost anything else you're having done, and can make other treatments last longer. But the golden rule still applies: always protect against sun damage with high-factor sun preps, big glasses and a close-woven, big-brimmed hat.

Non-surgical treatments can be divided into six basic categories: botulinum toxins (Botox), fillers, resurfacing, biorejuvenatioon, thread lifting and radio frequency skin tightening. Remember that most of these treatments are considered medical procedures so should be administered by a qualified and experienced doctor/surgeon, or in some cases nurse or dentist, who specialises in aesthetics and has an in-depth knowledge of facial anatomy.

BOTULINUM TOXIN

Originally a medical treatment for eye spasms and disorders of the central nervous system, botulinum toxin (marketed as Botox®, Vistabel® and Dysport®) is the most popular cosmetic treatment today, with a good safety record. Botulinum toxin is a purified protein made from botulism bacteria, which binds to the nerve endings, preventing the release of the chemical transmitter which activates muscles. Injected into the face, it paralyses the small muscles, which cause frown lines, crow's feet and other wrinkles. Medically, it's used under arms, and on hands and feet to reduce sweating.

It's truly a wash 'n' go treatment, and you can wear make-up immediately. Results will last from three to six months, so regular top-ups are essential.

Risks: if the toxin is not injected properly, it's possible (although rare) to get an eyebrow or eyelid droop; this should resolve on its own within two to three weeks. Some asymmetries are possible and can be adjusted. If you have a history of neuromuscular disorders, or are sensitive to albumin (which is a constituent), discuss this before undergoing treatment. For more information, go to www.botox.com. **NB** for information about Botox testing on mice, contact Fund for the Replacement of Animals in Medical Experiments, www.frame.org.uk.

FILLERS

For rapid results on frown lines, scars, creases, thin lips or sunken cheeks, injectable fillers are effective. The most common material is hyaluronic acid; others include collagen from cows or pigs, as well as synthetics and combination products. Fillers may be short-term – eg, hyaluronic acids and collagens – or longer-lasting, eg, poly-L-lactic acid and fat (your own). The most controversial category is the permanent and semi-permanent variety, such as liquid silicone. No filler can really give permanent results, because your face will continue to age around the injection site.

Fillers are classified as medical devices; there are currently more than 70 fillers on the market, with new ones under clinical investigation all the time.

The US Food and Drugs Administration has the most stringent criteria, so if in doubt check the product's status in America.

Biorejuvenation

Here is Wendy's list of the fillers she considers the safest and most effective. There may be some swelling and bruising for 24 to 48 hours, but make-up can be worn immediately. Fillers that contain anaesthetic can hurt less to inject but you can request a numbing cream with any of them.

This mesotherapy technique uses micro-injections to infuse hyaluronic acid, antioxidant vitamins or homoeopathic remedies into the middle layer of the skin to improve texture, tone and quality The main options are Restylane® Vital and Elastence to plump up dry, dehydrated, lined and/or sun-damaged skin on the face, neck, chest and hands.
RISKS: slight bruising and tenderness.
Biorejuvenation should last two to three months after three to four treatments.
INFORMATION: www.restylane.com, www.inamed.com.

Restylane®

The Restylane® family, the most widely used filler worldwide, is based on hyaluronic acid, a natural polysaccharide found in the body's connective tissues.
The options are: Restylane Touch for fine lines; Restylane for lines and wrinkles; Restylane Perlane for deeper creases and folds; Restylane SubQ, implanted to build up chin and cheek contours; Restylane Lipp for enhancing lips.
Risks: Restylane® is naturally broken down by the body over time and is considered very safe. If lumps do occur, they can be injected with hyaluronidase, an enzyme that breaks down hyaluronic acid quickly.

Restylane should last six to nine months or longer, depending on the particular product, where it's injected and in what quantity.
Information: www.restylane.com

Puragen®

Good for lines, wrinkles, lips and scars, this product, launched in 2004, has a complex molecular formation which may make it more lasting and durable. Puragen® Plus is the only hyaluronic acid filler available containing lidocaine, a local anaesthetic. It will last from six to

12 months, depending on how much is used, and where.
Risks: as for Restylane.
Information: www.mentorcorp.com.

Hydrafill® Softline

Hydrafill® Softline and Hydrafill® Softline Max are non-animal, hyaluronic gel fillers. Each varies in concentration and is suitable for a different area, including lips, fine lines, shallow scars and deep creases.
Risks: considered to be a safe filler. Hydrafill® should last for six months or longer.
Information: www.inamed.com.

Radiesse ™

This thick white substance, heavier than most hyaluronic acid gels, is made from tiny microspheres of calcium hydroxylapatite, which has a consistency similar to bone and has been used safely for many years. Mainly used for deeper folds, 'marionette' lines, and to fill out cheek contours and jawline; injections can improve facial scars/nasal defects, too.
Healing time: some swelling or bruising for a few days.

Risks: has EU licence as medical device for plastic/reconstructive surgery. Radiesse™ should last for 12 months or longer.
Information: www.bioforminc.com.

Evolence®

This pig collagen is fortified with a natural sugar substance, and injected superficially into shallow lines and wrinkles. Its uses are similar to Zyplast®, see below.
Risks: there is a small risk of allergic reaction, but pre-testing is not required. If you have had any sensitivity to another collagen product, check with your doctor first. Evolence® should last for six to 12 months.
Information: www.evolence.com

Zyderm®/Zyplast®

Collagen, the original filler, approved by the US FDA in 1981, is derived from cows (as with Zyderm® and Zyplast®(, or from human tissue banks (as with Cosmpderm® and Cosmoplast®). They contain a local anaesthetic.
Risks: allergy tests are required (usually one or two) – three per cent

of people may be allergic. It should last two to four months.
Information: wwwinamed.com.

Sculptra®

This is injected very deeply into hollows, folds and creases. It comes as a powder, and can be mixed with an anaesthetic before treatment.
Risks: lumps may occur if it's injected too superficially. Results are gradual. A course of three treatments will last for 18 to 36 months.
Information: www.sculptra.com.

Fat transfer

This process involves several stages. Fat is extracted by syringe from wherever you have it, cleansed, then re-injected into facial folds and creases, lips or hollows. Results are variable. Expect swelling and redness for several days, also bruising.
Risks: infection, asymmetries and overcorrection, or lumps and bumps, which may require fat removal

Fat transfer can last from six months to several years, The most mobile areas tend to last least time – eg, round the lips and mouth – because there's more muscle activity.

Isolagen

A skin sample is taken from behind your ear, the cells grown and then your own fresh, healthy fibroblast cells are injected into fine lines, scarring – including acne scars – neck and décolleté lines and ageing hands.
Risks: you can't be allergic to your own cells. Results are variable but cells continue to grow for 12 to 18 months and longer.
Information: www.isolagenuk.com.

RESURFACING

Skin resurfacing includes peels and microdermabrasion, light therapy and lasers.

Skin peels

A chemical solution is applied to cleaned skin, left for a specified period, then neutralised. Glycolic peels improve skin texture and tone, acne, hyperpigmentation or discoloration and fine lines. TCA (trichloroacetic acid) peels are used for more severe sun damage, acne scars and melasma (brown patches). Light peels need no recovery time, although there may be some pinkness and mild flaking. Deeper peels may lead to peeling, crusting and redness for seven days.
RISKS: skin lightening or darkening, blotches, scabbing, scarring, temporary redness or blistering.
Don't expose your skin to the sun for at least two to three weeks.
Superficial glycolic peels are given in a course, three to four weeks apart.
DIY peel kits are an alternative or you can use them as an in-between treatment (see page 36). Deeper TCA peels may be a one-off or repeated as needed to maintain the effects and improvement.

Microdermabrasion

This entails blasting the face with sterile micro-particles to rub off the very top skin layer, then vacuuming out the particles and the dead skin. Microdermabrasion can improve texture, tone and superficial lines, fade brown spots and enhance the penetration of topical products for ageing or acne.
Skin may be rosy just after, but make-up can be worn immediately.
RISKS: none, unless the therapist is too aggressive during the treatment and causes a scab or irritation.
Results are instant. A course of four to six treatments is recommended, two to four weeks apart, with ongoing maintenance treatment every one or two months. A DIY kit can also be used at home (see page 36).

Fraxel®

This new laser device can treat brown patches, melasma, sun damage, fine lines, wrinkles, skin texture and scarring, including acne, and possibly cellulite and stretch marks. It is quite uncomfortable and requires a numbing cream and a cooling device during the procedure.
Healing time is three to five days. Mild swelling and redness will occur, possibly with dryness and flaking. Make-up cannot be worn until skin is fully healed.
Around the eyes, swelling may be severe for several days.
RISKS: scarring, skin lightening and darkening with poor laser use.
Results may last 18 months after three to four treatments.
Information: www.fraxel.com.

INTENSE PULSED LIGHT THERAPY (IPL)

This intense light treatment is considered the safest of the 'non-ablative' resurfacing procedures, ie, those which do not cause trauma to the skin – unlike lasers (see right). IPL works well for acne, brown spots and for hair removal. You can also expect improvements in tone and texture.

There is usually no recovery time, though there may be slight redness and some minor discomfort afterwards. Dark spots may appear darker before they fall off. Treated red lesions may appear slightly bruised and acne or skin tightening may look like mild sunburn for a few days. Acne and rosacea should improve gradually over a period of a few months.

Risks: this is considered safe even for dark skins, though they are more at risk of darker or light patches, scars and blotches.

Treatments are usually done in a series of four to six, typically every three to six weeks.

RADIO FREQUENCY SKIN TIGHTENING

The new generation of devices offers alternatives for tightening loose skin on various areas of the face and body without surgery. Thermage® is the best known, but other models are being developed.

Radio frequency basically heats specific targets, literally cooking the collagen layers to shrink or contract tissues under the skin and produce a subtle lifting and tightening effect on areas of the face, neck and chest, including jowls and jawline. It also treats acne scars. New devices are used for thighs, abdomen, buttocks and hands.

Expect mild redness for some hours, but make-up can be worn immediately.

Risks: it's very uncomfortable and requires numbing cream. Scarring or irregularities may occur, but rarely.

The effects last for 18 months or longer; additional treatments may be done any time.

Information, www.thermage.com.

THREAD LIFTS

Tiny 'barbed' sutures or threads are inserted with a long needle through tiny incisions to lift and tighten the skin of the brows, cheeks and jowls. New collagen bundles form around the barbs.Thread lifting (aka suture suspension) is most suitable for people aged 35 to 55, with some sagging but still good tone and elasticity. It doesn't work well on very heavy faces or where a lot of skin needs to be removed, in which case a facelift is recommended. Thicker heavier threads are starting to be used to lift saggy breasts, upper arms, buttocks and inner thighs. But the technique, which is pretty new (the first brand Contour Threads® was approved for marketing in America in 2005), is controversial, because doctors can't seem to agree on the best method.

Healing time is between three and seven days and there may be bruising, swelling, redness or tightness.

Risks include infection, asymmetries, thread breakage, extrusion, pulling and surface irregularities.

Effects last from one to four years.

CO_2 laser: friend or foe?

Unlike IPL (see left), lasers work by causing trauma to the skin, literally burning away the top layer to reduce wrinkles, smooth and tighten skin, remove age marks and mottling and help scarring. But there are risks, including permanent pigment change, post-operative bleeding, burns and lasting scars. Reactions vary, as these two patients report:

LYNDA, 57: 'My facelift was a doddle – virtually no bruising, and no pain. The laser treatment, in contrast, was a week of hell – 24/7 burning, weeping, crusting, and itching – followed by two weeks of severe discomfort. I hardly went out for three weeks. The 'new' skin was raw, tender, felt like parchment and the redness was unbelievable, even after ten weeks. Apparently, it affects everyone differently, and it did fade in the end. I look much better now, but at a cost.'

ROSE, 59: 'As a smoker with sun damage, the surgeon said I was a good candidate. After an hour of treatment I felt very woozy, and was given painkillers, though I felt no pain. The next day my skin was bright red and swollen; over the next few days it went very papery and brown. Sometimes it would heat up like a hot flush. By the second week I could work again. And the third week, with foundation, my skin looked beautiful: fresh and clear with no lines round the eyes. My sun spots went and the skin round my lips is better. I feel absolutely brilliant.'

AESTHETIC PLASTIC SURGERY

The whole perspective of rejuvenating surgery has changed over the last few years. Today, as our expert, London-based aesthetic plastic surgeon Mr Rajiv Grover explains, 'We appreciate that gravity is not the only cause of the physical signs of ageing. Previously the emphasis was on tightening facial tissues, now it's clear that, even more than lines and wrinkles, ageing is influenced by face shape. The cheek area or mid face loses volume about seven years before the skin starts to succumb to gravity. So rejuvenation now targets volume restoration, as well as lifting facial tissue, to improve face shape and make you look younger.' Here's the latest…

SKIN LIFT WITH SMAS LIFT

The most commonly performed lift is the skin lift, where the surgeon cuts around the ear, pulls up the skin, tightens the musculoaponeurotic fascia (the deeper layer of fibrous tissue and the sling muscle which embraces the jawline), and then removes the excess skin. The results will last up to three years, at most.

Most surgeons like to combine the skin lift with an SMAS lift: the skin is lifted from the SMAS (subcutaneous aponeurotic system – the layer where the muscles are attached to the skin), through a cut which runs around the ears and down into the hairline. The SMAS and the muscle are repositioned and excess skin removed, to correct heavy cheeks, jowls and sagging neck in patients of any age. It can give quite dramatic results in older patients and usually lasts ten years, provided that patients keep a constant weight.

Recovery time: back to normal life within two weeks.

Risks: Permanent damage is extremely rare; short-term problems include haematoma, skin necrosis, and temporary facial nerve damage (very rare).

EXTENDED SMAS LIFT

The extended SMAS, which needs a very experienced facial surgeon, goes further down to smooth out heavy lines between nose and mouth more effectively than with any other SMAS lift.

Recovery time: usually about three weeks.

Risks: same as skin lift; there is a much greater risk of injury to the facial nerve in inexperienced hands.

SHORT SCAR FACELIFT

Most facelift operations which also treat loose skin in the neck require the scar, which is discreetly placed around the contours of the ear, to be extended into the groove behind the ear and on for a short distance into the hairline. Patients whose signs of ageing are mainly in the mid and lower face, with little loose skin in the neck, can instead have a shorter scar with no incision behind the ear; this also improves recovery time.

Recovery time: usually ten to 14 days

Risks: similar to skin lift with SMAS lift.

VOLUMETRIC FACELIFT

This aims to rejuvenate the face by restoring volume to the mid face in the cheek area. This can be done by moving it up from the lower midface and overlapping the soft tissues to improve cheek projection, or by transferring fat to the cheek itself.

Recovery time: about two to three weeks, with slightly more swelling in fat transfer patients.

Risks: similar to skin lift with SMAS lift.

Summary for facelift procedures:

- **OPERATING TIME:** 2¹/₂ to 3 hours
- **ANAESTHETIC:** general
- **NIGHTS IN HOSPITAL:** 1
- **TIME OFF WORK:** 14 days
- **SENSITIVITY PERIOD:** 10–14 days
- **BACK TO NORMAL/SPORTS:** 3–4 weeks

NOSE RE-SHAPING (RHINOPLASTY)

Surgery can either beautify or correct injuries. Bumps can be removed, a broad nose slimmed down or the tip altered. Underlying excess bone and cartilage are usually removed from inside the nose, leaving no scars. Noses can also be built up with cartilage or bone.

Risks: haemorrhage, unfavourable result, asymmetry.
Operating time: 60–90 minutes.
Anaesthetic: general.
Nights in hospital: 1.
Time off work: 10–14 days.
Sensitivity period: 2 weeks.
Back to normal/sports: 4 weeks.
Information: for more details, visit Mr Grover's website: www.rajivgrover.co.uk

EYELID SURGERY (UPPER AND/OR LOWER BLEPHAROPLASTY)

Eye bags due to age are caused by the weakening of the supportive structure designed to keep the fat in place. Modern eyelid reduction aims to remove the protruding fat if necessary, but where possible to replace the fat and tighten the supporting skin and muscle. This reduces the danger of creating a hollow-looking eye – a giveaway sign of surgery.

Scars, positioned in the upper eyelid groove just above the crease or under the lower eyelashes, should be virtually invisible. The only painful bit is removing the stitches. Operating from inside the eyelid (trans-conjunctival surgery) avoids stitches but is only suitable for young patients with minimal skin to remove.
Risks: pulling down of lower eyelid if excessive skin removed, excessive scar tissue formations, haematoma, dry eye syndrome (grittiness), watery eyes.
Operating time: 60–90 mins.
Anaesthetic: general for both lids, local for upper lid alone.
Nights in hospital: day case or 1 night.
Time off work: 10–14 days.
Sensitivity period: 14 days.
Back to normal/sports: 2–3 weeks.

ENDOSCOPIC BROWLIFT

Rejuvenating the upper third of the face involves correcting a drooping brow ('brow ptosis'). This used to need an Alice-band cut from ear to ear but is now performed with keyhole surgery, through three small incisions (12mm) behind the hairline, leaving no visible scars. The surgeon can also weaken the frown muscles to produce a Botox-like effect, but permanent and not 'frozen-looking'.
Risks: damage to the sensory nerve with numbness in forehead and scalp, or to the motor (movement) nerve to forehead.
Operating time: 60 mins.
Anaesthetic: general.
Nights in hospital: 1.
Time off work: 7–10 days.
Sensitivity period: 1–2 weeks.
Back to normal/sports: 2 weeks.

CHEEK IMPLANTS

These are traditionally made of silicone but the cheek may also be built up with collagen or the patient's own (autologous) fat. The most recent advance is hydroxyapitite, a synthetic with a similar composition to bone, which is mixed with the patient's blood to make a paste which can be moulded and applied directly to the bone. Recommended for cheeks or other bone-deficient sites, but not for chins where there is too much motion.
Recovery time: seven days.
Risks: asymmetry, infection.
The non-surgical alternative is Restylane® SubQ, an injectable cheek implant, without significant risk of asymmetry or infection.

BREAST REDUCTION AND BREAST UPLIFT (MASTOPEXY)

Over-large, pendulous breasts can be surgically reduced and uplifted. The nipple is detached from the skin but left attached to the breast tissue, an incision made vertically down and then under the breast, skin and breast tissue removed, the nipple replaced and wounds sewn up.

Scarring will fade but is permanent. More recent techniques avoid a scar under the breast but leave a wrinkled vertical scar which takes several months to become even.

Pregnancy must be avoided for one year to avoid stretching the scars.
Risks: haemorrhage, infection, skin and, very rarely, nipple necrosis, asymmetry.
Operating time: 2–2½ hours.
Anaesthetic: general.
Nights in hospital: 1.
Time off work: 14 days.
Sensitivity period: 2–3 weeks.
Back to normal/sports: 3–4 weeks.

BREAST AUGMENTATION

The controversy surrounding the safety of silicone implants has clarified since the UK government's independent safety review, published in 1998. Since then breast augmentation has become the leading cosmetic procedure. Similar confirmations of safety have been declared by the EU and, in 2006/7, silicone implants are due to be approved by the US government again. So far there have been no findings of increased risk of breast cancer, autoimmune disease or chronic fatigue syndromes comparing age-matched individuals with and without implants in any large clinical trial.

Cohesive silicone gel implants are now used, which do not leak even if the implant ruptures. Also, improvements in implant shape allow not only round but also teardrop shapes, so the procedure can produce as natural a shape as possible, even in individuals with relatively flat chests.

Risks: haemorrhage, infection (very rare), capsules contract and harden, asymmetry.
Operating time: 60–90 mins.
Anaesthetic: general.
Nights in hospital: 1.
Time off work: 1–2 weeks.
Sensitivity period: 10–14 days.
Back to normal/sports: 3–4 weeks.

LIPOSUCTION

The removal of fat by suction means that many areas of the body can be re-contoured, including face and neck (particularly double chins and back neck humps), breasts, arms, waist, abdomen, buttocks, inner and outer thighs and knees. It is suitable for removing stubborn localised areas of fat – it is not an alternative to exercise and sensible eating.
Recovery time: seven days, but allow four weeks for bruising to fade.
Risks: this can cause nasty problems if not done by an expert (one woman we know of ended up in intensive care after poor surgery and there have been deaths reported). If too much fat is removed, there may be

irreversible rippling or sagging. Poor liposuction can cause grooves and ruts. Weight gain can settle elsewhere, which can lead to odd shape changes.
Operating time: 2–2¹/2 hours.
Anaesthetic: general.
Nights in hospital: 1–2.
Time off work: 14 days.
Sensitivity period: 10–14 days.
Back to normal/sports: 4–5 weeks.

LIPOSCULPTURE

Another name for liposuction, which may involve injecting fat into depressed areas to recontour the body. 'Superficial liposuction' involves removing fat just below the surface of the skin with a very fine syringe. Results can be excellent when the procedure is carried out by an expert surgeon. Liposculpture can also be performed on the face and the jawline.
Risks: as for liposuction.

ULTRASONIC LIPOSUCTION

With the patient sedated and under local anaesthetic, tiny incisions are made in the skin and the ultrasound probe slid into the tissue. Surgeons using this technique claim that by employing a specific ultrasound frequency, the fat can be dissolved and suctioned off, more fat can be removed and the skin shrinks better. But others dispute the benefits and say the risks are higher.
Risks: as for liposuction, plus skin necrosis – which can be a serious complication, so this should only be done by experts.

stephen glass's tips for cosmetic surgery patients

Many women take a 'Sssh, don't tell a soul approach' after they have had cosmetic surgery. Make-up artist Stephen Glass, who has many clients asking for advice after facelifts, recommends:

• 'If you wear glasses, have a tint put in them before the operation: it will disguise bruising or puffy eyes.'

• 'Manual Lymphatic Drainage massage is the only thing to drain the face and disguise puffiness. But bruising can be effectively covered with a product like Estée Lauder Maximum Cover which stays put – and matte – all day.' (See page 74 for guidelines on how to apply cover-up make-up.)

• 'Use stronger toned lipstick to take the focus away from the eyes.'

• 'Stick to make-up colours that will play down any redness around your eyes. Pink, burgundy – even brown is a bad idea. Instead, choose greys, or greens or slate blues.'

• 'Get a new haircut or a make-up makeover. Then you have an instant explanation when anyone says, "You look great – what have you done?".'

• 'Women often take longer to heal than the doctor says – so give yourself plenty of time and don't make plans you may have to cancel.'

DIARY OF A FACELIFT

Ellen, now 55, is a successful international businesswoman, currently living in London. She wrote her diary for us over the last decade.

DECEMBER 1993 *Dinner with friends; my husband — 12 years younger than I am — says, 'Didn't Emma look beautiful? She must be about your age, but there's not a line on her face.' Ponder.*

APRIL 1994 *My 47th birthday. Realise that since 45, face has begun to sag. Focus on deep frown-line.*

SEPTEMBER 1994 *Particularly harsh bright morning — look in mirror and decide I need advice. Beautiful Emma suggests top London plastic surgeon - Barry Jones.*

OCTOBER 1994 *BJ says three procedures would make great difference. Brow lift would smooth away frown-line, removal of excess skin round eyes would get rid of hooded look, and then — rather frighteningly — he draws line with finger round my ears where the incision would be if I had lower part of my face 'lifted'. Leave, clutching information.*

DECEMBER 1994
Go to business function with husband where everyone much younger. Am convinced that after 50, gap between our ages will become more apparent. Mention possibility of having eyes done.

JANUARY 1995
Ring BJ's office to say will have all three operations. Mention facelift to husband who rejects it out of hand. Then is gradually won round.

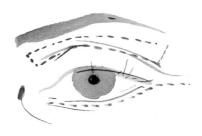

JANUARY 20th, 1995 – D-DAY *Jump in taxi at 6.30am. Arrive at Wellington Hospital in London, fill in forms, meet anaesthetist and theatre nurse. BJ draws lines on face where frown and sag. At eight o'clock sharp, clad in elasticated stockings (to prevent deep vein thrombosis), am wheeled into theatre. Op takes five hours. Wake up on glucose drip, worried as can't see very well. Nurse says eyes still 'seeping' slightly (due to ointment to stop eyes drying and getting sore).*

JANUARY 21st *Night of sickness; wake at last without nausea. Look in mirror. Horrible! Hair glued to head, eyes bruised, puffy, face swollen.*
Leave this afternoon. Go to bed early with head up on five pillows to help reduce swelling. Discover I have a circle of staples in my hair; cannot get comfortable.

JANUARY 22nd *Bruises improving. Eyes less puffy. Beginning to see shape of nose again. But still two black eyes surrounded by white sticky tape, bruising on neck and hard swelling under chin.*
Try to work but too tired. Very odd using phone as ears completely numb. And glasses too heavy for bruised nose and ears. Eyes sore in the night, so put on witch-hazel-soaked sterile eye pads.

JANUARY 23rd *Swelling down but still look like victim of domestic violence. Nurse takes tape off eyes and pulls stitches out — surprisingly un-painful.*

JANUARY 25th *Less bruising but skin looks jaundiced. Forehead smooth and rejuvenated. Swelling around mouth almost gone; lips beginning to regain shape.*

JANUARY 26th *Rest of stitching goes, so do awful staples. Taught how to massage face, eyes and chin.*

JANUARY 27th *Still enough bruising to keep me inside, but almost well again. Swelling under chin uncomfortable, numb ears strange, and sharp pain if raise eyebrows. Neck bullish with swelling both sides. Scalp still tender.*

FEBRUARY 3rd *Began week working normally, but by Wed evening was very tired. Nurse removed two stitches which should have dissolved but hadn't. First good night's sleep since operation.*

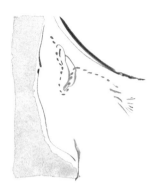

FEBRUARY 12th *Bad week. Fainted at theatre. Slept today and resolve to have snooze every afternoon next week.*

FEBRUARY 17th *Much better physically. Scalp incisions almost healed. Top of scalp and ears still numb. Begin having facial massages: cheeks and throat feel softer. BJ said it takes six months to get full effects of surgery so am relaxed.*

FEBRUARY 20th *People start asking guarded questions. 'You look great, what's happened?' Have hair restyled to give them a reason for transformation.*

MARCH 3rd *Swelling on cheek-bones going down, although neck still tender. Ears and edges of cheeks only half-numb. Went to hospital for well-woman check-up; doctor talked about my getting pregnant! Proof I've lost years off my face.*

APRIL 14th *My 48th birthday. Look as I did in my mid-thirties — eyes wide, cheeks don't sag, neck better than for 15 years, frown line just a slight crease.*

1998 *Husband now frightfully pleased and I look in the mirror every morning and say, 'Thank you, Barry Jones.' I look ten years younger, and I couldn't be happier.*

2000 *Can honestly say, once the initial pain had subsided, I never regretted my*

facelift. Only remaining sensation is in my neck when I press it, but even that isn't uncomfortable. In the last year, my cheeks have begun to sag slightly and my eyes are again a tiny bit hooded. As my tenth anniversary nears, I am seriously considering having another facelift.

2005 *Eyes still look good, slight hooding hasn't increased. But jowls coming back, forehead slightly wrinkled — though don't look nearly as old as before my lift. BJ advises another brow lift plus lower face and neck lift. Says techniques are less invasive now and recovery quicker.*

MAY 9TH *Went into the King Edward hospital in London much less scared. Three hours later I'm out, feeling ghastly and thinking why did I do it. But no sickness and less pain than before. By second day, feeling much better.*

MAY 25TH *Looking normal again. Lunch with parents-in-law: they don't notice a thing.*

AUGUST *We move to Salisbury where, I'm delighted to say, everyone thinks I am in mid to late forties, rather than my true age of 59.*

Prepping for surgery

Expert advice from surgeons Barry Jones and Rajiv Grover

One month before: get results of recent blood tests and/or ECG from your GP for the anaesthetist. Quit smoking and/or using nicotine substitutes as this reduces healing.

Three weeks before: avoid any medications which may cause bleeding and so post-op bruising, eg, aspirin and non-steroidal anti-inflammatories. Also vitamin E, its compounds, garlic, garlic capsules and ginseng.

Take high dose vitamin C (500–1000mg daily) to help wound healing.

Two weeks before: if you are having your hair cut, keep it long around the ears to cover up scars.

One week before: organise help at home for the week following surgery so you can rest. Stock up with good food.

Two days before: start taking arnica tablets to help reduce post-op bruising; continue until one week after surgery.

The night before: most cosmetic surgery is performed under general anaesthesia so eat and drink well the evening before but consume NOTHING in the eight hours before going to hospital, unless advised differently.

Aftercare: rest for the first three days and sleep with four or five extra pillows to help swelling go down. Always avoid any strenuous physical activity for the first two weeks.

If eyes are involved, apply pads soaked in witch-hazel and chilled. Shower and wash hair on alternate days to keep wounds clean. Avoid bleach-based hair colourants for six weeks; try vegetable colour after three weeks, if necessary.

At this age, there is an art to feeling fabulous. To waking up every morning refreshed

and full of life. To having the energy to do everything we need to do (and some

spare for what we want to do). When we were children, it came naturally. And it

still can – now that more is understood than ever before about superfoods,

HOW *feel fab* TO part 2

easy-but-energising exercise, health-protecting supplements – and the role hormones

play in our wellbeing. So we talked to the experts – worldwide. Uncovered the latest

thinking on ways to live life to the full. And spoke to real, glowing women about

their secrets for feeling fab forever – so that we could share them with you…

DESPERATELY SEEKING SLUMBER

More women complain of sleeping problems than men. For many of us, sleep is the sex of the new century – and, according to experts, most of us aren't getting enough.

At any age and every stage, the better we sleep, the better we feel – and the better we live. But unfortunately, not all mornings begin brightly. In general, sleep complaints increase significantly with age; some researchers believe that this is due to the reduction in levels of many hormones as we get older, especially around menopause. One problem is that the hot flushes associated with dwindling oestrogen levels tend to jolt women awake throughout the night, because oestrogen has a direct effect on sleep. And in midlife, we tend to have weighty responsibilities and worries which compound sleeplessness: unruly children, ageing parents, work pressures.

Many menopausal women, having previously relied on sleeping like babes, suddenly find that they are waking at 2, 3 or 4am – their bed more like a battlefield than a cosy nest.

Researchers like Dr Karen Moe in Washington are worried at the huge number of prescriptions for sedative-hypnotic drugs which people turn to for relief. The carry-over effect of these can, she says, exacerbate all sorts of problems, from sleep apnoea (snoring so extreme that it disrupts breathing) to the way your brain works – and may also contribute to the incidence of falls and subsequent fractures.

After a bad night – let alone a succession of them – your body feels achey and drained. You're irritable, foggy and edgy, because you haven't had the rest you needed. And you're not alone. Between five and ten million people in the UK have problems sleeping, and around half a million are estimated to suffer serious sleep disorders. In the US, 70 million people have trouble sleeping.

Today, most of us have so many commitments and chores to perform that sleep gets shuffled down the priority list. According to Stanley Coren, professor of psychology at the University of British Columbia and author of Sleep Thieves, 'We cheat our bodies of sleep every night because the pressures of modern life insist that we take less than evolution programmed us to get. Before electric light, people went to sleep before the sun went down and slept for an average of nine and a half hours – two hours more than now.' The knock-on effect of this shortage, he believes, 'is we are becoming clumsy, stupid, unhappy – and dead'.

Sleep deprivation undermines the immune system. When human guinea pigs were kept awake for four hours beyond their usual bedtime, blood tests taken the next day showed a marked dip in key defences against infections and cancer. Not getting enough sleep may even contribute to making us fat. Ignoring our need for rest makes us prone to overeating, seeking quick boosts from sweets and snacks because our energy reserves weren't topped up by adequate sleep.

But how can each of us tell what our individual optimum sleep quota is? If you can work efficiently and stay alert all day after a few hours' rest, consider yourself lucky – your nightly respites are satisfactory. If it's not enough, then daytime tiredness is likely to be the biggest symptom.

'The acid test for insufficient sleep is whether you have trouble staying awake during the day,' suggests Professor Jim Horne, who runs the sleep laboratory at Loughborough University.

If you find that you are tired all the time, try sleeping more – and tune in to what that does to your alertness. Set an earlier bedtime for a week and sleep longer. (If you don't experience improvements on the new regime, however, consult your doctor; there may be another physical cause.) Those who say they exist on four hours' sleep may only need that much, biologically. But if you're an eight-hour sleeper and you're only getting four, you will soon be running on empty.

how much sleep is enough?

Experts often tell us we need less sleep as we age. But when we asked Dr Joseph Pizzorno of Bastyr University in Seattle for his top anti-ageing secrets, eight hours' sleep was at the top of the list. 'Adequate sleep is absolutely necessary for long-term health and regeneration,' he explains. 'While many different processes occur during sleep, perhaps the most important for rejuvenation are, firstly, the scavenging effects of free radicals in the brain, and, secondly, increased production of growth hormone.'

Free radicals – responsible for a lot of the damage elsewhere in our bodies (including to our skins) – can build up in the brain. 'Sleep functions as an antioxidant for the brain, because free radicals are removed during this time,' says Dr Pizzorno. If you sleep for less than eight hours, however, the 'clean-up' task may not be completed. 'Most people can tolerate a few days without sleep and fully recover. But chronic sleep deprivation appears to accelerate ageing of the brain – so your brain will start to function less well.'

And as if that wasn't enough of an incentive to get the full eight hours, consider this: growth hormone – mostly produced during sleep – has been called the 'anti-ageing' hormone, for its ability to stimulate tissue and liver regeneration, muscle building, the breakdown of fat stores, blood sugar normalisation, 'and a host of other beneficial actions,' reports Dr Pizzorno. Basically, it helps convert fat to muscle.

It's certainly true that as people age, they tend to sleep less. 'The average person of 50 years or older sleeps almost two hours less than they did as a teenager,' observes Dr Pizzorno. 'But this diminished opportunity to secrete human growth hormone and scavenge free radicals in the brain probably plays a significant role in the degeneration of ageing.' He believes we should all try for the magic eight hours.

And to anyone who can't imagine they can get everything done that they need to do and manage eight hours' shut-eye, we'd say this: getting the extra sleep seems to make it easier to whiz through tasks. Whereas not getting enough can make for entire 'lost' days when life can be compared, at best, to swimming through treacle.

pay off your sleep debts

If you find that you 'get behind' with your sleep, then as soon as you can, pay off your 'sleep debts', as Professor Coren calls them. Losing one hour's sleep a night means we end up with a sleep debt of seven hours by the end of the week. 'This is the equivalent of losing a full night's sleep – and you start to show the symptoms of someone who's done just that.' Which might include itching or burning eyes, blurred vision, headaches and/or feeling chilly, as well as waves of sleepiness or fatigue, irritability or weepiness; short-term memory is also affected. The way to get back on track is napping and sleeping in on the weekend, when you have the opportunity. To avoid the knock-on effects of a nap keeping you awake at night, take it before 3pm.

sleep-easy strategies

Popping sleeping pills is always an option but managing stress, eating well and taking regular exercise will ultimately induce a far better quality of sleep. 'About 90 per cent of all insomniacs can be cured through self-care,' says Peter Hauri, director of the Mayo Clinic's Insomnia Programme, USA. So try these sleep-inducing tactics…

◆ Start preparing at lunchtime – if you keep your stress levels under control during the day, then you're less likely to be frazzled, come bedtime. Take a ten-minute break, around lunchtime, for some deep breathing or yoga.

◆ Avoid caffeine (in coffee and tea, chocolate, cola, guarana-based products and some pain-relievers) in the afternoon and evening; it takes nearly ten hours to leave your system. NB: decaffeinated doesn't necessarily mean caffeine-free.

◆ Regular daily exercise encourages deep sleep but do aerobic exercise early in the day, or you may be too revved up to nod off. (An early evening walk is a great way to wind down, we find.)

> If I'm exhausted, I clear my mind by imagining a blank, white canvas. When you're tired, problems escalate, so I go to bed as early as I can.
>
> **AMANDA BURTON**

◆ Avoid alcohol and cigarettes before bedtime. Alcohol may help you nod off initially, but as it breaks down in the system, it disrupts sleep later on, so you wake up and find it difficult to get back to sleep. Nicotine acts as a stimulant.

◆ For perfect slumber, the sleep 'hygienists' are agreed that we should establish a regular daily pattern of going-to-bed and getting-up times.

◆ Finish your main evening meal at least two hours before bedtime: digestion – and the blood sugar surge from food – can keep you awake. Sweet, sugary things are a particularly unwise choice at night.

◆ Have a warm, milky drink an hour before bedtime: it helps reduce anxiety and promote sleep.

◆ Have a warm pre-bedtime bath: it raises body temperature and the natural sleep-preparation mechanism is triggered as the body cools again.

◆ Ban TV and newspapers from the bedroom, and don't use it as an extension of the office, a place to eat, pay bills or talk on the telephone. Bad sleep rapidly becomes a vicious cycle; someone who's having problems sleeping will read or watch TV or look at work papers – which in turn stimulates them and can prevent sleep, or trigger poor-quality sleep. Experts believe that images of bad news or violence on TV can interfere with good sleep on an unconscious level.

◆ Keep the bedroom comfortably warm but not stuffy; try to ensure that fresh air is circulating.

◆ If there is a street light outside your window, or you wake early in the summer, invest in heavier curtains – or wear a sleeping mask in bed.

> I think sleep keeps you young. I like ten or 12 hours but I usually manage eight. I have trained myself to sleep in planes, trains, even cars.
>
> **CAROLINE HERRERA**

◆ Noise is one of the worst pollutants. Uncontrollable noise can disturb your sleep and result in physical tension next day. If you can't change it, make sure you have a battery of aids, from ear plugs to personal stereos; play soothing sounds or 'white noise', which blots out other noise.

◆ Write a 'to do tomorrow' list before bedtime – and keep it by the bed. Then if you wake up thinking of another task jot it down – and get back to sleep.

◆ Don't forget to get your oats! A bowl of porridge or muesli in place of supper is nutritious, good for the nervous system and an anti-depressant. (*See page 160 for natural sleep remedies.*)

SLEEPING BEAUTY

What if you could spend eight hours every night at a spa? Most of us would leap at the chance. Well, not for nothing is it called 'beauty sleep' – because the sleeping hours deliver the perfect opportunity for products to help skin to repair and regenerate itself. According to Manhattan dermatologist Dennis Gross, 'Studies have shown that wounds heal faster while you sleep. Your body ultimately goes into recovery. Your cells are not in overdrive producing antioxidants to fight free radicals. Instead, they are producing collagen and repairing DNA. Any topical actve ingredient with repair benefits becomes more efficient.'

Some skin experts, however – including Eva Fraser and Eve Lom – go so far as to suggest that skin should be left naked at night. (Although we've tried that, and given up, because for us it's just plain tight and uncomfortable; personally, we are big fans of facial oils for night treatments – see page 49 for suggestions – and serums, which seem to give our dry skins the extra nourishment we feel they need.) But whether you apply a special night cream – or use your favourite daytime moisturiser – is really a matter of personal preference. If you like the richer, nourishing texture of a night cream (or a facial oil), go for it – in the confidence that the shinier, more slippery texture won't interfere with make-up application. Night-time is certainly the right time for using heavier treatments on scalp, hands and lips that you wouldn't be able to get away with in the day, too – even sleeping in cotton gloves and socks, if a particular product demands it. After all, nobody has to be a beauty in the pitch dark.

tried & tested FACIAL OILS

These work best at night, when the rich, intense fusions of essential oils can work their skin-restoring magic, in rhythm with the body's own cell-repairing mechanism – which is at its most active while we sleep. (Also, oils are usually impractical for use by day, as they take a while to penetrate – so make-up slides right off again.) A bonus: many of the facial oils featured here contain aromatherapeutic, waft-you-sleepwards ingredients like lavender.

CIRCAROMA SKIN GENTLE FACIAL SERUM ROSE OTTO + APRICOT
Score: 8.22/10
This radiance-boosting facial oil really impressed our testers. Virtually all its ingredients are organic, and with softening apricot oil and rose otto, this will restore balance to parched and delicate skin, Circaroma promise.
Comments: 'Skin clearer, smoother – spot marks healing' • 'fine lines on brow and eye area smoothed' • 'people said I looked radiant' • 'skin softer, plumper, springy' • 'reduced redness on cheeks and nose after three weeks'.

CLARINS SKIN REPAIR BEAUTY CONCENTRATE
Score: 8.21/10
Clarins say this 'SOS' for skins should be used nightly for sensitive complexions, or as needed on skins that have 'flared up'. It includes soothing liquorice extract, soya and avocado oils, plus essential oils of lavender, mint and marjoram.
Comments: 'A miracle: skin's smoother, clearer, looks younger' • 'skin feels peachy' • 'immediately softer' • 'used on burnt hand: two weeks later hardly any scarring'.

CLARINS HUILE SANTAL FACIAL OIL
Score: 7.88/10
A second Clarins winner, this time a classic packed with sandalwood oil and lavender, and perfect, they say, for skins that are dry or have high colouring.
Comments: 'Immediate improvement in softness and radiance' • 'a godsend for dry skin after a new baby' • 'very economical' • 'forehead lines softer, acne scars faded'.

AROMATHERAPY ASSOCIATES RENEW ROSE & FRANKINCENSE FACIAL OIL
Score: 7.5/10
Intended for dry, more mature complexions and tired skin which may be losing its firmness, this anti-ager blends rose and frankincense in a base of vitamin E-rich oils.
Comments: 'Fantastic – skin is soft, smooth, fresh, glowing' • 'love the smell: beautiful to use' • 'really made a difference to fine lines' • 'skin looked plumper'.

natural sleep remedies

Millions of prescriptions for sleeping pills are handed out every year and though they will work – mostly – they traditionally do so by depressing brain function, resulting in a quality of sleep that's less restorative.

The body soon develops a tolerance to sleeping pills, so people may soon need to raise their usual dose after a while in order to get the same effect. Many sleeping pills are highly addictive and, in some cases, may actually lead to increased anxiety and stressful feelings during the waking hours; sudden withdrawal of the medication also leads to problems. In the last few years, some sleeping pills have had to be hastily taken off the market by manufacturers as unacceptable side effects emerged when millions of human guinea pigs put them to the long-term test in real life.

If you've tried our 'sleep-easy strategies ' (see page 158) and are still finding sleep elusive, it is worth trying the complementary route.

Acupuncture

Insomnia can be treated by a qualified acupuncturist. Or try sending yourself to sleep using acupressure: use your thumb to stimulate the acupuncture point in the centre of your abdomen, one hand's width below the navel.

Aromatherapy

To a warm bath add up to 15 drops of essential oils from the following list, blended into 1 teaspoon of 'base oil', such as jojoba or almond: camomile, lavender, rose, neroli, geranium, sandalwood or lime-flower oil.

Herbs

Herbal sleeping remedies are perfectly safe, says Andrew Chevallier of the National Institute of Medical Herbalists. 'There should be no significant side effects and you won't have a hangover.' **NB** Buy organic herbs whenever possible. Many dried herbs have literally been drenched in chemicals. Look for ready-to-use products or infuse your own herbal teas.

- German camomile *(Matricaria recutita)*
- Lime flowers *(Tilia)*
- Valerian *(Valeriana officinalis)*
- Hops *(Humulus lupulus)*
- Lavender *(Lavandula)*
- Skullcap *(Scutellaria lateriflora)*
- Passion flower *(Passiflora incarnata)*

Homoeopathy

Try one tablet of Ars alb 30C or Belladonna 30C – or consult a properly qualified homoeopath.

Hypnotherapy

Consult a qualified practitioner, buy a self-hypnosis tape or learn to DIY.

Relaxation tapes

Most music shops (and some natural-food stores) offer a selection of relaxing 'New Age' music that can help you unwind. Or listen to plainsong, or any favourite calming music.

Supplementing sleep

Some somnologists recommend a night-cap of minerals, including calcium and magnesium, to combat nervousness, muscle tension and aching joints.

And if all else fails, opposite are the top instant face wakers, to make you look as if you've had eight hours.

SLEEP AFFIRMATIONS

We find these are wonderfully effective at helping us chill out – particularly when we are worried about not getting enough sleep. Vary as you wish.

● Lie on your back and un-tense your body from head to toe – just run through your body from scalp to toes in your mind, letting all the tensions of the day gradually evaporate.

● Breathe slowly and gently – try visualising your breath as a wave on the beach, rippling gently up, pausing, then flowing out again.

● Say to yourself: 'Today is over and tomorrow is not yet here; now I'm going to have a restful/ delicious/restorative sleep and wake up gleaming.'

● Try noticing and appreciating nice sensations like the coolness of the pillow and sheets, softness of the duvet, supporting firmness of the mattress – or the feel of your partner's skin.

tried & tested INSTANT FACE SAVERS

Sometimes, even a good night's sleep isn't enough to make us look fab, first thing – and never mind those nights when sleep is totally elusive. So these are fast-fixes that belong in every woman's bathroom cabinet, for that morning-after beauty S.O.S. – useful, too, when skin's generally suffering, or before an important event.

CLARINS BEAUTY FLASH BALM
Score: 8.8/10

This is truly deserving of its place in the 'Beauty Hall of Fame', according to our testers. Over 20 years after its launch, it is still one of Clarins's bestsellers, known as their 'Cinderella in a tube' for the way it instantly plumps out lines, setting to a firming film that gives skin back its glow.
Comments: 'I got married recently and after little sleep was looking less than radiant – this restored a healthy glow!' • 'this should be every woman's beauty secret' • 'one of my must-haves – fab' • 'face glowed as soon as the product went on' • 'used it on combination skin – I'm 51 but it made me look 40'.

AVEDA TOURMALINE-CHARGED PROTECTING LOTION ✳
Score: 8.37

Aveda pitch this as a longer-term anti-ageing moisturiser – but were confident enough to ask us to test it in this category. It is based on crushed tourmaline – a crystalline, semi-precious gem – with antioxidants beta-carotene, lycopene and sugar extracts, and an SPF15 chemical sunscreen, plus seven skin-refreshing pure flower and plant essences. We like the fact that it's packaged in a partly recycled tube.
Comments: 'Sent my eye bags into the next millennium and really seemed to lock in moisture' • 'skin felt very fresh after application' • 'absolutely brilliant – infused my skin with radiance, restoring moisture balance' • 'glided on beautifully; to cheer up my winter-dull skin' • 'skin looked even – and full of vitality' • 'my whole face felt uplifted'.

DECLÉOR INSTANT DE BEAUTÉ INSTANT BEAUTY BOOSTER
Score: 8.22

Ingredients in this silky cream – which Decléor promise 'will eliminate all traces of fatigue in seconds' – include borage oil and antioxidant wheatgerm oil. If used regularly, it's claimed, it will refine and tone, improving skin texture – though our testers were asked to investigate only its immediate benefits – and is said to provide a great base for make-up. If your skin is dry, Decléor recommend you use your normal moisturiser over the top.
Comments: 'Felt 40ish instead of 50ish, – lovely' • 'like a facelift, at a fraction of the cost' • 'a fabulous boost for looks and confidence – like an instant facelift' • 'used it when recovering from a heavy cold and skin looked relaxed and radiant; a real find' • 'a fantastic base for make-up; I felt positively glowing'.

JURLIQUE HERBAL RECOVERY GEL ✳ ✳
Score: 7.88/10

An all-botanical, lightweight serum from a truly natural Australian brand. (Their founder used to work for Dr Hauschka.) We have trialled this before as an anti-ageing product, but this time it has done brilliantly as a quick fix. The potent botanicals and antioxidants include extracts from organic roses, liquorice, marshmallow, calendula, daisy, violet, aloe, quince and camomile, plus rosehip, evening primrose, carrot, macadamia and jojoba oils. Jurlique say it makes a great 'skin shield' – eg, when flying.
Comments: 'Magical – makes my easily irritated skin look calm, smooth and well cared for and has people commenting on how great it looks' • 'promised miracles – and delivered!' • 'saved me on New Year's Day as I'd drunk too much: should be available on prescription'.

beauty steal NEAL'S YARD REMEDIES ZEST SPRITZER ✳ ✳
Score: 7.66/10

The face-waking power of this 100 per cent natural preservative-free aromatherapy spray for face, body and space is down to its combination of essential oils of lemon, bergamot and palmarosa, blended with Australian Bush Flower Essences. It was the best buy among the less expensive face-wakers and, Neal's Yard promise, its aromatherapeutic power will also 'lift you out of your mid-afternoon slump'.
Comments: 'Felt awake – like a slap in the face, but nicer!' • 'zesty, lifting my spirits and leaving me revived' • 'I spritzed this on bed linen, and in wardrobes, too, for a very refreshing, clean smell' • 'a wonderful pick-me-up after a bout of flu'.

Forget aiming to look like Kate Moss or going for Jane Fonda's burn (and getting scorched). The new thinking on fitness is: take it easier. For the ultimate daily workout, scientists are now agreed that nothing beats regular, moderate exercise: a mix of cardiovascular, stretch and gentle weight-training. Think, too, of standing straighter, breathing better and acquiring grace. Sure, if you feel energetic, go for a run, play a game of tennis – or whatever you enjoy. But there's no need for exercise to leave you huffing and puffing, achey and flushed as a beetroot. (Which, if you're not used to it, can even be downright dangerous.) And the good news is: if you want to feel fabulously fit forever, it's never too late to start.

THE BREATH OF LIFE

In the beginning, we breathed. Rhythmically, deeply. Inhaling through our noses and filling our bodies and brains with oxygen. Exhaling through our mouths and breathing out all the waste carbon dioxide. Then life and all its stresses knocked the natural breathing pattern sideways, leaving us alternately gasping and holding our breath.

When we're anxious or nervous, we tend to breathe shallowly. Usually when we breathe we take in about the equivalent of a tumblerful of air – just one third of our lungs' capacity. If you could spread out the lining of your lungs, there would be 100 square metres (40 square yards) of it. In your lungs are 600–700 million air sacs, all waiting to be filled. Once the air gets to them, they pass the oxygen into your bloodstream. In turn, your blood sends back the waste carbon dioxide to be exhaled. Breathe inadequately – just at the top of your lungs – as most of us do, and a lot of the waste never gets expelled. (And you may puff as if you've been running for a train, although all you've been doing is walking to the phone.)

Getting back to breathing properly is

an almost instantaneous route to feeling better, in every way. What's more, like that other great health and beauty staple – water – it's completely free and under your control.

Try it now, wherever you are. Breathe slowly in through your nose, let the breath go down to your belly, put your hand there and inflate it like a balloon. Feel the breath go up to your head, clearing your brain. Now gently breathe out through your mouth. Try it again – and don't force it or your shoulders will go up, neck stiffen and jawline tense. Breathe as

lightly and softly as a puff of breeze on a calm day.

Do this all the time, everywhere, particularly when you feel anxious, and you'll notice how much better you feel instantly – more alert, relaxed, in touch. You may not realise that breathing is also calming your heart rate, helping to normalise your blood pressure and decrease your risk of heart disease.

Alternate nostril breathing – a mainstay of some types of yoga – has been shown to help brain clarity and concentration. It may seem confusing at first but you'll get the hang of it very quickly; then it's second nature and you don't even have to think.

◆ Keeping your mouth closed, push all the spent air in your body out through your nose.
◆ With your right thumb pressed firmly against the right side of your nose to keep it closed, take a deep breath through your left nostril.
◆ Now push your right forefinger against your left nostril, lift your thumb and breathe out through your right nostril.
◆ Pause for a second then repeat the other way around.
◆ Repeat this pattern several times and marvel at how well you feel.

You can use your breathing to express anger or frustration as well. In moments of fury, sit or stand with a straight back, take a long deep breath, hold it for about 15 seconds, shaking your hands and arms, then push it out vigorously – with a big roaring moan if no one else is around.

Last thing at night, as you lie in bed gazing at the ceiling, try closing your eyes, letting your mind roam and breathing your way to sleep. In through your nose to the count of four, hold for one, then out to a count of six, or eight, or…

straight talk

The inside story on how to lose five pounds – and get taller – in five seconds. Plus a lot more...

Posture may seem about as old-fashioned as pressing dried flowers, relevant only to Edwardian ladies. But, after breathing – with which it's intimately connected – improving posture is probably the cheapest, quickest and simplest method of improving your appearance and how your body systems work. If tension builds up in the muscles and connective tissue, the whole body's balance is disrupted, leading to a sagging tum, aching muscles and joints, and poor circulation, plus indigestion, headaches and even cellulite (because the body's detox systems are not flowing freely). Long-term wear and tear may lead to osteoarthritis.

Good posture
and real jewellery
are the only things that
can improve on nature
once a woman gets
to a certain age.

HELEN GURLEY BROWN

'Beauty and health are posture-deep,' says manipulative physiotherapist Warwick McNeill of Physioworks in London, an innovative practice which specialises in detecting and correcting the underlying postural problems that cause intractable chronic aches and pains.

Most of all, good posture means being effortlessly relaxed and at ease with your body – never tense or rigid.

quick fix: Just try this posture-perfecting exercise for starters

◆ Stand with your feet one hip-width apart, toes facing forwards, knees 'soft'.

◆ Make sure your weight is on the centre of your feet; roll forward on to your toes, then back on your heels to understand the wrong positions, then find the mid position.

◆ Breathe slowly and rhythmically, in through your nose and out through your mouth.

◆ Tighten buttock muscles, but don't stick your bottom out – again find the mid position between sticking out and tucked in.

◆ Draw in your tummy muscles – imagine you're sending your navel towards your spine.

◆ Remember to go on breathing – there is a tendency to hold your breath when you're tightening your muscles.

◆ Think tall – imagine a thread drawing the crown of your head to the ceiling, look straight ahead, letting your chin and jaw relax; let your shoulder-blades drop.

◆ Still breathing gently, prowl gracefully round like a cat. Try it with bare feet, on a lawn or sand, if possible. Your feet should be facing forwards, or at five to one on an imaginary clock face, second big toe leading, heel touching the ground first. Let your hips roll and arms swing gently.

◆ Keep breathing – and think feline.

◆ Some yoga teachers simply suggest you remember how you felt when you heard good news – then stand and walk like that, with chest lifted, shoulders back and head held high.

planning ahead

True postural fitness depends on long-term tactics. The key support system for the spine is the transversus abdominus muscle which wraps round your middle like a Victorian corset. If that is floppy, the spine suffers. Studies have shown that the muscle is far weaker in people with bad backs. Some gym workouts can actually make matters worse by emphasising limb strength: as the muscles in your arms and legs get stronger and shorter, a floppy middle tends to get even weaker.

Strengthening the 'corset' physically with simple exercises helps enormously, so – perhaps surprisingly – can visualising the muscle 'corset' in your mind's eye as you move about throughout the day. Visualise – strengthen. Visualise – strengthen...

Physically, you need to aim for exercise which incorporates limb and trunk strengthening so that you control the middle of your body. Postural fitness is best done slowly and gently. Yoga, t'ai chi, Pilates, Feldenkrais and ballet plus hands-on therapies such as Alexander Technique, hellerwork, rolfing and muscle-based physiotherapy (called physical therapy in America) are particularly suitable for anyone wanting to improve their posture.

physioworks perfect posture plan

Long-term strategy: find your corset and get your back in fine fettle.

1 Finding your corset

Locate your 'corset' muscles by kneeling on all fours and gently pulling in the wide belt of muscle over your tummy button and below – not the area above.

2 Single leg lift

Lie on your back with your knees bent, feet facing ahead. Place a hand on each hip-bone. Pulling in your 'corset', gently lift one knee towards you, raising the foot from the floor. Hold for a couple of seconds with your thigh as near vertical as possible then lower it gently. You will feel your pelvis roll very slightly from side to side – the object of the exercise is to use your corset to keep your pelvis as still as possible. Repeat on alternate sides for one to two minutes, twice daily.

3 Single leg over

Starting in exactly the same way, keep your left knee pointing to the ceiling and let your right knee drop out to the side, right foot planted on the floor. Slowly return it to upright. Use your corset all the time to control the pelvic roll. Repeat as for 2.

4 Shoulders right

Standing upright, find the correct position for your shoulders by having someone lay their hand on your lower trapezius muscle. Now draw it in very gently – imagine the hand pulling back your shoulder-blades – not your whole shoulder. (This is a subtle – not a big – movement.) Your shoulders should be square, rather than slouching and/or sloping like a ski run. Take care that your shoulders don't shrug up or your arms move backwards; keep your lower ribs still and don't let them lift up.

5 Behind basics

In a standing position, find the muscle in your bottom (the gluteus medius posterior) by imagining you are placing your hands over the back pockets of a pair of jeans. Now face a mirror and pull in those muscles. Let your legs turn out slightly from the hips and feel the arch of your feet lift.

6 Knee bends

This perfect basic exercise teaches your brain to have control over the alignment of trunk, knees and feet.

◆ Stand facing a mirror with your bare feet parallel, hip-width apart.

◆ Pull your navel in towards your spine without bending your back.

◆ Tense your bottom muscles, pointing the kneecaps straight ahead.

◆ Gently draw your shoulder-blades back to square your shoulders – don't let your lower ribs rise.

◆ Pull your chin in and back gently, lengthening your neck.

◆ Now bend your knees slightly; only go as far as you can while keeping your body in the same position and your knees directly over the middle toes.

◆ Repeat 20 times.

WATCHPOINT: don't stick your bottom out.

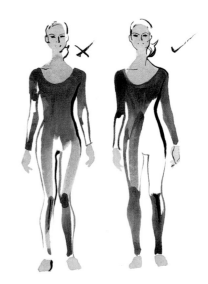

7 Nods for necks

Stand with your back to a wall, your heels about 5cm (2in) away (or sit on a stool); touch the wall with the back of your head, then start nodding your head gently. This will lengthen the back of your neck and you will feel your head slide up the wall.

chair in front of a mirror. Support your lower back and sit as above. Now gently draw your shoulders back into the correct position, without lifting your chest or sticking out your lower ribs. (It's easiest to monitor what your body is doing if you do it in a minimum of undies.)

9 Sit to stand

When you get up from a seat, the trick is to move from your hips and follow the crown of your head. Most people get out of a chair with their chin leading, straining the neck and spine. Instead, try putting your hands on your lower back, then bend at the hips, looking down at your toes so that your weight is well forwards. Then rise, keeping your lower back in its natural curve. Practise this ten times a day – or whenever you get up from a seat.

TIP: when sitting, change your position every 20 minutes.

8 Sitting pretty

Help align your lower spine when sitting by rocking forward on the bones of your bottom so you sit on the front side of the bones. Remember to keep the rest of your body relaxed, knees a hip-width apart, feet firmly planted on the floor. (Sitting habitually with your knees together turns off natural postural muscles and encourages bad posture.) Support your lower back with a fat cushion or a lumbar roll. Practise sitting well by putting your

10 Wrongs and rights

Sarah's first Alexander Technique teacher set her homework which involved looking at the way other people sat and stood. The problems are plain to see. The key thing to avoid when sitting is slouching and the goal at all times is to have ears and thighs in line, plus instep when you're standing. Not only will you look miles better but you'll avoid aches and pains and allow your organs to work optimally.

our *fabulously easy* fitness programme

Yoga-based routines, walking, dancing round the kitchen – or anywhere else – plus a DIY sleek and tone workout based on body-conditioning Pilates are our nominations for the greatest all-round gentle exercise. (Add in swimming, if you're a mermaid.) Think in terms of spending about half an hour every day, if possible – but at least five days a week – on these types of exercise. Get a mix – and, above all, do what you enjoy. Because the bottom line is that there's nothing more attractive and elegant than a woman who moves gracefully and with controlled vitality. Whether she's 30-something – or 80-something.

Exercise naturally induces many of the anti-ageing mechanisms that scientists try to bring about by much more complex means, from hormone supplements and calorie restriction to gene therapy. It builds muscles, burns fat, makes heart and lungs work more efficiently, lowers the density of damaging sugars in the blood and is a major factor in protecting you against osteoporosis – brittle bone disease – which causes 200,000 fractures a year in the UK, a horrifying 40 per cent of which prove fatal. Weight-bearing exercise makes bones stronger and more dense – try anything where your weight is directly pressing on the ground – walking, jogging, dancing, skiing, etc. (Cycling, although great exercise, isn't weight-bearing.) Resistance exercises, such as lifting weights and swimming, will keep bones and muscles healthy.

Remember: gentle exercise should be just that. If you have aches and pains, any medical condition, or you haven't exercised for a while, consult your doctor before starting any exercise programme. If you feel a twinge during exercise, stop pushing yourself and return to something gentle.

INSTANT ENERGISERS

● With your forefingers and thumbs on each ear, rub ear rims and lobes.
● Pull and wiggle the fingers of each hand in turn.
● Shake your hands vigorously, up and down, side to side.
● Pull, rub and wiggle the second big toe of each foot.

ARE YOU GETTING ENOUGH?

Here's the bottom line, from the Health Development Agency: half an hour of moderate-level physical activity, at least five days of the week – and preferably every day. Sarah Williams, spokeswoman for the HDA, explains: 'Moderate activity is anything that makes you feel warm and breathe a little more heavily. That could embrace anything from brisk walking to cycling, swimming – even vigorous housework or washing the car. People should try to find ways of fitting physical activity into their routine so that it doesn't become a chore – and vary the activity. If you're out of shape, split it into two 15-minute chunks – then increase to half an hour at a time. It's amazing how quickly fitness improves.'

GET GOING!

When exercising is the last thing you feel like, Champneys – the UK's leading health spa – suggests ways of getting off the couch and out of the door...

● Use aromatherapy oils such as grapefruit, geranium and frankincense to give you a boost.
● If you have an exercise bike or other exercise equipment at home, put it in front of the TV and promise yourself that you won't watch your favourite programme unless you are working out at the same time.
● Find an 'exercise buddy' so you can motivate each other.
● Have a massage every week, if you can; it will help your circulation and make you feel less sluggish in winter. Trade DIY massages with your partner or 'massage buddy'.
● If you feel unmotivated, tired or get the munchies during winter and can't face the great outdoors, try full-spectrum light therapy. Over-production of melatonin, the sleep hormone which is turned on by lack of light, will cause the same symptoms that make animals want to hibernate in winter. Bright light counterbalances these symptoms. (See page 235 for more details on winter depression, or SAD.) If you possibly can, remove your glasses or lenses and go out as often as possible on bright days.
● Eat a nutrient-rich diet to keep energy levels up (see pages 188–190).

EXERCISE FOR HAPPY HEARTS

Before menopause, the hormone oestrogen seems to help protect us from heart disease. But as oestrogen levels fall, so our risk goes up. Heart disease kills one woman in five, and it's the second biggest cause of premature death among women after cancer. What is certain is that taking exercise – in tandem with stopping smoking, eating wisely and reducing excess stress – is one of our best bodyguards.

For post-menopausal women, evidence is emerging that even a little exercise can go a long way. In a seven-year study of the link between physical activity and survival time in more than 40,000 women in Minneapolis, the Minnesota School of Public Health found that those who took moderate activity – such as bowling, gardening or a long walk – as little as once a week were 24 per cent less likely to die over the course of the study than those who weren't physically active at all.

But more is undoubtedly better. The fittest people live the longest and because the heart is a muscle it will get stronger and be more efficient if it's asked to work harder. You do this through 'aerobic' exercise. This means working relatively hard and steadily for a sustained period which makes your heart pump harder in order to provide the other muscles with supplies of fresh oxygenated blood.

Exercise helps you achieve two things: a more efficient pump which leads to a larger heart muscle; and a lower resting heart beat, or pulse (which also translates as a healthier heart). It happens like this. As your heart gets bigger, it can pump more blood per beat so it doesn't need to beat so often. So, as your heart gets fitter, the heart rate gets lower – at work, rest and play – and returns more quickly to a resting rate after exercise.

Getting your heart fit is simple if you follow our suggested exercise programme. If you do five 30-minute sessions a week, you're there. Alternatively, you can mix and match it with other aerobic activities from the list on the right.

If you are completely unused to exercise, start with eight minutes every other day for the first week, then add on three minutes per session each week.

Don't forget also to add on the three to five minutes' warm-up and cool-down time either end.

AEROBIC ACTIVITIES

For everyone:
Dancing/walking/dynamic yoga
Rebounding on a mini-trampoline
Swimming/aquarobics
Cycling
Jogging/running
Mountain hiking
Ball games (tennis, badminton, volleyball, basketball)
Martial arts (kick-boxing, karate, judo)

For more advanced exercisers:
Skipping
Rollerblading
Skiing, both downhill and cross country
Windsurfing, skin/scuba diving

Exercising once or twice a week reduces the risk of heart attack by 36 per cent, compared with no exercise; three or four times weekly by 38 per cent; five times or more per week by 46 per cent.

heart news

The American National Institute of Health recently recommended that people with moderately raised blood pressure and no risk factor for heart attacks (such as positive family history) should exercise regularly for a year and lose 4.5kg (10lb) in weight before resorting to pharmaceutical drugs. They should also stop smoking immediately, reduce salt intake, drink a maximum of two small glasses of red wine daily and, above all, relax.

The fittest people live the longest, but the good news is that exercise brings about the biggest jump in life expectancy, even for people who go from nothing to being moderately active. According to William Evans, director of the Knoll Physiological Research Center at Pennsylvania State University: 'If you're a sedentary person, any regular exercise of moderate intensity – even if it's mowing the lawn, house cleaning or climbing the stairs – will allow you to live longer.'

walking back to happiness

The problem with most of us is that we know we should exercise – but we don't, because it's boring, complicated, inconvenient (or a combination of all three). That's where walking wins, every time: it's free, it's easy, most of us are naturally good at it – and it's simple to fit into everyday life. (And walking from A to B is a double whammy: free transport and a free fat-burner.) So step right up for the perfect walking workout...

Our biggest health and fitness secret is that we walk, walk, walk, walk, walk – at every opportunity. Across the park, to meetings. In the evenings, with friends, as a social activity – or instead of taking the car to a restaurant.

We walk at weekends, in parks and in wide open spaces. And we've found that if we have to do without our walks, our stress levels soar and we feel decidedly unsparkling.

Today, research has confirmed that nature's greatest fitness and looks booster is walking, at a normal-to-brisk pace. Unlike jogging or running, walking doesn't jolt and jar the skeletal structure every time your foot hits the ground. Yet it can raise your heart rate to around 50–70 per cent of its maximum – similar to aerobics, cycling and swimming – which boosts your heart health.

Ideally, to feel the benefits, you need to walk for 20–30 minutes (or more), five times or more a week. (If you start to walk to get from A to B, instead of always driving, it's surprisingly easy to fit that into even the busiest lifestyle.) Yet according to the Pedestrian Policy Group, the average distance walked per person has actually plummeted by more than 20 per cent in the past 20 years – with disastrous consequences for our fitness, putting us at risk of heart disease, premature arthritis and osteoporosis through lack of exercise. The solution is simple: lace up those trainers (or those comfy brogues), and put one foot in front of the other.

Walking strengthens hips, thighs, stomach and bottom muscles (plus arms and shoulders if you swing your arms as you walk). It speeds up the metabolic rate so that calories are burned faster even when the walk's over.

What's more, walking also appears to boost our immunity. According to a study carried out by Dr David Nieman, PhD, a professor of health promotion at the Appalachian State University in Boone, North Carolina, 'Walking seems to prime the body's immune system, preparing it to fight disease before we even feel the first sniffle.' Among the women in Nieman's study, those who walked briskly for 45 minutes a day, five days a week, were sick with colds or flu for only five days during the 15-week study period – timed to coincide with the peak cold season – as opposed to ten days among the sedentary women.

My grandmother started walking five miles a day when she was 60. She's 93 today and we don't know where the hell she is!

ELLEN DE GENERES

STOMP AND STRETCH WARM-UP MARCH

Always warm up and cool down before and after exercising. This energising march can also be used to give yourself a speedy workout if you're short of time.

● **March briskly** on the spot for two minutes. Still stomping, add in some stretches.

● **Shoulder shrugs:** lift your shoulders up to your ears and down; with your elbows bent, circle your shoulders slowly backwards and then forwards.

● **Arm swings:** swing arms vigorously to front and back.

● **Knee lifts:** lift each knee high in turn so that your thighs are parallel to the ground.

● **Alternate knee lifts:** still lifting your knees, alternate your arms and legs: touch your left knee with your right arm and vice versa.

● **Chest presses:** bring your arms together across your chest so that the elbows, wrists and fists touch.

● **Hamstring curls:** with arms swinging loosely, bring your heels up to your buttocks.

● **Upper back squeezes:** squeeze your shoulder-blades together as you march.

● **Walk on the spot** for one minute, arms swinging, until you gradually come to a stop.

WALK-FIT SECRETS

Fitness expert and beauty editor Chrissie Painell is a great believer in the power of walking. But she says that for optimum exercise, you should go beyond a fast-paced stroll, and suggests incorporating these moves into your walk-out…

1 Walk tall. Lift up from the chest, keep your shoulders relaxed back and down. This will help you to breathe more deeply.

2 Breathe in through your nose and out through your mouth.

3 Keep your elbows bent at an angle of 90 degrees. (Imagine you are holding an egg in each hand.) This will help to ensure that your upper body movement is coming from your shoulders.

4 Your heel should land first. Then roll through to the balls of the feet and toes. Push off with the back leg as you bring your other leg forward.

5 Try to glide along. When your stride is too long, you break the forward motion and slow yourself down. If your hair is flopping up and down wildly, you may be over-striding.

6 Keep your abdominal muscles pulled firmly in to support your back.

7 Try to avoid swinging your hips.

8 Avoid dehydration. And avoid eating a large meal before your walk. Drink water before, during and after a workout, ideally sipping from your water bottle every 10–15 minutes.

9 Plan a well-lit route.

10 Remember: warm up and cool down for three to five minutes, walking more slowly at the beginning and the end of your workout.

STEPPIN' OUT – MUSIC TO WALK TO

Our top ten music suggestions to get you in the mood for walking…
1 **Simply the Best** by Tina Turner (to warm up)
2 **Do Ya Think I'm Sexy?** by Rod Stewart (to warm up)
3 **La Isla Bonita** by Madonna
4 **You Should Be Dancing** by the Bee Gees
4 **Good Vibrations** by the Beach Boys
5 **Everybody's Talkin'** by Harry Nilsson
6 **Cosmic Girl** by Jamiroquai
7 **Young Hearts, Run Free** by Candi Staton
8 **I'm So Excited** by the Pointer Sisters
9 **Hallelujah Chorus** from Handel's *Messiah* (to get you to the top of the hill or mountain!)
10 **The Long and Winding Road** by the Beatles (to cool down)

How can you tell if you're walking at the optimum pace? You need to have your heart rate raised – but don't overdo it. The easiest test is the 'talk' test: you should be able to pass the odd sentence as you walk, but if you can have a lengthy, effortless gossip, you're not working hard enough.

Eat within 60-90 minutes of exercising to reboost energy levels.

WHO'S WALKING

Walking advertisements – literally – include Michelle Pfeiffer ('walking burns fat and gives me energy for the day'), Hillary Rodham Clinton, Sophia Loren, Catherine Deneuve and L'Oréal 'face' Andie McDowell, who says she walks 'for vanity and sanity'.

SHOE SAVVY

The beauty of walking lies in its total simplicity: expensive gear and flashy Spandex are superfluous. But if you're planning to go walkabout regularly, do invest in a pair of supportive shoes. We are great fans of the Ecco range from Denmark, which get better and better with every season, combining style with amazing comfort; their shoes are often smart enough for meetings – but supportive enough for an eight-mile hike. Many are lace-ups, which stop the foot 'rolling' as you walk. The American range Aerosoles is fantastic, too.

Alternatively, look for a pair of walking trainers in a sports shoe store. If you can't find a pair specifically for walking, ask for 'cross-trainers', designed to be suitable for a range of sports, including walking. Ask for advice in a sports shoe shop, if you need guidance. Most of us have one foot bigger than the other, so always fit for your bigger foot (and, if necessary, wear an extra sock on the other foot), rather than squeeze your toes into a shoe size too small. Adequate toe space is vital. Heels shouldn't grip too tightly: leave enough space to fit a pencil between your heel and the back of the shoe, to avoid blistering. Half a size larger than usual may make the difference between exquisite pleasure and total torture. The soles should be flexible, so that you get a full range of movement through the foot. When trying on shoes, wear the socks you'll usually be walking in. (You might want to keep at least two pairs of walking shoes of slightly different sizes, one for winter and one for summer; replace pairs them every six months, if you walk regularly, as the heels get worn down.) And remember: for long, wet walks, two pairs of socks – or changing into a fresh pair midway – can prevent agonising blisters caused by damp-sock rub.

MORE SHOE TALK

All the shoes you choose to wear – at any time – are key to body alignment. High heels throw your weight forward to your forefeet. Compensating for the disruption can involve your entire musculoskeletal system: watch out for head, shoulder and back aches, not to speak of throbbing feet and injured calf muscles. The best advice is to wear low heels with plenty of room for your toes – crease marks on your feet mean toes are cramped.

Because your bones become more rigid as you age, high heels become even more of a problem from the age of 40 onwards. Wearing them very occasionally is OK – not at all is best, and certainly not for a standing-around sort of party or for dancing – or walking.

And if you are determined to get on your high heels, don't wear backless shoes or mules, and do protect corns with special tubing.

seven great reasons for walking

◆ Walking contributes to stabilising blood sugar levels, helping to avoid swings in mood and energy.

◆ Walking can lift your mood because it releases endorphins, your brain's mood-elevating compounds.

◆ Walking is weight-bearing exercise, so it helps fight osteoporosis.

◆ Research shows that people who combine exercise – like walking – with healthy eating are more likely to keep off weight than those who only diet. Not only that, it can peel off pounds. According to Dr Craig Sharp, professor of sports medicine at Brunel and Stirling Universities, 'At a moderate walking pace, you will burn up about five calories a minute; walking 20 minutes a day burns 100 calories a day – about three kilograms or eight pounds a year.'

◆ A regular walking programme builds endurance in the large muscle groups that stabilise and support the spine, helping to prevent (and even cure) back pain.

◆ It's great for the heart. Walking strengthens the heart, making it pump blood more efficiently through the body – and raising the level of HDL ('good') cholesterol, which helps cleanse the surplus fat from blood vessels and so reduces deaths from heart disease.

◆ Walking can even help to improve your reaction time – in tests, it's been shown that not only do exercisers' muscles work better – so do their minds.

BRAIN BAGS

If you carry a shoulder (or hand) bag, swap it from side to side. Don't use your shoulder as a hook; try to hitch a bag round the back. Preferably use a rucksack like the one Jo is striding out with below – very chic and savvy!

take strides, not Prozac

When you're feeling blue, walking can put you back in the pink. The Exercise Laboratory at the University of California claims that 'a vigorous walk can be more effective than 400mg of tranquilliser'. And since walking is suitable for everyone – from the overweight and the elderly, not to mention pregnant women – there really is no excuse not to lace up and step out.

no sweat

Everyone sweats, and when it's hot or we're nervous, we sweat even more. Research shows, however, that one in five of us is embarrassed by perspiration and nearly two thirds of women report wetness after using their regular deodorant.

There is a range of simple measures which may help to stop wetness and prevent body odour:
◆ frequent regular washing, plus thorough drying;
◆ shaving armpit hair;
◆ loose clothing made of natural fibres, eg, cotton or silk;
◆ shoes rather than boots;
◆ combined deodorant and antiperspirant products, such as Mitchum for Problem Perspiration;
◆ stronger products such as Driclor, which contains aluminium chloride; this is used at night then washed off in the morning before applying a normal product.

REACH FOR ▶ THE SUN

The Salute to the Sun is considered the perfect way to greet the day, stretching the body into wakefulness by unkinking muscles and banishing creakiness. It also helps de-mist foggy minds. Yoga sessions usually start with this gentle Salute to the Sun, to warm the muscles. You need to do it barefoot and make sure that you're on a non-slip surface – and don't try to reach for the sun immediately on getting out of bed; do some warm-up exercises such as the stomp and stretch warm-up march (page 169) or go for a walk first.

1 Stand straight with your feet hip-width apart. Toes should be spread and the weight evenly distributed between heels and toes; knees should be straight but not locked. Hold in your tummy. (You will feel your back straighten.) Breathe in slowly and deeply. As you breathe out again, bring your hands up and place your palms together at chest level, keeping your forearms straight but not stiff.

5 Inhaling, bring your left knee back so that it's next to your right knee, creating a box shape with your body. Hold your tummy in and ensure that your shoulders are directly over your hands. (Now you'll be looking at the floor.) Keep breathing deeply and naturally. (NB: if you are at all stiff or have neck or shoulder problems, we suggest you stop here. See note opposite and skip to step 8.)

6 Breathing in, slide your hands forward a few inches. Keeping your knees and feet on the floor, bottom raised, maintain your weight on your arms and lower your trunk very gently to the floor. Now lower your forearms to the floor. Lift your head slightly; keep your shoulders back and down and make sure you don't strain or over-arch your back and neck. Only come up as far as is comfortable – this may be a very small distance.

7 Breathe out and tuck your toes under. Without allowing hands or feet to move, raise yourself on your forearms as far as you can. Leaning on your knees, push your bottom up so you're back in the box position and then push your hips up. Tuck your head in, so that you're looking through your legs. (This is called the mountain position, because of the shape the body makes.)

WATCHPOINT: you can only do this with your toes gripping the floor. Remember to keep breathing, and try not to tense your shoulders.

2 Breathe in and stretch your arms over your head; hold your tummy in to prevent your back over-arching. Your arms should be in line with your ears, elbows and knees straight, palms a few inches apart, fingertips reaching upwards. Look straight ahead, but don't let your chin poke forwards.

WATCHPOINT: don't let your shoulders rise; feel your shoulder-blades sinking down even as you reach for the sky.

3 Bend your knees slightly. While keeping your arms and body stretched, breathe out slowly and bend forwards, keeping your head tucked in towards your knees. Bring your hands to the floor, next to your feet. (Don't worry if you can't reach that far; let them dangle, then take another deep breath – as you exhale, your hands will drop. As you become increasingly flexible, you may be able to straighten your knees and even touch your forehead to them.)

4 Breathe in, and with knees bent and palms flat on the floor next to your feet, stretch your right leg as far back as possible. (Fingers are spread and pointing forwards.) Drop your right knee to the floor. Your front left knee should be directly above your ankle. Eyes up, look straight ahead. Breathe out slowly.

8 Breathe in; bring your right foot forwards between your hands, letting your back foot uncurl and your body slide backwards so that once again you are in position 4. Make sure your front knee is aligned with your ankle and uncurl your back toes.

9 You are now going back to position 3, so breathe out, bringing your left foot forwards parallel with your right foot, several inches apart. Hands are by your side on or towards the floor (whichever is comfortable for you), forehead facing your knees, which are slightly bent.

10 Breathe in as you slowly and gently uncurl your body, with your head coming up last. When you're upright reach your arms forward and stretch them up over your head, eyes looking straight ahead, breathing naturally.

11 Breathe out and stretch your arms either side of your body until they come to a resting position, putting you back ready for position 1.

Repeat the whole sequence from start to finish, this time leading with your left leg in position 4. Build up until you can go through the entire cycle five or six times, to warm and loosen up the body. Keep the entire movement fluid and as smooth as possible, your breathing steady.

NOTE: if you have neck or shoulder problems, go through positions 1-5, then skip right to position 8. This will still be enough to get your energies flowing. Once you have reached for the sun, your muscles are warm – and you are ready for some individual yoga postures.

YOGA WISDOM

In the quest for grace, strength and flexibility, yoga has topped the charts for thousands of years. Yoga fans see it not as a form of exercise but as a way of life, thanks to the amazing physical and mental benefits it delivers, bringing mind and body into balance.

Yoga postures (aka asanas) exercise every part of the body, stretching and toning all the joints, muscles, spine and skeleton, as well as massaging the internal organs to make them work efficiently. **Yoga is something that you can literally enjoy forever. We know women in their seventies and eighties who took up yoga in mid-life – or even later – and as a result have stayed amazingly limber, with extraordinary elegance. What's more, you don't need expensive equipment or snazzy clothing – simply a few minutes of peace and quiet. And because of the emphasis on deep breathing, with movements that help the body's natural energy to flow, yoga exercises can quickly re-energise you when you're flagging.**

YOGA BREATHING

In yoga, it's important to breathe from the diaphragm, rather than from the chest – breathe in and out through the nose, not the mouth. Babies breathe naturally from the diaphragm – think of their little tummies rising and falling – but adults tend to breathe from the chest and the more stressed out we are, the shallower our breath becomes.

To learn diaphragm breathing, stand straight with your feet together, shoulders down, hands resting on your hips. Then inhale deeply and push your stomach out from the diaphragm; it will inflate like a balloon. When you breathe out, let your tummy contract again.

the tree

This is wonderful for improving balance – and surprisingly challenging at first. Stand up straight with your feet together. Shift your weight to your right foot; bend the left knee and place that foot against the opposite thigh/knee as high as you can get it. The knee should point outwards, with the sole of your left foot flat against the leg. Bring your hands together in the prayer position in front of your chest; keeping the palms together, slowly extend your arms above your head, elbows slightly bent. Focus on a point in front of you, breathing rhythmically and gently. Hold in position for 15 seconds to start with (building up to 30 seconds as your balance improves). Repeat, with the opposite leg.

the butterfly

This improves hip flexibility and stretches the groin area. Sitting on the ground with your back straight, bring the soles of your feet together. Take hold of your feet with both hands and draw them in towards the groin, being ultra-careful not to over-stretch. Keeping your back straight, hold the position for 30 seconds and gently release. Then repeat.

spinal twist

This boosts mobility and loosens up the spine, so it's good for muscle problems in the hips and back. Sit on the floor with both legs straight in front of you. Bend the left leg at the knee and place it over the right leg, with the foot flat on the floor outside the right knee. Put your left hand flat on the floor just behind your body. Then gently twist your torso and place your right hand on the floor, beside the left knee. Follow that line so that you are looking over your left shoulder, keeping your shoulders parallel to the floor. Very gently push your right elbow into the left knee. Hold for 30 seconds, then switch sides. Repeat. As always, be gentle and don't push yourself further than is comfortable. Practised regularly, the spinal twist will soon boost your flexibility more than you can imagine.

relaxation pose

This is the classic way to finish a yoga workout, relaxing the body and stilling the mind. Lie on your back with your arms by your side, palms facing upwards, legs slightly apart and eyes closed. Try to make your body as symmetrical as possible. Breathe deeply into your abdomen and then up into your chest so that your breath feels like a rolling wave. With each breath, allow gravity to help your body sink deeper into the floor. Be aware of all the parts of your body that are in contact with the floor. Bring your awareness to any tension in your body and let them gently relax. (This is a powerful time to repeat any affirmations to yourself.) Stay in the relaxation pose for at least three minutes or until you feel totally relaxed and ready to face life with a renewed charge of positive energy.

YOGA ESSENTIALS

◆ Exercise slowly.

◆ Don't stretch the body to the point where it's uncomfortable.

◆ Make sure the room is warm – or that you're wearing a cosy jumper.

◆ Try to turn off the telephone or exercise in a place where you won't be disturbed.

◆ Wear comfortable clothing and take off any jewellery that might get in the way.

◆ Always perform yoga exercises with bare feet, so that you don't slip, especially on wooden or tile floors.

◆ If you don't have a special exercise mat, you may want to use a thick towel to help cushion yourself against a hard floor.

LIZ EARLE

We're inspired by the way our friend Lizzie – formerly a bestselling health and beauty author and TV presenter, with a passion for natural living – took a business gamble to launch Liz Earle Naturally Active Skincare. And we're in awe of how she stays serene, despite juggling a growing global beauty empire with four children and her polo-playing, film-maker husband.

'I don't believe in obsessing about beauty; it's off my "to do" list. When my friend Kim Buckland and I created Naturally Active Skincare it was because, as busy working mothers, we wanted products that did the job beautifully, so we could get on with more important things. Yes, I worry about wrinkles – I certainly use more Smoothing Line Serum than I used to! – but my main skin bugbears were eczema and sensitivity, and my skincare has sorted those out. My husband loves me for who I am, and isn't bothered by the lines on my face, so I don't get hung up about it.

'You can eat to feed your face. Vitamins, minerals and essential fatty acids are our cells' building blocks, and my skin is stronger and more resilient if I take evening primrose oil and borage oil. I top it up with a good multivitamin, and specific herbs at different seasons – cleansing herbs such as dandelion, nettle and burdock, for instance, in January. But I don't take much of anything on holiday – partly because I can't be bothered to pack them, but also because it's important to break obsessions.

'Over the years I've found that eating low GI [glycemic index] foods suits me. During the week I avoid anything white: flour, pasta, rice, sugar, etc. If I'm travelling, I eat Japanese food if I can and I take a tub of home-made low GI muesli with me; if I blow it with a croissant for breakfast, that's the day gone haywire, blood sugar-wise. At home we eat seasonally – and organically, which matters to me for all sorts of reasons: traceability, nutrition, animal welfare. You wouldn't put two-star fuel into a racing car, so why put junk food into your body?

'Frankly I'd like to exercise more, but it's the first thing to go if I'm short of time. My metabolism slowed down once I hit 40 so I make more of a conscious effort to walk from A to B and I never begrudge carrying heavy bags because it's like lifting weights, in terms of strengthening my bones. I feel better if I've slept well – I have to have at least seven hours. What also works for me is ten to 15 minutes' activity to kickstart my metabolism in the morning: stretching, running on the spot – no complicated equipment. If I have more time, I'll exercise to a Pilates or yoga DVD.

'My skincare regime is based around my own range! Starting with Cleanse & Polish Hot Cloth Cleanser, because cleansing perfectly is the most important thing you can do for your skin. I love the instant skin-glowing effect of Instant Boost Skin Tonic, and I use the Dry Skin version of our Skin Repair, because it's got the highest level of skin-plumping avocado oil, GLA from borage seeds and natural-source vitamin E. At night, I put on Smoothing Line Serum, and if I'm having a tiring or stressful time, I'll slather on Superskin Concentrate. If I need a quick fix of radiance, I use Brightening Treatment or Gentle Face Exfoliator. Cosmetic surgery doesn't really tempt me – you can end up not looking like you and, in a way, become someone you're not, as a result.

'I became a Christian after I married my second husband. My faith has had such a positive impact and is increasingly what I rely on to get me through life. You can't literally "feel fab forever" until you've sorted out your relationship with God. I always look forward to church on Sunday and I certainly get a lot of my strength, peace of mind and sanity in this crazy world from the power of prayer. It also has a dramatic impact on how well I feel and look.

'Age is pretty irrelevant to me; I live so much in the present that I don't really think about how I'll be when I'm 80. I'm blessed to have four beautiful children so I rather hope that I'll be surrounded by 14 adoring grandchildren, being a very active grandma. But I'm certainly not about to buy a twinset, get a perm, and start dressing like one!'

SLEEK AND TONE PILATES STYLE

The body-conditioning technique known as Pilates – which several of the team working on *Feel Fab Forever* swear by – is a system of slow, sleeking and toning exercises that can be used to spot-target specific areas of the body – from bad backs to saddlebag thighs via weak pelvic floor muscles (these slacken after childbirth and naturally with ageing – sometimes leading to stress incontinence and/or reduced sexual pleasure). This ability to overcome physical problems non-invasively and/or improve angst areas makes Pilates one of the most effective all-round forms of exercise – and great for anti-ageing.

Pilates (named after its founder, Joseph Pilates) is increasingly being taught in workout studios or by personal trainers around the world. In this gentle but super-effective exercise, the focus of attention is the three main control centres of the torso: the deep inner and outer abdominal muscles, and the pelvic floor muscles. This results in a stronger spine, improved posture, reduced back pain (even in long-term sufferers), and an amazingly sleeked silhouette; even the notoriously hard-to-tone tummy area can be impressively tightened.

The following spot-targeted exercises tighten up the whole pelvic area. The result: a tighter tummy, more control – and better sex. Beat that!

PELVIC FLOOR
Exercise 1

◆ Sit on a straight-backed chair and place a firm cushion between your knees.
◆ Keep your feet hip-width apart. Lengthen your spine by placing your hands either side of you, and very slightly behind you, on the chair.
◆ Draw your sitting bones together – which will raise your bottom slightly in the chair – and squeeze your inner thighs together. Squeeze on the cushion for seven slow breaths. Inhale through the nose and, as you exhale, pull the abdominal muscles in towards your spine.
◆ Do three sets of this exercise. For the second set, move the cushion halfway up your thighs. For the third set, place it right at the top of your thighs.

PELVIC FLOOR
Exercise 2

◆ Same position as for Exercise 1, without the cushion, so your inside knees are around 7.5cm (3in) apart to start with. Place a strap or a belt around your thighs just above the knee. Keeping a firm, tight grip on the strap, push your legs outwards. Draw the sitting bones together and hold this position for a set of seven breaths, pushing against the belt for resistance, without releasing at any time during these breaths. Then release the strap and do two more sets of seven breaths each, moving the feet and knees very slightly further apart each time on each set.

WATCHPOINT: don't tense up your neck and shoulders, and keep lengthening the spine.

the good sex (and everything else) workout

PELVIC TILT

Lie on your back with your knees bent and your feet parallel, hip-width apart and facing forwards on the floor. Place a firm cushion between your inner thighs. Stretch your arms forward on the floor, palms down. Start with your spine in a relaxed position. (The small of your back will be slightly off the floor.) Slowly inhale in this position and then exhale, gently squeezing the inner thighs. Pull your navel down towards your spine and curl your tailbone slightly off the floor. You will now feel the small of your back pressing into the floor. Exhale and curl your spine down to a relaxed position. You are now back where you started; slowly repeat ten times.

PELVIC LIFT

Start in the same position as for the pelvic tilt. Go through the same movements and breathing as for the pelvic tilt, but this time peel your spine off the floor to the level of your shoulder blades. Hold the position and inhale. Make sure your feet stay firmly flat on the floor and don't roll in either direction.

As you exhale, bring the spine back down to the floor, vertebra by vertebra, returning to your neutral position. Keep tipping the pelvis upwards on the way down. Repeat ten times. (NB: if you feel any pressure on your back, place your feet on a low, wide stool.)

WATCHPOINT: make sure you keep your jaw and neck 'soft'; don't allow them to tense up, or your chin to jut out.

I'm not a health fanatic; I eat a reasonable diet and just add in extra vitamin C if I remember. But for the last 20 years I've been doing Pilates – a system of long, slow stretching exercises – at Alan Herdman's studio in London's West End. I'm convinced it's the key to suppleness and good health. You slowly develop a very strong, sleek musculature, which not only helps keep the figure but prevents back pain, because the stomach muscles become so strong. You're very closely supervised, so you have to do every exercise perfectly, ensuring the maximum results in just an hour and a half once or twice a week. On a cold winter's morning I always think, shall I go? But I always feel so fantastic afterwards that it's worth it. Lately I've also taken up fast-walking, a couple of times a week, because my doctor said I wasn't getting enough aerobic exercise. Together they mean total fitness.

HONOR BLACKMAN

THE BAKED BEAN WORKOUT

Stay full of beans forever and discover the strengthening and toning power of weight training.

Women lose about a third of their muscle mass between the ages of 35 and 80, but inactivity, not ageing, is the major cause for the slow slide into creakiness when steps seem steeper, groceries become heavier. According to Research Into Ageing, even healthy people lose strength at some one to two per cent a year, and some may decline even faster. Strong muscles are, of course, essential to support your bones.

The good news is that weight and resistance training can reverse muscle decline. Two groups of women were observed for a study at the Jean Mayer USDA Human Nutrition Research Center on Ageing at Tufts University, Boston: one group remained in couch potato mode, while the other group came in twice a week to lift weights. One year later, the inactive group was even less active than before; their muscles and bones had aged. But according to the study's co-ordinator, Miriam E Nelson, PhD, 'The women who lifted weights changed, too – but in a miraculous way: after one year of strength training, their bodies were 15 to 20 years more youthful.' And it really is never too late to

turn back the clock: a recent study showed that women aged 75 to 93 who exercised gently for a total of three hours a week improved the strength of their thigh muscles by around 25 per cent in only 12 weeks. This improvement is equal to a rejuvenation of strength of some 16 to 20 years. And in yet another study, it was found that muscles remain capable of improving with use even in the tenth decade of life.

You certainly don't need expensive equipment for weight training. If there are a couple of cans of baked beans in your larder, you've the recipe for a simple upper-body workout to regain strength – and improve posture. Holistic therapist Gloria Thomas (once a Bond girl and Pirelli pinup), gave us this baked bean workout. It's suitable for every woman because it can be done sitting or standing. Start slowly, but 'Do each exercise until your muscles become tired,' says Gloria. 'If you ultimately find you are doing endless repetitions, switch to a slightly larger can of beans!'

WATCHPOINT: don't forget to breathe!

SHOULDERS

Sit in an upright position. Your abdominal muscles should be pulled in, your shoulders back and down. Your head and neck should be relaxed. With a can of baked beans in each hand, bring your hands to shoulder level, with your palms facing forwards and arms straight. Inhale and take the can of baked beans up above your head to a count of two, then slowly lower to the starting position.

BICEPS

Keep the same sitting position as before, with your upper arms by your sides and your palms facing each other, holding the cans. Keeping your elbows close to the body in a fixed position, bend your arms, palms upward, and curl up towards your shoulders for two counts; lower to a count of four.

TRICEPS

Do this exercise one arm at a time, or both at the same time if you're used to exercising. Once again, keeping the same position as above, grasp a can of baked beans between the thumb and forefingers of each hand. Take your arms behind your head so that your elbows are just above either ear. Straighten your arms upwards until your baked bean can is overhead. Take care not to lock your elbows. Slowly return to starting position.

BACK

This is great for strengthening the muscles of the back and for posture. In the same sitting position as above, hold a can of beans in each hand and hold your arms out in front of you at shoulder level. Now take your arms around to the side, pulling your shoulder blades together, for two counts. Your hands should end up in line with your shoulders, making you into a T shape. Slowly go back to your original position.

swim to health

Some biologists believe mankind came from water. That, they say, is why we need to drink so much water, why we do so well on fishy food and why infants up to six months old have the same diving reflex as aquatic mammals like dolphins: drop a baby into water and it will submerge, stop breathing, slow down its heart rate, then re-emerge, turn its head to the side, breathe and dive again. (Dolphins' flippers, incidentally, have exactly the same bones that we have in our arms and hands.)

Whatever our evolutionary background, there is no doubt that swimming is wonderful exercise. Water's innate buoyancy makes it the perfect environment for workouts for all ages – whether it's for re-hab from injuries or keeping fit. Water exercise can improve the way your body works overall; in particular, it improves digestion and sleep patterns, reduces 'bad' cholesterol and, of course, makes regular swimmers sleek and toned. It is also a resistance exercise, so it helps protect you against osteoporosis. Water workouts in a swimming pool or the sea can be ultra-simple. You don't even have to know how to swim.

● Walk in water
Walk in chest-height water from one side to another, then walk backwards; keep your arms swinging.

● Crab walk
Now walk sideways, like a crab, across the pool, your body at right angles to

the side. Keep your feet pointing straight ahead and bring them together after each step. Don't turn when you reach the other side; simply lead with the other foot. Repeat both walks several times; work up to a run if possible.

● Trunk twist
Stand in shoulder-deep water, legs a shoulder-width apart, knees slightly bent. Extend arms straight out to sides, parallel to surface, palms facing forwards; swing body round to the right and the left.

● Front-back leg raise
Stand in chest-deep water at right angles to pool wall, holding on to bar. Raise your outer leg straight up in front of you. Lower leg and continue movement to the back, keeping your knee and back straight. Turn round and repeat on other side.

● Side leg raise
Stand in chest-deep water at right angles

to pool wall, holding on to bar. Lift outer leg directly to side, keeping toes forward. Repeat on other side.

● Arm pull
Stand in shoulder-deep water, legs a shoulder-width apart. Bend knees slightly. Extend arms directly in front of you, palms down and hands cupped. Keeping your elbows straight, pull your arms down past your body and behind. Then turn your hands around so your palms are facing down and push arms back to starting position.

WARNING: swimming is a wonderful form of exercise but, if you have a bad neck and/or back, beware of the breast stroke. London-based physician and back expert Dr Richard Petty says that it can exacerbate the condition unless you keep your face in the water. Some sufferers report that back crawl gives the most benefit.

CELLULITE: THE BOTTOM LINE

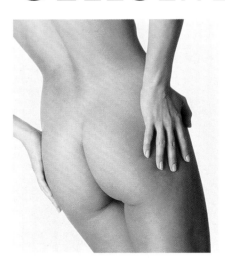

ACTION PLAN FOR DIMPLED DERRIÈRES

About 95 per cent of women have some degree of cellulite, the orange-peel skin on thighs and bottom, which ranges from dimples to the full-blown mattress look. American dermatologist Dr Howard Murad, author of *The Cellulite Solution*, explains that cellulite isn't down to too much fat, it's caused by dehydration and weakening of the skin cells, so that fat cells can push into the middle layer of skin (the dermis) and show through the surface. By eating well and taking carefully chosen supplements, plus applying skin preps (see opposite), you can 'repair, rehydrate and revitalise your skin – forcing stubborn fat cells back below the surface, and keeping them there,' he says. It's not insoluble, but equally it won't disappear overnight.

Allow at least four to six weeks on the programme, right, to see changes. (But just think how long it took to appear!) We're doubtful that cellulite ever disappears totally, but most women will see a big improvement.

DIY cellulite solutions

- Clean up your diet: exclude fatty sugary treats and fat/salt combinations.
- Feast on high-fibre fruit and veg, whole grains, protein-rich foods and 'good' omega-3 fats (see page 190).
- Balance your blood sugar by eating every two to three hours (see page 190).
- Avoid artificial additives, eg, pesticides, colourings, sweeteners, etc.
- Drink at least eight glasses of still, pure, room-temperature water daily.
- Reduce intake of alcohol as much as possible.
- Try this supplement programme, devised by pharmacist Shabir Daya, based on Dr Murad's advice (available online from Victoria Health):

All Natural Perfectly Balanced by Natural Nutrition Centre; one tablet three times daily, with or just after food.
Ultimate B Complex by Nature's Secret; one tablet daily, with or immediately after food.
Essential Oil Formula by Nature's Secret; three capsules daily, after food.
Glucosamine Sulphate 1000mg by Nature's Aid; two tablets daily after food.
Goji Berry Juice by Lifetime Vitamins, 1,000ml; 30ml daily, before breakfast.

- Try stretching and toning exercise, eg, yoga, dance; and swimming, plus a brisk daily walk.
- Brush your (dry) skin daily.
- Don't take diuretics/slimming pills.
- Investigate alternatives to the pill and HRT.
- Try manual lymphatic drainage massage (MLD, see page 61) or gentle self-massage with anti-cellulite oil.
- Most specific cellulite products improve skin appearance and feel, but any 'shrinking' may be short lived.

PROFESSIONAL CELLULITE SOLUTIONS

Ionithermie
A salon treatment combining plant and mineral preparation with a gentle electric current; good for tone and texture and may be useful in combination with a basic home treatment programme.

Mesotherapy
An expensive medical therapy where minute quantities of pharmacological drugs are injected into the cellulite deposits to boost circulation, stimulate drainage and digest hard-lump tissues around cells. Should be combined with a basic home treatment programme.

Endermologie
The only FDA approved treatment for cellulite: you're wrapped in a body stocking then massaged all over your body with two adjustable rollers. The process stretches and weakens the fibrous tissues and breaks down the fat cells. It also makes the skin more flexible and supple.

Surgery
No surgical intervention has been shown to remove cellulite – and it may damage circulation and the lymph system.

BEWARE! Clinics promising miracle cellulite cures spring up like mushrooms everywhere. Regimes are expensive, clients may be asked to pay up front and results seldom seem to match promises.

tried & tested
ANTI-AGEING BODY CREAMS

It is still our experience that women are reluctant to invest in body creams – unlike face-saving miracle creams. But, as these results show, anti-ageing body creams can deliver spectacular results, improving dryness, targeting flakiness and goose-bumps and even minimising age spots and cellulite.

LANCÔME ABSOLUE BODY ABSOLUT REPLENISHING BODY CREAM
Score: 8.79/10

A remarkable score for this product – although it comes at a sky-high price. With a stress-relieving fragrance and luxurious texture, its nourishing, firming action is combined with anti-age-spot properties.
Comments: 'Skin feels smoother and firmer' • 'legs and arms stay moisturised longer' • 'smells gorgeous; love the texture' • 'improved "bubbly" patches on my calves' • 'my skin is radiant'.

REN WILD YAM WITH OMEGA 7 BODY CREAM ✻
Score: 8.41/10

This has scored well in *Beauty Bible* trials as a body cream, but this time it wowed for its anti-ageing performance. With wild yam – long used for menopausal women – it also features EFA-rich sea buckthorn berry oil. Not totally natural, but high in botanicals, and no paraben preservatives.
Comments: 'The best I have tried: skin looks ten years younger!' • 'skin feels quenched and really soft' • 'easy to smooth in; could get dressed straight away' • 'excellent – skin lovely and soft throughout the day' • 'improvement to my legs and upper legs – a lot tighter'.

DARPHIN HYDROFORM FIRMING BODY CREAM
Score: 8.31/10

Darphin, now part of the Lauder empire, are seeing their popularity grow worldwide. With a revitalising fragrance of lemon, orange and bergamot essential oils, this is somewhere between mousse and cream and meant to promote all-over firmness.
Comments: 'Skin is more firm – toned and smoothed' • 'it's like whipped cream mixed with lemon curd, with a gorgeous, luxurious fragrance' • 'divine; absorbed very quickly' • 'bingo wings improved!'

CLARINS RENEW-PLUS BODY SERUM
Score: 8.05/10

We are never surprised when a Clarins product scores well – this is no exception. Created in response to pleas for an all-over anti-ageing treatment, it includes pro-Retinol, wintergreen, Madagascan white lily, olive and cashew nut oil, in a light fluid for twice-daily use, to firm, smooth and even out skintone. (NB: many testers commented on the small-ish bottle.)
Comments: 'I used this mostly on my thighs, which are marked with cellulite; you could have knocked me over when I saw the instant change' • 'definitely made a difference to my arms' • 'creamy without being greasy' • 'my skin glowed – instantly smoother' • 'love the smell'

L'OCCITANE FIRMING AND SMOOTHING ALMOND MILK CONCENTRATE
Score: 8/10

Rich in almond milk, oil and protein (to boost collagen synthesis), this cream – from Provence-based L'Occitane – is designed to show effects in three to four weeks. Testers were taken by softness rather than firming actions, and were mixed about the marzipan-y fragrance.
Comments: 'I used this while out in the sun, but my skin did look healthier' • 'smells lovely – doesn't overpower perfume; skin is smoother and softer'.

LAVERA LAVERÉ BODY CONTROL BODY LOTION ✻ ✻
Score: 7.9/10

An all-natural option from German brand Lavera's high-tech, top-to-toe anti-ageing range, targeted primarily at cellulite, with natural fruit acids and caffeine (as well as moisturising water lily essence and liposomes). But our testers found it a very effective all-over treatment for body skin.
Comments: 'tops of thighs and backs of legs much firmer' • 'dry patches on legs have been smoothed away' • 'skintone and texture much improved' • 'beautiful to use; lumpiness on thighs is reduced'.

beauty steal ★ ST IVES SKIN FIRMING BODY LOTION
Score: 7.75/10

We included this as a high-performance affordable option – featuring cocoa seed butter, ginkgo and rosemary. St Ives' own trials saw skin firmness improved by up to 31 per cent in eight weeks. Some testers saw great results; others felt it was no different to any other body moisturiser.
Comments: 'skin so soft, noticeably smoother' • 'stomach smoother and upper arms a lot more toned – for the price, it really performs' • 'reasonable improvement in tone and elasticity'.

guidelines for golden girls' wardrobes

The right choice of clothes can work figure-slimming, confidence-boosting miracles. So fashion expert Amanda Platt – a London-based wardrobe consultant and TV clothes guru – offers this wisdom on elegant dressing for all women *d'un certain age...*

● 'Treat age as something to be cherished, rather than something to fight. If you're at ease with who you are, you'll look better in everything.'

● 'Aim for more style and more gloss in clothes - like your hair and make-up. Buy fewer, better-cut clothes.'

● 'Dress appropriately for your age and the occasion.'

● 'Big outlays should all be in neutral colours. After 25, cut is everything. Save up for things that don't date.'

● 'If you wear a baggy jacket you'll just end up looking big all over. Invest instead in a tailored jacket that has been cut in at the "kidneys" – that area at the back, just above the waist – it improves every shape.'

● 'Larger bosomed ladies could consider small shoulder-pads, which can give a crisper line to T-shirts and knitwear, and balance the bust. (Not for the broad-shouldered, though.)'

● 'Sleeves and skirts should get a little longer as we get older. Elbow-length – or longer – sleeves are safest, to avoid underarms wobbling in the wind.'

● 'Frills and flounces are the kiss of death. Think crisp tailoring and clean lines – and keep it simple.'

● 'If you have any beautiful body part, dress to show it off – whether it's a neck, wrist, ankle, or waist. It distracts the eye from less-than-perfect parts.'

● 'Invest in good underwear, fitted by an expert. It's worth its weight in gold for the extra support and/or cinching-in that it delivers.'

● 'Get fitted regularly for a new bra. Bulging over your straps or cups makes you look as if you've put on weight.'

● 'Keep clothes dark from the waist down; dark tights, dark shoes and dark skirt creates a streamlined look. Then you can wear colour next to your face, to frame it.'

● 'Remember: the cut of a shoe is as vital as the cut of a suit.'

● 'Flat shoes are the most practical but they can make ankles look bigger. Try having a shoemaker add 1cm (1/2in) on to the heel – it can make all the difference.'

● 'Unless you have a divine figure, it's best to save jeans for gardening. Switch to well-cut trousers.'

WHAT ALL WELL DRESSED WARDROBES SHOULD CONTAIN...

◆ A good quality steam iron

◆ A professional steamer (or steam your clothes in the bathroom after your bath!)

◆ A special brush/sweater shaver for removing the 'pilling' from jerseys and cashmeres

◆ A sticky-tape roller

◆ Scotchguard fabric protector

◆ Sewing kit

◆ Button box

◆ Belt hangers

◆ Trouser hangers

◆ Skirt hangers

◆ Dress hangers

◆ A spot remover

◆ A tube of neutral leather cream

◆ A suede brush and spray

◆ Spray waterproofer for leather

◆ Moth-proofing spray (NB: use all sprays near a wide open window or preferably outdoors, particularly if you are allergic)

◆ Hanging bags, preferably cloth

MAKING SUMMER BARE-ABLE

As we get older, we love winter more – because it gives us the chance to hide less-than-perfect body bits under opaque tights and high-necked pullovers. But rather than sweat miserably through hot weather under too many layers, we thought we'd ask Belinda Seper – owner of ultra-stylish Belinda Boutique in Sydney's Double Bay, and a woman who regularly turns up on the 'best-dressed list' Down Under – for her advice on how to dress when the mercury's rising…

◆ 'You don't have to go bare-legged if you don't think yours are up to it: look for sheer, 9-denier tights which are like gossamer. They feel as if you're wearing hardly anything but disguise uneven skintone – and seem to suck in those little bits that hang over the kneecap!'

◆ 'Floaty silk palazzo pants are a terrific choice for your bottom half. If you want to wear tighter clothes, go for stretch fabrics, because they don't feel so restricting. A pair of the most expensive stretch pants that you can afford is a fantastic investment and will shave off years – and inches. Today's stretch fabrics look just like any other fabric – but feel fabulous on.'

◆ 'Linen makes a terrific summer fabric – if you can live with the crumples. Personally I like that layered linen look of a baggy shirt over trousers – but you have to give up being paranoid about not being perfectly ironed.'

◆ 'Check out tailoring in lightweight wools, which are almost as cool to wear as cotton – but slightly more structured and business-like, and don't crumple.'

◆ 'For summer jackets, try lightweight wool mixes, silk mixes, linen mixes – blended with viscose or acetate. They're light enough to wear over a T-shirt without expiring, if you'd rather not take your jacket off. An alternative to the summer jacket is a soft, knitted silk or viscose cardigan. With pants and a simple T-shirt in cotton or silk, they're the picture of cool summer dressing.'

◆ 'Spend the maximum on swimwear that you can possibly afford. With swimsuits, you want them fabulously constructed on the inside, with tummy panels and uplift if you need it, plus a flattering cut to the leg. Spend time – and money – finding the right bathing suit. Remember: no swimming costumes at the buffet table. Wear a sarong – or buy a couple of yards of chiffon and tie it around your hips. (And don't forget lashings of SPF15 on the chest.)'

◆ 'Steer clear of anything around the neck: scarves or high necklines. They make for instant hot flushes – even if you're not menopausal.'

◆ 'I prefer clean, simple lines: a T-shirt snug to the body is much more flattering than a loose blouse.'

◆ 'Layer a sheer blouse over a T-shirt if you're self-conscious about your arms. You can put on a bodysuit, a camisole or a skinny underpiece and fling an organza, silk chiffon or georgette shirt over the top. Or drape a piece of chiffon over your arms, shawl-style – it's a wonderful fabric for disguising little bumps and curves and blurring the edges a little.'

◆ 'Beware of dresses that are too loose and floaty – the Ghost look. The risk is that you end up looking like a walking fridge and nobody can tell that you've got a shape underneath. Try to buy dresses which are slightly more shaped at the waist, without being tight.'

◆ 'If summer dressing is a problem, go to a professional – or buy a book on how to dress stylishly and soak up the advice. People think that getting dressed and made up comes naturally – but it doesn't. You wouldn't mend your own lavatory; you'd get a plumber. If you don't want to go to a personal shopper, find a fashion sales assistant who's your age and whose style you like – not some skinny 16-year-old – for advice.'

◆ 'Age is a state of mind, not a number. Clothes can help – but there comes a point where women have to accept themselves for who they are, and the ageing process is part of that. We're all individual, and if we were all perfect, that would be boring. If I want to wear a sleeveless dress and it's a hot day, I wear it, even if I'm not that happy with my arms. I get a little bit funny about the veins in my legs but I'm too busy to get them fixed. There are plenty of people out there who specialise in helping you look and feel fabulous – so if there's something that really bugs you, deal with it. Otherwise, quit worrying and enjoy life.'

ANITA RODDICK

We've both known Anita for many years and we love her passion for life and living, for helping all sorts of people, particularly women in developing countries, and her invincible sense of justice. She's also fantastically good fun...

'Having energy is about feeling alive all the time and I feel SO alive. When I reached my forties, I decided that I was only going to be with people who move my spirit and educate me. I choose to live every day as if it's my last and act in order to have an effect. Action makes me feel alive: it's in my DNA. Some people find me irritating – they keep saying "oh calm down" – but I can't, this is my way of living.

'I sustain the energy because I actually live a quiet life a lot of the time. In my fifties I realised that I didn't want to be caught up in that hurry sickness. I can't sit still much but I'm not so obsessive now, partly because I like order – living has been so chaotic in the past. So I'm more reflective now. Also I read very well and I am always looking for inspiration.

'I always thought getting older would simply be a version of me with older skin but I didn't know how very physical ageing would be. It's not so much the wrinkles but gravity – the flesh dropping. Also a constant awareness of slowing down and of the movement of the body, its shape and the consternation of realising you're thinking about your health all the time. And I hate my hair getting thinner.

'But the good things like reinventing yourself are wonderful. It starts with knowing you did the best you could in terms of marriage, children and community. And with that comes a type of wisdom, which I think is knowledge with a canopy of good behaviour.

'The best thing about getting older is that you don't worry about the things you did in your twenties and thirties. I don't panic any more about what I look like. You don't angst so much about sexual attraction. In your fifties and sixties, you want to look good and healthy.

'I never smoke, don't drink alcohol and I eat really well – no red meat and lots of organic vegetables. I grow some in my own little veg garden and the greenhouse and make them sexy with olive oil and balsamic vinegar. I hate junk food and sugared waters. You have to protect yourself from fast food. I don't take supplements because I don't know what to take.

'Relaxing is simple: I go to our little local cinema – films are nice bite-size stories. I like putting my feet up and reading. I enjoy dinners at home with friends. And I love my garden. When I'm unhappy I write poetry. One thing I would like: to know how to take a holiday and enjoy it without feeling guilty.

'I do bugger-all exercise – I'm too embarrassed to go to the gym. But I like walking and I might buy a bicycle.

'I'm quite good at looking after my appearance, though my eyesight is so bad that make-up is hit-and-miss splodges. But looking good is a lot to do with posture and I do stand straight and proud. I am fashion oriented and I like the fact I make an effort, but it's really for myself: I say to Gordon, "Shall I wear that blue dress?" and he says, "Yes, do," – but there's no blue dress in my cupboard. I'm concerned now about elegantly covering up flesh rather than exposing it.

'My desert island must-haves would be salt – because it's a great exfoliator mixed with the Body Shop body butters. Exfoliating and moisturising are essential. Plus the most comfy bed and pillows!

'I couldn't take HRT because I have such high blood pressure but I loved the menopause, which happened in my late fifties, because nature was in charge – not me. So I revelled in the hot sweats, I just didn't wear silk.

'When we sold the Body Shop to L'Oréal [in April 2006], we made the decision to "give while we live". To really thank some of the people who helped shape our business, give a tranche to extended family, and the rest will be given away to human rights causes. But I'm not just going to sign a cheque; I want to get my hands dirty.

'I like that I'm really funny: I tell the worst jokes and I get lost halfway through. I want my life to be shaped by laughter. It gives you freedom against the bullshit of life.'

the fabulously simple guide to eating for health, beauty and happiness

We truly are what we eat (and drink). Each one of us is made up of about 63 per cent water, 22 per cent protein, 13 per cent fat and the remaining two per cent vitamins and minerals. Every bit of that comes from our diet. But the perfect fuel is not only nutritious – it's totally delicious. So your ultimate feel-good eating plan – to be enjoyed forever – starts here…

What we put in our bodies directly affects the way we look, our health (present and future), energy levels, our moods and even our brain power. So it's vital to get it right. It's politically correct nowadays to say that there is no such thing as good food and bad food. If you don't have enough, then of course all food is good. But most of us these days actually have too much – and we spend our time trying not to eat. So we're going to put our mouths where our money is and say we think there is a difference in the quality of food on offer.

Much mass-produced food – vegetables, fruit, meat and particularly cook-chill and processed food – is poor quality. It will keep you going but it may not give you the nourishment you need for gleaming health. The nutrients may have been leached out by intensive production and by processing. More worryingly, the food may well contain added chemicals which could impair our health – and the environment.

Many experts are now blaming sugar- and fat-laden processed foods for the pandemic of obesity, which leads inexorably to heart disease, diabetes and other life-threatening diseases. Over 30,000 new manmade chemicals, which the body is unused to, can be added to processed foods in the European Union. No wonder, you might think, that more and more people are finding that they suffer from food sensitivities.

Good-quality food for us is organic, grown and produced without the addition of unnatural chemicals. Both of us buy, grow and eat organic food. That's not every single mouthful – but as much as possible. (While we try to pick organic dishes on restaurant menus, for instance, we're not about to give up eating out just because there isn't much organic restaurant food around yet.) We like food the way nature intended, not put through umpteen chemical processes or genetically modified. And certainly *not* covered in layers of packaging, which contains more chemicals that harm us and the planet.

In the main, we eat vegetables, fruit, hardly any meat, a bit of fish, cheese, eggs, lots of grains and pulses, and plenty of good olive (and hemp) oil. You could call it eating like an Italian or Greek peasant – which is just fine because they've been proven scientifically to have the healthiest diets of all. We also love Japanese food and eat lots of soya and seaweed (see page 193). And we're very keen on the odd mouthful of organic chocolate, too.

Conventionally produced food simply doesn't taste as good as organic, and, as we've said, the battery of chemicals used on non-organic food – pesticides, antibiotics and growth hormones – may harm our health.

Actually, could someone please tell us what the point of intensively produced and/or genetically modified food is? (Apart from great profit to the vested interests in the food and chemical businesses, of course.)

The argument usually advanced against organic is that it's more expensive. But that partly depends on what you buy. If, for instance, you cut down on meat, in line with all the current medical recommendations, and use it as a garnish instead of the centrepiece of a meal, your bills plummet. Cost also depends on where you shop – supermarket or farm shop. Another way of cutting costs is to grow your own. Increasingly, people are growing at least some of their own vegetables and salads – in back gardens, allotments, window boxes, grow-bags – which not only saves money but is deeply satisfying.

Listening to all the different health lobby groups, it's easy to think that you should eat one way to help protect you against cancer, another for heart disease, and yet another for osteoporosis. And that's before you've got round to thinking about the food that's slimming, and gives you energy, sparkling eyes, glossy hair and clear skin.

The good news is that, actually, the way to fulfil all those food requirements is one and the same. It's very simple. And it's here in the *Feel Fab Forever* food guide. What's more, it's delicious. We know; we eat this way. We never diet – and we're pretty happy with our shapes. We never ever go hungry, we're bursting with energy, and we're always having treats.

The message is simple: eat fresh, eat organic, eat local. And please join our campaign to reduce unnecessary packaging by carrying your own shopping basket or bag.

EATING THE NATURAL WAY

◆ We are designed to graze, not gorge, in order to keep blood sugar levels steady (see overleaf). Aim to eat every two to three hours.

◆ Breakfast an hour or so after you wake up so your digestion has had a chance to get going. Never skip breakfast – you risk weight gain and low energy.

◆ Sit down at lunchtime for at least 45 minutes, if possible, and try to eat it in good company.

◆ Try not to drink too much with meals – it flushes the food through your body before it can be absorbed.

◆ Eat fruit between meals or at the beginning of a meal: it can get stuck in your digestive tract and ferment if eaten last.

◆ Have your last meal at least two hours before you sleep.

IDEAL FIGURES

Experts agree that for optimum health, what we eat should be divided up like this:

carbohydrate	70%
fat	15%
protein	15%

In fact, what most people eat looks like this:

carbohydrate	28%
fat	40%
protein	12%
sugar	20%

what's what in the food you eat

CARBOHYDRATE

Carbohydrate, which consists of sugars and starches, is the body's main fuel. It comes in two forms: 'fast release' (high GI) and 'slow release' (low GI). 'Fast release' foods include sugar, honey, malt, sweets and most refined foods; these give a spurt of energy as your blood sugar levels zoom up, followed by a slump as they crash down again. 'Slow release' foods include vegetables, fresh fruit and whole grains; these provide more sustained energy because they contain complex carbohydrates and fibre, which helps moderate the release of sugar into the bloodstream.

Aim to eat slow release, low GI carbohydrates as the mainstay of your diet, so that they make up 70 per cent of your total daily intake.

PROTEIN

This is absolutely essential, because it contains the 25 amino acids (forms of protein) which are the building blocks of the body. The best quality protein sources are fish, meat, beans, peas, lentils, quinoa, soya and eggs.

Aim to eat 35g (1^1/4oz) of protein daily, with one small serving of meat, fish, cheese, a free-range egg or tofu, to make up 15 per cent of your daily diet.

FIBRE

This absorbs water in the digestive tract, making food bulkier and easier to pass through the body; it maintains energy levels, and helps to prevent constipation and putrefaction of food (the underlying cause of many digestive complaints, including diverticulitis, colitis and bowel cancer). Eating a fibre-rich breakfast cereal is a proven way of helping to protect against bowel cancer. Fibre is found in whole grains, vegetables, fruit, nuts, seeds, lentils and beans.

Aim to eat at least 35g (1^1/4oz) of fibre daily, making up ten per cent of your calorie intake.

FATS

Fats or lipids are essential for the body, but in the right form – (see pages 194 and 195).

Bad fats
◆ Saturated fat is hard fat, found mainly in meat and dairy products, and is not essential for the body; it's linked to obesity, heart disease and a wide range of other illnesses.
◆ Hydrogenated (hardened) fats (aka trans fatty acids) are still found in some processed foods and are known to cause raised blood cholesterol and contribute to heart disease and some cancers.

Good fats (see also page 195)
◆ Unsaturated fat is found in cold pressed oils, nuts and seeds, and is thought to lower harmful cholesterol.
◆ Omega-3 is an essential fat found in oily fish with teeth (salmon, tuna, mackerel, herrings, sardines), linseeds, walnuts and walnut oil, flax seeds and oil. It is vital for the brain and nervous system, immune system, cardiovascular system and skin.
◆ Omega-6 is also essential, but we usually get enough in our daily diet, via sunflower and sesame seeds, safflower, soya and linseed.

Aim to eat: good fats only, and reduce fat intake from average 41 per cent of diet to a maximum of 30 per cent – and ideally 15 per cent.

THE BLOOD SUGAR CONNECTION

Stabilising your blood sugar levels is probably the most important factor in maintaining energy and weight levels, according to nutritionist Patrick Holford, as the amount of glucose (sugar) in the blood largely determines your appetite.

Glucose is raw material which your cells convert to energy. When the level drops, you feel hungry. When it's too high, the body converts the excess to glycogen, a short-term fuel stored mainly in the liver and muscle cells, or to fat, our long-term energy reserve. About three in every ten people find difficulty in keeping their blood sugar stable, rather than soaring (too high) and then dropping (too low).

Low blood sugar can trigger a whole raft of symptoms including fatigue, poor concentration, irritability, sweating, depression, headaches and digestive problems. It also contributes to hormonal problems, including PMS and menopausal symptoms.

The ideal is to keep our blood sugar levels on an even keel. Eating sugary foods is the biggest offender, with glucose – and foods which contain it – the worst of all. The best foods are pulses – peas, beans and lentils – and whole grains; all are high in complex carbohydrates and release their sugar content slowly. They are also high in fibre, which helps to stabilise blood sugar levels as well as aiding the digestive process. Follow the friendly foods on page 194 and don't skip meals.

the big question

There is a common belief that as women get older, it's inevitable that they get plumper. True or not? Not true, says leading expert Professor Michael Lean, head of the Department of Human Nutrition at the University of Glasgow, although we may change shape. The shift in hormone levels with the menopause (ie, falling oestrogen levels and comparatively higher testosterone levels) means that we are more likely to store fat around our middles rather than our hips. But hormone changes don't result in a major shift in appetite – and thus weight. It's more likely that we simply take less exercise and/or eat more, as we get older. 'People who keep using their legs (above 10,000 steps a day) don't gain weight,' he says.

Nevertheless, the huge problem of overweight and obesity in the so-called developed world should be taken seriously. Everyone can lose weight, according to Professor Lean, with a 'combined' programme of sensible diet (lower in bad fats, relatively higher in carbs, eg, veg) and exercise, plus psychological support.

Danger signs for obesity used to be predicted on Body Mass Index. Doctors have now simplified this and say that women of any height whose waist measurement is 80cm (32in) or more should try not to get bigger and, if possible, to take off some pounds. This emphatically does not mean crash dieting – it means lifestyle changes along the lines we suggest in *Feel Fab Forever*. With a waist measurement of 88cm (35in) or more, women are in danger of a serious medical problem and should consult their doctors immediately.

Professor Lean cautions most seriously against women consulting slimming clinics without their GP's referral and taking drugs which have not been scientifically validated and may be dangerous. 'Whether these clinics are in a village hall or in Harley Street in London, it's the same thing. They charge huge prices for drugs which cost pennies and patients are unlikely to receive the good multidisciplinary care they need,' he says.

Prescription drugs are available for truly intractable weight gain, but they can have serious and/or undesirable side effects. Surgery is a final option.

FOOD FOR FLATTER TUMS

Washboard stomachs are unrealistic for most older women, but almost everyone will be able to reduce a Rubens-esque belly. An efficiently working digestion and strong stomach muscles are the way to a flatter tummy. If you bloat easily, try cutting out all foods containing wheat, beans and all carbonated drinks. Explore food combining (see page 196), where fruit is eaten as a snack only, never at main meals, and protein foods are not eaten at the same meal as carbohydrates. All exercise helps, and re-bounding on a mini-trampoline has a marvellous effect on constipation. Also check out whether you may have food sensitivities, candida or Irritable Bowel Syndrome (IBS) (see pages 198-9). Then concentrate on the posture exercises on page 164 to improve your stomach muscles.

THREE GOOD REASONS NEVER TO DIET

◆ It doesn't work: 90 per cent of people who diet put the weight back – and more – within two years.

◆ Yo-yo dieting is a body and mind stressor, which contributes to hormonal problems, osteoporosis, cellulite, hair loss and chronic illness – and robs you of energy.

◆ Eating well – and taking exercise – will give you lots of energy and keep your body looking great at its natural weight. If you need to lose weight, try food combining (*see page 196*). Good food makes you thinner. Fill up on complex carbohydrates rather than quick-fix fatty or sugary snacks. 240 calories of stomach-satisfying potato are almost seven times more filling than the same amount of wouldn't-fill-up-a-bird croissant.

The opposite of fat is healthy – *not* thin.

Keep water, water everywhere: both sides of your bed, in the kitchen, even in the hallway. Bottled water is easiest – just grab and swig.

LAUREN HUTTON

SUPERFOODS FOR WOMEN

Scientists are learning more every day about the role of certain foods as disease-preventers, infection-fighters and potential life-extenders. And a new nutritional concept is emerging: eating more of certain foods so that we feel more vital and healthy and protect ourselves against illness.

We asked three of the world's top nutritionists – Joseph Pizzorno from Bastyr University in Seattle, Patrick Holford, founder of the Institute of Optimum Nutrition in London, and Kathryn Marsden, best-selling author on nutrition – to prescribe the superfoods that every woman needs as she ages.

why we should all eat organic...

In addition to agreeing about the importance of not assaulting our bodies with potentially harmful levels of toxic chemicals, every nutritionist we have ever spoken to is of one mind: organic is best nutritionally, too. 'Although so far there's been precious little research comparing the nutrients in organic with those in conventionally grown foods, that which has been done is highly compelling in favour of organics,' explains Dr Joseph Pizzorno. 'One study showed that the selenium content in organic food was four times that of conventional produce. In another study, the zinc content was 50 per cent higher in the organic food. We're talking about huge differences. The message is clear: organically grown foods are safer and much more nutritious.' Adds Patrick Holford: 'Although organic food is often 25 per cent more expensive than non-organic, it usually contains less water and more solid matter – including nutrients. So it really doesn't work out more expensive – yet it's so much better for you.'

SOYA

All three agreed that soy-based products like tofu, tempeh, miso and soya milk – which contain beneficial plant oestrogens called phytoestrogens – have important implications for women's health. During childbearing years, these plant chemicals can help prevent breast cancer; Asian women who eat large amounts of soy have a five-times lower rate of breast cancer than women who eat a typical Western diet. During menopause, when oestrogen levels drop by 60 per cent, phytoestrogens can help make up the difference. The optimum daily intake, according to our experts, is around 35–50mg of soya a day. 'The equivalent of a soya yogurt or a serving of tofu,' explains Patrick Holford. Although many vegetarian foods contain soya in the form of soya protein (burgers, frankfurters, etc), Dr Pizzorno warns that this may have been highly processed. We prefer organic tofu and soya milk or yogurt.

CRUCIFEROUS VEGETABLES

'Broccoli, brussels sprouts, cabbage and cauliflower contain substances which improve the ability of the liver to deal with both the toxins in our environment and those we produce internally,' explains Dr Pizzorno. 'They also contain useful cancer-protecting compounds.' Adds Patrick Holford: 'Research has shown that if you eat cabbage more than once a week, you are reducing your risk of developing colon cancer by two thirds.' Better still, believes Dr Pizzorno, eat 115–175g (4–6oz) a day – 'in any combination' – preferably raw or juiced, as cooking destroys vital enzymes. (Other cruciferous vegetables are cress, horseradish, kale, kohlrabi, mustard greens, radish and turnip.)

BLUEBERRIES

'Blueberries are rich in anthocyanidins, a type of flavonoid, which help protect the eyes from macular degeneration. Anthocyanidins are present in all berries with a blue/purple colour, ie, black grapes, blackcurrants and cranberries,' says Dr Pizzorno. You can also try supplementing with concentrated extracts. (Find berry extracts in natural food stores.) Eat daily, if possible.

BRAZIL NUTS and others

'An excellent source of selenium,' explains Dr Pizzorno. 'There is amazing data emerging on the link between selenium deficiency and increased rates of cancer. Selenium is a terrific immune-booster. In addition, it helps healthy thyroid function; often, people who have low energy levels may be suffering from selenium deficiency.' Three or four shelled brazil nuts each day can help.

Patrick Holford adds other nuts – particularly almonds, walnuts and hazelnuts – to the list of health-boosting nuts, together with seeds such as flax, sesame, sunflower and hemp. 'To get a balance, mix the seeds together and keep them in a sealed jar in the fridge. Grind a heaped tablespoon of these, and eat daily.' (NB: they're delicious sprinkled on salads.)

GARLIC

Explains Patrick Holford, 'Garlic contains about 200 biologically active compounds, many of which have a role in preventing disease – including cancer and heart disease.' Dr Pizzorno, like Patrick Holford, prescribes a clove a day, cooked or raw.

TOMATOES

Tomatoes help guard the eyes as we age as they are high in the substances lutein and lycopene, which protect against macular degeneration. Eat them juiced, raw, in pasta sauce or ketchup, or in ready-made products – around 50g (2oz) a day, to get the protective dose.

BREWER'S YEAST

'I'm a great believer in this old stand-by,' says Dr Pizzorno. 'It's a good source of protein, packed with B vitamins and high in chromium, which helps regulate blood sugar levels.' (And may also help with sugar cravings.)

SHIITAKE MUSHROOMS

These have immune-system enhancing properties; they contain lentinan, a powerful immunity booster. Shiitake are

one of the few vegetable sources of vitamin D, rich in calcium and phosphorus, with high levels of many amino acids. Buy them fresh or dry (soak before cooking); aim for one serving, twice a week.

QUINOA (pronounced keen-wa)

Known as 'the mother grain' because of its unique sustaining properties. 'It contains significantly more protein than any other

grain – and the quality of protein is better than meat,' says Patrick Holford. It offers almost four times as much calcium as wheat, plus extra iron, B vitamins and vitamin E. Find it in natural food stores. (It's also delicious in stir-fries with vegetables and tofu.) Go for one serving, twice a week (more if you're vegetarian).

FISH (if you're not vegetarian)

In addition to being rich in protein, vitamins and minerals (especially selenium), oily fish is a good source of brain-enhancing Omega-3 essential fatty acids. Fish to look for include mackerel, herring, salmon, trout, fresh tuna, sardines, anchovy and pilchards. Aim for three to four servings a week (unless pregnant).

EXTRA VIRGIN OLIVE OIL

This is packed with monounsaturates and is good for the heart. Olive oil seems to help blood sugar levels as well. Cook with it or pour on salads: 1–2 tablespoons a day. Hemp oil, now widely available, is also stuffed full of good fats.

AVOCADO

'A great skin food,' says Kathryn Marsden. 'Avocado is also rich in monounsaturates. Many women worry that avocado is fattening because of the high oil content, but there are only 190 calories in an average fruit. Avocado is rich in potassium, vitamin E (which is anti-hot flush), carotene, folic acid, B_5, biotin and vitamin C, plus the thyroid nutrient iodine. Piled high with hummus and a green salad, you've got a perfect, nutritious, filling meal.'

YOGHURT

'Sheep's and goat's yoghurt are best, as they're easier to digest than cow's milk, says Kathryn. 'A terrific source of calcium, it helps keep the digestive flora healthy, as it contains "friendly" bacteria. The levels of these bacteria diminish the longer you keep it, so buy it fresh in small quantities.'

SEAWEED

Our vote for a superfood goes to seaweed: when we're really tired and need to zing the next day, we have a Japanese meal with miso soup, seaweed salad and sizzling tofu steaks in ginger and soy sauce, with a side order of California rolls. Seaweed is one of the richest sources of calcium and other minerals, which help maintain bone mass, lower blood pressure, eliminate varicose veins and haemorrhoids, improve heart efficiency and relieve incontinence, vaginal dryness and hot flushes.

FABULOUSLY FRIENDLY FOODS

ALWAYS TRY TO BUY: fresh, organic food, locally produced
- **Vegetables** (unlimited): raw or lightly cooked. Aim for five portions a day
- **Beans, peas** (fresh or dried)
- **Lentils**
- **Whole grains** (aka cereals): eg, brown rice, millet, rye, oats, quinoa, wholemeal bread, corn, wholewheat pasta
Aim for one to four portions a day
- **Fruit:** aim for three portions a day as snacks
- **Soya foods,** eg, tofu, soya milk
- **Live yoghurt**
- **Seeds** (sunflower, sesame, safflower)
- **Brazil nuts** (buy unshelled)
- **Almonds, walnuts, hazelnuts** (ditto)
- **Extra virgin olive oil,** cold pressed

PLUS, IF YOU'RE NOT VEGETARIAN, ADD IN TWO TO THREE SERVINGS WEEKLY OF...
- **Fish and shellfish**
- **Eggs,** from organic-fed hens (salmonella and campylobacter are endemic in others)
- **Organic white meat** eg, chicken with skin off; also game

DRINK
- **Still pure water:** 1.5-2 litres (3-3¹/₂pt) daily
- **Organic herbal teas**
- **Vegetable juices** (home-made if possible)
- **Fruit juice** diluted with water
- **A little** (under two glasses daily) **good wine**

ENERGY-SAPPING ENEMY FOODS

TRY TO AVOID: processed, refined, ready-prepared, packaged and/or canned foods
- **Diet foods**
- **Refined white sugar/flour and other quick-fix carbohydrates,** eg, white bread, biscuits, cakes, candy bars
- **Low-fat cheeses or spreads**
- **Sauces with additives**
- **Cow's milk and products**
- **Refined wheat or sugar-loaded breakfast cereals**
- **Saturated (hard) fats,** eg, meat and dairy fat
- **Bran and bran-containing foods:** they can interfere with calcium absorption
- **Artificial flavours, colourings, sweeteners, preservatives**
- **Salt/salty foods**
- **Polyunsaturated spreads**
- **Processed, smoked, coloured fish/cheese/meat**
- **Pork/beef**

DRINK
- **Fizzy drinks** which are high in phosphate
- **Artificially sweetened drinks**
- **Coffee, tea**
- **Beer, lager, spirits**

the facts of fat

◆ Most of us eat too much of the wrong sort of fat. Over 40 per cent of our calories come from fat (you should aim for 15–30 per cent), and more than half from saturated fat.

◆ Saturated fat is a major 'baddie', particularly in terms of heart disease and strokes: too much meat, eggs and butter can pile up the fatty cholesterol deposits in our arteries and cause weight problems. Saturated fat is present in most animal foods, including meat and dairy products.

◆ Swapping from butter to margarine (which is made from vegetable oil) may not automatically be the answer, if the oil in the margarine has been 'hydrogenated'. Hydrogenation is a process that converts liquid oils into solid oils, but at the same time it produces substances called 'trans-fatty acids', which actually increase blood cholesterol and blood fats and are said to disrupt the vital functions of EFAs. 'Hydrogenated fats act as blockers, stopping the good fats getting through,' says Dr Udo Erasmus. So look for a margarine or spread which says 'non-hydrogenated' on the label – and be aware that many processed foods (including biscuits, cakes, ice cream and many ready-prepared meals) contain hydrogenated vegetable oils. (Margarines are also linked with allergies, according to research from Germany.)

◆ Heating oils for cooking – even in the process of stir-frying – destroys EFAs and may actually be harmful, according to Dr Erasmus. 'Burning oil, where you create smoke, may create carcinogenic chemicals' he says. Coconut oil is the best choice.

EAT (THE RIGHT) FATS
~ and oil your skin from the inside out

Low-fat mania is sweeping the world. But our bodies and our complexions – brains too – actually need fat. Because without it we may be fast-forwarding ageing. According to LA-based plastic surgeon Richard Ellenbogen, MD, 'Very low-fat diets suck the oils out of the skin. We see people in their thirties on low-fat diets who look like prunes.'

Dr Udo Erasmus, a leading international expert, agrees. 'Our bodies need to be oiled,' he tells us. 'Oils – which contain Essential Fatty Acids (EFAs) – do a wonderful job. If you get the right balance, they form a barrier on the skin against loss of moisture, giving soft, smooth, velvety skin; plus the fine lines and wrinkles that come from dryness will diminish.' Among other vital health-protecting roles, these 'good' fats transport the vital fat-soluble vitamins A, D, E and K round the body.

EFAs are found in vegetable oils (in particular, in flax seed and hemp oils), seeds, nuts and some other foods like oily fish. The EFAs that play such a vital role are Omega-3 (alpha-linolenic acid) and Omega-6 (gamma-linolenic acid or GLA), and we need a balance of about one third Omega-3 to two thirds Omega-6. The good news is that to save us the trouble of working out if we're getting the sums right, balanced mixtures of oil are available in capsules, or as liquid oils. (These oils can taste quite delicious swallowed from the spoon – or sprinkled on salads; aim for 1–2 tablespoons a day, or the equivalent in capsules.)

Fascinatingly, the fastest way to tell if you're getting enough EFAs is a DIY skin test. 'The skin is the last organ to get the oil; if it gets there, you know it's got everywhere.' Dr Erasmus suggests taking a sauna or a hot bath, towelling skin dry but not applying a body cream or lotion. 'If skin still feels papery and dry, you should up your intake of EFAs. When you're getting enough, you should reach a point where putting a moisturiser on your skin is no longer necessary – because your skin is being lubricated from inside by EFAs.'

Recently too, researchers have established that the benefits of EFAs – particularly Omega-3s, the ones we tend to get less of – extend to pretty well every area of your brain and body. So make sure you eat plenty and also look for topical products containing Omega-3, 6, 7 and 9 to slosh on.

FOOD COMBINING

Food combining, also known as the Hay Diet, has been around for some 75 years since Dr William Howard Hay devised it to help patients recover from chronic problems. The basis of it is not mixing foods that Dr Hay and his followers believe fight in your stomach – ie, proteins and starches – and keeping fruit separate. This way of eating, say its supporters (who include us), eases digestive and other chronic problems including allergies, headaches and skin problems.

Despite the fact that many people have found it of enormous help, most doctors are still adamant that it has no scientific basis and is simply a faddy way of eating, which has no point except that you are bound to lose weight because you are eating less. However, Professor Jonathan Brostoff, co-author of *The Allergy Bible*, is open-minded: 'It helps about half my patients who suffer from Irritable Bowel Syndrome (IBS) – the trouble is, I don't know which half. But it certainly can't hurt, so I often suggest they try it.'

Nutritionist Kathryn Marsden, who has written several best-selling books including *The Complete Book of Food Combining*, gives us the basics.

● Introduce this way of eating into your diet for one or two days a week to start with, to ease yourself into it.

● If you find that it suits you, increase that to three, four or five days weekly. But don't put yourself under pressure to follow it slavishly: healthy eating should not be a cult religion or make you feel deprived. Indulgence days are to be encouraged.

● Increase your intake of fresh fruit but eat it as a snack between meals or as a starter, not with your proteins or starches.

● Also try snacking on a handful of nuts or seeds.

● Drink plenty of water between meals.

● If you want to lose weight, aim each day for: one protein-based meal served with plenty of fresh vegetables or salad, one starch-based meal served with a good-sized portion of fresh veg or salad; plus one meal based on either a vegetable dish, eg, a big salad, stir-fry or stew, or a selection of any fresh fruits.

● If you aren't worried about your weight, try the alternative of one protein-based meal and two starch-based meals per day, with generous portions of fresh salad or vegetables.

how to food combine

Proteins in column A will mix with anything from column B.
Starches in column C will mix with anything from column B.
Don't mix column A with column C.

A	B	C
Proteins	**Mix with A or C**	**Starches**
Fish/shellfish	All veg except potatoes	Potatoes/sweet potatoes
Free-range eggs	and sweet potatoes	All grains including: oats,
Organic poultry	All salads	pasta, brown rice, rye, millet,
Lean lamb	Seeds	couscous, quinoa, bulgar
Cheese	Nuts	Sweetcorn
Yoghurt	Herbs	Flour
All soya products	Fats and oils including:	Bread/crackers
Milk (but keep to	cream, butter,	Pastry
a minimum)	margarine and extra	
	virgin olive oil	

NB Pulses (peas, beans, lentils) combine well with all kinds of veg and salads and
with other starches but can cause digestive problems if mixed with protein foods.

prevent dementia with green veg and party games

Dementia affects about one in ten people over 65, one in five over 75. Alzheimer's disease is the commonest form of dementia in the elderly. But heart disease, stroke and endocrine (hormonal) disorders, as well as rarer conditions such as the human form of BSE, can also bring about the brain deterioration which causes this infinitely distressing condition.

1 According to nutritionist Patrick Holford, author of *The Alzheimer's Prevention Plan*, research suggests that B vitamins (mainly folic acid, vitamins B_6 and B_{12}) have an even greater protective effect on the brain than they do against heart disease and stroke, cancer and maybe even multiple sclerosis. B vitamins help to lower high blood levels of homocysteine, a damaging amino acid. Supplementing with 800mcg of folic acid alone for three years has been shown to make you five years younger. Folic acid is in green leafy vegetables, beans, nuts and seeds. The best way to check you are getting enough of these B vitamins is to check your homocysteine level with a home-test kit (www.yorktest.com). If your score is above 8, consider supplements on top of improving your diet. The current recommended doses are 1,000mcg folic acid, plus 100mcg daily of B_{12} and 20mg of B_6. (Folic acid supplements should always be taken with B_{12}.) Higher Nature's H Factor or Solgar's Homocysteine Modulators provide these kind of levels.

2 Keep up oestrogen levels. HRT has been discredited as having a protective effect on the brain against the development of memory problems and Alzheimer's disease, but you can boost oestrogen levels by eating soya-based products and other phytoestrogens (see pages 192 and 219), which also have very high levels of folic acid.

3 The omega-3 essential fatty acids, found in oily fish (and specific supplements), may help ward off Alzheimer's, as they do heart disease.

4 Take regular exercise: research suggests that lack of it may be a risk factor for dementia.

5 Avoid stress and keep anxiety levels down. Too much stress has a damaging effect on the blood supply to the heart and the brain.

6 Don't vegetate: it's clear that continuous mental exercise helps protect the mind from decay. Try puzzles, crosswords, games, models, learning routes, etc. There is evidence that people who set about learning poetry, plays or new skills seem able to slow down deterioration or even improve their memory.

7 Keep existing hobbies going and try to learn new skills, especially musical ones. Those who learn to play an instrument seem less likely to get dementia, as do those who educate themselves or study with others. Gardening is particularly good for keeping mind and brain alert.

8 Pray and/or meditate. Time to relax, reflect and be at peace protects against not only dementia, but heart disease, cancer, depression, infections and other problems of ageing.

9 Keep in touch with friends and family and organise an active social life. Interact with agreeable people.

10 Consider herbs: there is evidence that ginkgo biloba, the Chinese maidenhair fern tree, improves the blood supply to the brain and may help slow down the progression of Alzheimer's disease. Sage may also help protect the brain. The nutrient Acetyl L-Carnitine has been shown to protect against dementia.

11 Live well, eat well, drink good red wine in moderation, stop smoking, sustain relationships and activities and, above all, be positive and enjoy life: all these help boost immunity, keep blood vessels unclogged, melatonin and DHEA levels high and your brain active and alive – and so diminish the risk of dementia.

WHEN FOOD IS UNFRIENDLY

Most of the time, food is not only necessary to sustain our bodies, it's also a treat for our minds. But for some people, it seems, things are going seriously wrong.

Some foods (among them tree nuts, shellfish and peanuts) clearly have a harmful effect on people who are allergic to them: they risk going into a potentially life-threatening condition called anaphylactic shock. People who suffer from coeliac disease have an allergy to gluten, the protein in grain crops, which damages the gut and can cause widespread illness. Asthma attacks and eczema are also known to be triggered by food allergens. So the link between some foods and ill health is firmly established.

Some doctors, though, have long believed there may be a wider problem – that in addition to severe food allergy, there may be a more widespread, less severe effect which they term food 'sensitivity' or 'intolerance'.

Until recently this was a cue for most

doctors to raise their eyebrows and mutter phrases about quack medicine.

Now all that has changed. In 1994, the British Government launched an ongoing research programme into food. It has produced a list of the 12 trigger foods which may cause serious reactions in sensitised people: cereals containing gluten, crustaceans, eggs, fish, peanuts, nuts, soybeans, milk, celery, mustard, sesame, and sulphur dioxide. Further offenders include tomatoes, oranges, chocolate, coffee and tea, plus artificial flavourings, preservatives and additives.

The non-fatal consequences of food intolerance can have a very distressing and debilitating effect on people's lives. According to *The Allergy Bible: Understanding, Diagnosing, Treating Allergies and Intolerances* by Professor Jonathan Brostoff and Linda Gamlin, the gamut of symptoms that can be expected may include:

- headache, migraine, fatigue, depression/anxiety (and hyperactivity in children); recurrent mouth ulcers;
- aching muscles;
- vomiting, nausea, stomach ulcers, duodenal ulcers;
- diarrhoea, Irritable Bowel Syndrome, constipation, wind, bloating, Crohn's Disease;
- joint pain, rheumatoid arthritis;
- water retention.

Symptoms may not be constant – stress, for instance, may make reactions vary widely between individuals. And there may be other symptoms of sensitivity which are not included in this list. Sarah suffers occasionally from wheat and other food sensitivities which can provoke extreme brain fuzziness (this is not a joke!), depression, lethargy, upset tummy and skin rashes.

Sensitivity may also swing with hormones: it's known that eczema tends to get worse in the pre-menstrual stage and sensitivity to food may be more marked then too.

Curiously, some 50 per cent of sufferers find they crave the very food to which they are sensitive. So when they eat – or drink – the offending substance, they may feel better initially, making it doubly hard to trace the culprit and to give it up.

Exactly what causes food intolerance is not yet certain but one thing is crystal clear: it's not all in the mind. So if you have unexplained health problems, explore the food link. There are food sensitivity testing laboratories which can pinpoint any problems. Start with your family doctor; some are still sceptical but most want to help.

candida – the cinderella illness

Candida, also known as candidiasis, responds both negatively and positively to food. One of the most common female conditions, it affects about three in four women at some point in their lives. It's often called the Cinderella illness because doctors have traditionally been reluctant to take it seriously – so many women seek help from natural medicine practitioners and nutritionists.

Candida is caused by overgrowth of a yeast-like fungus called *Candida albicans* which exists in the body anyway but causes trouble if it runs riot. It often occurs in the vagina (when it's called thrush), causing a thick white discharge which smells like baking bread, and/or itching in the genital and anal area.

Candida can also collect in the gut and start a fermentation process, leading to symptoms like those of Irritable Bowel Syndrome.

Bloating, flatulence and stomach pains are common, as well as irregular bowel habits, including constipation, and diarrhoea, bad breath and catarrh. You may also have aching joints, always wake up tired, and/or feel generally depressed and below par.

Some sufferers also get cravings, particularly for sugar, bread, alcohol and chocolate; you may put on weight for no apparent reason and not be able to lose it. Periods can become irregular and it may affect your memory, concentration – and even your libido.

Professor Jonathan Brostoff suggests that this portmanteau of symptoms, in tandem with tiredness, aching joints and depression, may all belong together as part of a condition that he calls 'gut fermentation syndrome'.

If you go to your GP, you may have a swab test to find out whether the fungus is present. The most usual treatments are antifungal creams for thrush and, if those don't work, a course of antifungal pessaries. There is also an antifungal tablet (Diflucan) available over the counter, but do be sure to discuss it with your doctor first.

Conventional antifungal creams or pessaries work better in combination with a low-yeast, low-sugar diet – because the fungus feeds on yeast and sugar. So try cutting out all forms of sugar (eg, chocolate, sweets, cakes, biscuits, and pudding – also fruit for three weeks), yeast (bread and bread-related food such as pizzas and pasta), dairy products (though you may find goat's or sheep's milk products are easier to digest than cow's – or try soya milk instead). You should particularly avoid blue cheeses, mushrooms, fungi and alcohol.

Many people say that food combining helps (see page 196). Experiment and see what suits you. Try to eat fresh food rather than ready-prepared or cook-chill; many sufferers prefer organic food. As well as diet, there are some other useful self-help options for thrush. Many women have benefited from using a tampon soaked in organic cider vinegar (one capful of vinegar to four of water) or natural bio yoghurt.

Probiotic supplements with bioacidophilus (to repopulate the gut with good bacteria) are helpful. Shabir Daya suggests Tanalbit (Anti Fungal Tannins) by Intensive Nutrition. Gillian Hamer, a nutritionist, also recommends Biocare's Oregano Complex for three months. (Check contraindications with all products.)

HOW I BEAT CANDIDA
AGE: 41
PROFESSION: food producer

'As an adult, I suffered chronically from sinusitis, asthma and lots of symptoms I didn't even realise were linked to candida: sore eyes, aching joints, fatigue, vaginal thrush, wind and diarrhoea.

'But I was starting a business, raising a family and felt too busy to tackle it. Then a couple of years ago, I read a magazine article (by Sarah Stacey), which prompted me to track down a nutritional consultant. The diet she suggested meant I had to cut out all my favourite foods: fruit, bread, chocolate and other sweet foods – and carrot juice!

'The first week, I felt dreadful. Giving up bread was hardest because I had been eating so much of it. I started to base my meals around brown rice, vegetables, salads, unrefined pasta, fish, peanut butter and oatcakes – plus supplements of B_6, biotin and immune-boosters. In week four, natural anti-fungal supplements were added in, together with garlic and EFAs. Gradually, the symptoms disappeared – I felt I was in control of my body. And I lost about a stone, effortlessly.

'It's an amazing feeling to be in control of my health. To anyone who thinks they might have candida, I'd say: try the diet. Don't be a victim. You can take control again – and live life more fully.'

A FABULOUS FRESH START

We live in a toxic world. Pollutants attack us from every quarter: petrol fumes, power lines, smoking, alcohol, sunlight, pesticides in foods, additives and flavour enhancers, office technology, mercury fillings in teeth, prescription drugs, chemicals used in common household cleaners, paints, glues, plastic containers and furnishings, and the biggest pollutant of today's world – stress – which affects both our minds and our bodies.

Many of us live in a state of toxic overload, assaulted by toxins from outside and inside our bodies. And the consequences are plain to see. As one friend, a high-powered, busy headmistress, said sadly, 'I can't remember the last time I got out of bed in the morning feeling gleaming.' Lifestyle-related illnesses are booming: at least one person in three suffers from anxiety, one in four from Irritable Bowel Syndrome, and one in five from some form of allergy.

An effective way of combating this unhealthy state is a regular gentle fast and detox which gives both body and mind a chance to regenerate. 'If you keep stuffing food and other toxins into your body, there is no point at which it

can rest and sort it all out,' explains nutritional therapist and psychologist Dr Marilyn Glenville. 'Fasting and detox can restore balance and give you a renewed feeling of energy and vitality.'

Fasting and detox cleansing are not the same thing. A fast is when you only drink pure water – a minimum of six to eight large (300ml/^{1}/2pt) glasses a day – and eat nothing. You do this first, for 24 hours, in peace: 'Give yourself permission to wind down – put on the answerphone, rest, sleep, have a gentle walk, listen to music,' suggests Dr Susan Horsewood-Lee. 'Or just stare into space.' You can fast at home, at a health hydro or anywhere peaceful.

Follow with a gentle cleansing period lasting from two to ten days or more (see opposite). Naturopath Dr Harald Gaier says it's important to remove as many toxins from your system as possible. So avoid chemical-laden foods (buy organic produce whenever possible), smoking, alcohol, drugs of all kinds and the stressors that make you feel out of control – whether that's 50 phone calls a day or noisy neighbours. During this period of two to ten days, the cells of the gut, which in ordinary life are constantly on arduous survival duty, have a chance to rest. 'You're turning the clock back in your gut so that the cells become youthful and bright,' explains Dr Horsewood-Lee.

You may feel worse before you feel better, both emotionally and physically,

warn experts (though some side effects can be allayed by colonic irrigation). Possible side effects include insomnia, coated tongue, dizziness and light-headedness, headaches, skin breakouts, aching limbs and muscles, hunger pains and nasal discharge. These are all good signs, though, that your body is getting to work and expelling the toxins.

You may also feel upset and tearful. 'So go to a health hydro or set up a lifeline – a friend to call – in case you need it,' says Dr Horsewood-Lee. Deep breathing and meditation (see pages 162 and 238–9) are enormously helpful to still disquiet of all sorts.

Also take this time to think about other longer-term detox measures – for instance, having mercury amalgam fillings removed: 'Mercury is a powerful neurotoxin,' says Gaier, and research now shows that it lodges in your brain and body (see page 141).

At the end of this cleansing process, you can expect clearer skin, better digestion, probably some weight loss and a flatter tummy, heightened senses, and possibly an improvement in problems such as arthritis. Most of all, you have given yourself a fresh start.

As you relaunch your system after this clarifying process, remember that everything is more sensitised. 'So go for pure, simple, good food,' recommends Dr Horsewood-Lee, 'and that applies to colour, texture and taste.'

cleansing and detox eating plan

Do fast first, if possible, as we describe opposite, then follow this two-to-ten-day plan – though you can go straight into it if you prefer.

This programme, which was devised by Dr Marilyn Glenville, acts as a cleansing diet to help many inflammatory conditions (including IBS, asthma, eczema and arthritis), and will also reveal whether you are allergic (or sensitive) to certain common foods.

If you feel worse for a few days remember it's a good sign, meaning you were probably sensitive to something you ate every day. When you stop eating the food, you get withdrawal symptoms (see opposite).

If you have a digestive problem (eg, pains, flatulence or bloating), cut down on raw food and poach or steam vegetables instead. Eating blander fruit (apples, bananas and pears) and non-crunchy salads and vegetables helps.

Generally, avoid citrus and acidic fruits and juices – particularly if you have migraine, arthritis or suffer from any kind of skin problem.

If you are in reasonable health, this is a safe cleansing programme. But don't fast for more than 24 hours.

Do consult your doctor before if:
- you are taking prescription drugs;
- you are severely underweight;
- you are pregnant;
- you are diabetic, have TB or cancer.

DETOX DAYS 1 AND 2

Eat only raw salads with olive oil and cider vinegar plus fruit. If you have digestive problems or have had a colonic irrigation, try steamed, poached and/or puréed vegetables, without fruit. Drink only bottled mineral water.

DETOX DAYS 3-9

If you have been eating only raw salads, add in some lightly steamed vegetables, including potatoes.

DAY 10 ONWARDS

DO EAT: raw salads (or wilted leaves), fruit, vegetables (raw, lightly steamed, puréed, in soups or stews), baked potatoes; fish (steamed, poached, grilled or baked, preferably oily fish such as mackerel, salmon, herrings and sardines); nuts and sunflower seeds; soya milk; rice cakes; sesame paste (tahini); olive and sunflower oil; cider vinegar; pulses (chickpeas, lentils, kidney beans, etc); brown rice.

Flavour food with miso dissolved in hot water, herbs and spices.

DO DRINK: spring water, fruit juice, vegetable juice (make your own or make sure bought versions are additive-free), herbal teas.

DON'T EAT: dairy products (butter, cheese, milk, etc), or foods containing dairy; bread or pastry, sauces or gravies made with flour; pasta, cakes or biscuits of any type; anything that contains artificial additives (colourings, flavourings, preservatives), flour, wheat or other grains, except brown rice; red meat; eggs; sugar; salt; 'instant' or cook-chill foods; sweets or chocolates.

DON'T DRINK: tea, coffee, alcohol.

NB The liver is the major organ of detoxification so it needs to function 100 per cent during this time. Drinking hot water with a slice of lemon will help, and you may want to take a supplement such as BioCare's Hep 194, or herbs such as milk thistle or dandelion.

prescription

FOODS TO FIGHT DISEASE

Like many researchers today, integrated physician Dr Rosy Daniel, founder of the Health Creation Programme, believes that what you eat can help you – and your family – fight cancer and illness of all sorts.

● Fresh vegetables and fruit – locally grown and ideally organic – should be at the heart of your diet.

● Try to eat a good proportion of vegetables raw. Don't overcook the rest and use cooking liquor in other dishes, eg, soups or risottos.

● Freshly made vegetable juices contain loads of protective vitamins, minerals, and phyto-(plant) chemicals.

● To retain the nutrients, store veg in cool humid conditions – the fridge is good – not in a vegetable rack.

● Think Oriental and make your diet 40 per cent vegetables, 40 per cent staples such as pulses and grains and 10–20 per cent protein and fat.

● An ideal meal contains a grain (brown rice, quinoa, couscous, millet or buckwheat), a pulse (peas, beans or lentils), plus salad or vegetables, and a soya product.

● Consider reducing animal fats – ie, meat and dairy produce – which carry an extra cancer risk factor.

● Replace cow's milk products with soya yoghurts, creams and ice cream – also try oat milk and rice milk.

● Ten per cent extra body fat puts up your risk of hormonal cancers by as much as 50 per cent, possibly because toxins and hormones are stored in the fat.

● Cut down on excess sugar and alcohol. (Drink grape juice instead.)

LESLIE KENTON

For three decades this American-born international bestselling author has worked to discover – and explain – treatments and foods that may help us feel better, live longer, look lovelier. The ultimate 'natural beauty', she inspired us with *Joy of Beauty*, *Raw Energy* and *Passage To Power* – which broke the menopause taboo and talked about alternatives to HRT.

'I am not in the least bit interested in growing old gracefully; I want to grow old disgracefully, with joy and just a touch of wickedness in my eye. I want to carry my own wood into my cabin on the day that I die.

'There is a real freedom in growing older. It can bring greater joy, freedom and richness. If we live from our soul and love, there's nothing to stop us living till we're 120 – and I mean really living – with radiance and vitality.'

'In my career, I've tried to investigate everything that can make us feel and look better, and live more from the core of our being. Periodic detoxification is essential both for the body and for the psyche.

'To live with real radiance, we need to continually clear all those false ideas, emotional pain and confusion housed in our cells, our DNA and our energy fields. Emotional Freedom Technique (EFT) is ideal for this. EFT [which developed from Thought Field Therapy] is one of the wonderful new energy medicines. It is a snap to learn and clears everything from aches and pains or fear of flying to the compulsive eating that makes us fat. It's based on tapping certain points on the body, identified long ago by traditional Chinese medicine. It brings a wonderful sense of freedom when you use it regularly – the freedom to be truly you. That's real beauty, [which brings] genuine charisma.

'If you detoxify the body, you rejuvenate and energise it so it heals itself. But it has to be done over and over again because we build up waste continually. Whenever I feel the need I eat nothing but raw food for a few days.

'I try to eat a huge variety of food: fresh vegetables and protein, with a little fruit and different seaweeds, choosing them because they're beautiful and I love the taste – not because this or that is "good". I grow most of my salad stuff and herbs organically among the flowers in my garden, and sprout seeds and beans on my kitchen counter. I harvest them just before lunch or dinner. For protein, I choose game like venison, wild boar, Thar (wild Nepalese goat), and fish. All are naturally high in Omega-3 fats – great for your skin and your heart. I loathe manufactured foods and never eat them. I seldom eat grains except wild rice and brown rice and I shun wheat completely.

'I don't eat processed food and always buy organic if I can. The soil our food is grown in is so depleted by intensive agriculture that we simply don't get the trace minerals we need for optimum health. What's more, the herbicides and pesticides that are sprayed on to conventionally grown food are oestrogen mimics, which leads to the hormonal imbalance that causes PMS, menstrual problems and a tricky menopause; I believe eating organic food helps protect you against that.

'It is really important to filter your drinking and cooking water; in London, I purify all mine with a reverse-osmosis water filter and I drink two to three litres a day. The more I drink, the more energy I have.

'I take supplements like Krill Oil – a powerful antioxidant and Omega-3 fat, the best anti-ageing multiple – Basic Immune Nutrients by Thorne, and 12 grams of vitamin C a day.

'I meditate at least once a day because this helps keep me connected with the core of my being so I am less likely to get lost in the labyrinth of silly mental thoughts that are irrelevant to what I really care about. I dance a lot – using movement to release feelings in a creative way. I row, I do weights, I swim and I run. But all the exercise I do has to be fun. I hate doing anything I am "supposed" to do.

'The cocooning world of my bed is also very important to me. Ideally I'd sleep seven or eight hours a night.'

SUPPLEMENTARY BENEFITS

Let's lay our cards on the table. As well as being passionate about eating the best possible diet, we're firm believers in nutritional supplements. Surveys in different Western countries shows that virtually everyone is deficient in key nutrients, however good their diet. This may be due to modern food production or to the extra stresses – physical, mental and emotional – that affect us now.

There is also increasing evidence that some supplements can help in the battle against ageing. The strongest contenders are antioxidants, which neutralise the harmful free radical molecules that cause cell damage and death (see page 13) affecting our health – and our looks. Says Professor Gladys Block of the University of California: 'There's ample evidence that nutrients can help prevent cancer and other diseases. Policy makers should back away from the position that you shouldn't take supplements. Antioxidant supplement use is inexpensive insurance.'

Ideally, we suggest you go to a qualified and experienced nutritionist or naturopath, or a doctor with detailed knowledge of nutrition. Otherwise, start with a good multivitamin and mineral supplement and an antioxidant preparation. If your skin and/or hair is dry, add in Essential Fatty Acids (EFAs see page 195). Always give supplements at least a month to see if they are of benefit. Some may take longer.

We asked pharmacist Shabir Daya, from our favourite natural health mail order company Victoria Health, to give us his tips for supplements to help us feel and look our best.

WHAT TO TAKE WHEN

Here are supplements that may help you down the decades... Remember: buy as good-quality supplements as you can afford, by a reputable manufacturer. It's important to take supplements as directed. Please don't exceed recommended dose levels or you may risk side effects. More is not better. Try using food-state formulations, where possible, because the nutrients are in their most natural state and have higher absorption and utilisation rates. Most supplements should be taken with or immediately after food. However, it's often helpful to take minerals at night, if you have sleep problems. Some experts advise a supplement-free day weekly.

TWENTYSOMETHING

+Multiple vitamin/mineral formula preferably containing minimum 50mg B complex and 400mcg folic acid. Adequate folic acid is specially important for women of childbearing age because the B vitamin folic acid (folacin) helps to prevent neural tube-related birth defects such as spina bifida. The evidence seems to show that, even with the best of diets, you can't eat enough folic acid to give optimal protection so a supplement is sensible (see also 'Prevent dementia with green veg', page 197).
Dose: as directed on label.

+Antioxidants
Look for sulphur-rich nutrients plus common antioxidants such as vitamins A, C and E, selenium and carotenoids. Sulphur, especially when found in nutrients such as cysteine, glutathione and lipoic acid, is one of the most powerful detoxifying agents. Sulphur is also a major component of hair, skin and nail tissue.
Dose: to protect against disease/ageing:
● vitamin A 800–1,000mg
● vitamin C 500–2,000mg
● vitamin E 100–400iu
● selenium 150–200mcg
● carotenoids 15–20mg
● L-cysteine 100–500mg (contains sulphur)
● zinc 15–25mg
● copper 1–2mg
● manganese 10–20mg
● lipoic acid 50–60mg
Most the of the antioxidants above should be included in your multivitamin; if they are not, look at red berry formulations such as acai, mangosteen, goji, blueberry, etc.

+Essential Fatty Acids (eg, GLA)
Certain fats are absolutely essential for your health as well as your skin and hair (see page 195). It's a matter of choosing the right type of fats in the right amount – and in a form that your body can use properly. The fats you need are known as Omega-3 and Omega-6 essential fatty acids
Dose: 100–150mg per day, in a ratio 1:1 Omega-3 to Omega-6.

For PMS Try Chaste Berry Extract, which allows the body to manufacture more progesterone hormone.

THIRTYSOMETHING

+**Multiple vitamin/mineral formula** with minimum 50mg B complex and 400mcg of folic acid.

+**Essential fatty acids**, as for twentysomething.

+**Antioxidants**, as for twentysomething. Particularly look for high doses of carotenoids, eg, astaxanthin. Add in 30mg daily muscle-supporting Co-enzyme Q10.

+**Calcium and magnesium** Bone density begins to be compromised now, so start a preventative approach against osteoporosis (see page 214). Magnesium is needed for calcium to be distributed properly.
Dose: calcium 800–1,000mg, magnesium 400–500mg.

+**Ashwagandha (Indian ginseng)** Strengthens and calms the nervous system, while giving inner strength; treats anxiety, sleep problems, and helps energy.
Dose: 400mg dry herb, taken up to three times daily.

+**Phytoestrogenic herbs** such as dong quai, red clover, black cohosh and soya would be of great benefit, as the ovaries start to shut down from the age of 34 onwards, leading to symptoms such as stress, anxiety, erratic/heavy periods, lack of concentration. Herbs often work best in multiple formulations. Phytoestrogens also will enhance the efficacy of bone building nutrients such as calcium and magnesium.

FORTYSOMETHING

+**Multiple vitamin/mineral formula** with minimum 50mg B complex.

+**Essential fatty acids** These should now be in a ratio of 2:1, Omega-3 to Omega-6.

+**Antioxidants,** as for thirtysomething. Consider adding Glisodin, a bioavailable/bioactive form of a vital protective nutrient called superoxide dismutase (or SOD, thus GliSODin).
Dose: as on label.

+**Phytoestrogenic herbs,** as for thirtysomething.

+**Calcium and magnesium** as for thirtysomething. If you do a lot of sports, add a specific joint formulation with glucosamine, chondroitin, type II collagen, hyaluronic acid, bromelain.

+ **Magnolia and L-Theanine:** to eliminate cortisol build-up, use extracts containing these nutrients (this is crucial for this age band and older).

FIFTY/SIXTY/ SEVENTYSOMETHING

+**Multiple vitamin/mineral formula** with minimum 50mg B complex. Remember to look for food-state formulas. Avoid 50+ products: they just tend to have more calcium, which you should be taking separately anyway.

+**Essential fatty acids** Especially relevant at this stage, to protect against cardiovascular disease and help hair and skin.
Dose: continue with a 2:1 ratio of Omega-3 to Omega-6.

+**Antioxidants**, as for fortysomething. The effects of free-radical damage will normally have been quite established by now. Aside from free-radical factors such as skin wrinkling, early stages of osteoarthritis may become apparent. Sulphur-rich antioxidants may be especially useful during the menopause, because sulphur is a major component of joint tissues and lubricating fluid. Look for red berry formulations, as before. Increase Co-Q10 to 100mg daily.

+**Phytoestrogenic herbs**, as for thirtysomething.

+**Calcium and magnesium**, as for fortysomething. Because magnesium becomes more vital as you get older, also supporting heart health, it's worth taking more (good at night for sleep problems).
Dose: 200–400mg daily, in addition to calcium/magnesium above, but no more than 500mg daily in total.

+ **Magnolia and L-Theanine**, as for fortysomething.

+**Soluble fibre formula** (eg, psyllium seed husks, pectin, flax seed, etc). Digestive abilities are typically much weaker in women over 50, often leading to intestinal sluggishness and symptoms such as constipation and/or diarrhoea. Soluble fibre can be used for improving intestinal function and detoxification, as well as relieving constipation and diarrhoea.
Dose: psyllium seed husks 1,000–3,000mg (with a full glass of water).

+**Ginkgo biloba** (see preventing dementia, page 197).
Dose: standardised extract 60–180mg per day.

+**Acetyl L-Carnitine** A crucial nutrient for the brain cells to produce energy, proven to be important in preventing dementia.
Dose: 500mg daily, half an hour before any meal.

FEEL FAB FOREVER FORMULATIONS

Because we know just how much some supplements have helped us in the past, including MenoHerbs2 (phytoestrogens), essential oils and GliSODin, we have put together our own Capsule Collection of the products we take. For more details, visit www.beautybible.com or www.victoriahealth.com

YOUR ROLLER-COASTER HORMONES

According to many men, hormones are the catch-all explanation for whatever ails a woman's mind or body. Whether we like it or not, these chaps may not be far from the truth. Every one of us (that includes men, too, of course) is governed by these powerful invisible forces which control every moment of our days: moods, desires, waking and sleeping patterns, the way we age – and, crucially, every woman's reproductive cycle.

From puberty to menopause, women live in a flurry of reproductive hormones – mainly oestrogen and progesterone – going up and down like a pearl diver. In a perfect world, these hormonal carousels wouldn't affect us. But, due probably to the stresses of modern life, many women now suffer a raft of problems, from PMS to the discomforts of menopause.

In some ways, you could argue that conventional medicine has made vast strides in treating hormonal problems, with the pill and hormone replacement therapy; also fertility treatment. There is, too, increasing interest in the so-called miracle hormones: melatonin, DHEA, pregnenolone and growth hormone.

But it's becoming clear that manipulating nature in this way may not be as desirable as doctors hoped. HRT, for instance, once viewed as the elixir of life for menopausal women, is now controversial, partly because of unpleasant side effects, partly because of the increased risk of breast cancer, heart disease and stroke, gallstones, and Alzheimer's disease. Many experts also say that while the hormonal system is a delicate precise mechanism, requiring a featherlight touch, HRT is a crude blunderbuss-like treatment.

Today many women want to explore alternative remedies for menopausal symptoms. And many experts, too, believe these can be equally effective, although there is much less scientific evidence – mainly because the pharmaceutical companies do not fund research into alternative therapies.

The most important thing for any woman to understand is that there is a range of ways to help menopausal symptoms. 'Where the reliance in the past was on HRT alone, emphasis should now be placed on the value of lifestyle changes and dietary supplements such as isoflavone phytoestrogens that can, for many women, help mild to moderate hot-flush symptoms,' says Mr Nick Panay, consultant gynaecologist at Queen Charlotte's Hospital, London.

Remember: it's your life – you should be in charge. So find out about all these different systems and trust your body.

THE MAIN HORMONES THAT MAKE US TICK

HORMONE	PRODUCED BY	WHAT IT DOES
Follicle stimulating hormone (FSH)	pituitary gland	stimulates growth of cells surrounding eggs in the ovaries and controls division of sperm in the testes
Luteinising hormone (LH)	pituitary gland	triggers ovulation of egg from ovary
Oestrogen	ovaries	controls menstrual cycle; levels fall after menopause
Progesterone	ovaries	also controls menstrual cycle; high levels support successful pregnancy
Testosterone	adrenal gland	a male hormone also found in women, may cause undesirable male features in women, also greasy hair/skin, acne, excess hair growth
Thyroxine (and other thyroid hormones)	thyroid gland	controls metabolic rate and levels of activity; too much = restlessness and hyperactivity; too little = weakness and lethargy; essential for normal menstrual cycles and fertility
Adrenaline and noradrenaline	adrenal gland	increases heartbeat and blood pressure in response to activity and stress
Cortisol	adrenal gland	many actions, including increasing the stressful effects of other adrenal hormones
Insulin	pancreas	controls the rate of sugar absorption

ALL YOU NEED TO KNOW ABOUT ROLLER-COASTER HORMONES

Q What is a hormone?

A Hormones are body chemicals produced by different glands which carry messages from one part of the body to another, via the bloodstream.

Q Can I see my hormones?

A No. Individual hormone molecules are so small you can't even see them under a microscope. But hormones are so potent that, in some cases, less than a millionth of an ounce of a hormone is enough to produce an effect.

Q What do they do?

A They control the chemistry of the trillions of cells in your body, determining, for example, the rate at which cells burn up food and release energy, which cells produce milk, hair or other products. They influence your mental and emotional state, your drive to succeed, your sexuality and appearance, as well as your menstrual cycle, immune system and your chances of getting osteoporosis, some cancers and even possibly heart disease. They also have an effect on the way you age.

Q What controls them?

A The headquarters is part of the brain called the hypothalamus which works with the pituitary, also in the brain, to send hormones to other 'endocrine' (hormone) glands in the body including thyroid, adrenals and ovaries.

Q What happens at puberty and menstruation?

A Around the age of 11 or 12, an increase in growth hormone triggers the spurt of growth which happens before the onset of menstruation. Next, the hypothalamus starts producing another hormone called gonadotrophin releasing hormone (GnRH); GnRH stimulates the

pituitary to produce follicle stimulating hormone (FSH) and luteinising hormone (LH). FSH works on the cells which surround the eggs (ie, the follicles) in both ovaries; all of a woman's eggs are present at birth, incidentally, unlike male sperm, which are constantly reproduced. Every monthly cycle, FSH ripens an egg ready for release and fertilisation and also tells the ovary to produce the female sex hormone, oestrogen. (There is actually a group of oestrogenic hormones: oestriol, oestradiol and oestrone. They all come under the oestrogen umbrella so, for simplicity's sake, we'll call them all 'oestrogen'.)

Oestrogen levels rise over the first half of the menstrual cycle, causing the lining of the womb to grow ready to receive a fertilised egg. In the middle of the cycle, LH triggers the release of an egg (ovulation). Oestrogen levels then fall off slightly and progesterone, the second female sex hormone, is produced. Progesterone makes the glands in the womb produce a nutritious fluid for the embryo and makes the womb receptive to implantation of the embryo in the lining. If the egg isn't fertilised, progesterone levels fall, causing a period as the womb lining is shed.

Q So what happens at menopause?

A Menopause comes from the Greek words 'meno', meaning month, and 'pausis', meaning ending. Menopause is medically defined as the time when a woman has had no periods for a year. The average age of the last period is 50 or 51 (although some experts advise continuing to use contraception for two years). During peri- and pre-menopause, which can start in the early 40s, levels of various hormones change gradually. As oestrogen drops, FSH goes up, menstrual flow becomes lighter and often irregular, until eventually it stops

altogether, when the ovaries finally run out of their supply of eggs.

Q Is there a point at which women stop producing oestrogen entirely?

A Oestrogen levels drop gradually as the ovaries stop working. After menopause, levels of oestradiol fall significantly. But there is still some circulating oestrogen in the form of oestrone produced in your fat tissue. The adrenal glands also produce androgens, which are converted to oestrone in fat. This is an important source around menopause, but the adrenals also produce our stress hormones, which can take priority. That's why stressed-out women are more likely to have hot flushes, etc. So it's vital to keep stress down so that the adrenals can help keep your oestrogen levels from plunging too far too fast. Progesterone, however, is only made in effective quantities when oestrogen is produced from the ovaries. Women also produce a small quantity of testosterone; during menopause, the ratio of testosterone to oestrogen becomes higher because of the falling levels of oestrogen.

Q How do I know when I'm coming up to menopause?

A In the early-to-mid-forties, women start

to notice changes – often minimal – in their menstrual periods due to erratic hormone production. Periods may be heavier (or lighter); you may get PMS for the first time; cycle length may be shorter, or you may miss a period. If you're worried, consult your doctor; make a diary of your symptoms beforehand. You may have a blood test to measure FSH levels and show whether you are in peri-menopause. If there is abnormal bleeding, the doctor may refer you for one or more of the following tests…

Endometrial biopsy: microscopic examination of sample of womb lining.

Hysteroscopy: the womb is examined through a tiny telescope on a narrow flexible tube inserted into the vagina.

Ultrasound: an imaging probe is inserted through vagina or abdomen.

Q What is surgical menopause?

A When periods stop because of a hysterectomy and removal of ovaries. Women whose ovaries are left may continue to produce oestrogen (although they won't menstruate), so will have an FSH test for menopause.

Q Am I bound to get uncomfortable physical symptoms of the menopause?

A A recent American survey of 851 women between the ages of 45 and 59 showed that 49 per cent had mild symptoms, which had little impact on their lives; 34 per cent had moderate symptoms, and 17 per cent severe ones.

Q So what are the most common symptoms?

A A survey of 500 women by the UK Menopause Awareness Alliance showed hot flushes affected 68 per cent, night sweats 49 per cent; 41 per cent report poorer skin and hair.

Q What causes hot flushes?

A They seem to be caused by an abnormal response in the message from the brain to the blood vessels, which upsets your ability to control your skin temperature. The nerves transmit 'red alert' messages via the blood vessels to the skin to sweat, when there's no need. Some women appear not to provoke this mechanism, possibly due to less stress, or lower consumption of stimulants, such as coffee and alcohol.

Q Does the change of life affect sleep?

A Oestrogen deficiency can affect serotonin levels and thus sleep patterns. Taking oestrogen in some form can help, as can daylight, exercise and a good diet with an adequate intake of B vitamins, vitamin D and selenium.

Q What about sex?

A Vaginal dryness and lack of libido are common. Although it's often still a taboo subject, experts say that about half of menopausal women are affected by vaginal dryness, which in turn affects libido. Less blood flow to the vaginal area results in loss of elasticity in skin tissues and cells of vagina and also bladder, which may lead to stress incontinence and/or cystitis.

Q Anything else physical?

A Women taking HRT seem most affected by intractable weight gain. However, almost everyone puts on weight as they get older, partly due to hormones, but also owing to a slower metabolism in tandem with a decrease in activity. Urinary incontinence and restless legs also affect many women.

Q What about the emotional side?

A Depression and anxiety are the most common complaints. Some women experience rapidly changing moods, irritability, low self-confidence, even panic attacks. Mood swings are exacerbated by almost any problems, including, as one woman growled, 'husbands!'.

hormone tests

Q Are there tests to see if I'm coming up to my last natural period?

A Your doctor may do a blood test to measure levels of follicle stimulating hormone (FSH); this can give a crude assessment of the stage of menopause and any significant hormonal deficiency but it's a signpost rather than a firm measurement. Two recently developed tests may also be useful: inhibin B and anti-mullerian hormone. Hormone levels go up and down like yo-yos, so the blood tests may need to be repeated. (One-off blood tests are generally considered unreliable.)

It's important that tests are done at the correct time of the month – ie, the early part of your cycle – and they will almost certainly need to be repeated several times to get a true picture. If you're not having periods, then they should be done on two or three occasions across a calendar month.

If you are considering taking HRT, an FSH test may be useful if the diagnosis of menopause is in doubt, also thyroid function. Oestradiol blood levels may be of some value in measuring dosage for non-oral routes (eg, implant). If you've had a blood clot or a strong family history of them, a blood clotting test may be appropriate, with blood lipids if you have a family history of high cholesterol or heart disease.

A mammogram and cervical smear should be part of your general health check and should be up to date before you go on HRT. You (or your doctor or practice nurse) should assess your Body Mass Index to make sure that you are within the recommended range of 20 to 25, again for general health.

LOWDOWN: HORMONE REPLACEMENT THERAPY

As we've explained, the menopause happens because ovaries stop producing eggs and that leads to a decrease in oestrogen production. So the logical thing seemed to be to replace it – and that's how hormone replacement therapy was born: as a treatment for a natural condition, which came to be labelled a 'deficiency disease'.

HRT was first launched in the 1930s when injections of oestrogen were given to ease symptoms. In 1942, an oral form of oestrogen was developed from the urine of pregnant mares. Around this time, scientists also realised that if a woman's ovaries were removed by surgery at an early age, causing premature menopause, she had an increased risk of developing osteoporosis (loss of bone density). In 1946, the first alarm bells rang. Doctors began to suspect that giving oestrogen alone ('unopposed') could increase the risk of cancer of the womb up to sevenfold. By the mid-1970s, more and more evidence had accumulated to confirm this. But by then, HRT had begun to gain its legendary status as a panacea for ageing women. Much of this was due to the evangelising of a Manhattan gynaecologist called Dr Robert Wilson.

Dr Wilson wrote a book called *Feminine Forever*, published in 1966, which outlined a doom-laden scenario for postmenopausal women who did not drink at the hormonal fountain of youth. They would become 'dull and unattractive'. Moreover, he said, the menopause is both unnecessary and harmful. But, abracadabra! – there was an answer: 'The deficiency disease created by ovarian decline with its painful, disabling and even fatal consequences is responsive to therapy.'

Oestrogen therapy could hardly be regarded as altering the natural state of life, he added: 'It is the case of the untreated woman – the prematurely aging castrate – that is unnatural.' His son Ronald later admitted that his father's work and expenses had been entirely financed by the pharmaceutical company concerned, whose oestrogen drug, derived from the urine of pregnant mares, went on to become America's fifth-best-selling prescription drug.

The uterine cancer scare peaked in 1975, with two studies documenting the link. There was panic and the drug's popularity plummeted. Then researchers came up with a solution: combining progestogen (another sex hormone) with oestrogen appeared to protect the womb lining. At the beginning of the 1980s, HRT was relaunched, hailed as the holy grail for middle-aged women, with a litany of health and beauty benefits in addition to easing menopausal symptoms.

Over the succeeding two decades, however, it's become clear that, for some women, the increased risks of heart disease, stroke and breast cancer outweigh the benefits. There is a role for HRT for certain women with intractable symptoms (or premature menopause), but it's vital you understand the risks – and the questions to ask.

QUESTIONS TO ASK YOUR DOCTOR ABOUT HRT

● What are the benefits of HRT for me, in particular?

● What are my long-term health risks, based on my own and my family's medical history?

● Why should I start HRT now, rather than waiting until I'm older?

● What product do you suggest and what does it contain: oestrogen, or oestrogen and progestogen? Does it also contain testosterone?

● Why is it best for me?

● Which method of delivery (route) is most suitable for me and why?

● Is this the lowest dose I can have?

● How long would I have to take HRT for?

● What side effects are likely?

● Do you have patient information leaflets and may I see the manufacturer's information? (NB: this is available on the internet.)

● If I decide to take HRT, what tests would I have first and what kind of follow-up would I receive?

● What alternatives to HRT are there for me – both conventional and natural?

● Can I talk to a specialist nurse, or a dedicated (independent) helpline before I decide?

WAYS OF TAKING HRT

There are all sorts of different forms of HRT – what doctors call 'routes of administration' or sometimes 'methods of delivery'.

The main options are tablets, patch, gel, cream, nasal spray and implant, as well as vaginal products. But not all preparations are available in all forms. If your doctor is rushed, you may not hear about all the choices, but do remember to ask, because different routes have different effects.

For instance, if your main problem is a dry vagina causing painful intercourse, you might just need a vaginal tablet of oestradiol, or oestriol cream. There is very little absorption of this into the blood stream from the vagina, so it won't improve hot flushes or benefit bones, but at the same time it shouldn't be linked to an increased risk of breast cancer. If you're only using a vaginal cream twice a week, on a relatively short term basis, you shouldn't need a progestogen. But if you find yourself using it daily and long term, your doctor may recommend adding in a progestogen to protect the womb lining.

If, however, you are taking HRT to stop hot flushes, you will need to take it via a route that allows adequate levels to get into your bloodstream, so the most likely route is oral.

possible side effects of HRT

Apart from the risks (see opposite), many women stop taking HRT because of the unwelcome side effects, which include:
- abdominal cramps
- bloating
- changes in libido – increase or decrease
- gastrointestinal upsets
- nausea and vomiting
- weight changes
- premenstrual syndrome
- breast tenderness and enlargement
- breakthrough bleeding
- heavy menstrual bleeding
- raised blood pressure
- thrombophlebitis (inflammation of wall of a vein)
- headaches or migraine (see below)
- dizziness
- leg cramps
- fluid retention
- depression, irritability, mood changes
- jaundice (see below)
- increase in size of fibroids in the womb
- intolerance to contact lenses
- skin irritation (especially with patches) and rashes
- hair loss
- runny nose and, rarely, nosebleed with nasal spray

Do not take HRT if you have:
- had a recent heart attack or stroke
- an undiagnosed breast mass
- an active blood clot in leg or lung
- recently diagnosed breast or uterine cancer
- active breast or uterine cancer
- acute liver disease
- undiagnosed vaginal bleeding
- are pregnant or breast-feeding

Think twice about taking HRT if you have:
- strong family history of breast cancer
- personal or strong family history of blood clots
- previous history of benign breast lumps
- untreated high blood pressure
- vaginal bleeding of uncertain cause
- endometriosis
- fibroids (benign womb growths)
- migraine
- previous history of gallstones
- any previous liver disease, even mild
- migraine/migraine-type problems
- bad varicose veins

Discuss these conditions with your doctor:
- epilepsy, diabetes, multiple sclerosis, asthma, inherited deafness, thyroid disease, lupus, kidney disease

WARNING HRT affects blood circulation and also the reproductive parts of your body – breasts, ovaries and womb. Stop taking HRT (or the pill) immediately and go to hospital if you have sudden chest pain, breathlessness, pain in the calf/stomach, unusual headache, loss of vision, hearing or speech, or jaundice.

THE MAIN RISKS OF HRT

ABSOLUTE VERSUS RELATIVE RISKS

To understand the increased risks of illness associated with HRT, it's important to understand the difference between relative risk and absolute risk, and put it in the context of the period of time.

Relative risk is the increased percentage: so, for instance, the risk of getting a clot in your leg around the age of the menopause is one in 10,000 for non-HRT users, which increases to three in 10,000 if you take HRT. That is a 200 per cent increase in your relative risk, which sounds terrifying. But the absolute risk is in fact an extra two cases of blood clots per 10,000 women.

There is still an increased risk, which is a personal tragedy for those affected, but it is not as vast as it's often portrayed.

KEY STUDIES

The Women's Health Initiative study in America, where about 8,000 healthy postmenopausal women took combined HRT and the same number a dummy pill, was halted in May 2002, just over five years into the eight-and-a-half-year trial. One woman in a hundred experienced some kind of 'adverse event' over the five years. The additional yearly threat to 10,000 women on combined HRT, compared with placebo, was:

- seven more heart attacks
- eight more strokes
- eight more blood clots in the lungs (pulmonary embolism)
- eight more invasive breast cancers

On the plus side they would be likely to have:

- six fewer colorectal cancers
- five fewer hip fractures

Two months later, in July 2002, the European Wisdom Study (Women's International Study of Long-Duration Oestrogen after Menopause) was stopped because of the risks. In March 2004, the oestrogen-only arm of the WHI trial was halted early because of the increased risk of stroke and of probable dementia and mild cognitive impairment.

In 2003, the Milllion Women Study, carried out in Britain, which looked at 1,084,110 women between the ages of 50 and 64 found that both combined and oestrogen-only HRT increased the risk of breast cancer. The risk rose the longer HRT was taken but returned to normal five years after stopping. The greatest increased risk came from implants, followed by oral, then skin patches. In July 2005, the International Agency for Research on Cancer, part of the World Health Organisation, reclassified HRT from 'possibly carcinogenic' to 'carcinogenic'. In the past, studies have suggested that breast cancer linked to HRT was less likely to be fatal but this has not proved to be the case.

Research is ongoing about whether HRT also increases the risks of:

- ovarian cancer
- endometrial cancer
- gallstones
- increasing the size of fibroids
- reactivating endometriosis
- migraine (some HRT users report fewer, however)
- asthma
- osteoarthritis
- venous thrombo-embolism, a potentially fatal blood clot

It all sounds frightening – and it is – but many women who are depressed, possibly suicidally, by intractable symptoms, believe these risks are worthwhile to help them reclaim their lives.

HRT: AN EXPERT VIEW

A decade can be a long time in medicine. HRT has gone from being seen as the first line of treatment for menopausal symptoms and osteoporosis, with a significant heart protective effect, to being headline news as public enemy number one. But it's still licensed, still prescribed and, according to many doctors, still has a valuable role. So just who might benefit – and how can the risks be minimised? Here's a straightforward assessment.

When we researched this book in 1997–8, the majority of doctors practising conventional medicine took the view that HRT was the universal panacea for heart disease (heart attacks and strokes) and osteoporosis, as well as treating unwelcome menopausal symptoms. In fact, doctors prescribed it as much to protect against heart attacks and for its purported general health benefits as for hot flushes.

Yes, they admitted, there did seem to be a slightly increased risk of women getting breast cancer, but they weren't likely to die of it. (The unspoken subtext was, 'So that's all right then.') Our experts back then, however, led by Howard Jacobs, formerly professor of reproductive endocrinology at the Middlesex Hospital in London, took a sceptical view, which proved extraordinarily prescient. Later research showed that not only did HRT not protect against heart attacks and stroke, it increased the risk in the first year and possibly later, as well as increasing the risk of breast and possibly other cancers.

Since then, Sarah has co-written a book on the menopause with British consultant gynaecologist Michael Dooley. *Your Change, Your Choice: The Integrated Approach to the Menopause* examines in depth the pros and cons of HRT, explains the research to date, and also gives information about the alternatives. In the following extract, you will find a summary of Michael and Sarah's findings, based on years of reading all the research, listening to women's experiences and talking to experts worldwide.

HRT: THE FACTS

The use of HRT is now controversial, except in cases of intractable symptoms or premature menopause, where the patient is fully informed about the risks and has no serious contra-indications. What has largely been left out of the medical equation until now is that there are effective alternatives to HRT. Unfortunately for their patients, few doctors have made themselves aware of these, although this situation is beginning to change. The tide is turning among British doctors, who have traditionally tended to continue supporting the use of HRT.

In a recent survey, 25 per cent of GPs said that, until very recently, they didn't recommend natural remedies at all to women at the menopause. Now nearly half say that they recommend HRT less often and, in March 2005, more than half of female GPs reported that up to four out of ten of their patients at menopause ask about natural remedies and dietary supplements.

One thing is clear: HRT is not a wonder drug that should be taken by all menopausal women. Evidence shows that the benefits are much fewer and the risks far greater than the manufacturers and doctors initially claimed – and that women hoped for.

But you should remember that all drugs (even aspirin) have potential risks and side effects, so the baby shouldn't be thrown out with the bath water. Anecdotally, many women say they feel well and happy on it. Equally, however, many report feeling better when they come off it.

Michael Dooley was one of the first leading gynaecologists to question publicly the benefits of HRT: 'I'm the first to admit that I was, in the past, an oestrogen evangelist. Now I feel that although it has an important role, especially for women who go through the change early, it is not my first line of treatment for most patients. Women need to be fully informed of the risks and benefits, kept up to date with new research and offered a full range of alternative options, as well as being counselled about the crucial role of diet, fitness and stress management.'

Here is a summary of the pros and cons of HRT, based on the available information:

● HRT has some benefits for some women.

● There are definitely some risks, but these are smaller than they may seem from headlines [as explained on previous pages]; women must always be counselled individually and the risks and benefits explained so they can make up their own minds.

● Unless contraindicated, HRT is very important for women who have premature menopause, either due to premature ovarian failure or surgical menopause, because of the risk of bone loss; diet and weight-bearing exercise are crucial too.

● If you have had a hysterectomy before menopause, without your ovaries being removed too, you may or may not need HRT; discuss this in detail with your doctor.

● While not essential, HRT is effective at helping hot flushes and night sweats, within four to 12 weeks of starting; if you take HRT for hot flushes, continue for a year because the symptoms will be likely to return if you stop.

● HRT does help to relieve hormonally related mood changes and insomnia.

● HRT can help with vaginal problems, including painful sex, but it may take several months: systemic HRT (oral, patch, implants or nasal routes) or oestrogen cream in tablet form applied to the vagina may ameliorate vaginal irritation, dryness, soreness and itching not due to infection or other skin problems; it may also help with painful sex, bleeding after sex, reduced sexual arousal, vaginal discharge or infections.

● HRT may help with urinary problems – but again, it may take several months before results are noticeable.

● HRT may also help to reduce skin and hair loss in some women, may improve wound healing, and alleviate age-related macular degeneration and tooth loss – but all these areas are in need of further research.

● If HRT is prescribed, it must be in the smallest effective dose for the shortest time.

● The routes of delivery must be tailored to individual women; the traditional oral route may not be appropriate, or as necessary as others (see page 210).

● If HRT is offered, the option of adding in a progestogen (known as combined HRT, as opposed to oestrogen only) must be fully discussed.

● Regular follow-up of HRT users is essential, not only for monitoring but to keep up with the latest research.

COMING OFF HRT

If you are on HRT and have concerns, do NOT stop abruptly unless there is an emergency (see page 210). You must tail it off gradually, just as you would go through the menopause gradually. The usual time frame is three to four months, during which you reduce the dose as your doctor suggests. If you have a womb and are taking a combined oestrogen and progestogen product, you need to talk about how you have a final bleed.

HRT AND OSTEOPOROSIS

As we've mentioned, it was recognised in the mid-20th century that you need oestrogen to achieve the optimal peak bone density, because oestrogen stops bone shedding. That's why missing periods for over six months under the age of 35 is a significant risk factor for osteoporosis, and why falling oestrogen levels at menopause can be a crucial turning pont in the life of your bones.

But on the basis of the recent research showing the risks of HRT, the European Expert Working Group from 28 countries concluded in November 2003 that HRT should not be recommended as the first line of treatment for osteoporosis in post-menopausal women (who would not naturally be producing oestrogen) – although it is still considered very important for younger women going through premature menopause (who would naturally be producing oestrogen).

The reason that experts decided HRT should no longer be the drug of choice for post-menopausal women with bone loss is two-fold: firstly, although it does help bone to stay stronger (and was shown to prevent fractures in the WHI trial and others) the benefits only last as long as you stay on the drug. Soon after you stop taking it, your bones play catch-up and return to where they were when you started. As long-term HRT is not advisable, the maths doesn't work. Secondly, the Group said the risks outweighed the benefits.

For more on osteoporosis, see over.

OSTEOPOROSIS

Osteoporosis, or thinning of the bones, affects about one in three post-menopausal women in Britain to some extent, according to the National Osteoporosis Society.

Bones consist of connective tissue (mainly collagen) packed around with solid crystals of minerals, rather like a honeycomb. Despite their inert appearance, bones are as much alive as the rest of our bodies, constantly building (due to the bone-making cells, osteoblasts, which mature into osteocytes) and shedding (due to the third type of bone cell, osteoclasts). They grow with us from birth, stop lengthening when we are about 16 to 18 but go on increasing in density to reach peak bone mass at 30 to 35. After that, problems may begin because we tend to start losing bone faster than we replace it.

Osteoporosis leads to a reduction in both the connective tissue and mineral content of the bone. This makes bones brittle and easily fractured and also results in curvature of the spine. Although osteoporosis runs in families, it can be prevented by plenty of weight-bearing exercise and good nutrition in early life when bones are forming. Current tests (see below) measure bone density, although in future there may be more accurate measurements of bone loss. If your bone density is low, you may be recommended to have follow-ups.

TESTING BONE DENSITY

The idea of measuring your bone mineral density (BMD) is to assess the holes in the honeycomb and thus your risk of fracture. Bone toughness and flexibility are also important, as are the internal structure of the skeleton and the rate of bone cell turnover, but at the moment BMD testing is the most reliable way of assessing risk.

The main procedures are:
● **DEXA (dual energy x-ray absorptiometry):** this x-ray based system uses two different energies to differentiate between soft tissue and bone. The two main sites tested are the lumbar spine and the hip. You lie flat during the scan, which is painless and lasts between five and 15 minutes. DEXA is the gold standard, but not everyone will be referred for it. However, if you have strong risks and are likely to need treatment, your doctor should make sure you have a DEXA. The radiation dose is extremely small – a fraction of the dose from a chest x-ray.

● **QUS (quantitative ultrasound):** this uses ultrasound to scan part of the body, usually the heel bone (calcaneum). It's an attractive method because the machine is easily portable and it doesn't use any radiation. QUS gives an indication of fracture risk rather than measuring bone density. It should be used for people who have risk factors already to see who would benefit from being referred for a DEXA.

Results: if your BMD is one SD (standard deviation) below the mean, you are normal; if your BMD is between one and 2.5 SD below the mean, you have osteopenia (your bones are thinning, but not badly enough for you to be diagnosed with osteoporosis); if your BMD is 2.5 or more below the mean, the diagnosis is osteoporosis.

RISK FACTORS

You are more likely to develop osteoporosis if:
● it runs in your family
● you are inactive and take little exercise
● you exercise to extremes
● you don't get out in the sunlight
● you go into premature menopause, ie, before 40
● you have had a hysterectomy before 50
● you smoke
● you consume a lot of animal protein, alcohol and/or coffee, and salt
● you have coeliac disease, rheumatoid arthritis, thyroid malfunction
● you take drugs including: corticosteroids (eg, prednisolone), laxatives, diuretics, thyroxine
● you have irregular periods
● you stopped having periods for more than six months at any time
● you are thin
● you have suffered from an eating disorder such as anorexia or bulimia
● you have a digestive problem, eg, Irritable Bowel Syndrome, diarrhoea, constipation, or a lack of stomach acid

QUESTIONS TO ASK YOUR DOCTOR ABOUT OSTEOPOROSIS

● What is my risk of osteoporosis, based on my own and my family's medical histories?
● What tests do you suggest I have?
● If I'm at risk, what treatment do you recommend – and why?
● What will this therapy do – halt bone loss or build bone?
● When would I begin treatment – before or after menopause?
● How long would I have to undergo it for?
● What are the possible side effects of this treatment?
● Are there any alternatives to conventional therapy?

simple helpers

There is no dispute at all that preventing bone loss through simple lifestyle measures is the best thing you can do at any age – these measures will also help build peak bone mass in the under-thirties.

● **Take regular weight-bearing exercise.** (See page 166.) In one study, 30 post-menopausal women increased their spinal mass by a significant 0.5 per cent in 12 months simply by walking 50 minutes four times a week.

● **Get out in the fresh air.** Vitamin D from the sun helps calcium absorption.

● **Reduce protein foods.** Some nutritionists now believe that a diet high in animal proteins may be a primary cause. One study compared meat-eating women with vegetarians. The veggies lost 18 per cent of their bone mass, while the meat-eating women lost 35 per cent.

● **Don't rely on dairy foods.** Their benefits are now disputed. The 'antis' point to Asian women, who don't drink milk or eat cheese, and yet have little problem with osteoporosis.

● **Have frequent regular meals** to avoid internal stress, which causes an acid body environment

● **Cut down on caffeine.**

● **Avoid bran and bran-containing foods.** They may interfere with calcium absorption. Get all-important fibre by eating lots of fruit and veg.

● **Drink one tablespoonful of cider vinegar and honey** in a cupful of warm water up to three times daily; naturopaths say this helps digestion and also absorption of calcium.

● **Chuck out aluminium pans:** aluminium can leach from cooking pans, foil and containers, and stop the body metabolising calcium. Switch to glass, enamel, stainless steel or cast iron.

● **Relax:** stress triggers adrenaline production which damages bone.

● **Look after your digestion.** As we get older, levels of beneficial stomach acid (hydrochloric acid) drop, often giving rise to symptoms such as flatulence, bloating and indigestion and interfering with nutrient absorption. Try food-combining and a digestive supplement, and/or consult a nutritionist, naturopath or doctor.

● **Don't smoke.** Smoking cigarettes lowers blood oestrogen levels and also has a dampening effect on the cells that make new bone.

DRUG TREATMENTS FOR OSTEOPOROSIS

As we explain on the previous page, HRT is now not recommended as a first-line treatment for osteoporosis . Here are the drugs that are used today. Check side effects on the net, by googling the drug name and selecting the manufacturer's information.

SERMs: selective estrogen receptor modulators, aka designer oestrogens, have been shown to reduce the rate of spinal vertebral fractures in post-menopausal women with bone loss. Raloxifene is licensed for prevention and treatment.

Tibolone: a synthetic steroid drug with mixed oestrogenic, progestogenic and androgenic action, currently licensed for prevention, but not treatment.

Calcitonin: hormone produced by thyroid, which reduces bone loss. Rarely used.

Parathyroid hormone: very costly, so for patients with severe osteoporosis, who are non-responsive or intolerant to other drugs.

Biphosphonates: eg, Fosamax and Actonel. The most effective group of anti-resorptive drugs, which stop the bone being shed and resorbed into the body. Can cause digestive side effects, but may be licensed as monthly or yearly injectables to overcome the problem.

Calcium and vitamin D supplementation: principally for sixty-plus women.

Strontium ranelate: the drug Protelos both blocks bone loss and stimulates new bone, useful for helping to prevent secondary vertebral fractures.

Black cohosh: this herb has shown some promise in helping bone metabolism, as well as its better known role in preventing menopausal symptoms. Researchers suggest it acts like a SERM (see above).

ALTERNATIVE HORMONE HELPERS

Many experts feel that an integrated combination of gentle alternative/complementary therapies, aimed at treating both body and mind, can ease the menopause (and of course many other conditions). As well as the stress therapies detailed on pages 238–9, there is a range of traditional herbal, homoeopathic and nutritional approaches such as the ones detailed below. It is always wise to consult a doctor with an interest in these remedies, or another appropriate expert – homoeopath, nutritionist, naturopath, herbalist or Chinese medicine expert are the most relevant – before starting out on a new regime. We recommend keeping your family doctor informed about what you are doing.

ALTERNATIVE MEDICAL SYSTEMS

The following systems have given help to women we know. In practice, they may overlap, and practitioners invariably also give general advice about lifestyle measures.

Homoeopathy

The homoeopathic approach involves exploring the woman's feelings about the menopause and what it represents to her, then supporting her with homoeopathic tinctures. Devotees include Queen Elizabeth II who, together with other members of the Royal Family, has regularly consulted London-based medical doctor and homoeopath Dr Ronald Davey, among others.

Dr Tessa Katz of the Women's Clinic at the Royal London Homoeopathic Hospital reported in 1997 that about 70 per cent of patients felt a definite improvement in menopausal symptoms while they were using homoeopathic medicines, about 25 per cent got some benefit and the remaining five per cent noticed no change. Most of those patients had tried HRT in the past and were either unhappy with taking possibly harmful medication daily, or had suffered 'intolerable' side effects. Some patients used homoeopathic treatments alongside HRT.

Chinese medicine

Menopausal symptoms are believed to be linked to kidney, blood and kidney/liver imbalances. Herbs such as dong quai (Chinese angelica) and ginseng are commonly prescribed. Acupuncture is used to balance hormones and ease pain. Chi gung, a system of mind/body meditation and gentle exercise, is also practised as part of Chinese medicine.

Western herbal medicine

The emphasis is on stimulating the hormonal changes to progress as easily as possible. Herbs which work like oestrogen are often prescribed for hot flushes, night sweats and flooding, eg, black cohosh, blue cohosh, agnus castus, hops and wild yam. Infusions of sage or motherwort, which also have an oestrogen-like action, are prescribed for vaginal dryness, pot marigold cream may be suggested for the vagina, and for stress, soothing herbs (eg, skullcap and vervain) with St John's wort (one of the best researched herbal antidepressants) for depression. Lavender, rose and ylang ylang oils may be recommended for the bath.

Bio-energetic medicine

This is based on the principles of homoeopathy and acupuncture, well known in Germany. Practitioners believe that behind every condition is a weakness in the system or a prolonged energy disturbance. The aim of the therapy is to balance the body so that it functions optimally.

Nutritional therapy

Higher levels of various vitamins and minerals may help as women get older, particularly the B vitamins 6, 12 and folic acid, vitamins D and E, plus magnesium, chromium and zinc. Vitamin E has been shown to improve vaginal dryness (see also seaweed, page 193), hot flushes, sweating, dizziness and fatigue, as well as helping to protect against heart disease.

Hydrochloric acid (HCl), which helps digestion and the absorption of minerals including calcium, seems to decline with age. Zinc and/or B_{12} deficiency, food sensitivities, rheumatoid arthritis, stress, coffee consumption, pollutants, and an over- or underactive thyroid may all affect it. By menopause, some women appear to have virtually no HCl. Eating papaya (pawpaw), which is rich in the digestive enzyme papain, or taking supplements such as HCl and/or pepsin with meals, may help. Chewing food thoroughly is vital.

alternative 'drugs'

Pharmaceutical drugs are not the only preparations which can help women through the menopause. Increasingly, plant-based products are proving their worth, alongside exercise systems such as yoga.

Medicinal plants have been used for millennia worldwide to help with menopausal symptoms, as with other problems. They came to prominence in the West when HRT was shown to increase the risk of heart disease and breast cancer. Although many conventional doctors tend to dismiss their efficacy and safety, in general there is consensus over the effectiveness of black cohosh (*Actaea racemosa*). According to an article in the *American Family Physician*, 2003:

'The roots and rhizomes of this herb are widely used in the treatment of menopausal symptoms and menstrual dysfunction. Studies have demonstrated that this botanic medicine, when standardised properly, appears to be effective in alleviating menopausal symptoms. Adverse effects are extremely uncommon, and there are no known significant adverse drug interactions.'

In one trial at the University of Göttingen, black cohosh (in a 40mg daily dose) was as effective as oestrogen at reducing menopausal symtpoms and helping bone metabolism. Researchers proposed that it acted like a SERM (Selective Oestrogen Reuptake Modulator), because of its good effects in the brain, bone and vagina, without causing changes to the lining of the womb which could lead to cancer. Most traditional medicines combine herbs, rather than using them singly (See 'Herbs', on page 219.)

Natural progesterone, made from wild yam and usually applied as a cream, has long been used to lessen the unwelcome symptoms of the menopause. Its benefits have now made this plant-derived product so much part of the mainstream that your GP can prescribe it on the NHS. It can also be obtained at health food stores and via the internet.

Dr Susan Horsewood-Lee has prescribed natural progesterone for many years. The patients she has found it benefits most are those who would never take conventional HRT but are at some risk of osteoporosis. 'These are patients who look after themselves already, eat well and take regular exercise. Then they have a bone density scan and the result is low. They spend the next year doing more load-bearing exercise, adding in a supplement such as OsteoPro – which is good – but the next scan is even lower.' At that point, she says, they are unsure what to do. About 90 per cent of the patients who have come to her in this situation and who have added natural progesterone to their routine have benefited. The sooner you start, the better. Women on natural progesterone also tend to have fewer hot flushes, according to Dr Horsewood-Lee, possibly because oestrogen levels drop more gently and may plateau at a higher level.

Do consult a knowledgeable health professional for advice, if possible.

KEEP YOUR ADRENALS HAPPY

Doctors are now accepting what natural therapists have been saying for a long time: that it's vital to take good care of your adrenal glands because they can produce your body's own natural HRT. This pair of glands, sitting on top of your kidneys, are the body's primary system for coping with stress – but as well as releasing stress hormones, they produce an androgen called androstenedione, which gets converted into a form of oestrogen in your fat cells. If, however, you are stressed out, pumping out stress hormones takes priority. So, instead of helping your body balance the hormonal fluctuations, it becomes ever more unbalanced, resulting in symptoms such as hot flushes. Erratic adrenals cause wide-ranging effects on your body, including weight gain on bottom, hips and thighs. Additionally, they can cause blood sugar levels to swing wildly, which also leads to mad moods, as well as other symptoms. Keeping your adrenals balanced is not rocket science. Detox your diet (see pages 200–201), cut down stimulants (caffeine, alcohol, sugar), eat slowly, chew food thoroughly, and keep stress levels in bounds by learning simple breathing techniques, practising yoga (we like therapeutic Iyengar yoga) and having fun! Many more details in Sarah's book, *Your Change, Your Choice: The Integrated Approach to the Menopause*, co-written with gynaecologist Michael Dooley.

NATURAL WAYS TO HELP HOT FLUSHES

TAKE CARE OF THE BASICS

● Eat every three hours: this keeps blood sugar levels steady, which helps with all hormonal problems, including hot flushes, according to research. So keep a glass of milk and an oatcake by your bed.

● Sip at least eight glasses of still water daily between meals and at night.

● Choose fresh food, low in animal fats and sugar: a high-animal fat, high-sugar diet seems linked to hot flushes. Eat lots of vegetables and non-citrus fruit, plus fish and plant oils, which are essential for balancing hormones, improving anxiety and depression; also skin, hair and nails.

● Cut out known triggers: hot spicy foods, chocolate, alcohol, hot drinks (particularly tea and coffee because of the caffeine).

● Don't smoke.

● Exercise daily for at least 30–60 minutes: it helps your adrenal glands release androgenic hormones that convert to a form of oestrogen (see previous page).

● Get out in the light for an hour a day. This helps boost levels of the feelgood hormone serotonin. Lack of serotonin is linked to poor sleep and low mood.

● Avoid sudden changes of temperature, eg, coming in from the cold and going into a hot room.

LOOK AFTER YOUR MIND

■ Keep stress levels under control – relax and laugh!

■ Stress may prevent the production of oestrogen-forming hormones from the adrenal glands, and may deplete serotonin levels.

Practise therapeutic iyengar yoga, to stretch your body, calm your mind and help with specific symptoms (www.iyengaryoga.org.uk).

■ Meditation and visualisation help too.

■ Breathe deeply, slowly, smoothly: it will help you sleep and can stop a hot flush in its tracks. Inhale to a count of three, pause for three, exhale to six, repeat five times, as often as possible.

■ Play relaxation tapes in bed: listen to soothing music such as Gregorian chants any time: research shows it slows your brain waves.

■ Give yourself little treats, and ask for help: lifting your mood helps everything.

LIFESTYLE HELPERS

● Spray face and neck from a small atomiser filled with spring water and a drop each of essential oils of juniper, clary sage and geranium.

● Carry facial blotters in your make-up bag.

● Consider using powder foundation, such as Susan Posnick's Colorflo range, which won't drip down your face as the heat rises (www.susanposnick.com).

● Carry a fan with you always – either an old-fashioned one, which is elegant and romantic, or a battery-operated, handbag-sized mini-fan.

● Ditch man-made fibres such as polyesters and nylon: they trap the heat and make flushes much worse. Wear easily removable layers of cotton, silk, linen or wool.

● Use pure cotton bed linen; and have layers of blankets or coverings, rather than duvets.

● If you are sharing a bed and you're casting off the bedclothes while your beloved freezes, consider separate covers – it can save separate rooms.

● Keep wet flannels in the fridge at home and have one by your bed at night; wring them out in cold water mixed with rose water, or a drop of essential oil of camomile, rose geranium or lavender.

● Make sure all rooms are well ventilated.

if a hot flush rises ...

■ Immediately sip cold/iced water (or tea) and breathe slowly and deeply.

■ Open the nearest window and/or get out in the fresh air as soon as you feel the flush coming on.

■ Reduce your body temperature by putting a bag of frozen peas or a chilled face cloth on your forehead.

■ Sniff essential oil of camomile (Roman or German) dotted on a handkerchief.

■ When you go out, carry a flannel wrapped around ice cubes inside a plastic bag, or a packet of facial wipes which has been in the fridge.

■ If you're at home, have a cool or cold shower.

NUTRITIONAL SUPPLEMENTS

Soy and other phytoestrogens

Many studies show that soya-based products (eg, tofu) which are rich in plant (phyto-) oestrogens and calcium have a moderate to good effect in reducing menopausal symptoms and may help protect against osteoporosis. About half of women with hot flushes can expect to benefit. Some experts have concluded that Japanese women escape hot flushes (there is no Japanese translation) and other menopausal symptoms because their diet is rich in soya and in ginseng. Also the rate of breast and other hormonally dependent cancers and osteoporosis is much lower in Japan.

Phytoestrogen-rich foods include wholegrains (oats, corn, barley, millet, buckwheat, wild rice, brown rice and whole wheat) plus soya flour and flax seed oil; also vegetables (fennel, celery, parsley, sprouts and the legume family – peas, beans and lentils).

Concentrated soya protein is also available in tablet form. Brands include Blackmores Phyto-Life Plus and Solgar's Iso Soy. Tofupill is a soy product which researchers in Israel say acts as a phyto-SERM (Selective Estrogen Receptor Modulators, aka designer oestrogen), significantly helping hot flushes, vaginal dryness, low libido, aches and pains and insomnia, without the risks of HRT (www.femarelle.com). NB: anyone who has been diagnosed as having a low thyroid condition should avoid excessive consumption of soy and vegetables from the cabbage family (brassicas).

Rhubarb, rhubarb

A preparation of rhubarb root called Phytoestrol gives a medium daily dose of plant oestrogens. Although not as fast acting as conventional HRT, it's said to create a lasting improvement in menopausal symptoms.

Gamma-oryzanol

For a gentle way of dealing with severe clusters of hot flushes, London GP Dr Susan Horsewood-Lee suggests taking three capsules daily of this rice extract, which has undergone extensive research in Japan.

> Japanese women escape hot flushes (there is no Japanese translation) and other menopausal symptoms because their diet is rich in soya and in ginseng.

Vitamins

Vitamin C with bioflavonoids (up to 1g daily) and vitamin E (400–500 IUs daily) have been shown to help with hot flushes and other menopausal symptoms. The vitamin C helps with accompanying skin problems, and vitamin E improves vaginal dryness and has been shown to help prevent heart disease and cancer.

HERBS

Unlike the 'magic bullet' concept of pharmaceutical drugs, herbal formulas tend to work best in combinations, according to many experts. Consultant gynaecologist Michael Dooley recommends his patients take MenoHerbs2, (which Sarah swears by, too) which includes a mixture of wild yam, black cohosh, dong quai, agnus castus, red clover, Siberian ginseng, nettles and protykin. We also like the flower remedy Women's Balance by Light Heart Essences.

MENOPAUSE SMOOTHIE RECIPE

Blend together

35–50g organic tofu

1 cupful red and purple fruit (buy frozen packs)

1 banana

with a little organic milk, yoghurt or pure apple juice.

This smoothie, devised by naturopath Roderick Lane, is based on organic tofu and berries. It is delicious, nutritious, quick to make and is a perfect labour-saving breakfast or meal replacement any time.

The secret of success with soy is consistency, consistency, consistency, according to Roderick. So try to have 35–50g of organic soya daily, rather than lots once a week. If you are vegetarian and using soy as your only protein source, go for 100–125g daily. Take a supplement if you don't manage to consume your daily amount. The antioxidants found in red and black berries can also help. Roderick emphasises that any milk you drink should be organic whole milk, not skimmed (unless your blood lipids are abnormally high) because it contains an important Omega-6 fatty acid called conjugated linoleic acid (CLA).

DO YOU BELIEVE IN MIRACLES?

The idea of a magic elixir to fight off age is the fulfilment of all our dreams, the holy grail of age researchers – and a billion-dollar prospect for pharmaceutical companies. But, despite a slew of much vaunted contenders, including the so-called 'miracle' hormones, international experts are sceptical. And so are we...

There is increasing talk of the so-called 'miracle' hormones – melatonin, DHEA (dehydroepiandrosterone), pregnenolone and growth hormone – which, according to some researchers, can keep us healthy and beautiful, bursting with vigour, our minds and memories alert. Like all hormones, they decline with age and the pro-lobby believes giving us back levels we had at our peak (about 25 to 30 years old) can rejuvenate both body and brain. But the National Institute on Ageing (NIA) in America warns potential consumers: 'The NIA does not recommend taking supplements of DHEA, growth hormone or melatonin because not enough is known about them. People who have a genuine deficiency of human growth hormone should take it only under a doctor's supervision.'

Despite these warnings, melatonin, DHEA and pregnenolone are classed as food supplements and are freely available over the internet. The UK Department of Health comments about its ban on melatonin: 'Melatonin is a very powerful hormone which has a marked physiological effect. Therefore it's a medicine, not a substance which compensates for a deficiency in your diet.'

As the NIA also points out, hormone supplements may not have exactly the same effects on us as our own naturally produced hormones, because the body may process them differently. Additionally, high doses of supplements, whatever form they come in, may result in higher amounts of the hormones in the body than are healthy. For instance, the usual dose of 2–5mg of melatonin is thought to be safe by researchers, but can result in blood levels of up to 40 times higher than normal.

When that happens, any negative effects may increase. And even tiny amounts of these powerful substances can have widespread effects on body chemistry. But large-scale studies are ongoing worldwide and there may come a time when these hormones are shown to be useful and safe. Meanwhile we do caution you to be sceptical about anti-ageing clinics who prescribe these and other powerful drugs. Although some doctors may be extremely knowledgeable, we were worried when we interviewed the owner of one such clinic in London. He routinely prescribed DHEA and also pharmaceutical drugs more or less on demand. Our concern was the lack of information given to patients about proven lifestyle factors, such as nutrition and exercise, and the emphasis on these so-called 'miracle' drugs. However, Dr Cecilia Tregear, editorial director of the *British Anti-Ageing Medicine Journal* and founder of the Wimpole Skin Care Centre in London, believes that by testing levels of a range of hormones and giving tiny supplementary amounts if needed, women can have their youth and wellbeing restored. She also emphasises the need for a really good diet.

In our view, antioxidants are the only anti-ageing compounds that genuinely justify the hype. What's more, they're safe, reliable and great for both health and beauty. (For more on antioxidants, see page 13.)

THE SO-CALLED 'MIRACLE' HORMONES

HORMONE	PRODUCED BY	WHAT IT DOES
Melatonin	pineal gland	regulates sleep/wake pattern and influences other hormones, affecting mood, libido, digestion and immune system
DHEA	adrenal glands	may be converted to hormones, principally oestrogen and testosterone
Pregnenolone	adrenal glands, ovaries (testes in men)	may be converted to hormones, including oestrogen, testosterone and cortisol
Growth hormone	pituitary gland in brain	regulates growth and maintenance of skin, connective tissue and organs

WHAT TO DO IF YOU FIND A BREAST LUMP

First of all, try to stay calm: 90 per cent of the time it's not serious. But if you do need treatment, you have rights and choices.

One woman in 12 develops breast cancer in Britain, one in eight or nine in America. Although doctors admit they do not yet have a cure, guidelines have now been agreed by UK medical experts (the British Association of Surgical Oncologists' Breast Group), who say that women should be treated in specialist cancer units by expert multidisciplinary teams who can give the best possible advice and treatment.

If you find a lump in your breast, make an immediate appointment with your family doctor to discuss it.

WITH YOUR DOCTOR

Detailed notes will be taken of your own and your family's medical history; then you will have a physical examination.

Don't leap to the worst conclusion, because nine breast lumps out of ten are benign. What you are feeling may not even be a lump but an area of nodularity; your GP will then suggest examining you again after your next period.

If your GP believes it is a true lump, he or she should refer you immediately to a specialist breast cancer unit. These units are now much quicker at organising appointments than they used to be, and will usually see you within a week, although you may have to travel. If your GP is really concerned, appointments and referral letters are now routinely organised by fax or email.

If your GP does not refer you immediately and you are concerned, you must be persistent, however vulnerable you feel. It is your body.

THE EXPERTS

If you are referred to a specialist unit, you will find the team has several key personnel: one or more consultant surgeons who specialise in breast work, a clinical oncologist (cancer expert), a breast-care nurse, a pathologist (who interprets the results of biopsies), plus a radiographer and radiologist who work on breast x-rays (mammography). Your first appointment will be with the consultant surgeon or a senior member of his or her team. Specialist breast nurses should always be available if you want to see one.

DIAGNOSTIC TECHNIQUES

Firstly, the consultant will examine your breast to confirm that there actually is a physical lump. Secondly, needle

aspiration will be carried out to draw off some of the cells. (This may be uncomfortable but it shouldn't be painful.) If it's a cyst – one of the commonest causes of breast lumps – the fluid can be drawn off there and then and the problem solved. If it's not a cyst, further investigations will take place. Thirdly, imaging techniques will be used to investigate the situation. If you are under 40, sophisticated ultrasound imaging with sound waves will be used to build up a picture of the breast. For the over-forties, mammography (x-ray of the breast) will be used. (Many surgeons believe that two views should be taken of each breast.) Frequently, both ultrasound and mammography are used in both age groups.

From this triangle of information, the consultant surgeon and team decide whether they believe the lump to be benign or malignant. In the most efficient clinics, you will have the result the same day, or within a few days. You should not wait more than one week.

If the results are inconclusive, the consultant may suggest a biopsy under general anaesthetic to remove the lump, for testing. The results should be available within a week to ten days.

If the tests suggest a malignant tumour – in other words, cancer – your next appointment will be with the consultant surgeon, the breast nurse and possibly the oncologist. Although the diagnosis should always be given to you in a warm and caring way, it's a good idea to take a companion with you. Some consultants will give you a tape of the meeting, others are happy if you or your companion take notes. You may want to go in with a list of questions. Now and throughout your treatment, you should be given information and choices and as much support as you feel you need.

CHOOSING A TREATMENT

Treatment options for breast cancer are surgery, radiotherapy, hormone therapy and chemotherapy (by drugs). Treatments may be used alone or in combination. Each case is different and treatment should be individually tailored. The consultant should discuss all the possibilities, and you have every right to ask as many questions as you like about the proposed treatment and any possible alternatives, side effects – both short and long term, including possible fertility problems – success rate, breast reconstruction (immediate or delayed) or prosthesis fitting service, and arrangements for follow-up after-treatment. The breast nurse will be there to give support and information throughout. Though you may feel pressured to make a decision, you should take as long as you feel is necessary to consider the options. You may find a second opinion reassuring – and most experts will refer you to another specialist without any fuss. If there is a problem, go back to your GP.

Surgery should be offered within two weeks. There are three possible operations: a lumpectomy, or wide excision, where the lump and some surrounding (healthy) tissue are removed; segmentectomy, where a larger area (but less than a quarter of the breast) is removed, leaving a natural shape and cleavage – usually performed when the woman has a lump under 2cm (3/4in) round; and a mastectomy, where the breast is removed entirely.

The lymph nodes will also be tested and may be removed to prevent the cancer spreading. Reconstruction of the breast can be performed at the time by a specialist breast surgeon, although some consultants suggest patients wait for six months before deciding. In this case, the reconstruction may be done by a plastic or specialist breast surgeon.

Radiotherapy is commonly given with a lumpectomy and segmentectomy to stop the disease recurring. There have been revelations recently about cases where patients have been damaged by massively misjudged doses of radiation, but meticulous checking systems are now in place to prevent mistakes. The number of sessions varies but usually falls between 15 and 30, given over several weeks.

Chemotherapy can be given in tablet form or intravenously and may be prescribed over several months, possibly starting before surgery in order to shrink a large tumour. Side effects may include sickness, fatigue, depression and hair loss.

Hormone therapy in the shape of the drug tamoxifen used to be the most popular back-up treatment. This synthetic hormone seems to block the effect of oestrogen (the hormone implicated in most breast cancers) on breast cells. Now, however, a range of innovative drug treatments mean that more women than ever are surviving breast cancer and not having a recurrence. Exciting advances include aromatase inhibitors for post-menopausal women, also for oestrogen-receptor positive (ER+) disease. These may be used instead of tamoxifen, or as a follow-up. The drug Herceptin has shown clear positive results for a group of women, who test positive for HER-2 growth factor.

TECHNIQUES TO HELP YOU

Part of the modern holistic approach of specialist units is to ensure that new patients meet others who have undergone similar therapy and to put them in touch with a local or national support group.

Cancer specialists increasingly work alongside complementary therapists to help patients cope with treatment. All relaxation techniques are helpful. Patients also recommend massage, reflexology, aromatherapy or homoeopathy to help combat nausea and tiredness; chiropractic to help after surgery; a good, balanced diet; nutritional supplements to help build up the immune system; and gentle exercise such as yoga and walking.

GET TO KNOW YOUR BREASTS

Being breast aware and knowing what is normal for you will help you to be aware of any changes. Learn how your breasts look and feel at different times. Examine them whenever is best for you (eg, in the bath or shower or when dressing).

THE NORMAL BREAST

Before the menopause, normal breasts feel different at different times of the month. The milk-producing tissue becomes active in the days before a period. In some women the breasts then feel tender and lumpy, especially near the armpits. After a hysterectomy, the breasts usually show the same monthly differences until the time periods would have stopped. After the menopause, activity in milk-producing tissue stops. Normal breasts feel soft, less firm and not lumpy.

CHANGES TO LOOK OUT FOR

Appearance: change in the outline or shape of the breast. Enlarged veins, puckering or dimpling of the skin.
Feelings: discomfort or pain in one breast, particularly if new and persistent.
Lumps: lumps, thickening or bumpy areas in one breast or armpit.
Nipple change: an inverted nipple or, very rarely, discharge from, or rash on, the nipple; bleeding or moist reddish areas which don't heal.

SUSAN GREENFIELD

Baroness Professor Susan Greenfield – as she's known in a mouthful – is one of the world's leading neuroscientists and, at the same time, a super-feminine woman who has never lost her passion for glamour. We admire her hugely.

'As much as possible, I do everything in my life because I enjoy it and want to do it. If you're not enthusiastic, there's no point in bothering. But anything I can delegate I do.

'I do care what I look like. If it's a 'bad look day' – hair not right, outfit not working, feet hurting – I feel less effective. My 50th birthday was one of the most difficult, because then you know you're seriously middle-aged. Nonetheless, I still have long hair – coloured – and wear miniskirts.

'I've never had a strategy for my appearance but I'm very much a clothes-y, certainly compared to most women scientists, and I love reading glossy magazines and shopping. Fatally, the Royal Institution [of which Baroness Greenfield is director] is right by Bond Street in London. I like Vivienne Westwood, Armani, Moschino – and Top Shop, where you can come out with an armful of clothes that costs you less than a fancy restaurant meal.

'Product-wise, I have to have mascara, face cream, a mild face wash and hair conditioner by the gallon because my hair drinks it up. And perfume every day: I've always loved Shalimar by Guerlain, who also make floral waters – I wear one with grapefruit and another with lemon for daytime.

'I'm still like a kid in many ways. The funniest thing was when two young graduates brought their parents round for a drink and I realised I was treating the parents, who were the same age as me, as if they were my parents' age – calling them Mr and Mrs, offering them chairs... Not having children of my own brings a certain sense of irresponsibility, too. Also my parents are still alive, which perhaps allows you to retain a rather juvenile mindset.

'My favourite role model is Queen Elizabeth I. She was a wonderful woman who had a shaky start in life but became hugely powerful and clever, also very glamorous and sexy. I like original people with a sense of style and a sense of humour. I don't take myself too seriously: after all, in the end we'll all be dead.

'For sure, I feel low sometimes. I deal with it by phoning a close friend. I have an inner circle of about a dozen, most of whom I've known since I was a teenager. Talking to them restores my sense of balance. The thing that makes me happiest is sitting on the terrace on a warm summer's evening with a glass of wine and friends, with the conversation ebbing and flowing. To relax, I like collapsing in front of soap operas – and sleeping.

'I'm pathetic about keeping fit. My gym phase didn't last because my life is so busy and irregular, combined with a natural distaste for exercise. I do eat quite well but I love chips and eat chocolate, and my great weaknesses are champagne and coffee – instant cellulite. I can see the benefits of HRT, although there are some real concerns, and it's vital women know the risks in the context of their own medical history.

'There are light-bulb moments all the time in every area of life. The problem is if you don't take notice of them. I've learnt that you have to go with the things that feel right, and take your foot off the gas pedal when they don't. The most significant moment for me professionally came in relation to brain and consciousness, which has led to the research project I'm leading at the Oxford Centre for the Science of the Mind (OXSCOM). Scientists trying to work out how the brain gives you that highly subjective inner experience we call 'consciousness' have always thought living beings were either conscious or unconscious. I realised it might be more like a dimmer switch – that perhaps consciousness grows as brains grow. So the most modest form of consciousness would be that of infants, non-human animals or adults who have taken (recreational) drugs, while the greatest degree of consciousness might be humans in transcendental or meditative states.

'My mum says: "Be yourself and you're magnificent; if not, you'll always be second rate". You should be considerate of other people, but not live your life to please them, or try to keep up all the time. Life's too short for worrying that you're not as young/thin/rich/pretty as others. You are what you are.'

This part of feel fab forever is all about you the human be-ing. (Not the human do-ing.) When all's said and done, friends, lovers, children, employers, even pets won't be with us forever – and the people we're left with are ourselves. Asking our medical experts worldwide for their suggestions on looking after the emotional and spiritual side of life inspired the most wonderful input.

HOW TO *be fab* part 3

Looking after yourself is emphatically not selfish, says consultant clinical psychologist Dr Elspeth Stirling: **'You've got to look after yourself first and meet your own needs before you can be fit to look after anybody else's. Stop thinking of others first and you'll do yourself – and them – a favour.'** Neither of us has had a smooth ride (though we're both happy now) and you probably haven't either. This section suggests ways to help your soul sing…

FACE YOUR DEMONS

The factors that really make women look old are psychological, not physical, according to one of the most attractive and interesting women in the world, supermodel Lauren Hutton. Just as we develop wrinkles on our faces so we do in our minds…

Few of us – perhaps none – escape the sort of life experiences that leave us feeling less than blithe and often downright miserable and frightened. They frequently come from childhood as well as the decades of trying to be grown-up. They may be big or small, short or long term, but they have a profound influence on the women we are now. The problem is that, however much we suspect they affect our lives, they're often the things we least want to explore. But, as Lauren Hutton puts it, 'Every woman has to face her demons.'

The supermodel is now in her mid-sixties and, in 2000, survived a near fatal motorbike accident, which put her out of action for some time. When Sarah interviewed her earlier, she was open about the deep-seated problems that led her, in middle age, to consult a Jungian therapist. 'In my mid-forties, I was at a very dark time in my life. I broke my leg and for the five months I was recovering, I had to confront myself. I liked nothing about my life. Nothing. I had been in a very long relationship which had broken up. Then I had been with someone else, but I hadn't done what I should have to that. And I didn't like my work.'

'Put out to farm' from modelling at 40, Lauren reckons that she had become 'a cheesy movie queen, making five bad movies a year which I didn't want to see'. But the biggest problems – her inner demons – were the evils of her childhood. 'That's the thing we put the lid down tight on,' she says.

She never met her father, who went missing in the Second World War. Her stepfather had a profound effect on her life. 'He was brutal, mad and alcoholic… but he was also a great reader, knew all about the stars and loved nature.' He had a lot to do with her passionate championing of the environment and underprivileged people of all sorts, from women everywhere to the Kalahari tribespeople of Botswana. But at the same time, he made her, she says, into 'Deeply Disturbed of the Ozark Mountains'.

Jungian therapy delves into the subconscious and explores dreams. Lauren Hutton had grown used to regular appalling nightmares of holocaust landscapes, zombie-like men chasing her, and – the worst one – constantly trying to find a place to sleep. After therapy, her dreams turned to gorgeous houses and lovely plants.

Hanging on to the wrong man is a bad mistake, she believes. 'If you have a mate and it hasn't worked for ten years, it's not going to change. Bag him, get rid of him! First, you'll be much happier alone; second, if you don't, it stops you having a shot at real love.'

Her ongoing success as an older model, and others like Dayle Haddon and Carmen dell'Orefice (see page 91), proves, she believes, that 'womanhood can be celebrated in the bloom, not just in bud'. In 2005 she posed nude for *Big* magazine, explaining: 'I want them (women) not to be ashamed of who they are when they're in bed.'

Few of us will have to face the same demons as Lauren Hutton, or need the same level of professional therapy. But we believe that everyone benefits from looking at their lives and sorting the wrinkles in their minds.

re-start your life

We all want to feel at peace with who we are and how we live our lives. 'I want to really like the woman I see in the mirror each morning,' one nearly 50-year-old said to us. So start by auditing your life.

Running away from emotional pain is natural. We may then think it's gone but stored-up pain invariably comes back to haunt us. And demons in your cupboard make it pretty well impossible to live in a comfortable state of mind.

Life is about people, and the root of most problems (and much disease) is how we get on with others, according to Dr David Peters, past chair of the British Holistic Medical Association. Sorting out our relationship with ourselves is the first step to getting on well with others.

One of the hallmarks of not valuing ourselves is thinking we have to go through hard times on our own. So face your demons with the help of a confidant(e) – one or more trusted friends, a support group or a professional therapist, doctor or priest.

The key questions for your audit are: 'Do I like myself?' and 'Do I like my life?' A good place to start is by sorting out your past, then move on to your present. (Do it vice versa, if that's more comfortable.) Write your life story, exploring your feelings about your experiences and about the people who have coloured your life. If you've done things you really dislike yourself for (and who hasn't?), make a list of people to apologise to – you'll feel vastly better.

Be honest and take your time; there's no one to answer to but you.

Now look at the present day. Go through a week or more, being your own emotional shadow. Note your feelings about yourself and your life: try saying 'I feel…' and see what comes

out. Record your dreams. Note what – and who – makes you happy or sad, jolly or snarly, fulfilled or frustrated. Do you, for instance, feel happy at your work? Who do you feel good around? Are you happy with what you do or is there a nagging desire in the back of your mind to do something different? Are you a perfectionist – always trying to achieve the impossible for two women, let alone one? Do you give yourself time to relax and do what you want to do?

Pay attention to your senses: record the music you like, the paintings, books and films which enhance your life.

When you're writing, try not to worry about what has happened, or what may happen. Live in the present moment: it's the only reality we have. If you find that worries keep popping up, make a list of them; then you can plan how to tackle them – if necessary.

You could write your life story in the third person if you want (using 'she' rather than 'I'); it sometimes helps objectivity. If you find it hard writing things down, say them into a tape-recorder. Or try drawing or painting them.

Discuss what's happening with your confidant(e). If you feel really troubled, consider consulting a professional therapist, for a short time at least. Brief cognitive behavioural therapy, usually three one-hour sessions with a follow-up three months later, is an increasingly popular option and can be very helpful.

THE 'DIFFICULT' QUESTIONS
We found these tough to face up to but also the most constructive:

● Do I criticise myself overmuch? Or am I complacent and/or boastful?
● Do I worry what other people think of me? Or do I tend not to consider other people's feelings and wishes?
● Do I have enough self-confidence to do what I want as long as it doesn't hurt anyone else? Or do I often give in to what other people want?
● Do I usually tell the truth?
● Do I say I'm sorry when I've done something wrong?
● Am I loyal to family, friends and colleagues? Or do I gossip and/or criticise them behind their backs?
● Do I know what I want in most areas of my life? Or do I feel aimless?
● Do I think that I'll get on with most people? Or do I feel I have to be a saint for other people to like me?
● Am I contented by and large – and do I say so? Or do I complain a lot?
● Do I like what I do? Which bits of my life and which people make me feel 'up', engaged, passionate? Which make me feel bored, irritable, anxious?
● Do I feel in charge of my life? Or have I let someone/something else take control?

WHEN TO LOOK FOR PROFESSIONAL 'TALKING' HELP
● If you feel your emotions are out of control.
● If the inability to make a decision is affecting work and/or relationships.
● If you're trapped in a painful situation and can't see a way out.
● If you have a pattern of unhappy relationships.
NB Be sure to consult a qualified counsellor or psychotherapist.

THE NEXT STEP

All of this should help you come to terms with the demons from your past. Now, armed with all this information, you are in a good position to see the parts of your life you may want to change. Remember: small changes make a big difference, so try the five per cent rule.

One of the big problems about changing our lives is that by the time we see the red light flashing we are usually at such a pitch of desperation that wholesale 100 per cent change seems like the only option. Fast. And all at once. Job, house, man, haircut, clothes, that thread vein on your cheek that's been bothering you for so long. And on, and on. It happens to most of us.

You can't do it, of course, and the only alternative seems to be to do nothing. So you do. Or rather don't. And feel worse. But there is another way. Consider changing five per cent. Keep on with what you're doing but change a few small things – the ones you've identified

> Live in the present. The only time you have is now.

in your life audit. A small change really can make a big difference. Think of it as the art of doing what's possible.

'We're conditioned to thinking in absolutes,' says psychologist Professor Cary Cooper, 'but in fact most people who contemplate major change are unsuccessful in achieving it. A major change work-wise might be something like, "I'm going to leave my job entirely and have a good life," or, "I'm going to stop being a primary school teacher and become a lawyer." For some people that will be achievable, but the vast bulk don't know what that change will bring. So their vision of what will happen with

total change doesn't dovetail with reality and they end up thinking, "My God, I wish I'd known."'

The trick, he says, is to bite off what's chewable. 'Chew that first mouthful and if it feels good, chew another chunk and

> Perfection is impossible – admitting to imperfection is human and lovable.

so on.' So when you're considering major change, try smaller ones to begin with. 'Aim at getting the practical information to know what the change might mean to you, get a taste of it without burning your bridges – you might need them as a support system when you're in transition.'

If you are one of the great biters-off-of-more-than-you-can-chew, there's a tendency to feel dejected if you don't achieve 100 per cent. You know from experience you won't manage it – so you procrastinate with everything. The joy of five per cent change is that it's almost always achievable. And the rewards tend to be greater than the initial effort. Think of how your life would change if you threw out the tube of toothpaste which has lost its cap and is oozing all over your mascara, in your make-up bag. Or put the door key where you could find it – every time. Or took your alarm clock to the menders. See?

'It sounds good to try for 100 per cent but you'll never achieve it in anything,' says Professor Cooper. 'If you have any sort of big task in front of you, break it down into do-able chunks.'

The neat thing is that you can apply

EINSTEIN'S MOST IMPORTANT QUESTION

Scientist Albert Einstein said the most important question for all of us is whether we think the world is a friendly place or not. If you truly believe it is friendly, you will be able to relax and be optimistic about your future – for the next ten minutes and the next ten years. Optimists believe the world is essentially good, even if they don't understand why. People who send out positive messages very often get positive responses, so optimism is a self-fulfilling prophecy. But those who think the universe is unfriendly expect the worst and tend to focus on bad things that have happened to them and to other people; so pessimism, like optimism, is largely self-fulfilling.

Gratitude is the key emotion linked to optimism, and so is feeling in control of a situation and not blaming yourself. Revenge is associated with pessimism, also depression and anger, plus not feeling in control. Pessimism can be transformed into optimism with the help of cognitive therapy and also techniques such as neurolinguistic programming.

this to pretty well everything in your life. Nothing is too small to be insignificant. For someone suffering from anxiety or depression, simply getting out of bed

The only person you can really change is yourself.

can seem impossible – let alone getting dressed. So the five per cent change could be rolling out on the floor and down to the kitchen. Next day, it could be getting dressed before noon. The next, going out of the house.

Never underestimate what changing a situation slightly can do. 'Shifting a small log at the bottom of the pile causes the whole lot to move,' points out psychologist Dr Keith Stoll. Behaving in a more pleasant way and being good at negotiating, compromising and giving way are recognised as very important factors in improving close personal relationships. 'Pay compliments instead of criticising, smile instead of scowling, take an interest and listen without judging while other people tell you about themselves. Do nice things for other people, such as giving them little presents and looking after them,' suggests the late Professor Michael Argyle, author of *The Psychology of Happiness*.

The reason we feel the burden of having to do 100 per cent perfectly – or

Don't live in the problem, live in the solution.

often 120 per cent – is, of course, insecurity. It's all very well saying smugly that to be human is to be insecure, but it's not very useful. 'Give yourself

permission not to be perfect,' advises Philip Bacon, counsellor and family therapist. 'Many of us are too good at criticising ourselves, which sets up constant conflict in our minds. It's OK to feel selfish, cross, guilty or any other negative emotion. The trick is to acknowledge it, both to yourself and, if it's appropriate, to other people. Then move on.'

A useful five per cent tip is to develop the habit of saying 'no' occasionally. With adulthood comes the obligation to please other people – at home and at work. The result is that most of us feel guilty if we say 'no', and resentful when we give in and say 'yes' instead. Sorting things out every morning in your mind into the things you definitely want to do and those you don't can help to clarify

Happiness is just another way of saying you have your stress load under control.

these issues. American stress management expert David Sobel says he makes more time for important things – like himself and his family – by assessing invitations and demands, asking himself: 'In five years' time, will I care if I did or didn't do this?' He turns down a lot of things that way.

The underlying fear we have that other people will dislike us for saying no – nicely – is usually unjustified. Invariably they like and respect you more for knowing your own mind.

Following the five per cent rule helps put you back in control of your life. And that's the key to dealing with stress, according to experts. It's also a way of being kind to yourself. Which is about the most important thing you can do.

hear yourself

Listening is essential to peace of mind and body. Listen to yourself and to other people without interrupting or riding roughshod over the messages, spoken and unspoken. Bodies usually shout their needs (food, water, loo, sleep, etc); minds may whisper. Listening to other people's unspoken messages is called using your intuition. Women are very good at it, according to biophysicist Dr Luca Turin. (But not always so good at using it for their own benefit.)

mind and body

Remember that mind and body are never separate. Aches and pains in your body affect your mind and vice versa. Falling in love can banish your back pain, and chronic illnesses often disappear on holiday. (Although you're more likely to get a cold.) Food and drink can make you behave differently: you may feel speedy after coffee, lethargic after wheat. Exercising makes most of us feel (and look) brighter.

You can use this mind/body synergy to help transform your life. Before you start saying 'I can't possibly change', try this…

Sit on a chair facing a window with a view. Ask someone to put their hands on your shoulders. Focus all your attention on a far, high-up point – the top of a building or a tall tree. Both of you will feel the immediate change in your body as your mental and physical energy focuses positively.

small changes in difficult times

PHYSICAL

● Start by breathing – anxiety is often allied to shallow breathing.

● Untense your body from top to toe, uncrossing arms and legs, straightening spine and neck.

● Take more exercise generally – it's been proved to lift your mood as well as tone your body. Practise yoga.

● Ask a friend to give you a hand and foot and/or neck and shoulder massage for a minimum of 15 minutes once a week, and reciprocate. Allow yourself to relax completely and accept it as a present you deserve.

● Investigate possible food allergies: wheat, for instance, can profoundly depress some people, and simply cutting it out of your diet can lift the depression. Read *Food Allergy and Intolerance* by Professor J Brostoff.

● Quit smoking and drinking alcohol and caffeinated drinks (coffee, tea, cola, chocolate), which have been linked to depression.

● Drink lots of still pure water.

● Get enough sleep – try to go to bed early – 10pm is ideal.

● Improve your diet, making sure you have enough Omega-3 fatty acids (oily fish, olive oil and linseed are good sources) and consider taking supplements. Low levels of B vitamins have also been linked to depression; other important mood food supplements are vitamin C and magnesium and the Omega-6 fatty acids. Consult a qualified nutritionist if small changes don't help.

● Always take a lunch break – try for 45 minutes, at least.

MENTAL

◆ Lie or sit comfortably and picture in your mind somewhere you love being, where you have once been happy.

◆ Take a worry break: confront one of your worst fears and really worry about it for the next five minutes. The deal is, however, that the worry is confined to that time only and you don't worry again for the remainder of the day.

◆ Unclutter your work space and living space.

◆ Count to five – or preferably take five minutes – before you yell at anyone.

◆ Don't watch the news.

◆ Read an enjoyable novel.

◆ Smile at someone; laugh at a joke; see a funny film. Smiling and laughing (even if you fake it) trigger feelgood hormones. Try shouting 'Happy!' and beaming.

◆ Listen to music you enjoy – the rhythm can help your mind.

EMOTIONAL

■ If you feel low, remember you're not the only one – one out of every three women you see each day is likely to have felt the same way.

■ Be your own best friend: imagine the help, love and support you would give a friend in the same situation and know that you deserve the same.

■ Don't get caught up in other people's problems or write yourself roles in their movies when you needn't even have a walk-on part in their lives.

■ Take a few calming drops of Bach Flower Rescue Remedy or Jan de Vries Emergency Essence in water.

■ Practise feeling joy in small things – a phone call from a friend, a beautiful flower, not getting a parking ticket, a delicious meal.

■ Burn vetiver essential oil, the oil of tranquillity, in a vaporiser – or simply put some on your heel.

■ Allow yourself to wear your favourite clothes, do your hair and put on make-up.

SPIRITUAL

▲ Light a candle in a holy or inspiring place – which could be your own home.

▲ Make a wish to whatever force you believe gave you life.

▲ Believe that there are other people on your side.

quick lifts

✳ Drop 'if only' from your vocabulary.

✳ Turn on some music and dance.

✳ Buy yourself your favourite flowers.

✳ Think of five things you've done well – anything from exquisite ironing to cooking a delicious meal, adding up your bank statements to helping a friend, not losing your temper with someone really irritating to finishing a job of work.

✳ Sit in the sun (with an SPF on, please).

✳ Wrap your arms round yourself and give yourself a hug.

✳ Tune in to your favourite comedy show.

✳ Think about times and places when you are happy; store away the memories to revisit when you feel low.

✳ Think of one thing you can do – big or small – which would make you feel better, and either do it, or take positive steps to make it happen.

✳ Plan a trip or holiday.

✳ Go to sleep with a happy thought in your mind: a compliment someone paid you; a joke; a lovely view; a person you like.

✳ Wake up and decide to enjoy the day as much as you possibly can.

✳ Do something you really want to do, whether it's learning something new (see Creativity, pages 240–1) or playing your favourite record.

✳ Consider cognitive therapy – tweaking the way you view the world and your place in it can re-colour your life.

✳ Try a herbal anti-depressant such as St John's wort, which 23 studies have shown to be as effective as drugs for mild to moderate depression, with very few potential side effects.

get a life, get a pet

Simply watching a dog bound joyfully round a park or a cat stretch in the sun is cheering. But evidence is now growing that being close to an animal is positively health enhancing. 'Having a pet can improve your life,' says Professor Donald Broom, who researches into people's physiological responses to animals. By making people calmer, animals can help lower blood pressure and boost the immune system. Plus, of course, some animals such as dogs and horses prompt owners to take more exercise. And animals can be powerful antidepressants in themselves. Research with elderly women showed that puppies could persuade even the most depressed and reclusive to come out of their shells. 'A warm and wiggly puppy has the power to make an old and tired spirit soar,' said Professor Gloria Francis of Virginia Commonwealth University.

BEATING THE BLUES

Can't be bothered to get out of bed in the morning? Nothing seems worthwhile? Feel you're trying to turn a mighty river upstream? Millions of others feel the same. But there are positive answers...

Although we are both on a pretty even keel now, we have personal experience of depression and stress. According to Government figures, one woman in five suffers 'unwelcome stress', and the peak time is between 35 and 54. The World Health Organisation forecasts that depression will be the leading cause of incapacity by 2020. Virtually everyone feels blues-y at times, but a staggering one woman in three will experience a more severe form of low mood in her life. Twice as many women as men suffer from depression, probably because they have more stress, less support and more hormonal ups and downs.

The anxiety-to-depression spectrum is a complex one. Both are internal states: anxiety is being wound up too tight, and depression is sinking down into a low mood. Both are responses to external stressors. Depending on how we cope with stress, it can be positive – the sort of thing that makes you rise to an occasion – or negative – when we feel things are out of control and too much is expected of us.

'Feeling low' is one of the most common reasons women consult their doctor and, in a hectic world where most doctors have little time to talk, prescriptions of anti-depressants are rocketing. Drugs may temporarily mask the pain but they won't tackle the root cause. The encouraging news is that there is a range of non-drug ways to improve it. For women, it's frequently allied to exhaustion – simply doing too much and having too high standards. And, of course, being expected to live a double life as carers and workers. Talk to your doctor if he/she is sympathetic and also consider exploring naturopathy, homoeopathy, herbalism as well as counselling or psychotherapy.

Reasons for feeling low

Disentangling the strands in the web of depression may be difficult. Obvious problems are the four big stressful life events: moving house, job worries or unemployment, bereavement, divorce or separation.

Stressful life events can all be exacerbated by physical conditions including hormonal changes (see pages 206–223), not eating properly, food allergies, specific vitamin/mineral deficiencies, pollution, not taking

> Share any worries and also be a good listener for those who may need you.
>
> **FRANCES HUNT**

exercise or simply being tired out. Other physical problems which may result in a low mood include an underactive thyroid, anaemia, candidiasis, hypoglycaemia (the shortage of sugar most often linked to diabetes) and post-viral symptoms.

Pain – whether it's back, shoulder or neck ache, or the pain of long-term or life-threatening illness – is both a cause and a symptom of depression. Skin problems such as acne rosacea and psoriasis also often depress patients, according to London GP Dr Susan Horsewood-Lee. Post-natal depression may linger for years, if not treated.

Alcohol can lower rather than enhance your mood, and too much too often can result in profound depression.

Symptoms of anxiety

- feeling wound up and restless
- thinking and worrying about tomorrow
- feeling panicky
- having trouble getting to sleep
- wanting to avoid people and challenges
- getting indigestion
- setting unrealistic expectations for oneself
- feeling constricted in the throat; hyperventilating

Symptoms of depression

- feeling isolated and misunderstood
- feeling tired or exhausted
- sleeping badly; waking too early
- feeling sad for no apparent reason
- losing your appetite and losing weight or eating much more than usual and gaining weight
- not wanting to do anything or be interested in anything
- having no motivation at work
- feeling worthless and/or hopeless
- having no self-confidence
- having thoughts of suicide

winter depression

Depressed between autumn and spring? So lethargic and sleepy you can hardly function? Comfort-eating like crazy? Any of these can be symptoms of Seasonal Affective Disorder. Now recognised by the medical profession, SAD is sometimes known as 'winter depression' because it tends to strike when the days shorten and the nights draw in, and can endure until the lambs are frolicking in the fields the following spring.

SAD is thought to affect as many as ten per cent of us, three times as many women as men, although doctors don't yet know why. But unlike other forms of depression, the cure is simple – good old daylight.

SAD is triggered by lack of daylight. During the night, the pineal gland – our 'third eye' – produces a hormone called melatonin, which makes us drowsy. At daybreak, the bright light of dawn causes the gland to stop producing melatonin. But on dull winter days, especially when we're indoors, not enough light is received to trigger this waking-up process. New research is also starting to link bright light with the increased production of serotonin, a neurotransmitter; lack of serotonin is known to be a cause of depression. While most people adjust perfectly to the seasonally changing day length, the body-clock mechanism which tells SAD sufferers when to wake up and when to sleep doesn't function properly.

The solution, for as many as 85 per cent of sufferers, has proved to be light or photo-therapy. This means getting out into bright light as much as possible. But since that isn't always practical, consider investing in a full-spectrum light box, which sits on your desk, or some other convenient place where the light can reach your eyes for a minimum of 30–45 minutes daily. The light must be suitably bright; at least 2,500 lux (the technical measure of brightness) is needed – that's about five times brighter than a well-lit office. It must also be full spectrum, which gives you the same light waves as daylight, unlike normal electric light bulbs. (It's not like a sun-bed light, however, and won't either tan you or damage your eyes.) We both suffer from SAD during winter months and have invested in full-spectrum lights for our desks; we've found them to be literally life-changing.

SAD SYMPTOMS

If you experience these five major symptoms during autumn and winter months you could be suffering from SAD, according to Dr Norman Rosenthal, a US government researcher generally credited with discovering SAD.

1 Noticeable lack of energy to the point of debilitation.
2 A fairly constant feeling of sadness or depression.
3 A desire to sleep as much as possible – or to sleep briefly and become nocturnal.
4 Feeling listless and less creative than usual.
5 Having less control of your appetite – perhaps to the point of weight gain.

NB If you suffer from a skin or eye condition which might be affected by exposure to bright light, check with your doctor before beginning light therapy.

HOW IS IT FOR YOU?

Probably the biggest myth in the world is that everyone else is having an earthshaking sex life. And it becomes truer as we get older. That's not to say, however, that more – or different – wouldn't be better. We talked to experienced psychosexual therapist Frances Emeleus, accredited by the British Association of Sexual and Marital Therapists, about the particular problems of sexual love and ageing.

'Our sex lives can lose their sparkle as we get older and, in consequence, become relegated to late at night when both partners are tired. Also, most women struggle to a greater or lesser extent with the menopause and that can affect our body image, so a lot of middle-aged women no longer feel sexually attractive,' says Frances. The reason for this, she suggests, is largely the media. 'Magazines in particular have constructed a culture which says only one thing is attractive – youth and slimness. It can be difficult for women who don't think that they match that idealised photofit to feel sexy. And that's very destructive.'

To help overcome this, she suggests that women look at themselves in the bath, or in front of a mirror naked, and attempt to suspend judgement on their bodies. So, instead of saying 'Oh help!' and rushing for the nearest total tent-like cover-up, she recommends describing your body objectively – 'as if it were a building or a statue; for example "those are nice long curves, that's a striking shape and there's an interesting slope"' – because in doing so you are able to move away from judging your body, and finding it wanting.

Afterwards, she suggests, 'Let yourself think about the woman you saw in the mirror as if she was a close friend – you might be surprised at just how many pluses there are.

'Being sexy doesn't mean wearing black lace suspenders,' she continues. 'It does mean each of us seeing sexuality as an integral part of our bodies – and souls. Sexual energy is creative energy – part of the life force even when we can't have children any longer.'

Touching and stroking are 'absolutely crucial' to loving your body and discovering its sexuality. And that applies to both partners. 'Remember that men feel exactly the same thing about their bodies – their tummies, their waistlines, their balding heads – but if you can spend time celebrating rather than criticising and condemning, you begin to develop something to help you over your feeling of regret for your youthful body.'

After menopause, women may find that intercourse is uncomfortable as vaginal walls thin and there may be less vaginal lubrication. Frances recommends two lubricating products: Sensilube and Sylk (see Directory).

A lot of people have very mixed

messages going through their heads about touching themselves and others. To counter this, Frances recommends sensate focusing exercises (described in detail in the box below) which essentially involve stroking each other's bodies (or your own), in silence, without progressing to intercourse.

'This hurtling towards penetrative sex is like going for a plane or train – it's just how to get from here to there in the shortest possible time. As if we're saying, "This is the only bit that counts and everything else is irrelevant".' A good sex life is also about tenderness and intimacy, she emphasises.

The most important relationship to cherish is the one nearest you. 'Spend time and thought and care on your partner and that will help your sex life,' says Frances. And communicate! 'Couples have often adapted to "doing it" in a particular way,' she says, 'with very little conversation, very little knowledge of what the other wants and an attitude of he (or she) should know what I like…by now. But in fact they never actually ask what the other one wants or

> ## What's my ultimate health secret? Sex. It keeps you young. Let's face it, after an orgasm you feel better.
>
> **ZSA ZSA GABOR**

likes, or say what they would like themselves. So neither of them knows.'

Many women may have a satisfying sex life but feel that there is still something missing. This may be because they are not fully connected with their own bodies and emotions or with their partner's, Frances believes. One of the problems, she says, is that many couples subconsciously base their relationship on getting the other to do what they want. 'All of us want our own way all of the time. A good relationship is where I acknowledge that you have a different point of view from me and I don't need you to hold my view for me to feel secure. Sex is not about overwhelming the other, but recognising you are each different people with different needs.'

Frances also recommends relaxation breathing exercises (see page 162; specific techniques are detailed in *The Joy of Sexual Ecstasy* by Margo Anand). And, although the idea of sexual therapy is still a taboo, Frances believes it could help many people. 'I've seen people turn their sexuality around after 25, 30, even 40 years of mediocre sexual relations.'

Finally, Frances recommends taking your love-making out of the fifteenth division. 'Bodies are magnificent things and sex shouldn't be a third-class activity. It should be a celebration, so spend time and imagination on it.'

sensate focusing exercises

These can be done to another person or to yourself. Remember, do these for yourself – don't get tempted into giving the other person a massage.

TOUCHING: with a partner

● Take it in turns to silently explore your partner's body with different degrees of touch – hard and gentle, circular or long strokes; spend 15 minutes each on the back and 15 minutes on the front, caressing everywhere except breasts and genitals. If you can, talk about it afterwards.

● Notice which parts gave you the most pleasure – or not.

● Remember to indulge all your senses while you're doing this, with music, warmth, soft lighting and body or massage lotion for your stroking hand.

TOUCHING: on your own

● Do the same – and remember that just because you are on your own, it doesn't mean that you have to go without sex; solo sex can be a rich and rewarding experience.

QUESTIONS TO ASK YOURSELF ABOUT YOUR SEXUALITY

■ What do I really think about sex?

■ Has that view changed over the years?

■ Is this what I really want to think?

■ Am I fulfilling my sexual desires?

■ Has my sex life gone wrong?

■ Where and when did that start?

■ Am I simply giving in if I give up sex now?

■ Would it be possible for me to change?

■ Do I really want to become a sexual being?

HOLISTIC HELP FOR STRESSED MINDS AND BODIES

Our state of mind is a major factor in our state of health. When you're feeling like screeching – or climbing into a deep, dark, miserable pit – some TLC from an expert pair of hands can soothe your mind and boost your health. There is also a range of complementary therapies to help wellbeing: some you can do yourself, like meditation, others are done to you, like acupuncture.

We asked three experts in the field, Dr James Hawkins, a member of the British Holistic Medical Association, Dr George Lewith of the Centre for the Study of Complementary Medicine in Southampton, England, and Anne Woodham, author of *Beating Stress at Work* and *The Encyclopedia of Healing Therapies*, for their top suggestions (see right).

Stress-related and chronic conditions, including high blood pressure, allergies, muscle tension, pain, migraine and headaches, tend to respond particularly well to these types of therapy.

We've tried out many complementary therapies and are great supporters. As well as helping the way we feel, these tension busters can help the way we all look, smoothing out worry lines and putting a sparkle in tired eyes. Our particular favourites are aromatherapy massage, Bach Flowers, reflexology, healing and herbal medicine.

HANDS-ON THERAPIES
● **Healing**
● **Massage**
● **Reflexology**
● **Tragerwork**

ALTERNATIVE THERAPIES
● **Acupuncture**
● **Bach Flower Remedies**
● **Homoeopathy**
● **Herbalism**
● **Music therapy**
● **Nutritional therapy**
● **Flotation therapy**

SELF-HELP
● **Autogenic training**
● **T'ai chi**
● **Qi gong** (aka Chi kung)

DIY...NOW!
● **Meditation**

Meditation helps calm mind and body: circulation improves and muscle tension disappears. As a result, you can deal better with whatever the day hurls at you. Some doctors already recommend meditation to patients to combat stress-related illness. Try the basic principles below, and then decide whether you want to go further.

1 Don't attempt to meditate with a full tummy or when you're hungry.

2 Find a quiet spot where you won't be interrupted; unplug the phone and put up a 'do not disturb' notice.

3 Experiment with dimmed lighting and closed curtains or blinds.

4 Lie or sit comfortably, with your hands in your lap; make certain your body is relaxed, uncross arms and legs, straighten your spine. (Meditation teachers often suggest sitting so you won't drop off!)

5 Breathing gently, imagine your whole body relaxing; start with scalp, hairline, every feature, then move down your body, feeling tension ebb away.

6 The aim of meditation is to stop stimulating thoughts or niggling problems taking up mind space. The easiest way is to concentrate on one calm thought, eg, the colour blue, mountain tops, a sunset, the sea.

7 Transcendental meditation gives you a mantra (word) to repeat over and over in your mind. Try choosing a word you find soothing and repeating it.

8 Allow your breathing to settle into a natural rhythm. Focus on your breath: feel the air as it enters your nostrils moving down to fill the lungs; rest a moment then let it go gently, emptying your body. Try to breathe from abdomen rather than chest and feel your tummy swell as you inhale. Count slowly as you breathe: count to four as you inhale, rest for a beat or two, then exhale to a count of four.

9 Whenever a distracting thought breaks in, simply acknowledge it and let it go. American meditation master Ram Dass suggests transforming it into a cloud and watching it float away in your mind's eye.

10 Start with a couple of minutes and gradually spend longer. Don't worry if you feel you can't focus at first; just go on practising. Try to establish a regular time to start off with: early morning and last thing at night are very helpful.

Creative visualisation

This can be a form of meditation and uses the same general principles detailed above. With visualisation, however, you are going to focus on creating healing pictures in your mind and employ other senses to re-create that memory of wellness. These visualisations or mind pictures can come in thousands of different forms – whatever suits you. Think of it as targeted daydreaming. Once you get used to it, you can do this virtually anywhere, any time, even when there's noise and people around you. Try variations on these themes, then make up your own.

● When you feel flustered, think of a place where you have been happy and secure and calm, eg, a garden in the summer, a beach, a meadow; now feel the sun and the breeze, smell the flowers, hear the mew of seagulls or the buzz of bees; let your mind and body sink into the 'film' in your head.

● If you have a problem, or more than one, bedevilling you as you try to go to sleep, try putting it/them into an air balloon, releasing the balloon and watching it drift away, far up into the sky and out of sight.

● Alternatively, take your problem and put it into a file, put the file in a folder, and the folder in a lower desk drawer or filing cabinet, shut the drawer, turn the key and put that away. You can do this at any time, but the deal is that you must sort out the problem at the next practical opportunity.

● If your left – organising – brain is on overtime and you can't stop your mind whirring, try transferring over to your right – creative – brain like this. Feel yourself in your left brain then turn your back and walk along a path – whatever you like – over to your right brain. Imagine yourself going through a door – turn the handle, open the door, and shut the door again behind you. Notice where you find yourself – in a walled garden, perhaps, or a peaceful room. Make yourself comfortable and either do nothing – smell the roses – or wander round and see what or who else is there.

● If you're frightened or uncomfortable in a situation, visualise winding a lovely lavender-coloured cocoon around yourself, up and down, round and round, until you feel entirely safe.

● Or do as actress Amanda Burton does and imagine beautiful golden angels putting their wings around her and shielding her from all harm.

See Directory for contact details for all organisations mentioned.

UNLOCK YOUR CREATIVITY

We are all creative. But exploring that playful, artistic, creative side often gets put on a back burner in a flurry of family commitments, deadlines and the general, overwhelming feeling that there isn't the time to do the things we have to do – let alone the things we'd like to do. But if you want to experience a real jump in your quality of life, it's time to tap into your creativity.

Psychologists believe that we should all make time to indulge and explore our creative potential. 'You never know where that may lead,' says Nick Williams, who runs highly successful seminars to help people unlock their creative potential. 'Sometimes, women discover a whole new path in life – and turn what started as an enjoyable hobby into a career. Others simply find a way of dealing with stress, not just forgetting their problems for a while, but discovering creative solutions – a whole new way of tackling them.

'As children,' explains Nick, 'we are all naturally creative and have no problems with singing/drawing/being natural. But we lose that as we grow up. My recommendation to women is that they get back in touch with that creativity in some area of their life – whether through singing or dancing or writing or flower arranging.'

Nick agrees with Leslie Kenton that midlife can be a time of tremendous creative potential. 'The children have flown the nest – or maybe you're not striving so hard to get to the top of the career ladder, which may allow you more time for creative pursuits.'

BLUEPRINT

So many of us, however, just don't know where to start. So here is Nick Williams's blueprint – to encourage each and every one of us to tap into our creativity…

- **Start now.** 'We do sometimes forget that life is not a rehearsal. Don't wait for a crisis – an illness, a bereavement – to do the things you really want to do.'

- **Give up on perfectionism.** 'What often deters people is the idea that if they paint a picture, it won't be "good enough". Paint for yourself, not because you want to put a painting in an exhibition. There is no right or wrong way of being creative – it's about self-expression. You don't have to show anyone: write for your own joy, arrange flowers for your own joy, sing to your heart's content – out of earshot, if you prefer. However you connect with your soul is just fine.'

- **Never tell yourself** 'I'm not creative'. 'Everyone's naturally creative – but we often lose touch with that, over the busy years. If you're not sure which area to express your creativity in, cast your mind back ten, 15, 20 – maybe 30 – years and ask yourself, "What did I love doing then?" I believe that everyone has a vein of gold – their creativity – running through them; sometimes they just have to dig a little deeper to find it.'

- **Keep a creativity journal.** 'I am a big fan of Julia Cameron's book *The Artist's Way*. This is a 12-step programme for rediscovering creativity, and a key step is to get up every morning and write – about whatever you want to write about; how you feel, whether you're in a lousy or a great mood, what inspires you. Sometimes you feel totally uninspired and hate doing it – and other days you are brimming with ideas and possibilities. Because creativity is like a muscle that needs to be exercised.'

creative inspirations

It really is never too late – or too early, for that matter – to find out what you love to do, what fires you up and makes you tingle with alive-ness. So: here are some shining examples of adventurous, creative, daring women who've inspired us…

Anna Murdoch, writer, born 1945 – who gave up journalism to marry Rupert Murdoch (they divorced in 1998), but tapped into her creativity again in her forties – and became a bestselling author: 'I have a lot of energy and I think women should do things. I don't write to be independent or for the money. I do it for the satisfaction.'

Karin Clements, painter, born 1944, whose canvases now sell for over £1,000: 'I'd never picked up a pencil in my life till I was 47 and signed up for drawing classes at a local Adult Education institute. I went on to take an A-level in art, not for the qualification but to learn more. Suddenly, I felt there had been a huge hole in my life that had been filled.

'My upbringing was: you grow up, get married, have children, it's your job and you should enjoy it. At the end of the day, I didn't; I would ask myself, "Why aren't I blissfully happy?" But painting changed my life. And although I now make my living out of painting – I've been commissioned to paint portraits of Gillian Shepard, MP, and the Duke of Kent, and had sell-out exhibitions – I do it because I want to, not to make money. I can completely lose myself in my painting. If you can just find that fulfilment, it absolutely shines out of you and makes you so much more attractive as a

person. My message would be: it's never too late to start something new – and get so much more out of life.'

Lynne Franks (pictured above), legendary PR turned author, entrepreneur and lifestyle guru, born 1949. We have both known Lynne (one of life's 'whirling dervishes') for years. If you're looking to start a business, perhaps, or just to tap into the inner creative 'you', we heartily recommend Lynne's books *GROW* (which stands for Gorgeous Real Original Women, and we're all for that) and *The SEED Handbook: the Feminine Way to Create Business*. They have inspired lots of women we know to get up off the comfy sofa and explore life! For more about Lynne and her books, log on to www.lynnefranks.com, where you'll also find details of workshops that Lynne leads in Deia, Majorca.

MORE CREATIVE INSPIRATIONS

For every single one of us, there is a way of expressing ourselves – of making our souls sing – just waiting to be discovered. We both garden (see opposite for Jo's horti-heaven) and, at 52, Sarah finally followed her dream of having horses and has never ever been happier or more in love with life.

As Leslie Kenton says: 'Creativity lies at the core of what it is to be a woman. One of the many gifts growing older has brought me is learning to dedicate my life to creativity. Each day I follow my passion for whatever I long to create. This could be anything from decorating a room to putting together a new television documentary or book. The menopause and post-menopause years hold the greatest creative potential in a woman's life. If you're waking in the night tossing and turning, get up and start writing, trying to tap into your inner creativity. Look ahead at what you want to do with your life – and start to live a life that's authentically yours. Creating what fascinates you is the most satisfying thing any woman can do with her life. Let your passions drive you to create what most excites you day after day and you will have discovered the best-kept anti-ageing secret in the world.'

There are extraordinary stories of ordinary women who have reinvented their lives by unleashing their creative souls. If you haven't yet read Jane Juska's book *A Round-Heeled Woman: My Late-life Adventures in Sex and Romance*, then you should – not just because it holds out hope for those of us who want to stay sexy in our sixties and seventies (yes!),

but because it's this former teacher's first book. An unorthodox way to tap into your creativity, perhaps, but California-based Jane's adventure began with a lonely hearts ad, placed after she felt she'd been celibate too long. The romantic – and not-so-romantic – experiences that she had as a result inspired her to write this poignant, funny, unique memoir, proving that it's never too late to pick up a pen and write your life story.

Jill Connolly (above) brought out her first CD in her forties: *Venus in Transit*, inspired by Joni Mitchell, Ella Fitzgerald and Sarah Vaughan, which you can listen to on www.jillconnolly.com. (Before then, she'd worked as a singer and voiceover talent.) Her advice? 'If you haven't quite discovered your passion yet, tune into the things that make you feel whole. Then listen to your body, and just choose one.' And if you're dyslexic or can't sing a note – don't worry: what were formerly considered 'old lady's hobbies', like

crochet and knitting, can be hugely creative too.

Jo belongs to a knitting group, which takes turns on a Monday night clicking and chatting at each other's houses, while producing gorgeous garments for all ages. Wren Ross also discovered how healing knitting could be when going through a painful divorce. She began creating a 'story coat', in which she incorporated images and symbols (such as an open heart, and tap dancers with hats and canes), that she felt reflected her new, single life. She is now so passionate about her 'contemplative craft', that she teaches people with cancer to use knitting to tell their own stories. Wren has recorded a CD with the wonderful name: *Wren Ross's Greatest Knits*. She has also written a book, with Daena Giardella, called *Changing Patterns: Discovering the Fabric of Your Creativity*.

You could even combine creativity, company and cash by setting up an investment club like Geraldine Puxtey and Liz Thomas, co-founders of The Glamorous/Grumpy Old Women Investment Club. The Glam Grumpies' only rule seems to be: no men.

Above all, remember – as Jo's 95-year-old great aunt used to tell her 93-year-old sister: 'Use it or lose it!' Because, as the adage goes, 'An unused engine rusts. A still stream stagnates. An untended garden tangles.'

Creativity is good for the soul and work is a process of self-definition, of finding out who you are. But once you find out – you can lie down.
BETTE MIDLER

IF IN DOUBT, GARDEN

When the going gets tough, where will you find us? Up to our wrists in dirt, dead-heading the roses, worrying out the stringy roots of bindweed or planting out lettuce seedlings (that's Jo, above, keeping an eye on the degree of floral growth on her plot). It's small wonder, perhaps, that gardening – one of the most accessible forms of creativity for many of us – is soaring in popularity. As May Sarton said in her *Journal of a Solitude*, 'Everything that slows us down and forces patience, everything that sets us back into the slow cycles of nature is a help. Gardening is an instrument of grace.'

Whether of window-ledge proportions or a matter of acres, gardening offers tremendous potential for stress-busting and creativity. We can switch off – or use

that time, in touch with nature, to think about how we want to spend the rest of our lives. We admire fashion entrepreneur Dianne Benson, who – having owned four stores in Manhattan – changed tack in her late forties, turning a hobby into a career by writing an utterly inspirational book on gardening – *Dirt* (iUniverse.com, 2000), a great read for the green fingered, if you can find a copy.

But more than that, gardening also has the potential to heal our souls. There is actually a new movement – 'horticultural therapy' – creating gardens in unlikely places, such as prisons and inner-city community centres, where stress levels might otherwise be soaring. Horticultural therapists use gardening to improve people's physical, mental and emotional wellbeing. Explains Kathleen Fisher, editor of *The American Horticulturalist*,

'Research shows that we don't just imagine that plants make us feel good, but that their presence can hasten physical healing and produce psychological changes similar to those brought about by meditation or other highly relaxed states.'

Nancy Stevenson, Friends' Chairperson of the American Horticultural Therapy Association, believes that gardening is a powerful restorative for the body and spirit. 'In the garden, we witness the natural, cyclic rhythms of birth, life, sickness and death. We see ourselves as part of that process, fit our own lives into the bigger picture of experience. It is a deeply comforting experience.' And at the end of it, we have roses for our house and (organic) vegetables for our table. And as creative pursuits go, beat that.

Last but not least – the late BEATRICE WOOD, known as the 'Mama of Dada', an artist and sculptress who died at the age of 105 just before we were due to interview her for this book. And who was sculpting, drawing and flexing her creative muscle right up to that day...

HOW TO GIVE YOURSELF MORE TIME

What wouldn't you give for another hour a day? Not many people know this – as Michael Caine might say – but our bodies think there are 25 hours in each day; the natural body clock runs to a 25-hour not a 24-hour cycle. For reasons known only to evolution, Something Went Wrong and most of us ended up like the White Rabbit in *Alice in Wonderland* – always hurrying through life.

But there are tricks to claw back that hour and reduce stress – 'worry hurry sickness' as one psychologist calls it. The simple answer is to get up earlier. Try setting your alarm clock five minutes earlier every day. By the end of a fortnight (lie in on Sundays – but not too long, or you risk the whole exercise), you will have re-set your waking mechanism by an hour. Great time-saving tips:

1 Do one thing at a time, focus all your attention on that task and finish it before moving on.

2 Make a 'to do' list each day. With each job, ask yourself... Is it really necessary? What would happen if: I junked it? asked someone else to do it? took a short cut? Does it really need to be done today? If not, decide when you should tackle it – and do it then.

3 Plan what you need to prepare today to make tomorrow easier, eg, collect dry cleaning, plan supper, check route.

4 Keep running short- and long-term lists in your diary: eg, shopping, birthday and Christmas presents, when to collect shoes and laundry.

5 Practise saying 'no', the greatest time-saver ever invented. It's absolutely legitimate to say 'no' at home or at work when: the request is unreasonable; it's

less important than the job you're working on; you don't have the required knowledge, skills or information; you're angry or upset; or it need not be done by you at all.

6 Make a place to put everything – think of the time you spend looking for the car keys, your diary, guarantees...

7 Fill the car with fuel before it's on its last gasp and you have to spend hours looking for a petrol station.

8 Don't get cross, resentful or give in to road rage: they all waste energy as well as time.

9 Allow other people to do things for you, even if they don't do them quite as well as you would. And always accept offers of help with washing up saucepans: it saves your very valuable time and your equally valuable hands.

10 Make a year plan including time off daily, weekly and monthly, plus proper holidays. We all know about 'lost' time; now try 'found' time, which means those periods of a few minutes – usually waiting for something or someone – which can either irritate the hell out of you or make your day. Make the most of found time by always carrying a notebook, pen, postcards, address book and a good paperback or magazine, plus a personal stereo and tapes/CDs if you can.

find time!

1 Sit on a bench in the sun and daydream – it's good for your health.
2 Do your pelvic-floor exercises – pull up your internal muscles and think thin (see page 178).
3 Plan tomorrow.
4 Deep breathe, meditate or do a spot of creative visualisation (see page 239).
5 Read your book or magazine.
6 Plan any big event coming up, eg, your birthday party.
7 Write 'keep in touch' postcards.
8 Between appointments, use the time to stock up on birthday cards, wrapping paper, presents.
9 Give yourself a relaxing head massage.
10 Listen to a tape/CD of a book or your favourite music.

directory

When writing to any of the organisations listed in this book, always enclose a large stamped addressed envelope.

NB Virtually all the nutritional and herbal supplements listed in this book are available from:

Victoria Health, tel: 0800 3898 195, www.victoriahealth.com

Most products from the beauty companies and natural health brands listed in this book are widely available in beauty departments, pharmacies or natural food stores – or you can try the following mail order/website addresses; some stores listed also ship worldwide. All websites should direct you to a stockist/mail order source in your country. If you're still having trouble, try the search engine www.google.co.uk or www.google.com.

Calling UK telephone numbers from abroad, dial 0044, then drop the first '0' of the following number.

● **Beauty Bible** www.beautybible.com
A quick route to most of the companies listed here is to use Speedshop on our own site: we list all the brands, and at the click of a mouse you'll be whisked to their site.

● **Boots the Chemist** Information, tel: 0845 070 80 90, www.boots.com
Sells a very wide range of beauty and health products, including prestige brands, eg, Chanel, YSL, etc.

● **Calmia** Mail order UK and worldwide: www.calmia.com
Products for holistic lifestyle, including clothing, skincare, yoga products, health supplements, music and books.

● **Farmacia** Mail order UK and worldwide, tel: 0870 1118 123
www.farmacia123.co.uk, www.clfshop.com

● **Fenwick of Bond Street** Mail order UK and worldwide, tel:: 020 7629 9161
No catalogue, so you need know the brand/product you want and ask for it by name.

● **Fresh & Wild** www.freshandwild.com

● **Garden Pharmacy** www.garden.co.uk
Sells leading health and beauty brands online.

● **Harrods From Home** tel: 0870 732 1234, www.harrods.com
Ask for brand/product (as with Fenwick).

● **Harvey Nichols** Orders, tel: 020 7235 5000, www.harveynichols.com
Ask for brand/product (as with Fenwick).

● **HQhair.com** www.HQhair.com
Sells many 'cult' brands online.

● **www.qvc.co.uk**
A terrific selection of hard-to-find and 'cult' brands.

● **Selfridges** tel: 0870 8377 377, www.selfridges.com
Ask for brand/product (as with Fenwick).

● **So Organic** www.soorganic.com
A wide range of truly natural skin/hair/body care.

● **Space NK Apothecary** Enquiry line, tel: 020 8740 2085. Mail order, tel: 0870 169 9999. www.spacenk.com

a

ACUPRESSURE
See Acupuncture

ACUPUNCTURE
British Acupuncture Council
Tel: 020 8735 0400
www.acupuncture.org.uk

AROMATHERAPY
Aromatherapy Consortium
Tel/fax: 0870 7743 477
www.aromatherapy-regulation.org.uk
Aromatherapy Associates
Call for stockists/mail order
of blended oils.
Tel: 020 8569 7030
www.aromatherapyassociates.com

AUTOGENICS
The British Autogenic Society
Royal London Homoeopathic
Hospital NHS Trust
Tel: 020 7391 8908
www.autogenic-therapy.org.uk

Aveda
Tel: 0870 034 2380
www.aveda.com

Ayurvedic Massage
Ayurvedic Medical Association UK
Tel: 020 7631 0156
www.haleclinic.com

b

BACD (British Academy of Cosmetic Dentistry)
Tel: 020 7612 4166
www.bacd.com

Bach Flower Remedies
A Nelson & Co Ltd
Tel: 020 8780 4200
www.nelsonbach.com

Barefoot Botanicals
Tel: 01273 823 031
(Mail order, tel: 0870 220 2273)
www.barefoot-botanicals.com

Bates Method
Tel: 0870 241 7458
www.seeing.org

BeneFit Cosmetics
Tel: 01245 347138
www.benefitcosmetics.co.uk

BKamins Chemist full skincare
range is available in UK at
John Bell & Croyden, London W1,
tel: 020 7935 5555

Blackmores
Tel: 0870 7700 976
www.blackmores.com

Bobbi Brown Essentials
Tel: 0870 034 2566
www.bobbibrowncosmetics.com
Available at Harrods, who will
mail order (*see the listing for
Christian Dior, right*)

The Body Shop
Tel: 01903 844 554
www.bodyshopinternational.com

Boots
For nearest branch, tel: 08450 70 80 90
www.boots.com

Borghese
www.borghese.com
For mail order and enquiries,
tel: 01273 40 88 00

Dr Fredric Brandt
www.drbrandtskincare.com

Bristol Cancer Help Centre
Tel: 0117 980 9500
www.bristolcancerhelp.org

**British Association of
Aesthetic Plastic Surgeons**
Call for list of fully accredited
cosmetic plastic surgeons.
Tel: 020 7405 2234
www.baaps.org.uk

**British Association of
Dermatologists**
Tel: 020 7383 0266
www.bad.org.uk

**British Association of Nutritional
Therapists**
Tel: 0870 606 1284
www.bant.org.uk
To find a nutritional therapist in the
UK or for general information send
£2 and a large sae to:
BCM BANT
27 Old Gloucester Street,
London WC1N 3XX

**British Association of Plastic
Surgeons**
The Royal College of Surgeons
Tel: 020 7831 5161
www.baps.co.uk

**British Association of Sexual
and Relationship Therapies**
Tel: 020 8543 2707
www.basrt.org.uk
Email: info@basrt.org.uk

**British Association of Skin
Camouflage (BASC)**
Tel: 01625 871129
www.skin-camouflage.net

**British Society for Allergy,
Environmental and Nutritional
Medicine**
Tel: 01547 550380
www.jnem.demon.co.uk

CACI
For nearest salon contact
Micromode Medical Ltd
Tel: 020 8731 5678
www.caci-international.co.uk

Cellex-C
Cellex-C (UK) Ltd
Tel: 01273 401604
www.cellex-cuk.com

Champneys
Tel: 0870 3300 300
www.champneys.co.uk

Chanel
Tel: 020 7493 3836
www.chanel.co.uk

Charles Worthington
Products available at
Boots, Selfridges and
John Lewis

Chelsea Nail Studio
Tel: 020 7225 3889

Chinese Herbal Medicine
Register of Chinese Herbal
Medicine
Tel: 01603 623994
www.rchm.co.uk

Christian Dior
Tel: 020 7172 0172
www.dior.com
Direct mail order service
available at Harrods,
tel: 0870 732 1234

Circaroma
Tel: 020 7359 1135
www.circaroma.com

Clarins
Tel: 0800 036 3558
For stockists, tel: 020 7307 6700
www.clarins.co.uk

Clinique
Tel: 0870 034 2566
www.clinique.co.uk

**The Colonic International
Association**
Call for a list of qualified colonic
irrigation practitioners in the UK.
Tel: 01442 823555
www.colonic-association.com

Coudray
Available at Les Senteurs, who offer
a mail order service.
Tel: 020 7730 2322
www.lessenteurs.com

Creed
Available at Les Senteurs, see
listing for Coudray

Crème de la Mer
For stockists, tel: 0870 034 2566.
Mail order from Harrods, see listing
for Christian Dior
For international mail order
tel: 001 212 753 4000
www.neimanmarcus.com

Demeter
Available at Harrods; see listing for
Christian Dior

Dermalogica
Tel: 0800 591 818
www.dermalogica.co.uk

Decléor
Decléor UK Ltd
Tel: 020 7313 8787
www.decleor.co.uk

Diamancel (foot files)
http://diamancel.com
Available from Space NK

Diptyque
Available at Les Senteurs, see
listing for Coudray

Disfigurement Guidance Centre
Fax: 01337 870310
Write to The Disfigurement
Guidance Centre, PO Box 7, Cupar,
Fife KY15 4PF enclosing a stamped
addressed envelope for a reply
www.skinlaserdirectory.org.uk

Mr Michael Dooley
Lister Hospital
Tel: 020 7730 8298
www.thelisterhospital.com
Tel: 0870 240 8745
www.mdooley.co.uk

Dr Mervyn Druian
London Cosmetic Dentistry
Tel: 020 7722 1235
www.fresherbreath.com

Eclectic Institute
www.eclecticherb.com for
international mail order

Efamol Ltd
Information service: 0870 606 0128
www.efamol.com

Electrolysis
British Association of Electrolysists
Email: electrolysis@fslite.co.uk

Elemis
www.elemis.com
For mail order and product
enquiries, tel: 01278 727830

Lucinda Ellery
Tel: 020 8741 8224
www.lucindaellery.com

Elizabeth Arden
Tel: 020 7629 4488
www.reddoorsalons.com

Udo Erasmus
www.udoerasmus.com

ESPA
Tel: 01252 352 231
www.espaonline.com

Essential Care
Tel: 01284 728416
www.essential-care.co.uk

Estée Lauder
esteelauder.co.uk
For stockists, tel: 01730 232 566
Direct mail order service at Harrods,
see listing for Christian Dior, left

Eylure
Original Additions Ltd
Tel: 020 8573 9907
www.originaladditions.co.uk

Flotation Therapy
The Floatation Tank Association
UK/EIRE
Tel: 020 7627 4962
www.floatationtankassociation.net

Gengigel
www.gengigel.com

Stephen Glass at Face Facts
Fortnum & Mason
Tel: 020 7735 8040

Green People
Tel: 01403 740 350
www.greenpeople.co.uk

Mr Rajiv Grover
Tel: 020 7486 4301
www.rajivgrover.co.uk

Guerlain
For stockists,
tel: 01932 233 875
www.guerlain.com

Guinot
R Robson Ltd
Tel: 01344 873 123
www.rrobson.co.uk

Sally Hansen
Tel: 01276 674 000
www.sallyhansen.co.uk

Jo Hansford
Tel: 020 7495 7774
www.johansford.com

Dr Hauschka
Tel: 01386 791 022 for mail order,
01386 791 022 for skincare advice
www.drhauschka.co.uk

HEALING
Confederation of Healing Organisations (Government-recognised body)
www.confederation-of-healing-organisations.org
Tel: 020 8800 3569

HERBALISTS
National Institute of Medical Herbalists
Tel: 01392 426022
www.nimh.org.uk

Karin Herzog
Tel: 0800 056 2428
www.karinherzog.co.uk

HOMEOPATHY
Society of Homeopaths
Tel: 0845 450 6611
www.homeopathy-soh.org
Or: **The Homeopathic Medical Association – UK**
Tel: 01474 560336
www.the-hma.org
Or, to find a doctor who is also a homeopath:
Faculty of Homeopathy
Tel: 0870 444 3950
www.trusthomeopathy.org

Dr Susan Horsewood-Lee
Tel: 020 7352 6748
www.chelseadoctor.com

Institute for Optimum Nutrition
For in-depth health checks,
including hair analysis,
tel: 0870 979 1122
www.ion.ac.uk

Integra Facecare System
Tel: 0870 850 1467
www.integra-skincare.com

Janina International Oral Cosmetique
At Boots, Selfridges and
independent pharmacies or,
for information,
tel: 0800 915 2914
www.janina.co.uk

Jenny Jordan Eyebrow & Make-up Clinic
Tel: 020 7483 2222
www.jennyjordan.com

Jurlique
Tel: 0870 770 0980
www.jurlique.co.uk

Kiehl's
www.kiehls.com
Available from Space NK,
see opposite

Krill Oil and Thorne Basic Immune Nutrients
Tel: 01664 810011
www.health-interlink.com
International mail order and
further information about
Thorne products online at
www.thorne.com

Lancôme
Tel: 020 8762 4040 (head office)
For product information:
www.lancome.com

Roderick Lane
Tel: 0845 094 3224

L'anza
www.lanza.com

Laura Mercier
Available from Space NK,
see opposite
Available by mail order
from Selfridges,
tel: 0870 837 7377
www.lauramercier.com

Lavera
Tel: 01557 870 203
www.lavera.co.uk

Léonor Greyl (Paris)
Tel: 00 331 42 65 32 26
www.leonorgreyl.com

LifeTime/Nutritional Specialties
www.lifetimevitamins.com
(Available from Victoria Health)

Light Heart Essences
Tel: 01986 785216
www.lightheartessences.co.uk

Liz Earle
Naturally Active Skincare
Mail order, tel: 01983 813 913
www.lizearle.com

Look Good...Feel Better
To find a workshop in your area,
and/or to obtain a copy of their free
leaflet, tel: 01372 470 900.
Or see www.lookgoodfeelbetter.org

L'Oréal, nationwide,
Tel: 0845 399 1949
www.lorealparis.co.uk

Professor Nicholas Lowe
The Cranley Clinic
Tel: 020 7499 3223
Email: cranley@aol.com

MAC (Make-up Arts Cosmetics)
Tel: 0870 034 2999
www.maccosmetics.com

Maitre Parfumeur et Gantier
Available at Les Senteurs,
see listing for Coudray

Manual Lymphatic Drainage (MLD)
Tel: 01592 748 008
www.mlduk.org.uk

MASSAGE
For a list of local practitioners of Eastern and Western massage:
British Federation of Massage Practitioners
Tel: 01772 881063
www.jolanta.co.uk

Max Factor
Available nationwide
www.maxfactor.com

MUSIC THERAPY
Association of Professional Music Therapists
Tel: 020 8440 4153
www.apmt.org

National Institute on Ageing (USA)
National Institute of Health
Tel: 001 301 496 1752
www.nia.nih.gov

National Osteoporosis Society
Tel: 01761 471771
Helpline: 0845 4500230
www.nos.org.uk

The National Register of Hypnotherapists & Psychotherapists
Tel: 01282 716839
www.nrhp.co.uk

Natural Progesterone Information Service
For a booklet or information,
tel: 07000 784 849
www.npis.info

Nature's Best
Tel: 01892 552118
www.naturesbestonline.com

Nioxin
For details of your nearest scalp
health clinic, tel: 0845 458 9350
www.nioxin.com

OPI
For mail order and stockist
enquiries, tel: 01923 240010
www.opi.com
www.lenawhite.co.uk

Organic Food
*For information about where to
obtain organic food contact:*
The Soil Association
Tel: 0117 314 5000
www.soilassociation.org

The Organic Pharmacy
Tel: 020 7351 2232
www.theorganicpharmacy.com

Origins
Products available at Harrods,
John Lewis, or for further stockists
(who all offer mail order),
tel: 0800 731 4039
www.origins.com

Physioworks
Tel: 0845 331 6116
www.physioworks.co.uk

Phytoestrol
Available by phone only, from the
NutriCentre, tel: 020 7436 5122

Pilates
The Pilates Foundation
Tel: 07071 781 859
www.pilatesfoundation.com
Or: **Body Control Pilates
Association (BCPA)**
Tel: 020 7379 3734
www.bodycontrol.co.uk

Susan Posnick
Tel: 020 8997 8541
for stockists
www.susanposnick.com

Prescriptives
Tel: 0870 034 2566
www.prescriptives.com

Privé (USA)
Tel: 001 866 351 1193
www.priveproducts.com

Q Switch Ruby Laser
Used by Professor Nicholas Lowe
at The Cranley Clinic (see above)

Redken
Tel: 0800 444 880
www.redken-uk.com

**REFLEXOLOGY
The British Reflexology
Association**
Tel: 01886 821207
www.britreflex.co.uk

**REIKI
The Reiki Association**
Tel: 0901 8800 009
www.reikiassociation.co.uk

**Relate National Marriage
Guidance**
Tel: 0845 456 1310 or
01788 573241
www.relate.org.uk

Revlon
Tel: 0800 085 2716
www.revlon.com

Romanda Healthcare
Tel: 020 8346 0784
Email: jan_romanda@hotmail.com

Mr John Scurr
Lister Hospital
Tel: 020 7730 9563
www.thelisterhospital.com
www.jscurr.com

**The Seasonal Affective
Disorder Association**
SADA, PO Box 989, Steyning
BN44 3HG
Tel: 01903 814942
www.sada.org.uk

Sebastian
For international mail order log on
to www.sebastian-intl.com
The new Original Range from
Sebastian is available from
Martyn Maxey online:
www.martynmaxey.co.uk

**SHIATSU
The Shiatsu Society**
Tel: 0845 130 4560
www.shiatsu.org

British School of Shiatsu-Do
www.shiatsu-do.co.uk

Shu Uemura
Mail order, tel: 020 7235 2375
For stockists worldwide, log on to
www.shuuemura-usa.com

Sisley
Tel: 020 7491 2722
www.sisley-cosmetics.com

**The Society of Chiropodists
and Podiatrists**
Tel: 0845 450 3720
www.feetforlife.org

Space NK
Tel: 020 8740 2085
www.spacenk.com

Superdrug
Tel: 0800 096 1055
www.superdrug.com

**T'AI CHI
The UK T'ai Chi Association**
Tel: 020 7407 4775
www.taichiuk.co.uk

Therapeutic Touch
The Sacred Space Foundation,
Emmers Farm, Sparket, Dacre,
Penrith, Cumbria CA11 0NA
Tel: 017684 86868
www.sacredspace.org.uk

Tibetan Buddhism
Tel: 01387 373232
www.samyeling.org

Tigi
Tel: 0870 330 0955
www.tigihaircare.com/uk

Tragerwork
Trager UK
Tel: 01903 717987
www.trager.co.uk

Trayner Pinhole Glasses
Tel: 0800 071 2020
www.trayner.co.uk

Trilogy
Available from Xynergy
Products Ltd
Mail order: 08456 58 58 58
www.xynergy.co.uk

Tweezerman
Tel: 020 7237 1007
www.tweezerman.com

Umbrella Smiles
Tel: 020 7612 9810
www.umbrellasmiles.co.uk

Vaishaly Patel
Tel: 020 7224 6088
www.vaishaly.com

Victoria Health
Tel: 0800 3898 195
www.victoriahealth.com

White Cliffs Hair Studio
Tel: 0800 028 0486
www.whitecliffsgroup.com

Nick Williams
For information on workshops:
Alternatives Workshops
Tel: 020 7287 6711
www.alternatives.org.uk

**YOGA
Iyengar Yoga Association of the
United Kingdom**
Tel: 020 8997 6029
www.iyengaryoga.org.uk
Orange Tree Yoga
Tel: 077251 20043
www.orangetreeyoga.com

Yorktest
Tel: 0800 074 6185
www.yorktest.com

**Yves Saint Laurent
YSL**
For stockists,
tel: 01444 255 700
www.ysl.com

Zinopin
Tel: 0800 028 0037
www.zinopin.com

BOOKS

The 21st Century Beauty Bible
by Sarah Stacey and
Josephine Fairley
(Kyle Cathie, 2006)

**The Allergy Bible:
Understanding, Diagnosing,
Treating Allergies and
Intolerances**
by Linda Gamlin,
Jonathan Brostoff
(Quadrille Publishing Ltd, 2005)

**Anam Cara: Spiritual Wisdom
from the Celtic World**
by John O'Donohue
(Bantam Press, 1997)

The Art of Hair Colouring
by David Adams and Jacki
Wadeson (Thomson Learning
Vocational, 1988)

**The Art of Sexual Ecstasy:
The Path of Sacred Sexuality
for Western Lovers**
by Margo Anand
(Aquarian Press, 1992)

The Artist's Way
by Julia Cameron
(Tarcher/Putnam, 2002)

Beating Stress at Work
by Anne Woodham
(Health Education Authority, 1995)

Better Sight Without Glasses
by Harry Benjamin
(HarperCollins, 1992)

**Bobbi Brown Beauty: The
Ultimate Beauty Resource**
by Bobbi Brown and Annemarie
Iverson (Ebury Press, 1997)

**The Cellulite Solution: A
Doctor's Programme for
Losing Lumps, Bumps,
Dimples and Stretch Marks**
by Dr Howard Murad
(Piatkus, 2006)

**Changing Patterns: Discovering
the Fabric of Your Creativity**
by Daena Giardella
(Hay House, 2006)

**The Complete Book of
Food Combining: A New,
Easy-to-use Guide to the
Most Successful Diet Ever**
by Kathryn Marsden
(Piatkus Books, 2005)

**The Complete Book
of Hair Styling**
by Charles Worthington
(Carlton Books Ltd, 2003)

**The Complete Guide to Food
Allergy and Intolerance**
by Prof Jonathan Brostoff
and Linda Gamlin
(Bloomsbury, 1998)

**Eco-Friendly Houseplants:
50 Indoor Plants That
Purify the Air**
by Bill Wolverton
(Weidenfeld Nicolson, 2000)

**Encyclopaedia of
Healing Therapies**
by Anne Woodham and Dr David
Peters (Dorling Kindersley, 1997)

**The Encyclopedia of
Natural Medicine**
by Michael Murray and Joseph
Pizzorno (Little, Brown, 1998)

Fats That Heal, Fats That Kill
by Dr. Udo Erasmus
(Alive Books, 1998)

Food Allergy and Intolerance
by Jonathan Brostoff and
Stephen J Challacombe
(Saunders Co Ltd, 2002)

**GROW: The Modern Woman's
Handbook: How to Connect
with Self, Lovers, and Others**
by Lynne Franks
(Hay House, 2004)

The Handbag Beauty Bible
by Josephine Fairley and
Sarah Stacey
(Kyle Cathie, 2005)

**Healing Environments: Your
Guide to Indoor Well-being**
by Carol Venolia
(Celestial Arts 1988)

**Heal Yourself with Flowers
and Other Essences**
by Nikki Bradford
(Quadrille Publishing Ltd, 2006)

Hotline to Health
by Kathryn Marsden
(Pan 1998)

**How to Keep Your Feet & Legs
Healthy for a Lifetime**
by Gary Null and Dr Howard
Robins (Seven Stories Press, 1990)

Journal of A Solitude
by May Sarton
(Women's Press, 1985)

Joy of Beauty
by Leslie Kenton
(Doubleday, 1983)

**Juice High: Experience the
Power of Raw Energy**
by Leslie Kenton and Russell
Cronin (Vermilion, 1999)

**The Meditator's Handbook:
A Comprehensive Guide to
Eastern and Western
Meditation Techniques**
by Dr David Fontana
(HarperCollins, 1994)

Menopause
by Jan de Vries
(Mainstream Publishing, 2001)

**Mind-Body Medicine – A
Clinician's Guide to
Psychoneuroimmunology**
edited by Dr. Alan Watkins
(Elsevier Health Sciences, 1997)

**New Natural Alternatives
to HRT**
by Marilyn Glenville
(Kyle Cathie, 2003)

Passage To Power
by Leslie Kenton
(Century Vermilion, 1998)

**Patrick Holford's New
Optimum Nutrition Bible:
The Book You Have to Read
If You Care About Your Health**
by Patrick Holford
(Piatkus, 2004)

The Psychology of Happiness
by Prof Michael Argyle
(Routledge, 2001)

Raw Energy
by Leslie Kenton
(Century Vermilion, 1994)

**A Round-heeled Woman:
My Late-life Adventures in
Sex and Romance**
by Jane Juska (Vintage, 2004)

**Secrets of a
Fashion Therapist:
What You Can Learn Behind
the Dressing Room Door**
by Betty Halbreich, Sally Wadyka
(Harper Resource, 2005)

**The Seed Handbook:
The Feminine Way to
Create Business**
by Lynne Franks
(Piatkus Books, 2005)

Sleep Thieves
by Stanley Coren
(Simon & Schuster, 1996)

**The Spiritual Tourist:
A Personal Odyssey
Through the Outer
Reaches of Belief**
by Mick Brown
(Bloomsbury, 1999)

**Stress at Work: Causes,
Effects and Prevention –
A Guide for Small and
Medium Sized
Enterprises**
by Michiel Kompier,
Lennart Levi
(European Communities, 1995)

**SuperYou: Be the
Best You Can Become**
by Anne Naylor
(HarperCollins, 1996)

Total Wellness
by Joseph E Pizzorno
(Prima Publishing, 1998)

**The Wellness Book – The
Comprehensive Guide to
Maintaining Health and
Treating Stress-Related Illness**
by Herbert Benson and
Eileen M Stuart
(Scribner, 1993)

**You Can Look Younger At
Any Age: A Leading
Dermatologist's Guide**
by Nelson Lee Novick, MD
(iUniverse.com, 2000)

**Your Change, Your Choice:
The Integrated Approach to
Looking and Feeling Good
Through the Menopause –
And Beyond**
by Michael Dooley and
Sarah Stacey
(Hodder Mobius, 2006)

Your Skin: An Owner's Guide
by Joseph Bark
(Prentice Hall USA, 1995)

American books can be ordered
via www.amazon.com.
Out-of-print editions can be
sourced at www.abebooks.co.uk

acknowledgements

This mammoth project wouldn't have been possible without a great deal of help and co-operation. Firstly, we would like to thank the 2,500 women on our ten-woman product-testing panels, who diligently reported back on their experiences.

We would also like to thank our 'Inspiring Women' – Evelyn Lauder, Carmen Dell'Orefice, Anita Roddick, Susan Greenfield, Nigella Lawson, Leslie Kenton, Jennifer Guerrini-Maraldi and Liz Earle – for sharing their experiences with us. In addition we would like to thank the following, who were all interviewed especially for this book…

The make-up artists: the late Kevyn Aucoin, Bobbi Brown, Liz Collinge, Barbara Daly, Darac, Sharon Dowsett, Olivier Echaudemaison, Stephen Glass, Mary Greenwell, Ruby Hammer, Jenny Jordan, Vincent Longo, Trish McEvoy, Laura Mercier, Noriko Okubo and Tricia Sawyer.

The fashion experts: Betty Halbreich, Amanda Platt and Belinda Seper.

The hairdressers: Susan Baldwin, John Barrett (and George at John Barrett), Nicky Clarke, Andrew Collinge, Daniel Field, John Frieda, Léonor Greyl, Jo Hansford, Louis Licari, Christophe Robin and Charles Worthington.

The foot and nail experts: Mara Caskin at John Barrett, Robyn Opie, Katharine Royston-Airey and Clare Wolford (educational director of Supernail of LA).

The skincare professionals: Dr Karen Burke, Christina Carlino, Eva Fraser, Susan Harmsworth (founder of ESPA, UK), Marcia Kilgore, Dr Jurgen Klein (founder of Jurlique cosmetics), Eve Lom, Dr Daniel Maes (vice-president of research and development for Estée Lauder Worldwide), Dr John McCook (Elizabeth Arden), Vaishaly Patel, Edith Poyer (assistant director of product development for Fashion Fair), Germaine Rich of Aromatherapy Associates, Lydia Sarfati, Barbara Simpson-Birks and Dr Patricia Wexler (New York).

The doctors, scientists, fitness, nutritional and personal development experts: Philip Bacon (UK), Glenda Baum (London), Prof Etienne-Emile Baulieu (Paris), Dr Mary Ellen Brademas (New York City), Prof Carol Brayne (Institute of Public Health, Cambridge), Prof Jonathan Brostoff (King's College London), Prof Robert Butler (Dept of Geriatrics, Mt Sinai School of Medicine, New York City), Dr Rosy Daniels (Health Creation UK), Jan de Vries (Glasgow,) Mr Michael Dooley (London and Dorchester), Torje Eike (chartered physiotherapist, London), Frances Emeleus (British Association of Sexual and Marital Therapists, UK), Dr Udo Erasmus, Dr Linda Fellows (UK), Dr Justin Glaister (London), Dr Marilyn Glenville (Hale Clinic, London), Prof Jean-Alexis Grimaud (University of Paris), Dr James Hawkins (Scotland), Patrick Holford (London), Dr Susan Horsewood-Lee (London), Prof Kim Jobst (UK), Mr Barry Jones (London), Prof Kay-Tee Khaw (Clinical Gerontology Unit, University of Cambridge), David Klaff (British Academy of Aesthetic Dentists, London), Prof Michael Lean (Dept of Human Nutrition, University of Glasgow), Wendy Lewis (London and New York), Dr George Lewith (Centre for the Study of Complementary Medicine, Southampton), Prof Nicholas Lowe (Cranley Clinic, London), Dr Tony Maltby (Depart of Social Policy and Social Work, University of Birmingham), Dr Andrew Markey (London), Kathryn Marsden (Spain), Warrick McNeill (Physioworks, London), Anne Naylor (France), Kate Neil (Institute of Optimum Nutrition, London), Chrissie Painell, Prof Ian Philp (UK), Joseph Pizzorno (Bastyr University, Seattle, Washington), Prof David Purdie (UK), Dr Deborah Rozman (Colorado), Dr Hugh Rushton (London), Mr John Scurr (London), Gloria Thomas (London), Dr Alan Watkins (UK), Dr Ian White (UK), Nick Williams (Alternatives, London) and Anne Woodham (London).

Thanks also to the following organisations: Action Research, Age Concern, Society for Endocrinology, British Geriatric Society, British Heart Foundation, British Psychological Society, British Society for Research into Ageing, Institute of Gerontology, Institute of Human Ageing, Public Health Forum and Research Into Ageing.

We would also like to say thank you, thank you, thank you to the colleagues, family and friends who have given unstinting time and effort, including our doughty helpers Jessie Lawrence, Rhian Hepple, Lily Evans, Elizabeth Guy, Amy Eason, Margaret Sams, Dave Edmunds and Nicki at Hastings Old Town Post Office. And thanks to Craig Sams for his patience! Also thanks to David Downton for his fabulous illustrations, and to designer Jenny Semple and copy editor Simon Canney. Thanks as ever to Sue Peart, editor of YOU magazine, and Catherine Fenton, deputy editor. And finally, a big thank you to our agent, Kay McCauley, for being there…

index

photographic acknowledgements

The publishers wish to thank the following photographers and organisations for their kind permission to reproduce photographs in this book.

2 The Image Bank/Meola Studio

8 Stay Still/Evan Arnstein

10 Tony Stone Images/ Laurence Monneret

11 Robert Harding Picture Library/Wesley Hitt

13 The Image Bank/Bokelberg

14 Francesca Yorke

19 Francesca Yorke

23 Robert Harding Picture Library/Caroline Hughes/© IPC Magazines Ltd/Options

24 Tony Stone Images/ Bill Heinsohn

25 Time & Life Pictures

26 Tony Stone Images/ Mark Lewis

27 Guerlain

28 Corbis Outline/ Naomi Kaltman

30 Images/Jay Freis

33 Science Photo Library/ Alfred Pasieka

34 Camera Press/Brigitte

39 Marie France/Barbro Anderson/Dominique Eveque

42 Tony Stone Images/James Darell

44 Corbis

47 Andrew Lawson

49 Angela Hampton Family Life Pictures

52 Jennifer Livingston

54–55 Jekka McVicar

59 Superstock

61 Tony Stone Images/ Jerome Tisné

63 Hulton Getty

65 Robert Harding Picture

Library/Jake Chessum/ © IPC Magazines Ltd

66 Telegraph Picture Library/ Bavaria/Bildagentur

71 Robert Harding Picture Library/Rene Dupont/© IPC Magazines Ltd/ Options

72 Francesca Yorke

75 Francesca Yorke

77 TonyStone Images/ Jerome Tisné

78 The Kobal Collection

80 Tony Stone Images/ Steven Peters

81 Eyevine/Simon Songhurst

82 Telegraph Colour Library/ J P Frouhet

84 Francesca Yorke

88 Attard

89 London Features International

90 Eyevine/Mike Owen

92 Guerlain

93 Tony Stone Images/ Dennis O'Clair

94 Action for Blind People

95 Tony Stone Images/ Claudia Kunin

98 Associated Press

100 Retna Pictures/Phil Loftus

104 Francesca Yorke

107 The Stock Market

109 Marie France/Barbro Anderson/ Catherine de Chabaneix

111 Time & Life Pictures/ Kevin Winter

114 Tony Stone Images/ Christopher Bissell

116 Retna/Bruno Gaget

117 Rex Features/Erik Pendzich

118 Reuters/CORBIS

119 Bobbi Brown

120 Tony McGee; make-up by Maggie Hunt

122 Retna/Jenny Acheson

123 Retna/Jenny Acheson

124 above Tony Stone Images/ Donna Day; below Retna/Jenny Acheson

125 Retna/Jenny Acheson

126 Tony Stone Images/ Antonia Deutsch

129 Robert Harding Picture Library/© IPC Magazines Ltd/ Woman's Journal

132 Superstock

135 Tony Stone Images/ Laurence Monneret

137 Hulton Getty

138 Tony Stone Images/ Jerome Tisné

143 Tony Stone Images/ Christopher Bissell

154 Tony Stone Images/ Laurence Monneret

156 Attard

158 Francesca Yorke

160 Garden Picture Library/ Lynne Brotchie

162 The Image Bank/M Regine

168 The Image Bank/ John P Kelley

171 Francesca Yorke

176 Craig Fordham

180 Francesca Yorke

181 The Image Bank/ Tracy Frankel

182 The Image Bank/Gio Barto

184 Belle

186 Brian Moody

188 Katz/Outline/Art Streiber

193 Tony Stone Images/ Robert Holmgren

195 Robert Harding Picture Library/© IPC Magazines Ltd/ Options

196 Tony Stone Images/ Catherine Panchout

197 Tony Stone Images/ Chris Everard

198 The Image Bank/Dingo

200 The Image Bank/ Tcherevkoff Ltd

202 Doug Blanks

221 The Stock Market/Sanai Shahram

222 Tony Stone Images/ Stephanie Rushton

226 Katz/Outline/ Jeffrey Thurnher

228 above Colorific; below Sylvain Gaboury/Rex Features

233 Francesca Yorke

235 Explorer/Bordes

236 The Kobal Collection

239 The Stock Market/ ML Sinibaldi

240 The Image Bank/ Weinberg/Clark

241 Michel Bocandé

242 Troy House

243 Francesca Yorke

244 Marlene Wallace

245 Hulton Getty